PRESS, POLITICS AND SOCIETY

Press, Politics and Society

A HISTORY OF JOURNALISM IN WALES

Aled Gruffydd Jones

CARDIFF
UNIVERSITY OF WALES PRESS
1993

British Library Cataloguing-in-Publication Data

A catalogue record for this book is available from the British Library

ISBN 0-7083-1167-9

Typeset by Action Typesetting Ltd., Gloucester
Printed in Wales by WBC Print Ltd., Bridgend

I'm rhieni, am gyfeillgarwch diamod

Contents

Preface ix

Acknowledgements xi

Introduction 1

1 **Journalism** 10
- Editing 10
- News gathering 23
- Life-style and social status 55

2 **Production and Distribution** 61
- Management 61
- Advertising 66
- Technology and labour 72
- Markets 90

3 **Ownership and Patronage** 113
- The pattern of ownership 113
- The religious press 118
- The political press 124
- The politics of patronage 141

4 **Conflict and Culture** 152
- The 'moral machine' 153
- Authority and dissent 162
- The contours of culture 177

5 **Traditions and Transformations** 202
- The press in twentieth-century Wales 203
- The press and the new media 228

Conclusion 239

Abbreviations used in the notes 242

Notes 243

Glossary of Welsh-language titles 294

Bibliography 296

Index 311

Preface

Henry James once remarked of Anthony Trollope that 'he did not write for posterity; he wrote for the day, the moment; but these are just the writers whom posterity is apt to put into its pocket.'[1] Journalists in the past also wrote for the moment, with little time for reflection or revision, yet, as writers, they too have been pocketed by posterity. Immediate and ephemeral in nature, weekly and daily newspapers have been transformed by being bound, microfilmed, catalogued and preserved by librarians and archivists into texts that are as permanent and durable as books. The social value of the press has also been changed by this process, and if old newspapers are no longer read in order to appraise the 'latest intelligence', they are, nevertheless, constantly being referred to by historians and other scholars who are drawn to their pages by the breadth and comprehensiveness of the primary evidence that they provide. But posterity, as usual, has been selective. The writing of journalists in the past may survive and continue to be utilized in the present, but the industry that produced and published this writing has fared less well. The energies of hundreds, then thousands, of editors, reporters, sub-editors, engravers, illustrators, photographers, 'penny-a-liners', local and amateur correspondents, managers, compositors, printers, street-sellers, distributors and readers were harnessed by a dynamic, if at times chaotic, newspaper industry. Furthermore, the press, being, to use Raymond Williams's term, a 'privileged institution', interacted in important but complex ways with the economy, politics and culture of the society in which it developed.[2] The historical study of journalism must therefore take into account the contexts of the writing, and the purpose of this book is to attempt to place the origins, growth and transformation of a particular popular press within a particular history. To accomplish this it has been necessary both to reconstruct the history of that press as an industry, and to consider its changing relationship with the broader society.

The particular circumstances for this study of the popular press are provided by the history of Wales over the past two centuries.

Historians of the British press have indicated for some time that the development of journalism in Wales needs to be considered separately from that of the rest of the United Kingdom. Alan J. Lee observed in the introduction to *The Origins of the Popular Press in England 1855–1914* (1976) that Wales 'could do with a separate study', and Stephen Koss, in the prologue to his two-volume *The Rise and Fall of the Political Press in Britain* (1981), adds that, in the nineteenth century, English newspapers were 'satellites that revolved around the metropolitan base . . . Wales and, still more, Ireland, lie outside the orbit'. Both historians acknowledged that, for a variety of reasons, the history of the press in Wales could not simply be reduced to the pattern of events that obtained elsewhere. The energies that created and sustained the popular press in Wales were substantially different from those that were responsible for the growth of journalism in England, Scotland or Ireland, at least in the nineteenth and early twentieth centuries. In its journalism, as in so many other respects, Wales needs to be explained in its own terms.

Aled Gruffydd Jones
Aberystwyth, 1992

Acknowledgements

This study of the history of journalism in Wales has been facilitated by the generous and often invaluable assistance of a large number of individuals and institutions. Grants from the following bodies enabled me to extend my research into areas that would otherwise have been difficult if not impossible to reach: the Twenty-seven Foundation of the Institute of Historical Research; the Sir David Hughes Parry Award, University College of Wales, Aberystwyth; the British Academy, for a personal award to fund a separate prosopographical research project on Victorian journalists on which I have drawn heavily in this study; and the Vice-Principal's Fund, University College of Wales, Aberystwyth, which helped to defray expenses incurred in travelling to seminars and conferences in Britain, Canada and the USA to deliver papers based on earlier drafts of this book. I also wish to thank my colleagues in the history department, University of Wales, Aberystwyth, for permitting me a light teaching term in 1988 to complete the primary research.

Thanks are also due to the staffs of County Record Offices and Archives at Bangor, Caernarfon, Hawarden and Rhuthun, the university libraries at Aberystwyth, Bangor, Swansea and Warwick, and other libraries at Swansea, Cardiff, the British Library Newspaper Library at Colindale, the British Library, London, and the Newberry Library, Chicago. Above all, I wish to record my thanks for the friendship and endless patience of the staff of the National Library of Wales, Aberystwyth, without whose exquisite manuscript and printed collections this book could not have been written. My pursuit of other sources was aided by the valuable advice and guidance of Mr T. W. Baker-Jones, Company Archivist of W. H. Smith and Son Ltd.; Mr Ralph Gee, Librarian, T. Bailey Forman Ltd.; Dr Ann Matheson, National Library of Scotland; C. E. Phillips, Local Studies Library, Nottinghamshire County Council, and Dr Richard Storey, Modern Records Centre, University of Warwick. Thanks are also due to Mr Gary Cullum, Head of Press and Public Affairs, The Newspaper Society; Mr Cymric Mytton-Davies, Past-President, Institute of Journalists; Mr J. R. Hart, General Secretary, Institute of Journalists, and the late

Mr Angus McDermid. Other journalists and newspaper manager who kindly responded to my often impertinent enquiries and extended invitations to visit their offices included Mr M. L. Beardall, Financial Director and Company Secretary, South Wales Argus Ltd., Mr Ray Bower, Editor, *North Wales Chronicle*; Mr Raymond Crabb, Editor, *Chester Observer*; Mr M. J. Davies, Editor, *Penarth Times*; Mr Rowland Davies, Editor, *Aberdare Leader*; Henry R. Douglas, News Group Newspapers Ltd.; Mr Eric Edwards, Editor, *Y Gwyliedydd*; Mr A. George, Chief Librarian, *Western Mail*; Mr Roy Hancock, Editor, *Cambrian News*; Mr G. A. Jarvis, Managing Director, Shropshire Weekly Newspapers; Mr Clive B. Jones, Managing Director, North Wales Weekly News Group; Mr Graham Jones, Managing Editor, Celtic Newspapers Ltd; Mr G. F. Keighley, Editor, *Gwent Gazette*; Mr Jim Mansell, Editor, *Daily Post*; Mr Jeff Morris, Editor, *Abergavenny Chronicle*; Mr Alan Osborn, Editor, *Carmarthen Journal*; Mr Haydn Rowlands, Editor, *Y Llan*; Mr Dudley Stephens, Editor, *Pontypridd Observer*; Mr D. R. Thomas, Vice Chairman, North Wales Newspapers Ltd; Mr Dennis J. Underwood, General Manager, *Cardigan and Tivy-Side Advertiser* and Mr D. D. Voyle, Editor, *Pembroke County Guardian*.

Many of the approaches and arguments contained in this book were tested in seminars and conferences before being commmitted to paper in the present form, and I would like to thank in particular the following for their criticisms and suggestions: the interdisciplinary Periodicals Group at the University of Wales, Aberystwyth; Professors Joel H. Wiener, J. Don Vann, Barbara Quinn Schmidt and other colleagues in the Research Society for Victorian Periodicals; and Dr Michael Harris and Dr Virginia Berridge of the Media History Seminar in the University of London.

Finally, I wish to record my thanks to Professor Royden Harrison, whose teaching kindled and sustained my curiosity about the social history of the press in Wales, and to Professor Ieuan Gwynedd Jones, whose engagement with the complexities of nineteenth-century Welsh political culture has made it possible to ask new questions. I have also benefited immensely from the friendship and expertise of Yasmin Ali, Laurel Brake, Joanne Cayford, Catrin M. S. Davies, Neil Evans, Dennis Griffiths, Deian Hopkin, Philip Henry Jones, Paul O'Leary, Lionel Madden, Michael Roberts and Huw Walters. The responsibility for any errors of fact or infelicities of style that remain is, however, my own.

Introduction

On the evening of 4 March 1797 the lieutenancy and magistrates of Carmarthen met in the Shire Hall to express public relief following the repulsion the previous month of an attempted French sea-borne invasion of south-west Wales. The meeting noted with pride how the people of Carmarthen had risen in patriotic defence of their country, and praised, in the form of self-congratulatory resolutions, the 'loyalty, spirit and unanimity' of the town in the crisis. It was also felt that such loyalty should be made known to a wider public, and a decision was taken to send copies of the resolutions to selected representatives of the two most efficient broadcasting media of the time, the clergy and the newspaper press. Unfortunately, since no newspapers were at that time being produced in Wales, the notices were published instead in the nearest available titles, the *Hereford Journal* and the *Bristol Journal*. A century later, the patriotic gentlemen of Carmarthen would have found no difficulty in advertising their loyalty within Wales. By 1897 the periodical press was a flourishing industry, spanning two languages and a wide spectrum of political and religious opinion. During the intervening century a printing industry had developed, publishing enterprises had been launched, styles had been fashioned and a readership had grown. The emergence of this new medium of communication, and the conditions that made it both possible and necessary, are the subjects of this study.

The origins of periodical publishing in Wales lie in the early eighteenth century when, in 1735, Lewis Morris attempted to launch *Tlysau yr Hen Oesoedd* in Holyhead, Anglesey, an unsuccessful venture that was followed in 1770 by Josiah Rees's *Trysorfa Gwybodaeth, neu Eurgrawn Cymraeg*. The French Revolution stimulated further periodical production in Wales in the 1790s, including *Y Cylchgrawn Cynmraeg* by Morgan John Rhys in 1793, *The Miscellaneous Repository, neu y Drosorfa Gymmysgedig* by Thomas Evans (Tomos Glyn Cothi) in 1795 and David Davies's *Y Geirgrawn* in 1796. Religious fervour led Thomas Charles and

Thomas Jones to start *Trysorfa Ysprydol* in 1799, an example followed by adherents to other Nonconformist denominations, including the Wesleyan *Yr Eurgrawn Wesleyaidd* in 1809, *Seren Gomer*, associated with the Baptists, in 1814, and *Goleuad Cymru* and *Y Drysorfa*, established in 1818 and 1831 respectively by Calvinistic Methodists. The Independents were connected with *Y Dysgedydd* from 1832, and the Unitarians with *Yr Ymofynydd* from 1847. By the early nineteenth century, however, weekly newspapers also started to appear in Wales. Beginning in Swansea with the *Cambrian* in 1804, the *North Wales Gazette* in Bangor in 1808 and the *Carmarthen Journal* in 1810, the early weekly press was, unlike the magazines, dominated by the English language. *Seren Gomer*, the first Welsh-language weekly, was launched by Joseph Harris (Gomer) in Swansea in 1814, and was followed in 1836 in Mold by *Cronicl yr Oes*, and *Yr Amserau* in Liverpool in 1843. The number of titles in both languages increased rapidly following the Repeal of the Stamp Act in 1855, including a spate of new denominational weeklies, *Baner ac Amserau Cymru* by Thomas Gee in Denbigh in 1859 and the first daily paper, again published in Swansea, the *Cambrian Daily Leader* in 1861. Other dailies followed in Cardiff in 1869 and 1872 and in Swansea in 1893. The transformation of newspaper publishing in Wales in the course of the nineteenth century was, in British terms, exceptionally rapid, but so too were the changes that had occurred more broadly in Welsh society.

The press emerged during a turbulent period in which the Welsh economy and society were as a whole transformed. Industrial expansion and demographic movement were changing an overwhelmingly rural population into an increasingly urban one, and the growth of the periodical press was in large measure the product of these developments. Dependent as it increasingly became on advertising revenues and the new technologies of production and distribution, the newspaper press in particular acted as an index to this uneven process of economic modernization and as an indicator of the vibrancy of commercial life. But although the general social and economic circumstances of nineteenth-century Wales provide a context without which it would not be possible to explain the emergence of Welsh journalism, the history of the periodical press cannot simply be reduced to those developments. On the contrary, the press possessed its own internal dynamic, and its expansion must be studied in terms of its own rhythms and within its own chronology.

The relationship between the press and the broader society was further complicated by ideology and the question of press influence. Journalism was not perceived simply as having emerged from a favourable set of social preconditions, rather it was very firmly believed that the role of the press was precisely to *change* that society. The mere presence of a new and popular press in Wales altered social relationships in both material and ideological ways. As Elizabeth Eisenstein has argued of the social impact of the press in early modern Europe, 'one cannot treat printing as just one among many elements of a complex causal nexus, for the communications shift transformed the nature of the causal nexus itself'.[1] The powerful impact of the periodical press on social and political life has been widely acknowledged in the historiography of modern Wales, in which the press has often been described as an agent of modernization and change. Gwyn A. Williams has noted how 'the new political consciousness broke in along the railways and through the press',[2] and Kenneth O. Morgan, commenting on religious life in Wales, agreed that, 'the growth of the Welsh press and its early association with the outlook of nonconformists was a fundamental factor in shaping the outlook and sensibilities of people throughout Wales'.[3] Ieuan Gwynedd Jones sees the emergence of the press as 'the great turning-point in Welsh political life', adding that it is 'impossible to exaggerate the importance of this change which was beginning to take place in the reading habits of the people'.[4] The belief that forms of communication materially affect both social consciousness and behaviour remains deeply rooted in the political culture as well as in the historiography of Wales. The mobilization of opinion that led to the establishment of Sianel Pedwar Cymru (S4C) in 1982, for example, rested on a collectively held assumption that a medium of communication, in this case television, could play a major part in rescuing the Welsh language from its precipitous decline. Such beliefs regarding the connections between the communications media and society were formed early in the history of the press, in the main during periods of intense social conflict, and endure in a largely unquestioned way in the present. The battles that were fought by journalists in the past continue to have their uses in the present in one other respect. Modern journalists, according to one recent account, turn to the 'bounteous umbrella of nostalgia' in order to gain temporary refuge from the realities of the present state of the press, not least because many of them 'want to believe that the past was somehow filled with nobler venture'.[5]

The complex mythology of press power was largely a product of the nineteenth century. The image of the newspaper as 'a gigantic engine of thought', a guiding, even a determining, ideological power, was clearly expressed by one journalist writing in 1849:

> . . . the periodical press of this country is, in fact, the ruler of its thought and action. It exercises a sway which neither kings, Lords nor commons has ever attained; for it rules not only men's outward deeds, but their inward thoughts also. Its energies are tremendous, because they are chiefly directed to the intellectual and moral portion of our nature.[6]

Others also shared the view that journalism exerted an influence over 'men's outward deeds'. C. D. Collet, for example, advocating the repeal of the Stamp Act before 1855, argued that the 'Rebecca Insurrection in Wales . . . would never have taken place if the aggrieved parties had had any easier and cheaper method of making known to Government their grievances', by which he meant, of course, a popular and untaxed newspaper press.[7] Ironically, however, large claims were often made for the influence of journalism by a society that generally knew remarkably little about the actual operations of the press. 'Few people have a definite notion of what a newspaper really is', wrote Sir J. F. Stephens in 1862,[8] a view echoed thirty-five years later by A. Elliott, who remarked that it was 'curious to reflect how very little is known by the general public of the conduct and management of newspapers'.[9]

The significance of the press as a social agency in nineteenth- and twentieth-century Wales has thus been acknowledged by modern historians and contemporary journalists, political activists and general readers alike for a considerable time, yet the mechanisms whereby this agency actually wielded its influence, and wove its magic, have received astonishingly little sustained attention. For a variety of reasons, then, it may be seen that the origins and growth of popular journalism in Wales warrant a re-evaluation in the form of a separate study. But it will also be appreciated that this study necessarily encompasses a number of paradoxes. The first is that the periodical press is most often regarded as a source of historical information, rather than as a subject of historical enquiry. Secondly, plentiful collections of nineteenth-century periodicals have survived in spite of the ephemeral nature of the product. And finally, this plenitude of surviving material conceals quite as much as it reveals. It is a surface only, and one which is at best exasperatingly opaque. The industry that created it and the motivations that defined its character must be reconstructed mainly from other sources. Furthermore, the purpose of this study is to place the evolution of journalism within its historical contexts – professional, industrial, political, religious and cultural – rather than to provide a succession of in-depth studies of individual titles or the biographies of journalists and publishers, important though that work undoubtedly is.[10]

It will also be seen that the primary focus here is on newspapers published in the counties of Wales, Monmouthshire and the city of Liverpool. The other two important categories, periodicals and the newspapers that circulated in Wales but were published in England, receive far less attention. The monthlies and quarterlies played an enormously significant role in the intellectual life of Wales, as did their counterparts in Scotland and England, and there were numerous interconnections between them and the weekly and daily newspapers. Many carried news stories and entertainment items as well as instruction and religious, political and literary discussion, and were popular in the sense that they were accessible to large numbers of readers through subscriptions, lending libraries and reading rooms. However, the sophistication of their contents and the complexity of the motivations of their editors and contributors deserve fuller treatment than can be afforded here. It should also be borne in mind that English newspapers, that is to say newspapers printed in England, circulated in Wales in increasingly large numbers as the nineteenth century proceeded. It is difficult to estimate the extent of their distribution, but, unlike the situation in the twentieth century, nineteenth-century newspapers produced within Wales dominated the market in the face of external competition. It is with these newspapers and their producers that this study is primarily concerned.

As a case study of the origins of popular journalism, Wales contains a number of special features. In the first place, journalism in Wales did not crystallize around the affairs of a sovereign state. The press was sustained instead by a variety of voluntary organizations, social movements and the affairs of local politics. All newspapers in nineteenth-century Wales were local in the sense that they were associated with specific places or communities of belief, although the intention to create a 'national press' for the whole of Wales was an enduring ambition. Many in Wales felt that they needed to be represented in an autonomous press largely because of their palpable exclusion from English journalism. G. Osborne Morgan noted in 1888 that:

> . . . the systematic 'boycotting' of Welsh intelligence by every London newspaper, with the single exception of the *Daily News*, has passed into a proverb. We shall be told, perhaps, that this neglect is the penalty we pay for our language and our nationality'.[11]

The drive to compensate for this exclusion of Welsh news from the English press was a most powerful motive for the expansion of journalism in Wales, but the geographical distribution of that growth was necessarily uneven, and was determined largely by the economic conditions that prevailed in the places of its production. Nineteenth-century advertisers helpfully divided Wales into four economic regions, comprising agricultural, manufacturing and mining districts and tourist centres. Different kinds of societies were to be found within each region, and each produced its own distinctive type of journalism.[12] These regions, however, were not static categories, and the social geography of the press in Wales shifted in the course of the nineteenth century from the older market towns, such as Brecon or Carmarthen, towards the larger centres of population in Caernarfon, Swansea, Cardiff and Newport.

A third distinctive feature of Wales as a case study is its use of two languages, English and Welsh. Titles were produced in both languages, and while only a small minority were bilingual in the sense that they contained as much editorial material in one language as in the other, many weekly and daily English-language newspapers contained Welsh-language columns. The use of either of the two languages signified more than a simple linguistic choice: it embodied geographical, social, religious, cultural and even political difference. The fourth characteristic of the Welsh press is this very diversity, particularly the fragmentation of journalism as a result of its predominantly religious and political sectarianism.

The absence of a centralized state, the wide disparities in social circumstances, the condition of bilingualism or disglossia, and an endemic denominationalism each served to mould the peculiar shape and character of the newspaper press in nineteenth-century Wales, and to a considerable extent continued to do so in the twentieth century. But in other respects the press in Wales shared the characteristics of journalism elsewhere in Europe and beyond. The dynamism of the rationalist, liberal tradition that regarded the press as 'mind's machine' and the 'chief mover of all progressive doctrines . . . the very safeguard and protector of the rights and liberties of the people . . .', was as powerful among journalists in Wales as it was amongst those in England or France.[13] Furthermore, the Newspaper Stamp legislation of 1836 and 1855 affected the press in Wales in much the same way as in the rest of the United Kingdom. Finally, Victorian Wales was as keenly self-conscious of its journalism as was Victorian England, and demonstrated its preoccupation with a similar vast array of critical studies, eisteddfod competitions and public debates on the styles and future prospects of the newspaper press. The Victorians were anything but passive readers of newspapers: many engaged actively with their texts and volubly evaluated and criticized their forms and functions. This stream of commentary constituted a public critical discourse that explored and contested the purposes and effects of journalism.

Journalism, however, was a problematic, ill-defined term. The publishers of the *Caernarvon Advertiser* in 1821 described the role of the 'Journalist' as one of 'reporting discoveries', linking such reporting with 'the Progressive advance of Philosophical Knowledge'.[14] From the inception of Welsh journalism, newspapers had embraced a very catholic definition of 'news' that combined general information and entertainment with a world-view. Early newspapers comprised a package that included advertisements, leader columns, general and local news, market and shipping prices and readers' letters. The *Silurian* of 1838, without doubt the finest of the early weeklies, for example printed in addition to foreign and British news stories and advertisements, lists of market prices, poems, gardening notes and readers' correspondence in both English and Welsh. It also campaigned in support of further Parliamentary reform, the anti-slavery movement and the Political Unions.[15] The package of general information, entertainment and politics, combined with its regularity, provided the readers of newspapers and the wider community which they were able to reach by word of mouth, with a complex narrative of the times in which they lived. This narrative enabled people, both rich and poor, urban and rural, to make sense of their environment in new and different ways. 'The Newspaper is the chronicle of civilization', wrote the editor of *Y Byd Cymreig* in 1862, 'It shows us the only world that we can see and feel'.[16] Exactly a century later Claude Morris recorded the same sensation when he bought his own Welsh newspaper and was able to aim his 'own press at last at the big, dirty, wonderful target of the outside world'.[17]

The intelligence thus gathered not only aided readers in the making of day-to-day decisions, such as finding a job, participating in voluntary societies, voting, buying or selling commodities, or emigrating, but also in detecting general social trends. This early-warning system, however, was politically ambivalent in the sense that it was simultaneously accessible to all sections of society, and was emphatically not privileged information limited to a ruling élite. It was simply a matter of reading the 'signs of the times', of finding and interpreting the clues in the narrative provided by the press in a critical and informed way. One writer in 1847 observed how newspapers, although

> . . . sympathizing with, and speaking for the class that rules the hour, yet, being apprised of every ground-swell, every Chartist resolution, every Church squabble, every strike in the mills, they detect the first tremblings of change.[18]

It was widely held at the time that newspapers, by empowering their readers in this way, were formidable instruments in the democratization of Welsh society.

The narrative was regarded by some as being so important that they maintained that the newspaper ought not to be treated as ephemeral literature at all, but rather as an essential component of a community's identity, its remembrancer. All newspapers thus deserved to be 'read, re-read, and saved for binding, as a record of local acts and facts'.[19] This reverence for the press bordered on the mystical as journalists began to speak of 'the soul of a newspaper', and of journalism's ability to lift 'out of the invisible and the inaudible the fuel and nourishment of an enormous universal curiosity'.[20] Such hyperbole, of which there were many instances throughout the nineteenth as well as the early twentieth century, indicates the difficulties that were faced when individuals attempted to come to terms with the existence of a new medium of communication and felt obliged to try to explain its possibilities and its fascination. Although some elements of continuity remained, these explanations changed over time as older paradigms were dismantled and more appropriate or fashionable ones were offered in their place.

This book has three objectives: to outline the way in which a newspaper press emerged in Wales; to examine the changing social relations of journalism, particularly with regard to religion, politics and culture; and to consider some of the twentieth-century legacies of this nineteenth-century process. It seeks to give a balanced weighting to the writing, the industry and their contexts by focusing in turn on the production of the text, the production of the commodity, its distribution and the broader political and cultural *milieux* of nineteenth-century Wales. Thus, in addition to the practices of journalism and printing, such issues as the ownership and control of newspapers, and the conflicting contemporary attitudes towards the powers of the press will also be addressed.

Finally, it should be noted that journalism produced only one kind of published text among many that could be found in Wales during the past two centuries. Books, including popular biographies and encyclopaedias, pamphlets, published sermons, essays, ballads, poems, popular songs and hymns all made their contributions to literary culture. But the newspaper press was exceptional in that it included elements of all these forms of writing and combined them with other components such as rumour, news and correspondence to create a new kind of popular literature with its own highly distinctive properties. This literature engaged with its audience in a very direct way, and its text changed, and was changed by, the society in which it circulated. This study of the emergence of the popular press seeks to make its own small contribution to the history of modern Wales by helping to place that particular text in its context.

1 *Journalism*

Journalism in Wales developed in a relatively short space of time during a period of rapid social change. Industrialization, urbanization, migration and the extension of roads and railways affected all the regions of nineteenth-century Wales, although in different ways and at an uneven pace, and developments in the production and distribution of the press followed closely the general patterns of economic and social change. Journalists observed this changing world, and, in their writing, provided for it a complex, unbroken chronicle. In writing this chronicle, however, they did not simply hold up a mirror to their society. Journalists were from the beginning both news-gatherers and news-makers who, in a variety of ways, helped to shape the society whose politics, religion, accidents and indiscretions they earned their living by reporting.

The work of the journalist in relation to this changing society was at no time unproblematic, and in consequence journalism was seldom capable of being defined clearly in commonly agreed terms. The history of journalism is at its core a study of the evolution of a craft, but the relationships between journalists, correspondents and reporters changed as the newspaper industry became more highly structured and professionalized. Despite this, the appeal of 'the journalist', which powerfully combined the qualities of writer and activist, remained strong long after the conditions in which it had originated had changed. Other difficulties in defining the journalist's craft lay in the fragmentation of journalism into the sectarianism of politics and religion, into profitable and less-profitable sectors of periodical publishing, and, above all, into the hierarchies that controlled the public flow of information. Editors, particularly editor-proprietors, were at, or were very close to, the apex of this hierarchy.

Editing

In the words of one recent historian, editing was 'at the core of the Victorian experience'. Situated 'at the nucleus of the Victorian world',[1] editors determined the contents and shaped the formats of a new medium, they tested its early potentialities and its limitations, they imagined a readership and, with varying degrees of success, communicated with it. Victorian editors not only invented new forms of printed communication, but established styles and ground-rules that were later to influence journalism in both the older and the newer media. Editing thus required a multiplicity of skills. The ability to write quickly and accurately was essential, but, as the American journalist David G. Croly observed in 1873, editors also needed 'the judging, suggesting, selecting, discriminating faculty' that distinguished them from 'mere phrase-mongers . . . mere writers'.[2] The skills that allowed editors to perform their pivotal social roles, and which differentiated them from other writers, had their origins in the printing trade.

Early printing technology, developed by, among others, Johann Gensfleisch zum Gutenberg in Mainz in Germany around 1450, and by the Chinese some five hundred years earlier, reached Wales in the middle of the sixteenth century when Sir Siôn Prys of Brecon printed devotional works in 1546, and William Salesbury in Llanrwst printed a dictionary and collection of proverbs a year later. From 1586 an illegal press printed Welsh Catholic tracts, including *Y Drych Cristnogol*, from a cave near what is today Rhos-on-Sea, near Llandudno. This followed the success of the first Catholic book in the Welsh language which was printed in Milan in 1568.[3] Journeymen printers were allowed to start their own printing businesses from 1695, when some of the repressive publishing laws that had been imposed after the Civil War, in particular the Licensing Act of 1662, were relaxed. For much of the late seventeenth century, printing was allowed only in London, Oxford and Cambridge, and the liberalization of 1695 effectively made provincial printing, and in turn provincial journalism, possible. Seven years later, in 1702, the *Daily Courant*, the first English daily newspaper, began publication, and in the same year Francis Burges launched the *Norwich Post*, the first English newspaper to be published outside London. Other new regional newspapers appeared in Bristol in 1702 and Exeter in 1704. The reform of 1695 was also the signal for the Corwen-born printer, Thomas Jones, to leave his adopted London for Shrewsbury, where a Welsh reading public was closer at hand. The Welsh-language almanac which Jones had published each year since 1680 was thus transferred from London to the Welsh border, where it continued publication until 1712. The *Almanac* could justly be described as the first Welsh news periodical, for in addition to astrological prophecies, it contained information on fairs, instruction on reading and writing, poetry and ballads, a historical chronology and a compendium of facts, such as the length of roads and numbers of churches and MPs. This general miscellany, moreover, was aimed at a plebeian readership, and was at the time the only publication to reach monoglot Welsh-language communities. Thomas Jones had acquired some experience of journalism whilst in London, where in 1692 he had acted as the publisher of Tom Brown's *London Mercury*. Later, possibly in 1704, he had also published, in Shrewsbury, *A Collection of All the Material News*, which according to the later recollection of one reader contained 'merely gleanings from London papers, rather than local news'. Thomas Jones also began to establish a distribution network in Wales for selling books, pamphlets and other printed material, a task that was also being undertaken at about the same time by the Society for the Propagation of Christian Knowledge (SPCK), who by April 1725 had developed a network that extended even into the Welsh prisons.[4]

By the end of the seventeenth century there existed in Wales a rudimentary system for the distribution of printed material, but there was no significant indigenous printing activity until the early decades of the following century. Isaac Carter, the earliest of the Welsh printers, established a business in Trefhedyn (now Atpar) in Newcastle Emlyn in 1718 before moving the press to Carmarthen in 1725, where Nicholas Thomas had been printing religious material since 1721. In 1730, John Breden set up yet another printing works in the town. The first three presses in Carmarthen were also the first three in Wales, but from the middle of the eighteenth century printers emerged in many other centres. Miles Harry opened a press in Pontypool between 1740 and 1742. In 1759 a press was established in Bodedern, Anglesey, John Ross began to print in Carmarthen in the 1760s, and a host of others were established in the 1770s and 1780s, including Rhys Thomas in Cowbridge, Evan Evans in Brecon, John Theophilus Potter in Haverfordwest (whose son, Joseph Potter was to establish the first newspaper in the county, the *Pembrokeshire Herald*, in 1844) and

Daniel Evans in Swansea. In 1791, William Wilmot established a printing house in Tenby, as did John Bird in Cardiff and Charles Heath in Monmouth.

Carmarthen was the first major printing centre in Wales, and the first attempts to establish a home-grown Welsh journalism were made there. John Ross and other printers issued numbers of *Y Cylchgrawn Cynmraeg* and *Trysorfa Gwybodaeth, neu Eurgrawn Cymraeg*, pioneering and challenging, if short-lived periodicals which set important precedents for the future. Morgan John Rhys, a Baptist minister of Jacobin persuasion, brought out *Y Cylchgrawn Cynmraeg* in 1793, with the help of Joshua Watkins, another Baptist minister and printer. Unlike the religious periodicals that preceded it, the five issues of Rhys's *Y Cylchgrawn Cynmraeg* signalled the emergence of a Welsh intelligentsia radicalized by the American War of Independence and the French Revolution, and which drew its energies largely from the London-Welsh societies, in particular the Gwyneddigion. The printing trade in London and Wales attracted such radicals in surprisingly large numbers, and was regarded by them in the optimistic political climate of the early 1790s as the main instrument of political argument and the means of inaugurating the Age of Reason. It is significant that the first Welsh-language monthly periodical, *Y Geirgrawn*, appeared shortly afterwards, from February to October 1796.

The early nineteenth century witnessed a sharp acceleration in Welsh printing activity. New businesses were established in Merthyr in 1801, Aberystwyth in 1809 and Newport in 1810, and almost exactly a century after the first non-metropolitan newspapers had appeared in England, Wales began to produce its own newspaper journalism. The *Cambrian* was launched in Swansea in 1804, and three years later a Chester printing firm opened an office in Bangor, and Charles Broster, its first manager, almost immediately started to publish the *North Wales Gazette*. The *Carmarthen Journal* then appeared in 1810. After an abortive attempt by Mark Willett to launch the *Cambrian Messenger*, a sixpenny weekly in May 1809, Monmouthshire eventually acquired its first paper in May 1829, the *Monmouthshire Merlin*. Others, including the *Welshman* and the *Merthyr Guardian*, were established during and after the political crisis of 1829–30.[5] The early nineteenth century also saw the emergence of small printing dynasties that were to exercise an undue influence over Welsh journalism. Notable examples include the Rees family in Llandovery, who between 1829 and 1856 published *Y Gwyliedydd*, the *Cambrian Quarterly Magazine*, the *Cambro-Briton*, *Yr Efangylydd*, *Yr Haul* and *Y Cylchgrawn*, the Welsh version of the Society for the Diffusion of Useful Knowledge (SDUK) periodical, the *Penny Magazine*. The Clark family performed a similar role in English-language journalism. James Clark, who had been apprenticed as a printer to the *Gloucester Journal* and had worked in London and Portsmouth, settled in Chepstow in 1823 and in June 1855 published the *Chepstow Weekly Advertiser*. His son, James Henry Clark, published the *Illustrated Usk Observer* between 1855 and 1907, and also brought out the monthly *Usk Gleaner and Monmouthshire Record* between 1875 and 1878. His eldest son, William Henry Clark, in turn left Usk in 1866 to publish the *Brecon County Times*.[6]

Early periodical and newspaper journalism thus emerged directly from the many small printing works that sprang up across Wales during the eighteenth and early nineteenth centuries. Printers were motivated to issue newspapers by both commercial and ideological considerations, and not infrequently by a combination of the two. Weekly newspapers were acknowledged as being excellent means of attracting advertising revenue, often to subsidize other less profitable book-printing work, but they were also regarded as being cheap and effective means of furthering the cause of a movement, sect or party. Printers were quick to learn the skills of news collection and editing, copying the formats and pirating the contents of English newspapers. Between 1804 and 1822 the *Cambrian* was edited, managed, printed and published solely by Thomas Jenkins,[7] and other examples of printer-editors abound in this early period, although the practice was not by any means universal. The *Carmarthen Journal* in 1812 to 1817 was printed first by John Daniel, who had served his apprenticeship with Ross, and later by David Rees and John Evans, and edited by Richard Phillips, but briefly in 1820 was both printed and edited by the latter. In general, the skills and functions of printers and editors in this period were virtually indistinguishable.[8]

During the second quarter of the nineteenth century, a shift in emphasis occurred as journalism ceased to be marginal to other printing activity, and newspapers became flagship enterprises with growing advertising clientele and readerships. Even then, the links between printing and editing remained strong. Many of the most prominent editors in nineteenth-century Wales had served printing apprenticeships, and had been legitimately inducted into the 'mysteries of the printers' trade'. Samuel Evans (Gomerydd) had learnt the printing trade with John Evans in Carmarthen before becoming editor of *Seren Gomer* in 1835 and of *Seren Cymru* in Cardiff in 1852,[9] and Josiah Thomas Jones, a prolific publisher of newspapers in both Welsh and English, including *Y Gweithiwr* and the *Merthyr and Cardiff Chronicle*, had abandoned his ministry with the Independents in 1831 to take up full-time printing and editing. Similarly, William Roberts (Nefydd), the son of a shoemaker, set up his own press in Blaenau in 1863 in order to publish *Y Bedyddiwr* and, later, to edit *Seren Gomer*. Printers were also prepared to take financial risks to launch or sustain their titles. Richard Mason of Tenby, for example, produced *Archaeologia Cambrensis* in 1850 'at his sole risk', and started the *Cambrian Journal* in 1854 'as a private speculation'.[10] In 1837 Thomas Gee, who in later life would become the most successful printer, publisher and editor of his time in north Wales, had followed what was by then a familiar path to the London offices of Eyre and Spottiswoode, a 'rat house' for which he retained a lively dislike for the remainder of his life.[11] The career of Edward Dobbins clearly illustrates the occupational fluidity of the nineteenth-century printer-editor. Born the son of a yeoman farmer in Gloucester in 1865, Dobbins grew up in Newport, Monmouthshire, and was apprenticed on the *South Wales Weekly Telegram*. He then studied law, but returned to journalism as a reporter on the staff of the *Sussex Daily News* in Brighton. Returning to Newport in 1890, he became a master-printer and bought the three papers of the Monmouthshire and South Wales Newspaper Co., the *South Wales Weekly Telegram*, the *Evening Telegram* and the *Monmouthshire Merlin*. Two years later he brought out a penny daily newspaper, the *South Wales Morning News*, but its failure three months later induced him to leave Newport and to take a reporter's job with the *Falmouth and Penryn Times* and the *Falmouth Packet*, and then to work as editor of the *Hertfordshire Standard* in St Albans. In March 1896 he returned to Wales as commercial editor of the *South*

Wales Daily News, and between 1902 and 1904 brought out the first illustrated newspapers in Wales, the *South Wales Graphic* and the *Western Counties Graphic*.

The geographic, as well as the occupational, mobility illustrated in the case of Edward Dobbins, was to prove to be of particular significance for the growth of journalism in Wales. Journalists and printers, apprenticed in a much older and better established trade in England and Scotland, were drawn to Wales by new work opportunities provided by the more recent expansion of printing. James Hews Bransby, Presbyterian pastor and kleptomaniac, left Dudley in disgrace in 1829 and settled in Caernarfon, where he took up teaching and journalism, and where, in 1831, he was one of the founders, and an early editor, of the *Caernarvon Herald*.[12] John Gibson, editor and proprietor of the *Cambrian News*, had started his working life as a printer's help in Lancaster in the early 1850s, and had graduated to the *Cambrian News*'s parent paper as a compositor in 1860, remaining a journeyman printer until 1870.[13] Gibson's transition from printer to editor had involved a long process of self-education and the reading of borrowed books that included Smith's *Arithmetic*, Heley's *Grammar and Exercises*, Bacon's *Essays*, and Pitman's *Shorthand*.[14] Lastly, it should be noted that both David Duncan and Lascelles Carr, of the *South Wales Daily News* and the *Western Mail* respectively, had moved to Cardiff after serving their apprenticeships elsewhere, Duncan from Perth in 1856 to found the *Cardiff Times* and Carr from Knottingley, Yorkshire, via the *Liverpool Daily Post*, to serve as the founding sub-editor of the *Western Mail* in 1869. The migration of editors into Wales was more noticeable than the traffic that went in the other direction, but some nineteenth-century Welsh printers and journalists did become editors in England and elsewhere. David Edwards, for example, was apprenticed at the *Herald* office in Caernarfon and worked for the *Liverpool Daily Post* before returning as manager of the *North Wales Observer* group in Caernarfon from 1884 to 1891. For the following six years he was employed as managing editor of the *Nottingham Daily Express* and the *Nottingham Evening News*, and between 1897 and 1902 served as assistant manager and then as editor of the *Daily News* in London. For the last eight years of his life, from 1908 to 1916, he returned to Nottingham to serve as editor and managing director of the *Express* and the

Evening News.[15] The route from the print-shop to the editor's desk had become such a common one by the early twentieth century that Aaron Watson insisted on maintaining the principle that 'an editor from the composing-room should be entitled to the same privileges as if he had come from the Bar',[16] indicating by so doing that inequality of status between these two routes to editorship continued to exist.

Not all editors, however, emerged from the printing trade. Robert Parry (Robyn Ddu Eryri), editor of *Y Wawr* between 1850 and 1852, was the son of a Caernarfon tailor and bonesetter who arrived at journalism via a career that included working as a schoolmaster, a lawyer's clerk, a preacher, a temperance lecturer and a Mormon missionary. Robert John Pryse (Gweirydd ap Rhys), an auto-didact master weaver, earned his living by freelance writing before becoming editor and publisher of *Papur y Cymry* in 1863, and Thomas Jones (Glan Alun) was apprenticed as an apothecary, and after editing the short-lived *Y Wenynen* in 1835 was ordained as a Calvinistic Methodist minister. Excommunicated for 'intemperance' he then became a candle-maker and a commercial traveller. John Pryse, founder of the *Llanidloes and Newtown Telegraph* in 1859, and Jenkin Howell, editor of the *Gweithiwr Cymreig* from 1885 to 1890, had both been apprenticed to shoemakers, whilst Ellis Roberts (Elis Wyn o Wyrfai), Anglican rector and editor of *Yr Haul* for ten years after 1885, had started his working life as a miller. John James Hughes (Alfardd) had been a farm labourer, a stonemason's labourer and a policeman before ascending to the editorship of *Yr Herald Cymraeg* in 1868, and Evan Probert, publisher of the *Blaenavon and Brynmawr Express* between 1871 and 1873 had previously been an accountant working in various truck shops in south Wales. Wholly ignorant of printing, Probert had engaged a journeyman to teach him the basic skills of the printer's trade, and to advise him on the organization of his print-shop.[17] Henry Tobit Evans, editor of the *Carmarthen Journal*, was a headmaster who had also learnt to print from a press set up at his home.[18] Religious organizations provided a vitally important route to editing, and, like many others, John Hughes (Glanystwyth), a farmworker, lead miner and quarryman, turned to editing after joining the Wesleyan ministry in 1867, and Daniel Silvan Evans, editor of *Y Brython* from 1858 to 1860 and *Archaeologia Cambrensis* from 1871 to 1875, was a minister of the Church of England who became Professor of Welsh at Aberystwyth in 1875. Welsh editors in the nineteenth century thus came from widely differing social and occupational backgrounds, and whilst for some editing was a career, for others it was a political or religious duty, and for a third group it was merely a passing phase, an opportunity briefly seized to make a mark on public life before poverty or lack of interest or the allure of another occupation drew them away. But what this diversity of backgrounds and experiences demonstrates is that in the period before production costs began to soar in the late nineteenth century, editing was a relatively open and accessible occupation.

The accessibility of journalism, however, did not make for a well remunerated profession, and pay for the majority of editors remained low throughout the nineteenth century. The editor of the *South Wales Reporter* in 1838 was paid £2 a week by the paper's printer and publisher,[19] and in 1840 Hugh Jones (Erfyl) complained to an aspiring journalist friend of the prohibitively low wage he received for his work. 'Owing to my other several engagements,' Jones explained,

> I feel inclined to relinquish the Editorship of the *Gwladgarwr*, and the Publisher, if he continues it, will be on the look out for another Editor. No one, I am confident, would be more capable than yourself should you feel disposed for such employment; but the emolument, I must confess, is but trifling, therefore I cannot conscientiously recommend the situation.[20]

Evan Jones (Ieuan Gwynedd) was in continuous financial difficulties during his short but brilliant career as a journalist in Wales. In 1851 he admitted that he augmented his paltry income from writing by letting his house to lodgers. Journalism brought him only £5 from the *Adolygydd*, with an additional £1 or £2 for occasional reports to the London press. In 1851 receipts from *Y Gymraes* came to £40, but his printing and other debts stood at twice that sum.[21] Welsh language editors were particularly prone to low income and to incur heavy losses. Robert Isaac Jones (Alltud Eifion) lost a livelihood and £300 of his own money when *Y Brython* died a cruel and sudden death 'by financial starvation' in 1863. Not surprisingly, even forty years after the event, he remained bitter about the experience.[22]

There is some evidence to suggest that editors' incomes in Wales were generally lower than in many other parts of Britain. In 1851, Archibald Henry Hamilton, editor of the *Carmarthen Journal*, earned £80 a year, whereas in 1846, as editor of the *Nottinghamshire Guardian*, he had earned a salary of £250 a year.[23] Fred B. Mason, editor of the *Oswestry Advertiser* and hailing from a family of journalists (his father was a newspaper proprietor and editor in Hemel Hempstead, and his brother the editor of the *Worcester Chronicle*) complained to Lord Rendel in 1888 that his income was not sufficient to meet his household expenses.[24]. Later in the same year Mason doubted whether he would be justified in remaining for an indefinite period as editor in view of his income, which, with his growing family, he found to be insufficient.[25]

The payment of salaried editors was in some instances tied to the circulation figures of their papers. In Caernarfon, John Davies (Gwyneddon) was paid £2 a week for editing *Y Goleuad*, with a £20 bonus should circulation reach four thousand.[26] Salary levels were also employed as means of enabling directors and shareholders of printing firms to exert a degree of influence over editorial policies. During the reorganization of the management of *Y Tyst a'r Dydd* in August 1891, it was suggested that a discretionary 'sweetener' of £100 per annum might be made to the editor, Dr J. Thomas, and his staff 'for good behaviour',[27] and in July 1895, the salary of Job Miles, editor of *Y Tyst*, was raised from £18 to £23 a year at the Independents' annual conference at Pwllheli.[28] The rewards of denominational loyalty were not inconsiderable.

In general, however, editors were paid little for their work, and one complained in 1910 that the editors of weekly papers received wages lower than those of the compositors who set their copy.[29] Much of the work was done voluntarily or on a part-time basis, and a readiness to sacrifice time and money were essential requirements for a successful editor's job. William Williams (Caledfryn) edited six periodicals for little or no remuneration, and claimed to have lost a considerable sum of his own money.[30] Editors therefore needed to do other work simply in order to be able to afford to be journalists, and many took on work as Welsh correspondents for the national British newspapers. T. J. Hughes (Adfyfr) admitted to Rendel in 1891 that he had recently 'become so prostrate with nervous exhaustion and attacks in the head that the Doctor compelled me to give up all night work . . . I have kept my *Daily News* correspondentship and my *Manchester Guardian* correspondentship through all my illness'.[31] Other editors drew salaries from parallel occupations. It was said of John Thomas (Eifionydd) that he could not have made a success of *Y Geninen* were it 'not for the fact that he held another job as secretary to the Gorsedd of Bards which acted as a handmaiden for him' in his work as an editor and publisher.[32]

The condition of the editor in mid-nineteenth-century Wales confirms the contemporary view of 'a much abused man', overburdened by hard work, constant anxiety and wearing responsibility.[33] Moreover, it was commonly assumed that 'to be a salaried editor, confined to the daily drudgery of an editorial chair, was not perhaps quite the thing for a gentleman'.[34] The editing of newspapers was an exhausting, poorly paid and relatively low-status occupation. In his valedictory address in March 1837, the editor of *Y Papyr Newydd Cymraeg* complained of being worn out by the work of producing the paper, and vowed never again to undertake the task. He added mournfully that he had lost much and gained little by the experience.[35]

Despite the generally poor pay, editing was a difficult occupation that required a wide range of technical, literary and communication skills. Shrewdness and resourcefulness were essential prerequisites, and it was not uncommon for a local editor to write the leading articles, collect and write the local news, correct the proofs, help illiterate customers to write out their advertisements, keep the sales and advertisement accounts, and even at times to work the printing press.[36] Richard Jefferies's graphic description of an editor's office in rural England in the late nineteenth century might also apply to the interior of a Welsh county newspaper of the same period: 'Upon one side is a large desk or bureau; the account books lying open show that the editor, besides his literary labour, has to spend much time in double entry'.[37] The absence of trained assistance often meant that much of the accounting and administrative work also devolved on the overburdened editor.[38] The incompetence or wilful fraudulence of local correspondents also required constant vigilance. Jeffries's 'village tailor with literary tastes' was a staple of all local journalism in nineteenth-century Wales.[39]

Whether they edited part time or full time, voluntarily or salaried, editors were of necessity polymaths, and the notoriously unspecific nature of newspaper work made accurate contemporary job descriptions very difficult to formulate. Hugh Jones (Erfyl) was offered the editorship of *Y Gwyliedydd* in May 1829 by the publisher, Rowland Williams, on condition that he furnished 'the news, recent, local and political, and to look over and assess the various contributions from occasional correspondents with of course the power of rejecting and admitting.' Williams added rather nonchalantly that 'This seems to me very easy provided you have time for the execution of it'.[40] The paper, printed in Bala, was edited in Chester, and despite the distance, this was not considered to be a difficulty either by the publisher-printer or by the editor. Even in the 1880s, a successful Caernarfon weekly such as the *Y Genedl* was put together by a part-time editor. W. J. Parry, who had irons in many other commercial and political fires, spent only one or two days a week editing the paper. On Mondays he would be 'engaged all day in the house putting Newspaper in order', and mid-week he would attend a 'staff committee at Caernarfon', where his overall reponsibilities were decided. He then travelled back to Caernarfon from his home in Bangor once a week to supervise the printing of the paper.[41]

Despite the apparent inconsistencies in editors' work-loads, it was increasingly acknowledged in the course of the nineteenth century that the editor did much to provide a paper with its distinctive identity. In the absence of clear editorial direction the cohesion that was so necessary for commercial success was weakened. The failure of the Pwllheli weekly, *Udgorn Rhyddid*, in 1888, was ascribed by John Grigg to the sharing of the editorship by David Lloyd George, D. R. Daniel and others.[42] Even in Wales, editing was not considered appropriate work for a committee.

Editorship conferred clear identity and the prospect of commercial success on a newspaper, and a degree of status if not wealth on the editor, but it also carried considerable legal obligations. Among the most serious of these was the ever-present danger of falling foul of the laws of libel. Editors were constantly exercised by this difficulty, and were necessarily well-versed in a corpus of libel legislation that underwent considerable change during the course of the nineteenth century. The Newspapers

Act of 1836 stipulated that publishers were to append their names to all published material covered by the Stamp Acts, and that a surety would be required to cover the cost of any libel case brought against the publisher. In the Printers and Publishers Act, 1839, the names of printers were also required to be published alongside those of publishers. Lord Campbell's Libel Act of 1843 provided some protection for editors, with a defence of no malice if a full apology and payment of amends were made to the aggrieved party. The Newspaper Libel and Registration Act, 1881, gave further protection to publishers against criminal libel, and introduced the compulsory registration of newspapers and their proprietors. Legal protection, however, did not cover the author of the libel if it could be proved that the author was unconnected with the production of the paper, and a newspaper reporter was not in law a person responsible for the publication of a newspaper and no order was required to launch criminal proceedings against him.[43] Summaries of the libel laws were specially provided for editors and sub-editors as guides through the legal maze, but the responsibility remained an onerous one,[44] and the loss of a libel case could signal heavy financial losses for publishers, dismissal for editors or reporters, and even the collapse of a newspaper. Where papers were run on narrow margins of profitability, the loss of even relatively small sums in libel cases could lead to disaster. The finances of *Gwalia*, a Tory weekly, were said to have been close to being critical after the loss of as little as £75 in a libel suit in 1884.[45] W. J. Parry paid £150 on behalf of the Liberal Welsh National Press Company in May 1889, followed by another £26 in June 1891,[46] and the editor of the Conservative *North Wales Chronicle*, David Williams, also paid £83, and issued a public apology, after losing a libel case against Professor Keri Evans in 1893.[47] One result of this anxiety was self-censorship, and Lloyd George complimented W. J. Parry for keeping his 'fire and brimstone' articles in *Y Genedl* firmly within the law.[48] The possibility of libels slipping through unnoticed was a particular worry for Frederick Coplestone, proprietor of the *Chester Chronicle*, the *Caernarvon and Denbigh Herald* and *Yr Herald Cymraeg*. As he did not read Welsh, this obliged him to be especially careful in his choice of editor.[49]

Others took a lighter view of libel as an occupational hazard.

John Gibson, returning from London in 1893, stopped in Newtown to buy furniture worth £350. 'Of course,' he assured a friend, 'this is not quite the cost of one libel suit, but libel suits are in the way of business'.[50] Also, if defendants could give a good account of themselves, libel cases could successfully be fought in the courts. The editor of *Tarian y Gweithiwr* was not alone among Welsh newspaper editors when he won a libel case brought against the paper by John Benyon in November 1886 when justices ordered the summonses to be withdrawn and each party to pay their own costs.[51]

News gathering

The principal function of an editor, however, was to organize, and if necessary personally to undertake, the collection of news and other editorial material, and as far as possible to ensure the veracity and legality of these items. General information was hardly ever in short supply, but the difficulty for editors was to render it sufficiently interesting and important to attract readers, and thus, for the commercial press, advertisers.[52]

Editors had at their disposal a number of useful sources of news, not least of which were other newspapers. Editors turned to their advantage the time-lag between London and Wales, and local newspapers routinely and inexpensively culled articles from the metropolitan or foreign press and reset them into their own columns.[53] H. Findlater Bussey recalled collecting American newspapers from the Liverpool docks for use in the *Albion*,[54] and in Wales it was common practice for editors similarly to scour the London dailies and other English provincial weeklies for suitable material for republication in their own papers.[55] The most cursory glance at the attributions of news columns in the Welsh press bears this out. *Y Papyr Newydd Cymraeg* regularly carried translations from the *Globe*, the *Hampshire Independent*, the *Spectator*, and the *Patriot*,[56] and the *South Wales Reporter* spent £6 in thirteen weeks up to July 1838 on 'London newspapers etc', which amounted to only 2.5 per cent of the total cost of producing the weekly paper.[57] *Cylchgrawn Rhyddid* in 1841 proudly advertised the fact that its editor was able to publish privileged information gathered from the pages of the 'main British newpapers' including the *Morning Chronicle* and the *Examiner*, as well as such local papers as the *Caernarvon and Denbigh Herald*.[58] *Y Gwyliedydd*, in its reviews of the London papers, simply drew attention to conflicting news stories without expressing its own view.[59] The dependence of Welsh newspapers on metropolitan journalism was most evident in times of war, when the absence of foreign correspondence and war news could spell disaster for a newspaper. The *Liverpool Daily Post* acknowledged its own weakness when, in 1904, shortly after the end of the Boer War, it vowed to its readers that in the event of another international conflict it would make arrangements with the London *Standard* and Reuters, as well as sending its own correspondents to the front.[60] In the absence of such resources, however, many editors had little alternative but to resort to other printed sources. The Sudan crisis of 1884–5 was extensively covered in *Y Gweithiwr Cymreig*, for example, but only by means of translations from the *Daily News*.[61] Distance from centres of political power also disadvantaged Welsh journalism in relation to the London press, and political scoops were virtually impossible to secure, even when a paper employed a London correspondent. John Griffith (Y Gohebydd), grandson of John Roberts, Llanbryn-mair, had, at the suggestion of William Rees (Gwilym Hiraethog), been appointed by Thomas Gee as *Baner ac Amserau Cymru*'s 'special correspondent' in London in 1857, but despite his extensive contacts, including a close friendship with Samuel Morley, there were political events to which even he could not gain access. Griffith did not conceal his admiration for the *Pall Mall Gazette* when, for example, he reported in *Baner ac Amserau Cymru* its exclusive revelation of the previous week of Gladstone's imminent resignation.[62]

The Welsh religious press was also dependent on the better resourced journalism of England, and translations of articles on temperance from the *Alliance News* and the *Methodist Times* appeared, for example, in *Y Gwyliedydd*.[63] The practice continued well into the twentieth century, as is shown in various newspaper account books.[64] *Y Dinesydd Cymreig* from May 1912, significantly, drew its foreign news from the pages of the American weekly, *Y Drych*, and its political reports from the *Merthyr Pioneer*. Ironically, towards the end of the nineteenth century, English-language papers began to publish regular reviews of the contents of the smaller circulation Welsh-language papers, for example the *Liverpool Daily Post and Mercury* published details of the contents of current issues of *Seren Cymru*, *Y Llan a'r Dywysogaeth*, *Y Goleuad* and *Y Tyst*.[65]

This kind of second-hand journalism, though convenient and cheap, did present editors with certain difficulties. The most intractable of these was how to establish the reliability of the reprinted item. A mistake, corrected in a later edition of the original paper, might be repeated without correction in another. This occurred to Mr Hemming, editor and manager of the *Glamorgan Gazette*, in March 1878 when a reprinted paragraph referring to an inheritance case caused him some considerable embarassment. He admitted to a solicitor that 'the paragraph in question was copied from the *Swansea and Glamorgan Herald*. Assuming it was an accurate statement, I inadvertently omitted to compare the reprint with your letter in the *Western Mail* in order to test its accuracy'. Hemming was fortunate to escape with an apology to the complainant.[66] On other occasions, a complainant would insist on taking action against the original version. Thus in July 1888 the Revd Glanffrwd Thomas took exception to an item which appeared in the 'Lloffion' column of the Church paper *Y Llan*, and demanded 'proof or retraction'. Failing that, he threatened legal action. The complaint, however, rested not on the original article in *Y Llan* but on a copy of the same article which had appeared in another newspaper, *Gwalia*. It was presumed that the writer in *Gwalia* had made a mistake in the transcription 'and this the Rev. G. Thomas charges *Y Llan* with'. The cleric who brought this complaint to the attention of the editor of *Y Llan* added 'your long experience as journalist will tell you what course of action you had better adopt'.[67] 'Long experience', however, did not necessarily safeguard editors against this kind of error, nor against its consequences for their reputations or their pockets.

In the second half of the nineteenth century, press agencies formalized and improved this largely informal scissors-and-paste journalism. Even in the early part of the century editors had recognized the limitations of other newspapers, and some had employed local journalists to provide their own digests of local, national and foreign news. In November 1841, for example, Hugh Jones (Erfyl), accepted an offer from the editor of *Yr Athraw* to contribute to that paper two pages per issue of home and foreign news at a cost of two and sixpence and three shillings per page. The editor from time to time also required items of Parliamentary news, reports of the Corn Laws controversy, and accounts of 'amazing accidents'. Jones was warned not to become too closely associated with either Whigs or Tories, but to provide unbiased reports of political events.[68] In effect, Jones was operating as an early, amateur version of a news agency. The emergence of professional news agencies later in the century, however, transformed the news coverage of the Welsh weekly press and also for the first time made possible a viable daily press. Before the 1860s conditions generally did not favour daily newspapers, but with the removal of the paper duty in 1861 and the establishment of the Press Association in 1870 new opportunities presented themselves which in Wales as elsewhere were swiftly grasped.[69] The *Western Mail* was launched in 1869, to be followed in Cardiff in 1872 by the *South Wales Daily News*. But for these daily papers, and even more so for the weeklies that sought to compete with them, a reliable and regular supply of inexpensive Parliamentary and general news was essential for their survival. News agencies were formed in response to this news-hunger and vied with each other to meet the pressing demands of an expanding newspaper press. The Central News Agency, initially the Central Press, was established by William Saunders in 1871, and was purchased by the Conservative Party Whips in 1873. A Liberal Press Agency was formed in response in the spring of 1873, and in June of the same year was reconstituted as the National Press Agency, promoted in turn by the Liberal Party Whips. Both agencies produced their own daily newspapers for newspaper proprietors, the *Central News* and the *National Press Journal*, printed on one side of the paper only and designed to be cut up and pasted into position in the preparation of other publications. There is little evidence to suggest that they were widely used by the major provincial papers, who by this time had other reliable sources of editorial material,[70] but from the early 1870s weekly newspapers in Wales were to draw heavily on these and other agencies. In February 1878, Central News supplied the *Glamorgan Gazette* with the text of the Queen's Speech,[71] and regular payments were made to the same agency by the Conservative newspaper, the *North Wales Chronicle*, from at least 1885.[72] The news agencies were also important sources of employment for journalists. The Swansea-born Howell Arthur Gwynne worked as the Romanian correspondent for Reuters from 1893 to 1904, before taking up the editorship of the *Standard*, and later the *Morning Post*, in London.

One of the services provided by the news agencies was the stereotype. This consisted of metal plates, for flat or rotary presses, on which columns of news and other items had been pre-typeset at the agencies' foundries. Advertisements and pictorial matter were also available in this format. The column plates were cast with longitudinal flanges, and were mounted at the provincial office on slotted softwood blocks. These plates of syndicated material could then be combined with columns of local news, comment, letters and advertisements to make up the normally eight-paged weekly newspaper. On completion of the print run, the plates were returned to the agencies for melting and recasting. Newspapers run on tight budgets were the most dependent on such stereotypes for cheap national and foreign news, 'London Letters' and so forth. The Typographical Association reported in 1886 that in many parts of the United Kingdom 'a good many newspapers were simply struggling for existence, and which had, so to speak, to live on stereotype'.[73] Some journalists and printers may have found the use of such stereotypes offensive to their professional sense, but there can be little doubt that such purchased pages imparted an enviable degree of sophistication, knowledge and wisdom to the columns of even the most parochial local newspapers. Stereotypes were also found to be useful in the political co-ordination of newspapers, for example the *Daily News* supplied stereotypes to the *Morning Post* until 1868. Also, they enabled provincial newspaper syndicates, such as Alexander Mackie's *Guardian* series in Cheshire in the 1870s, to be run cheaply and effectively.[74] In the main, however, the use of stereos, and the 'split-printing' of local papers which they entailed, was regarded with suspicion by many journalists, and many newspapers were eager to 'knock' their competitors with allegations of their use of stereotypes. The *Western Mail*'s praise for a new Conservative newspaper set up in Coleford, Gloucestershire, in 1874 was criticized by the *Forester* in the following terms, 'The WEAKLY paper to which [the *Western Mail*] refers contains four pages, two of them being printed in

London and two in Coleford . . . the news is stale and second-rate'.[75]

The business correspondence of J. Hemming, manager of the *Glamorgan Gazette*, reveals very extensive dealings with a number of different stereotype news suppliers between 1878 and 1882. At the start of this period he was making regular purchases of five to seven columns per week, including six of general news, from Leader and Sons, Sheffield,[76] and at the end of one week returned as many as ten columns of used metal to the Leader foundry.[77] In the following year he began to complain that the Leader stereos were too easily detected in his paper, and experimented with other suppliers, including the Exelsior Stereoptype Co., Birmingham, whose fonts bore a greater resemblance to his own.[78] If stereotypes were to be used, Hemming implied, it was better if the readers were not aware of it.

The contents of these columns varied from general news to literary notices, but it is clear that Hemming was unhappy with the quality of much of the material he received. 'The fault we find with stereo supply', he complained to the Manager of the National Press Agency in 1880, 'is this – we don't get concise paragraphs or late intelligence, but long accounts and stale news',[79] and in a missive to the Griffin and Hawkes Co., Birmingham, in the same year, he implored them to send him 'five columns of stereo . . . of *well-selected* general news; what we received this week was not satisfactory. We want epitome of news; short concise pieces . . .'.[80] Turning in despair to yet another supplier in 1881, Hemming asked whether he could 'give your Patent News Stereo a trial, and shall be glad if you will send us 7 columns, with blocks for use in our issue of this week. I shall leave the selection to you, trusting you will send us well assorted News, and as late intelligence as possible'.[81] The advantage of purchasing weekly stereotype items was that it gave the editor considerable flexibility. Whilst he could print eye-catching reports on the 'Attempted Blowing Up of Liverpool Town Hall' and equally sensational Irish news, for example,[82] without sending out correspondents, or even typesetting the report himself, he could also use such material to fill in space left by unexpected shortfalls in local news coverage. Thus Hemming informed yet another supplier in 1882 that 'when I sent you Order for Supplement yesterday, I expected an overwhelming quantity of Local reports, but finding the pressure is likely to be less than expected, I wired to countermand the order.'[83] Other newspaper offices in Wales took advantage of stereotype plates, including the Conservative paper *Gwalia*, which introduced new printing machinery in January 1882 specifically so that they might use stereotype plates 'as used by the *Times* and other leading London papers'.[84]

A more direct way of receiving the latest news was through the use of telegrams and the telegraph. The General Commercial Telegraph Co. was provisionally registered as a Joint Stock Company in September 1845, and a further nine telegraph companies were registered between October 1856 and March 1858, including the News and Entertainment Telephone Syndicate and the Newspaper Advertising Supply Co.[85] In Wales, as elsewhere, the telegraph followed the laying of railway tracks. The first messages from London were received in Swansea in 1852, and Carmarthen in 1853.[86] By the late 1870s, newspapers in south Wales were beginning to set into type news received from agencies by telegram, a form of news collection that was to prove most useful during times of international crisis. Hemming in February 1878 requested from Central News an additional supply of 'Telegraphic News . . . which we can publish in Second and if necessary Third Editions' on the entry of Russia into Constantinople.[87] The added advantage of telegrammed news was that editors could receive updated items up to the hour of printing.[88] Two other areas which required constant updating were Parliamentary affairs and market news, and Hemming, along with many others, relied on telegrams from news agencies to supply this kind of material. 'I am', Hemming told the Central News Agency in February 1878 'most anxious to give our readers the best information up to the hour of going to press, and shall bear in consideration the publishing of more frequent intervals, being of course guided by the turn affairs may take'.[89] The fascination with this new communications technology was also reflected in the titles of such ventures as the *Abergavenny Telephone* of 1887.

Hemming's dealings with the press agencies reveal two difficulties with the telegraphic news service that they provided. The first was the problem of reliability, and in particular the danger of errors made by postal clerks. In 1878, Hemming complained to the Post Office in London that an omission had occurred which the sender claimed was the fault of the postal officials who despatched it. The mistake, Hemming added, had put him to much loss and inconvenience.[90] A second difficulty was how to justify the payment of higher prices for such up-to-the-minute news, and Hemming stopped all further Central News telegrams in September 1882 on the grounds that his sales did not cover his costs. 'I have no complaint to make of the service,' he explained 'but much of the apathy of local readers who in a time of feverish excitement respecting the War in Egypt appreciated Newspaper enterprise (only) if they could learn the latest News for nothing'.[91]

The telegraph was slower to reach north Wales. D. R. Daniel celebrated the arrival of the telegraph in Fourcrosses, Llŷn, in June 1890. 'At last the thing is done . . .', he wrote in his diary, 'it originated in an idea that struck me at Llangefni nearly two years ago'.[92] In mid-August, Daniel sent the first wire to W. D. Owen in Liverpool, and was delighted to receive from him an immediate reply.[93] Newspapers were eager to take advantage of this new facility, and *Ye Brython Cymreig* informed its readers in its first issue that it had reached agreements with Central News and other companies, 'to send to us any important news item by telegraph up to the moment we begin printing'.[94]

Editors could also get publishable material directly from those who gave out the news. The relationship between editors and the private or public bodies which had news to communicate became a pivotal one, on which rested the ability of a newspaper to attract and maintain readers. Unlike stereotype and telegram news, the acquisition of this type of material relied more on the editor's personal contacts and powers of persuasion than on the amount of money with which he was prepared to part. Official bodies were important sources of information, and editors were eager to be included in their lists of approved newspapers. Hemming pleaded with the Registrar of Bank Returns in 1878 to be placed on the official list of papers authorized to publish the Bank Returns on the grounds that Bridgend had three Joint Stock banks.[95] The receipt of direct political news could also be negotiated between a politician and the editor, particularly in cases of speeches and statements. Fred Mason, editor of the *Montgomeryshire Express*, informed Lord Rendel in April 1890 that he was anxious to give as full a report as possible of a speech Rendel was to give at a forthcoming meeting in Newtown. However, in view of the fact that the Cambrian trains were 'extremely inconvenient', and that in consequence his reporters would have to return by a train which would not reach Oswestry until after midnight 'and we have to go to press with our Montgomeryshire edition at 2.30 a.m.' he delicately suggested that it would be 'an immense advantage' if he could be sent a copy of the speech beforehand.[96] It was Lloyd George's practice to confer with English-language journalists the evening before delivering a speech in Welsh in order to appraise them of its contents, and important sources, such as government ministers, would send advance copies of their speeches to the *Western Mail*, principally to avoid any errors being made in the reporting.[97] William Davies, editor of the *Western Mail*, also attempted to persuade judges to send him copies of their decisions in key court cases before they were delivered in open court. Judge Bryn Roberts agreed to this request, apparently as a favour granted on the grounds that he and Elliss Hughes, a senior reporter on the paper, attended the same church. Sales of the *Western Mail* the following week increased substantially.[98]

News collection of this kind, unlike news agency material, required the active participation of the editor in its acquisition and in checking its content and style. In time, editorial work began to be subdivided into different tasks, largely as a result of the growth of newspapers into larger and more elaborate enterprises. Thus there emerged newspaper workers who were not primarily writers themselves, but rather controllers and revisers of the writing of others.[99] Sub-editors, originally made necessary by 'prolix penny-a-liners', were first recorded in 1834.[100] In many parts of Wales, however, the work associated with sub-editing was conducted often by the editor himself. The work of preparing a manuscript for publication was clearly an onerous one. A letter to the editor of the *South Wales Reporter* by a 'Poor Workman' in 1837 was printed only after extensive alteration, and corrections of spelling and grammar.[101] Not all letters were accepted for publication, although a copy of a letter rejected by the editor of the *Merthyr Telegraph* was subsequently sent to the *Aberdare Times*, and was printed at second attempt only after considerable editing.[102]

In the larger newspaper enterprises, however, sub-editing became a common and essential occupation, and was likened by Mansfield to a 'constructive metabolism [which] is the process by which nutritive material is built up into living matter'. It was the sub-editor above all who was responsible for ensuring that news items were readable, accurate and legal. Often, the sub-editor was at the same time a reporter, or had 'graduated in the arduous school of reporting'.[103] Others were recruited from the ranks of occasional feature writers. T. E. Ellis was approached by John Duncan of the *South Wales Daily News* in 1885 to work as a sub-editor on his paper. 'Of course' he admitted, 'we are aware that you are inexperienced in Sub-Editorial, but we have no doubt you would rapidly acquire the necessary ability to do the work'. He was offered a relatively generous salary of £2.10*s*. a week, the only conditions being that he stay with them for a minimum of two to three years, and 'owing to the constant intrigues of the *Western Mail* people' that he would agree not to join their staff within twelve months of leaving Duncan's employment.[104] Alternatively, sub-editors, like many editors, graduated from the composing rooms. Thomas Catling described a not untypical experience when he recalled how for him 'the change from composing to sub-editing came quite suddenly and in an unexpected way'.[105]

Wage rates in the early years of sub-editing in Wales varied greatly. In 1885 and 1886, the sub-editor of the *North Wales Chronicle* was paid the same sum as was offered Ellis in Cardiff, £2.10*s*. a week. Sub-editors on *Gwalia* and *Y Cloriannydd* (John Williams) in the same period, however, were paid only £1.18*s*. and £1.10*s*. respectively.[106] In his application for a sub-editor's post at a proposed new paper published in Liverpool in 1902, J. H. Jones, from Wrexham, indicated that he would be prepared to accept a wage of two guineas a week in the first instance, whilst expecting this sum to be substantially raised in the course of time.[107] Working conditions and self-perceptions were similarly diverse. The work, as shown by Mansfield, was commonly performed 'in most offices in a drab room, and those who toil at night are cut off from the currents of outside life . . . A life of isolation and intensive labour'. Yet, being the 'brains department' of a newspaper office, it was a place of 'romance and zest to the born journalist'.[108] Writing in 1932, Mansfield conceded that 'the woman journalist is in many offices still a rarity', and that this was especially so in sub-editing, which remained a male preserve long after the National Union of Journalists (NUJ) had drawn up safeguards against sex discrimination in salary, hours and working conditions at its inception in 1907.[109]

Local news was gathered and submitted to editors by enthusiastic amateur correspondents as well as by full-time reporters, and for much of the nineteenth century, journalism in Wales was very largely a part-time occupation. At least until the early 1850s few papers could afford regular local reporters, and poor transport rendered travel in search of local news difficult and slow. Many editors relied on what R. D. Rees termed 'chance paragraphs gratuitously sent' for much of their local news.[110] As late as 1897, an article in the trade magazine the *Journalist and Newspaper Proprietor* commented that 'Welsh periodical literature, generally speaking, is the work of amateurs and the production of voluntary effort',[111] and even at the turn of the century many regular correspondents remained amateurs. Few Welsh newspapers employed permanent staffs, and most continued to depend to a considerable extent on the voluntary efforts of Nonconformist ministers, clergymen and schoolmasters, though artisans, especially shoemakers, tailors, miners and quarrymen, were prominent in the work of writing and distributing newspapers and magazines.[112] Where there were established staffs, newspapers commonly employed 'a large class of journalistic irregulars . . . a large body of literary casuals'[113] to augment their reportage. Such correspondents were drawn from a wide variety of occupations. A bookseller from Ystalyfera, for example, sent weekly reports of local news to the *Leader*,[114] while W. Williams of Liverpool estimated that in 1877 he had sent three hundred articles and letters to various Welsh newspapers, including *Y Genedl* and *Yr Herald Cymraeg*, and a similar number in 1880.[115] Hill farmer Richard Griffiths (Carneddog), writing under a number of pseudonyms, contributed prolifically to *Y Genedl Gymreig* (as 'Carn'), *Baner ac Amserau Cymru* (as 'Syr Rhisiart') and *Yr Herald Cymraeg* (as 'Carneddog').[116] For many writers, submitting reports and essays to the local press was a form of creative self-expression, and voluntary correspondents were often the most committed of auto-didacts. David Davies recalled in 1925 how his grandfather, a weaver who wrote extensively for *Seren Cymru* under the *nom de plume* 'Daniel Ddu', began to learn Greek at the age of fifty-five so that he might read his

Greek Testament.[117] The cultural implications of such widespread plebeian literary creativity are discussed more fully in a later chapter.

Part-time reporting of this kind was also a route to permanent work. In 1909, S. Gwilly Davies, a reporter with the *Western Mail* in Cardiff, was offered the editorship of *Y Cloriannydd* and the *Welsh Coast Pioneer* on the basis of a series of weekly columns he had written for J. H. Jones's *Y Brython*. Richard Hughes Williams (Dic Tryfan) was essentially a short-story writer, drawn towards newspaper journalism through the Eisteddfod. In 1911 he was appointed sub-editor of the Liberal *Herald Cymraeg* and in 1913 rose to be editor of the Conservative *Aberystwyth Observer*. He ended his rather unhappy career as a journalist on the staff of the Liberal *Cambrian News*.[118] Others came to reporting from other occupations. D. M. Richards worked as a teacher and a clerk on the Pontypool to Hirwaun railway before becoming in 1886 a reporter for the *Merthyr Express*, and later the *South Wales Daily News*, and Robert David Rowland (Anthropos) was apprenticed as a tailor before joining the staffs of both the *Herald* and the *Genedl* papers in Caernarfon, where he distinguished himself, under the pseudonym 'John Brown' as one of the most trenchant satirists of his day.

Newspapers also served as minute books and publicists for friendly societies, local clubs, trade unions and other associations, and the officials of such organizations voluntarily sent news material to local papers. D. Tyler, an official in the Pentyrch Lodge of the Tin Department of the Ironworkers' Association, regularly sent copies of resolutions passed at their meetings to the union's official organ and to a local Merthyr newspaper, the *Workman's Advocate*, which he claimed circulated widely through Glamorganshire and Monmouthshire.[119] Similarly T. Z. Jones, secretary of the Sailor's Union in Cardiff, was a frequent correspondent to the *Glamorgan Free Press*.[120] Occasional unsolicited articles sent to editors by such voluntary contributors served both to fill the pages of local papers with local news which would otherwise have been difficult if not impossible to obtain, and to provide an essential training in method and style for aspiring journalists. The inevitable rejection of letters and reports could teach a writer how better to gauge the public, that is to say the editorial, taste.[121]

However, not all these occasional reporters worked voluntarily, and commissioned writers were paid small sums for their contributions. In 1880, £1 was paid per printed page for articles in such magazines as *Nineteenth Century*, the *Contemporary*, the *Edinburgh Review* and the *Quarterly*.[122] In contrast, *Y Traethodydd* paid its contributors considerably less. One correspondent in 1865 was paid £2.10*s*. for writing two articles covering twenty-three pages.[123] For writing articles in weekly newspapers, Revd H. C. Williams, a Baptist minister from Corwen and President of the Welsh Baptist Union in 1892, acting as the Welsh correspondent of the *Freeman*, a Baptist journal published in London, was paid fifteen shillings in 1890 and thirty shillings in 1892.[124] The payment of local enthusiasts for their contributions, however, raised its own difficulties for editors. Many such correspondents might be called, with some justification, penny-a-liners. 'The "liner" ', one critic observed in 1899,

> is a man not only of resource and industry, but of verbosity. . . . As his remuneration depends on the amount of his copy which is inserted, he generally writes about five times, or even ten times, as much as is ever printed. His powers of amplification are indeed enormous. Whatever may be said of him, he cannot be accused of not dragging in every petty detail of the murder, fire, suicide, or burglary which is the subject of his paragraph or report.[125]

Texts submitted by such 'liners' required close and time-consuming editing. It was also a much sought-after job. Hemming, of the *Glamorgan Gazette*, was from time to time importuned by amateurs inquiring whether they could be employed as one of his many local correspondents.[126] In May 1878 he agreed to take on one such unsolicited applicant. Frank Williams from Maesteg was paid £4 a year, payable quarterly, the standard sum for local reporters, and was sent post-free a weekly copy of the paper. Much of the work involved the reporting of police and court news, and Hemming issued terse instructions that he,

> . . . should like to get Reports by Thursday mornings' post, and anything occurring during that day might be sent per post that night. In case of any important event occurring you could send per train on Friday. We could despatch to you Stamped envelopes to pay cost of train carriage.[127]

The work was also insecure, and the termination of a contract could be brutally delivered at the whim of a dissatisfied editor. In April 1878, Hemming informed another of his local correspondents, who had for the previous year provided 'excellent reports' from Neath, that he was no longer required to send Police and other news as he had made 'fresh arrangements as to the collection of Neath news'.[128]

Local part-time correspondents were expected to be both inquisitive and accurate, and were given by their editors detailed instructions regarding which local events were likely to be newsworthy. In 1892 the sub-editor of the *South Wales Daily News* reminded D. M. Richards of an imminent funeral in Aberdare, and instructed him to 'see that we are furnished with a report of any remarks that may be made on the subject'.[129] Also Kennedy Jones, of the *Daily Mail*, London, wrote to Richards asking for material for the Sunday edition of the paper, and to 'make such arrangements as will ensure the supply to us on Saturday evening of all the important items of news occurring on that day in your district'.[130] On occasion, editors would approach trusted friends to provide them with the names of reliable local reporters. William Davies of the *Western Mail*, for example, approached H. Haydn Jones in 1905 with the request that he inform him whether he knew of a 'good reporter' in Merionethshire whom he could recommend, 'one who understands the education difficulty in general, and the Merioneth difficulty in particular'.[131]

Editors were constantly frustrated by the tardiness and the poor writing style of such local reporters, many of whom they rarely met and communicated with only by letter. Tired of exhorting reporters to submit copy by the stated deadlines, some editors chose to explain, through the pages of the newspaper, how the paper was managed and edited, to describe the means whereby the paper was printed and to offer advice on the composition of news articles. The editor of *Y Gwyliedydd*, in one such appeal to his reporters in February 1888, described in detail the weekly timetable of his paper, and urged all correspondents to be mindful of the deadlines that the editor and the printers were also obliged to meet. The compositing, he explained, began at noon on Wednesday, and by Saturday a full half of the paper was ready for the press. By the evening of the following Monday, or at the very latest the Tuesday morning, the whole paper, including local reports and advertisements was set up in type. It was vital, therefore, that local news reports be submitted by the Saturday morning. The editor then appealed to all reporters to pay close attention to the three basic rules of good journalism, namely punctuality, clarity and accuracy in handwriting and expression and, thirdly, brevity and neatness. Of these, he added, the last was the most important, as too much of his time was spent deciphering and rewriting reporters' contributions.[132] 'Only one in a hundred' he complained, 'know how to write for the press'. Few adequately understood what the editor meant by 'news', and many of the reports received by *Y Gwyliedydd* were not only poorly written, but uninteresting. Every January, he complained, his office was inundated by reports of 'watchnights', and quarterly church meetings. Many were virtually identical, but when he wielded the editor's blue pencil the infuriated reporters would demand to know why their reports were not being printed in full.[133] Advice regarding style was also given by other Welsh editors. In 1868, the editor of *Y Dydd* implored his reporters in and around Dolgellau to 'write without ostentation, simply, briefly and clearly' and to avoid minor matters of local detail which were of little general interest.[134] Hemming also complained that local reports were arriving at his office too late for inclusion in the paper. He informed one local reporter that:

> Your letter was not despatched until the Mail last night and much of the space was forestalled. We sent a representative to Neath on Wednesday who reported two meetings and his 'copy' was put in hand Thursday morning. There is no reason in sending us news which reaches us a week after date. We hope, therefore, you will despatch your copy by installments and as early as possible in the week. The police report . . . does not appear to improve in your hands, I am bound to say'.[135]

The quality and accuracy of reports were also difficult issues with which editors were obliged to deal. Some were misleading and others were found to be deliberate falsehoods. *Y Rhedegydd* once found itself in an awkward position after printing an account of a local wedding. The groom named in the report angrily replied that he had been married for some years and demanded compensation. The editor, John Davies, subsequently discovered that the complainant was the author of the initial news report, and rather than take legal action against him ensured his public humiliation by reporting the deception and its consequences prominently in the paper.[136]

Other part-time correspondents included occasional special columnists, feature writers and the ubiquitous and prolific authors of 'letters to the editor'. Five years before he set up his own printing press, and began to edit and print his own newspapers, William Roberts (Nefydd), then a Baptist minister in Blaenau Gwent, Monmouthshire, wrote constantly for the weeklies. His diary shows how between 14 and 17 March 1859 he wrote two letters to the *Caernarvon Herald* and two articles on Dissent for the *Star* and *Gwron*.[137] Aspiring Welsh-language journalists also found a niche for themselves in the English-language papers as editors of 'Welsh columns'. Jonathan Owain Reynolds (Nathan Dyfed), a farm labourer and wheelwright, for example, edited a number of such columns before his death in 1891, including one in the *Merthyr Express*.

Occasionally, regular correspondents acquired prominence in their field, and thus became highly prized by their editors. Duncan, proprietor of the *South Wales Daily News*, wrote to T. E. Ellis in August 1886 to congratulate him on his election to Parliament. 'Now that your Parliamentary duties are about to begin,' Duncan continued,

> . . . it has occurred to me that you may possibly have the leisure and disposition to contribute more largely to our columns. You are aware that we are already represented by a London Correspondent (in confidence I may inform you it is Mr T. P. O'Connor MP for Scotland Ward, Liverpool) who covers pretty well all the ordinary Parliamentary work. Scenes in the House etc. But beyond these general topics there must be a great deal of discussion of matters and measures specially affecting Wales and Welshmen, which never come before the House, although they may largely occupy the thoughts and wishes of Welsh Members.[138]

Earlier in the year Ellis had been paid around 10*s*.6*d*. per article, but it is evident from this correspondence that from August Ellis could state his own terms.[139] Contributions made by key lay individuals over a long period of time were clearly of great importance to the Welsh weekly press in the late nineteenth and early twentieth centuries. Richard Jones Owen (Glaslyn), a quarry overseer from Nantmor in Caernarfonshire, wrote under a variety of pseudonyms hundreds of articles and letters for more than a dozen newspapers and magazines between the late 1860s and his death in 1909.[140] Bob Owen, Croesor, also made a distinguished contribution to Welsh learning through the pages of the weekly newspapers in the early decades of the twentieth century.[141]

Though of undoubted value to editors struggling to maintain and extend their readerships, such occasional and essentially non-professional correspondents could also get an editor and the paper into legal difficulties. One of the issues which highlighted the ambivalent relationship between an editor and such correspondents was anonymity and the associated question of the confidentiality of a newspaper's sources. Thomas Gee routinely denied all reponsibility for the contents of readers' letters, which were simply 'handed over to the editor and principal compositors'. Seldom did he admit to reading the proofs before publication. Gee, it appears, also instructed his sub-editors to refuse to take moral responsibility for the letters which they printed 'so far as is expedient, and so long as a letter is not libellous or indecent'.[142] But in the case of a correspondent whose letter or article was libellous, or aroused the indignation of a reader, it was far from clear whether or not the editor or publisher would protect the source if the item had appeared anonymously or pseudonymously. The matter was raised with some urgency in January 1888 when letters by two local miners were printed in the radical colliers' weekly in Aberdare, *Tarian y Gweithiwr*. 'Reformer', a miner from Birchgrove, rehearsed at length his reasons for joining the miners' union, and 'Leo' supplied a report of the most recent meeting of the miners' union. An enraged pit manager demanded from the paper's editor the authors' true names, and, to the astonishment of the miners, these were duly given without consultation with the correspondents. The union condemned the editor for 'muzzling the mouths of the miners, and preventing them from defending their rights through [the] paper', and called a meeting to consider what action the union should appropriately take against the paper and its editor.[143]

A comparable situation arose in June 1892 when an anonymous letter (by 'An Anti-Margarine Grocer') was printed in the *Haverfordwest and Milford Haven Telegraph*, implying that G. G. Fisher, brother of Sir Charles Philipps of Picton Castle,

Pembrokeshire, was of illegitimate birth. The paper's editor, William Lewis, was asked to hand over to Fisher's solicitors the writer's name and to make a 'full apology in terms to be approved by us' in the next issue 'in as conspicuous a part of your paper as you did this libel'. He was warned that unless the terms were agreed to within four days the case was to be taken to law.[144] Philipps, the Conservative baronet, was advised by his brother to turn the affair to his advantage by using William Lewis's discomfiture to ensure that his Liberal paper would cease its attacks on the Pembrokeshire Tories. 'I think if we could get either the apology or the writ kept before him [William Lewis] during the Election he will continue to ignore you'.[145] An apology was duly printed in the *Telegraph* on 7 July 1892, and in so doing, Lewis as editor took full responsibility for the contents of the anonymous letter. Sir Charles was subsequently advised by Fisher's solicitors that this was as far as he could take the case against the paper, and that the editor was not bound to disclose the name of the writer of the article if the editor had chosen to take the responsibility himself for the article, which in this case 'he has seemingly done by the insertion of the apology'. Contrary to his legal advice, however, Fisher demanded that the apology be printed twice, and that the editor be responsible for all the legal costs.[146] A second apology was duly printed in the *Telegraph* on 13 July, though the paper was not pressed for costs. The name and address of the anonymous correspondent, however, was secretly revealed by the editor to the legal representatives of the Philipps family.[147]

The issues of editorial responsibility, the confidentiality of sources and the protection of correspondents, whether anonymous or not, were raised in different ways by the appointment of permanent staff to newspaper offices. This occurred increasingly towards the end of the nineteenth century as journalism became professionalized and newspapers began to employ full-time trained reporters. In the course of the nineteenth century, recruitment and training practices evolved in response to the changing needs of newspapers and of the functions they performed in Welsh society.

Writing of the 1890s A. Patchett Martin recalled that a new kind of reporter was demanded by newspaper proprietors and editors. In choosing his staff, one such proprietor

> . . . did not care for men of broad views, sound common sense, and correct principles. Give me a clever, disappointed man, of morbid mind, who 'wants to get his knife' into as many of his fellow-creatures as possible. That's the kind of man who can write what the public like to read.[148]

The priorities of the New Journalism as expressed above may not have been shared in every cynical detail by all editors in Wales, but the subsequent change in style did permeate into Wales, and did influence the style of Welsh journalism. Wales was not isolated from the English press, and many Welsh journalists acted as correspondents for English newspapers. Henry Russell Evans, founder of the *Advertiser of Wales* and the Monmouthshire and South Wales Newspaper Co. Ltd., in 1865 and 1888 respectively, was also a correspondent for the *Times* by 1871, and Evan Vincent Evans, a reporter on the *South Wales Daily News*, was also a Parliamentary correspondent for *Baner ac Amserau Cymru*, *Y Brython* and the *Manchester Guardian*. Thomas John Hughes (Adfyfyr), erstwhile private secretary to Alfred Thomas, the First Baron of Pontypridd, sub-editor on the *South Wales Daily News* and the editor of *Cymru Fydd*, also acted as Welsh correspondent for, among others, the *Daily News* and the *Manchester Guardian*.[149] John Evans, a Llanberis quarryman self-taught in the skills of shorthand and sometime private secretary to Thomas Gee, acted as Clwyd correspondent for the *Liverpool Daily Post*, the *Liverpool Echo* and the *Manchester Guardian* for more than fifty years until his death in 1942. The careers of individual correspondents thus frequently crossed the boundaries of language within Wales, and also those between the Welsh and British newspapers. One route for the transmission of new forms of reportage was the influence of the editors of London newspapers on their Welsh correspondents. In 1904 the news editor of the *Daily Chronicle* appointed D. M. Richards to act as one of the regular Welsh correspondents for the 'new' *Chronicle*, and instructed him that it was no longer necessary 'that reports of ordinary political meetings, religious, labour and other conferences and matters of only local importance be supplied, unless these are ordered'. What was needed instead were 'early, accurate and full accounts . . . of events of general public interest'.[150] This was generally what editors came to demand of their correspondents throughout Wales. William

Davies of the *Western Mail* instructed a new recruit to the paper in the 1890s not to write long articles, as he had been trained to do on the weeklies, and advised the young journalist to condense rather than to elaborate, and to do so without losing anything of importance in the story.[151] Journalists, in the main, were obliged to learn these skills on the job, since well into the twentieth century methods of journalist recruitment and training remained haphazard and informal.[152]

It was generally agreed that the surest means of acquiring suitable reporting staff was to employ young persons, and to train them informally in the accomplishments that were required by specific circumstances. Many editors made strenuous efforts to persuade young people that journalism offered good career opportunities, and in so doing began a process of defining, explicitly, both the functions and the skills of journalism. The editor of *Y Dydd* declared in 1868 that he would make every effort 'to support young reporters',[153] some of whom appear to have been attracted to journalism by the promised diversity of the work. Picton Davies's route to journalism began at school in 1898 when Lewis Giles, the proprietor of a local newspaper, charmed him with accounts of the journalist's existence. 'That's how to see life', Giles informed him, 'you meet people, go to all kinds of meetings, the County Council, the Courts, concerts, eisteddfodau and all sorts of things'. Thus was the romance of journalism transmitted to one Welsh schoolboy at the close of the nineteenth century.[154]

Young and inexperienced journalists could expect to assume major responsibilities at an early stage in their careers, particularly in the smaller circulation Welsh-language press. In 1852, John Roberts (Ieuan Gwyllt) found, to his evident surprise, that his response to an advertisement in *Yr Amserau* for a post on that paper had been successful. Anxious as to whether he should accept the post, Roberts wrote to the religious leader, Dr Lewis Edwards, 'as to a father', seeking his advice. His previous work experience, he explained somewhat nervously, had consisted of teaching and seven years' work as a solicitor's clerk. The *Amserau*, on the other hand, required, for only thirty shillings a week, a journalist to write and edit virtually the entire paper with the exception of the leading article, which would continue to be written by the founding editor, William Rees (Gwilym Hiraethog). Lewis's reply is not recorded, but Roberts was taken on as a reporter and assistant editor in 1852 and in the following year replaced Rees as editor. He eventually became the paper's proprietor before the merger with Gee's *Baner Cymru* in 1857.[155] Roberts failed to sustain *Yr Amserau*, perhaps as a result of his strong support for Russia during the Crimean War which was said to have halved the paper's circulation from eight to four thousand copies a week,[156] but this did not dissuade him from continuing to work as a journalist. In 1858 he founded *Y Gwladgarwr* in Aberdare, published and edited *Y Cerddor Cymraeg* from 1861 to 1873 (though Hughes and Son, Wrexham, took over the publishing in 1865), and finally, from July 1871 to October 1872, was editor of *Y Goleuad*.

By the 1870s, however, success in journalism was measured by the speed of a reporter's promotion from the weekly press to a daily paper. Editors of weekly newspapers were quick to acknowledge this, and to turn it to their advantage. The most effective route to the dailies, they argued, began with a good job on a weekly. Hemming, manager of the *Glamorgan Gazette*, made this abundantly clear in his reply to a job enquiry in January 1878:

> I may ask you if you have any literary tastes and would like to make the press your future vocation. If so our office would be an excellent opening for gaining probationary knowledge. We have had some Juniors who have obtained good situations on daily papers. The highest terms we could offer would be £2 a week, and one should expect the holder of the situation to make himself generally useful.[157]

Junior reporters on the *Glamorgan Gazette* in 1878 received only a pound or two a week, but were given the security of a month's notice of dismissal and were assured that they would gain valuable work experience in other departments, including distribution and advertising. This arrangement, Hemming concluded, provided an excellent opportunity for young journalists to learn 'the various details of newspaper work – both in the Reporting and Commercial departments' and one which enabled them 'to obtain what [they] desire, a connection with the Press'.[158] In return, Hemming required of a prospective junior good shorthand note-taking, 'steadiness, willingness and general attention'. [159]

Picton Davies's apprenticeship as a journalist to the *Carmarthen Journal* in 1899 was based on distinctly different terms. He agreed to stay with the paper for three years, pay his employees £10 for learning the craft, and in return received three shillings a week in wages in the first year, four shillings in the second, and a crown on the fourth. During his interview with the editor, Henry Tobit Evans, Davies and his father were served tea, which greatly impressed the aspiring young reporter. It was the first time he had tasted marmalade. Lewis Giles, the paper's proprietor, promised him a feast of a different kind, and advised him to spend half a crown to join the local library and reading room, and to read at least half a dozen of the novels of Charles Dickens with a dictionary at hand, 'and not to go past a single new word without consulting the dictionary'. This, he was told, was to be an essential part of his training as a writer. In 1901 Davies was appointed to a post on the *Western Mail*, starting on a wage of 25s. a week, five times his pay as an apprentice. Had he been recruited by the *South Wales Daily News*, he recalled with evident relief half a century later, 'the editor, Henry Read, would have asked me if I was a teetotaller and tested my shorthand'. Read, however, was commonly regarded as a good employer who would pay from his own pocket for his apprentice reporters to attend night classes. William Davies of the *Western Mail* did not subject his new reporters to such a test, nor did he enquire about their religious affiliations.[160]

The vast majority of those recruited to journalism in the nineteenth century were men. Very few women succeeded in entering the profession, in sharp contrast to their experience in England where, as Lucy Brown has shown, 'journalism was exceptional and noteworthy in its employment of women', and where women journalists were often to be found in key positions well before the appearance of women's pages.[161] Eluned Morgan became both editor and compositor of *Y Drafod* in 1893, but that was in Patagonia, not Wales. Women made more of an impact on periodicals than on newspapers. Sarah Jane Rees (Cranogwen) founded and edited *Y Frythones* from 1879, a magazine aimed specifically at Welsh women. Merged with *Cyfaill yr Aelwyd*, *Y Frythones* ceased publication in 1891 but was followed in 1896 by *Y Gymraes*, edited by Alice Gray Jones (Ceridwen Peris), and a far more aggressive defender of women's rights.[162] The south Wales dailies began to include women's pages and issue women's supplements in the early 1890s; the *Western Mail* introduced a four-page 'Ladies' Supplement' in November 1894, a development which signalled the emergence of women as an important segment of the readership and a valuable market for advertisers.

Fluency in Welsh, though not a general requirement, was regarded as a desirable skill for young reporters in both north and south Wales. To his intense disgust, H. Findlater Bussey was refused work on the *North Wales Chronicle* in 1846 on the grounds that he 'had no knowledge of the Welsh language'.[163] Later in the century, the editor of the *Western Mail* also indicated his preference for reporters who were able to listen to a Welsh speech and report it in English shorthand, although Pitman's shorthand had been adapted to Welsh by Richard Humphrey Morgan in 1878. Welsh-speaking journalists were thus in demand in both English- and Welsh-language newspapers in Wales, and considerable numbers received their initial training in the Welsh-language press before being recruited by English papers in Wales and in England. J. O. Jones, for example, who had made a name for himself as a radical contributor to *Y Werin* and *Y Genedl* in Caernarfon in the 1880s took up the editorship of the *Merthyr Times* in 1895 before moving on to work with his erstwhile manager, David Edwards, at the *Nottingham Daily Express*. Among the journalists who had started with the *Herald* in Caernarfon before 1914, Samuel Evans took up a reporter's job on the *Sheffield Independent* in 1880 before being appointed private secretary to Sir Edgar Vincent, financial adviser to the Egyptian Government and emigrating to Johannesburg in 1897 where he was a founder of the University of Witwatersrand. Arthur Jones and Evan Henry Ellis also went to work on daily papers in England, as did William Eames, who left *Y Genedl* in 1916 for a post as financial correspondent of the *Manchester Guardian*, and who, in June 1920, founded the *Manchester Guardian Commercial*.[164] The *Guardian* circulated widely in north Wales at the turn of the century, and was described as the 'secular Bible' of the Caernafon journalists, largely as a result of the efforts of its 'Welsh editor', F. E. Hamer. John Gwyndaf Jones, also from the same office in Caernarfon, moved to Chester as manager of the *Chester Chronicle* and served in 1956 as President of the Newspaper Society.

The traffic also flowed in the opposite direction, from the

English- into the Welsh-language sector. Beriah Gwynfe Evans abandoned the *South Wales Daily News* in 1892 to become managing editor of the Welsh National Press Company in Caernarfon, publishers of *Y Genedl Gymreig* and other weeklies. A quarter of a century later the 22-year-old Haydn Morgan, an ex-reader on the night staff of the *Western Mail*, and who occasionally deputized for Cemlyn Jones as author of the paper's 'Welsh Column', applied for a post on the Welsh-language socialist weekly newspaper, *Y Dinesydd*, on the grounds that he wished to write in his own language and to speak his own mind 'even if it is of the same opinion as the Russian bear'.[165] Work mobility of this kind was relatively common and led to the much needed cross-fertilization of ideas between the various sections of the industry, particularly the main language groups, the political and religious denominations and the weeklies and dailies. A cause of greater concern was the outflow of journalists from Wales to more lucrative work in England and elsewhere. Even John Gibson, proprietor and editor of the *Cambrian News*, was at one time almost lost to Welsh journalism. During a lengthy convalescence in London in 1891 he was so delighted to have had articles accepted by the *Daily News*, the *Chronicle,* the *Star,* the *City Press* and the *Athaneum* that he wrote excitedly to a friend to say that his future life had become an 'open question', and that a new career in London journalism awaited him. Within a matter of weeks, however, he had returned to his 'long exile' in Aberystwyth.

Partly as a consequence of the mobility of journalism, and despite the attractions of the work for growing numbers of young people, it was clear by the 1890s that the demand for journalists in Wales far outstripped the domestic supply. David Davies, editor of the *South Wales Daily Post*, complained in 1897 that 'much of the talent which in other countries gravitates naturally to the newspaper' continued to be attracted to the ministries of the religious groups. As a result, the staffs of Welsh newspapers, particularly the dailies, were 'recruited chiefly in England'.[166] Competition with English and Scottish journalists had, by the 1850s, become a feature of the Welsh domestic labour market. Newspapers in Wales formed part of a wider informal network that linked journalists across Britain, by means of personal contact as well as advertisments, and which kept them in touch with job vacancies wherever they might be, even in the most remote areas of the country. The network opened up new opportunities for both reporters and the managers who employed them, and newspapers were often more concerned to take on experienced journalists with good track records than they were to employ people simply because of their local knowledge and connections.[167] For obvious reasons this applied more to the English-language press than to the Welsh, although neither segment of the industry lacked applicants from the larger British, and even international, pool of labour. In March 1882, for example, K. W. Douglas of the *North Wales Chronicle* took on one George H. D. Webber, from Guildford, Surrey, to be apprenticed for three years 'in the art of printing, journalism and newspaper work'. But job mobility of this kind, which could attract into Wales the best young talent from England, might also impoverish domestic journalism as reporters, once having learnt their trade, were attracted by more lucrative prospects elsewhere. Apprenticeship contracts sought to impose some constraints on this free movement of labour, and K. W. Douglas was so eager to prevent his highly-prized new apprentice from being drawn towards the local competition that he inserted into the contract a clause that stipulated that Webber was forbidden 'to engage on any paper or in any business apart from that of the said K. W. Douglas within 30 miles of his place of business without his consent in writing for the term of seven years from this date'.[168]

The Welsh-language press also attracted its share of interest from journalists working outside Wales. Vacancies advertised in the national British papers for posts on a proposed new Welsh-language newspaper in Liverpool in 1902 drew enquiries and applications from a number of highly experienced journalists from England and beyond. One, a 27-year-old secretary to John R. Lord, the assistant editor of the *Journal of Mental Science*, currently living in Wilmington, Kent, admitted to having 'considerable experience both in Journalism and in secretarial work' and to having travelled 'over a large portion of the world mainly in a Journalistic capacity'. An expert shorthand writer and typist, he could speak or translate French, German and Japanese. He had worked in Japan on the *Japan Mail* and been the business manager of the *Japan Gazette*. He claimed to have 'considerable experience in missionary matters' and, above all, he emphasized that he could 'write an interesting article on many subjects'. He suggested that a salary of £2 a week would be acceptable. A second experienced applicant with considerable skill in languages requested further clarification regarding the language of the new paper. 'Is it' he enquired,

> . . . a paper printed in the Gaelic language? I ask this question, because, although well versed in English, French, German, and to a minor extent in Portuguese and Italian, I do not understand Welsh. If the knowledge of the latter therefore is a *sine qua non* my application will be useless.

He added that he was thirty-five years of age, and had

> . . . some knowledge of the Newspaper business on account of my having contributed to some leading papers abroad, and considered a good all round business man.

A third applicant, fifty-year-old Patrick McSweeney from Liverpool, summarized his experience as being 'a blending of journalism and business'. He had worked as a reporter on the *Belfast Morning News*, an editor of the *Whitehaven Guardian*, and a reporter on the *Worcester Herald* and, for the previous three years, the *South Wales Daily News*. He had also been employed for eight years as a shorthand and general clerk in the office of a large firm of solicitors in Swansea. In addition, he had served as a reader, reporter and translator on the *Catholic Times* in Liverpool for over six years. For the past two and a half years he had worked as a French Correspondent and shorthand and typist (Remington) clerk with an engineering firm, which he had left following the closure of their Liverpool branch. He emphasized his punctuality, his experience as an 'all-round journalist' and verbatim shorthand writer, and, after eleven years in Swansea and Cardiff, one who possessed a sound knowledge of Wales.[169] Applications of this calibre for posts on a Welsh-language newspaper indicate that, however unrealistic many of them might have been in practice, the Welsh press was not so remote from the wider world as to isolate it from the pressures and the ambitions of the generality of British journalism.

In addition to the recruitment and training of journalists, working methods also developed in parallel with those in the profession elsewhere in Britain. Towards the end of the nineteenth century knowledge of shorthand, for example, became an essential skill for most, if not all, reporters. Such important Welsh journalists as Beriah Gwynfe Evans never mastered shorthand, and wrote accounts of political speeches and so forth from minimal longhand notes. This method enabled Evans to write several different versions of a single speech, each intended to suit the views of a different newspaper editor. But if his was the mastery of the political and literary imagination over the verbatim account, Evans was among the last of the gentleman journalists in a world increasingly dominated by the reporters' imperatives of speed and accuracy. Given the range of events and the affairs of public and private institutions that journalists were expected to cover in the course of their work, shorthand was an essential skill. During his years as Rhondda correspondent of the *Western Mail*, Picton Davies spent twelve days of each month in the courts, where the accuracy of reporting was an essential requirement.[170] In other situations, however, reporters' verbatim accounts of the proceedings of public bodies were interpreted as unwarranted invasions of privacy. In 1907 Frank Mason, editor-proprietor of the *Tenby Observer*, was prevented from attending meetings of the local council because of protests by councillors outraged by Mason's publication of their deliberations. The High Court defended the councillors' actions and, astonishingly, ruled that all council meetings were private events. The ensuing controversy, which threatened to undermine local political journalism throughout Britain, resulted in 1908 in the passing of the Admission of the Press Act which overruled the High Court decision and allowed Frank Mason to resume his seat in the Tenby Council Chamber.[171]

Unlike the part-time local correspondents who had formed the mainstay of so much Welsh journalism in the nineteenth century, professional reporters were required to travel often long distances to gather news. In the 1900s, Picton Davies was expected to cover upwards of twenty towns and villages in and around the Rhondda Valley without recourse to either trams or buses, and to report it promptly to the news office in Cardiff. Davies admitted that the work could not have been done at all without the help and co-operation of the police, with whom 'it paid always to be on friendly terms'. One journey from Carmarthen to Cardigan in 1900 involved taking a train, followed by a nine-mile walk before completing the journey by horseback. Journalism at this time was as much a 'tramping' occupation as printing or, indeed, the ministry.

The intense competition between the major titles, and in particular between the two Cardiff dailies, the *Western Mail* and the *South Wales Daily News*, imposed barely tolerable strains on their respective reporters. Picton Davies recalled that had an item of news from the Rhondda been covered by the latter paper but not by the former, a printed form would promptly be despatched from the *Western Mail* office enclosing a copy of the offending item pasted onto a blank page on which the hapless reporter would be required to explain the reason for his omission. Reporters from other papers faced similar trials as a matter of course.[172]

Full-time reporters, however, were free to send news to newspapers or agencies other than their own. 'Linage' was most common before 1914, after which the emergence of new national and international news agencies reduced the demand for the practice. Low wages in journalism were justified by employers, and tolerated by reporters, largely on the grounds that linage work augmented their earnings,[173] and some reporters earned more from linage than they did from their regular employment.[174] In practice, however, the 'linage merchants' were most frequently members of the senior staff, sub-editors and other office-based newspapermen who, according to T. A. Davies of the *South Wales Daily News* in 1911 'never went out for a story but simply milked the reporters' copy as it came into the office'.[175]

The competition between reporters, actively encouraged by editors, and which manifested itself also in linage work, instilled into journalists a deeply individualistic work ethic. However, on certain occasions, collective action between reporters from different, and perhaps even competing, newspapers was tolerated. Evidence of such 'reporters' rings' may most easily be found in the verbatim accounts of long political and election speeches which formed such an important part of the Victorian newspaper. To avoid unnecessary duplication, and to lighten the load of each individual, reporters co-operated by taking turns, often of three minutes each, to make verbatim shorthand notes. These notes would then be written out in longhand while each of the others in the 'ring' duly undertook his three minute's work. A corrected, longhand verbatim report would thus be ready within minutes of the end of a speech, and if promptly telegraphed (there is evidence that reporters also shared the cost of telegraphing such accounts) the newspapers' compositors could begin to set up the reports in type before the meeting had even closed. Reporting a speech by Lloyd George in Caernarfon, Picton Davies found it expedient to co-operate in this way with J. H .Roberts from the *Courier*, Humphries from the *Daily Post*, and Brocklehurst from the *Guardian*.[176]

The shorthand skills of reporters were also found to be in demand outside journalism. Clubs, societies and trade unions hired newspaper reporters to provide accurate minutes of their proceedings. Lewis William Lewis (Llew Llwyfo), a reporter for *Baner ac Amserau Cymru*, charged two guineas for reporting a speech at an eisteddfod in 1862, plus the cost of his travel,[177] and J. T. Morgan, editor of the *Workman's Advocate*, was in 1873 appointed offical minute-taker of a number of trade-union district meetings in south Wales. Public bodies also employed full-time journalists on a part-time basis. Thomas John Hughes (Adfyfr), whilst a sub-editor on the *South Wales Daily News*, worked for a number of years after 1894 as an official shorthand writer in the bankruptcy court at Pontypridd, and Picton Davies took the minutes for the Board of Trade Commission on Shipwrecks and worked as a recorder at the conference held to discuss the constitution of the new Church in Wales after disestablishment.[178]

The reporter's skills of news gathering and accurate shorthand were by themselves insufficient to ensure the success of newspapers in a highly competitive market. Journalism involved also the imaginative presentation of news in formats that would attract and maintain readers. The development of new forms of feature articles and the growth of specialization were two editorial responses to the changes demanded of the Victorian press. As early as the 1850s and 1860s, the Cardiff press was sensationally discovering 'visions of Hell' in the poorer quarters of the city. In 1869 the *South Wales Critic* promised 'local investigative journalism',[179] and by the 1890s this kind of journalism had become commonplace even in the Welsh-language press. In the second issue of *Y Cloriannydd* in August 1891 the editor promised a series of investigative features, written by specially commissioned correspondents, on the public institutions of north Wales which would include the prisons, the lunatic asylums and the workhouses, and in 1893 the *South Wales Daily News* printed a disturbing series on 'Darkest Cardiff'. Both were strongly reminiscent of the type of 'social conditions' features that had been pioneered by Henry Mayhew in the *Morning Chronicle* in 1849 and 1850 and James Greenwood in the *Daily Telegraph* in 1874.[180] The growth of specialization in Welsh journalism was more problematic, and its course was mediated by countervailing cultural pressures. Financial reporting was from the very beginning an acceptable part of reportage, and due attention was paid to stock market prices from the earliest issues of the weeklies in the 1800s, and a regular back-page column in the south Wales dailies. Sport coverage, however, was a different matter which was scorned in particular by Welsh-language newspapers until at least the 1890s. A football column featured in the *Caernarvon and Denbigh Herald* in 1912, but, significantly, not in its sister paper *Yr Herald Cymraeg*.[181] Front page news had replaced advertisements in the *South Wales Echo* by 1916, and from 1895 the *South Wales Weekly News* carried 'Special Features' that included 'Workmen's Topics' (by Mabon), fiction, 'Gossip of the Day', gardening notes, womens' columns (by a 'Lady Journalist'), children's columns, humour, 'Queer Stories: Grave and Gay: True and otherwise', extracts from the 'society papers' and 'Welsh Echoes from London'.[182] Women's columns and pages appeared in the *South Wales Echo* on its expansion to six pages on 7 May 1881, and a six-page illustrated 'Ladies' Own Supplement' was supplied free with the *Western Mail* in the 1890s. A 'Ladies' Column' written by Catherine Pritchard (Buddug) also appeared in the *South Wales Radical and Nonconformist* in November 1892. 'Buddug' had been the most trenchant of the early Welsh women journalists, a member of the Bardic Order since 1860, and the author of a challenging series of articles in defence of women in *Udgorn Cymru*.

The development of specialist political journalism in Wales was impeded as much by structural obstacles as by the constraints imposed by distance from London. The affairs of the Lords and the Commons had been reported by Welsh newspapers from the start, but attempts to formalize the relationship between the Welsh dailies and the Houses of Parliament in the early 1890s met with only limited success. The entry of reporters into the Lobby of the Commons had been restricted in 1871, and further tightened after a bomb scare in 1884. The modern Lobby system was formed in 1885, when entry was restricted to journalists whose names appeared on a list drawn up by the Serjeant at Arms. Entry into the Lobby after this date, particularly for newspapers from the provinces, often proved to be extremely difficult.[183]

In 1892 David Duncan, proprietor of the *South Wales Daily News*, began a long campaign to gain admission to the privileged Parliamentary sanctum of the Lobby. The refusal to admit Vincent Evans, the paper's Parliamentary reporter, in March 1892 led Duncan to protest to Sir Edward Reed that the criteria for admission to the Lobby were being inconsistently applied. It was untrue, he argued, that the Speaker only granted Lobby tickets to those newspapers who previously held seats in the Gallery. His enquiries into the operation of the Lobby revealed that, 'differences exist alike as regards the English, Scottish and Irish press, but they only tend to strengthen the claim we make in regard to the only cause likely to arise in connection with the Welsh papers'.

With regard to the English newspapers, Duncan found that the *Birmingham Daily Post* had been granted a Lobby Ticket despite the fact that it had never held a seat in the Press Gallery. The *Birmingham Gazette,* the *Sheffield Telegraph* and the *Newcastle Journal* had formed themselves into a small syndicate for securing Lobby news, and had between them one Lobby ticket. Again, not one of them had previously held seats inthe Gallery. 'Some years ago', Duncan observed, 'the Press Gallery was extended and various seats allotted to provincial journals. In many cases seats have never been utilized for the purpose of reporting the proceedings of the House, but have simply been used by various syndicates of papers for Lobby purposes.' As an example he cited the case of the *Manchester Courier*, the *Liverpool Courier* and the *Yorkshire Post* who between them had one box in the Gallery but no Lobby ticket, their Parliamentary reporting being undertaken by the Press Association, Central News and other agencies. Unlike these provincial papers, Duncan argued, the *South Wales Daily News* was a national newspaper, and as such deserved certain privileges. His case rested on an impassioned and revealing self-assessment in relation to what he regarded as a distinctive Welsh journalism.

> Ours (with the exception of our contemporary the *Western Mail*) is the only daily paper for the whole of Wales, and if so many tickets have been granted to English, Scottish and Irish papers, surely ONE can be granted for Wales. Even if the *Western Mail* also applied (which is unlikely as it already has access to the

> Lobby) the number for Wales would never exceed two. Further, a large number of papers at present in possession of Lobby tickets are surely local papers, that is they circulate in their own towns and immediate districts. In the case of the *South Wales Daily News*, its circulation is of a national character, so far as Wales is concerned, although in addition it also covers a large part of the West of England.

Duncan sought to supplement his case by the application of political pressure. He warned that he could mobilize some thirty Welsh MPs from both Liberal and Conservative parties in support of his application, as well as, for good measure 'the four Monmouthshire members and some of the Gloucestershire members'. T. E. Ellis, a regular contributor of political articles to the paper, was one of the MPs approached by Duncan, who cleverly sought to persuade him that the effective coverage of Parliamentary affairs through the Lobby would enable 'the actions of the Welsh members [to] be daily chronicled and in every way rendered effective in support of the Government throughout the Welsh constituencies'. Despite such appeals, Duncan's application for admission to the Lobby was again rejected in May and December 1892. The *Western Mail*, on the other hand, adopted a different tactic and obtained access to Lobby news in the early 1890s by reaching a mutually advantageous arrangement with the Lobby correspondent of the *Sheffield Telegraph*.[184]

Foreign news was an essential part of any newspaper, including the religious papers. Few, however, were sufficiently well endowed to employ foreign correspondents and most resorted to scissors-and-paste methods or to the stereotype services of the news agencies. However primitive the method the fact remains that from a very early date a high priority was given to foreign coverage in Welsh newspapers and journals, although the coverage was in many cases mediated by the political and cultural perspectives of the individual editor, and of Welsh society as a whole.[185] In the first issue of *Yr Haul* in July 1836, for example, in addition to literary reviews, six and a half pages of Parliamentary and British political news and reports of British robberies, murders, suicides, accidental deaths, poisonings, attacks of rabies, shipwrecks, religious news and items of financial and trading interest such as a calendar of fairs and markets and a list of wool prices, included also articles on events in Ireland, France, Spain, Portugal, Germany,

Greece, Tunisia, the West Indies, Egypt, the East Indies, South America and Mexico. The range was as impressive as anything in the era of the New Journalism in the 1890s.

Finally, it should be remembered that journalism, even in the early nineteenth century, did not rely on writers alone. Artists and engravers were from an early stage employed to illustrate newspapers and magazines. *Y Punch Cymraeg*, for example, used cartoons and line drawings extensively between 1858 and 1864, and cartoons in the *Evening Express* were advertised daily in the *Western Mail* in the 1890s,[186] whereas portraits of political and religious leaders were a popular feature of most Victorian newspapers. David John (Dyer) Davies, born in Llandeilo and educated in art schools at Kidderminster and Antwerp, was a popular illustrator for a number of Welsh publications at the end of the nineteenth century, including *Wales*, though perhaps his best cartoons are to be found in *Dafydd Dafis*, Beriah Gwynfe Evans's political satire of 1898. He worked also for the *Graphic* in 1899 before emigrating to South Africa where he worked as a free-lance artist and journalist.[187] 'Portfolios of photographs' were also sold by newspapers through their agents, and photojournalism emerged as a specialist occupation at the turn of the century, in line with developments in London and elsewhere, and has ever since been an important element of newspaper reporting. Whereas, at the beginning of the 1890s, a reporter 'specially equipped with a camera' could be reprimanded by the editor of the *Western Mail* for failing to take photographs of a hanging in Carmarthen, by the early twentieth century news photography had evolved into a more specialized branch of journalism, and in 1915 a company of press photographers, the 'Welsh Topical Press' was operating in Cardiff.[188]

Life-style and social status

The emergence of more rigid divisions of labour within journalism, and the fragmentation of the work of the early printer-editor generalists into specialized occupations, affected not only the organization of the press but also the ways in which journalists were perceived socially. The definition of a reporter as 'an uninvolved person sent to some public occasion to make a record for publication' was first recorded in the *Oxford English Dictionary* in 1813, where it was used specifically in relation to political reporting in the Press Gallery of the House of Commons.[189] In the course of the following century reporting acquired other, less favourable definitions. In 1893 Emily Crawford was irritated by 'applications from the relatives of persons who may be classed as failures to try to get some "light newspaper work" for them. There is no such thing, so faras I know', she retorted.[190] H. C. Strick offered an explanation for the low esteem in which journalists were held by the public which rested precisely on the professionalization of the occupation. 'In pre-shorthand days', he argued, 'the journalist was a creative literary artist . . . [but] with the introduction of type-setting machines, making possible the publication of long, verbatim reports, the man who had no other credential than a shorthand speed could become a journalist'.[191] Arnold Bennett described what he believed to be the generally held outsider's view thus: 'A newspaper office is a retreat where, amid cigarette smoke and the rumour of continual events, clever people write what they like when they like'.[192]

These external impressions were of considerable importance since a journalist's perceived social status was an essential condition of his trade, enabling him to attend public and private meetings, and to make detailed enquiries, rather like a policeman, into a community's patterns of behaviour. That the journalist's job was regarded as 'respectable' *mattered* because it could affect directly the journalist's capacity to obtain information. The growing preoccupation with defining the social status of journalists prompted a debate on whether or not journalism was a profession. Used loosely, the term 'profession' was freely interchangeable with such terms as 'trade' or 'craft', but if a more rigorous definition involves the possession of 'a systematic body of knowledge acquired through a long specialized training', it is doubtful whether journalism in nineteenth-century Wales approached professional status. However, increasingly towards the end of the century, journalists in the daily and sections of the weekly press were being professionalized through training, experience and a privileged access to information.[193]

The general view that the social status of journalism was a low one, however, survived at least until the mid-1850s. Reporting the death by suicide of a journalist in January 1845, the *Printer* observed that he had been 'a victim to that baneful habit which has ever been the curse of the profession – drunkenness, a scourge which has robbed the trade of its fair name, and defeated its pretensions to a proper position in society'.[194] But in the second half of the 1850s there is ample evidence to suggest that journalists throughout Britain were beginning to be accepted as responsible public figures, high in social regard, who deserved to be thought of 'in company with medical practitioners, and well above such meanly paid objects of occasional charity as ushers and schoolmasters'.[195] It was a measure of this new-found respectability that, having won the right to report Parliamentary proceedings, places were also being reserved for reporters in law courts, local government meetings and commissions and meetings of voluntary associations and trade unions. By 1874, Arthur Murphy, writing in the *Contemporary Review*, cautiously welcomed the fact 'that journalism is slowly but surely rising into a much better social position than it has occupied for the last hundred years. . . . But its position even for the last twenty years has been anything but satisfactory'.[196] By 1887, William Hunt could congratulate his 'brother journalists upon the greatly improved circumstances under which they now conducted their business, and the extraordinary increase of influence and respect that newspapers have secured during the last fifty years'.[197]

Doubts, however, remained. Thomas Frost in 1886 complained of the 'deterioration of journalistic work' and of the entry into journalism of 'uneducated men – illiterate, illogicial, ill-everything'.[198] As late as the 1930s the NUJ, anxious about the continuing poor esteem in which their work was publicly held, considered drafting a journalists' 'code of honour' in addition to a code of practice.[199] But as the NUJ readily acknowledged, the status and self-image of journalists as professionals was determined largely by pay and conditions, which were commonly agreed to be respectively low and poor. Job security in the Welsh daily press was generally good. Sir William Davies of the *Western Mail*, or John Duncan of the *South Wales Daily News* rarely sacked reporters, but the price paid for security in both papers was a low wage.[200] Competition, particularly in the lower reaches of journalism, further depressed wages,[201] and Wilfrid Meynell (John Oldcastle) reported in 1880 that some two-thirds of British journalists received 'less than the wages of a good mechanic'.[202] As late as the 1940s, E.

Morgan Humphreys complained that Welsh-language journalism was failing to recruit new talent principally because wages were 'less than that of a county school teacher, but the hours are longer and the work harder'.[203]

Actual wage rates for journalists in this period are difficult to ascertain for three reasons. Firstly, there was much local variation. The wages of reporters on the *North Wales Chronicle* in the late 1880s ranged from thirty-five shillings to over £2 a week,[204] but by 1902 an applicant for a post on a Welsh-language newspaper in Liverpool conceded that it was 'hard to mention a figure definitely, not knowing extent of duties', but suggested thirty-five shillings a week, a 'bricklayer's or a printer's wage'.[205] Even in 1916 the weekly earnings of the Merthyr correspondent of the *South Wales Daily News* still reached only thirty-five shillings, at a time when few working journalists in Britain earned more than £3 a week. In 1920 the Cardiff journalist T. A. Davies informed the National Arbitration Tribunal that when his wage first reached forty-five shillings a week he was living next door to a docker who was earning £8 a week.[206] Another explanation for the difficulty in estimating real incomes is that reporters were able to supplement their pay, however irregularly, for instance by linage and minute-taking.

A third reason for the scarcity of information on wage rates can be attributed to the fact that journalists were understandably secretive about their pay. It was generally felt that public confidence in their integrity might be undermined were it known that they actually earned thirty-five shillings a week instead of the £4 a week which, to judge from their speech, their dress and their gentlemanly ways, they were assumed to command. T. A. Davies complained that in 1916 his £3 a week wage could hardly sustain his 'rent, insurance, maintain and educate a wife and family of four children, and at the same time keep up a good social position', and spoke of the humiliation felt by his fellow reporters who 'obeying the rule of the office, had to attend the brilliant banquets held in the city of Cardiff in regulation evening dress and pictured their thoughts when they realised that most of the waiters who served them were much better off than themselves.'[207]

Such internalized resentment, combined with a 'professional' self-image, ironically served to inhibit their capacity to bargain collectively for higher pay. But the toleration of low wages reflected also the lower middle class origins of many Welsh journalists. Recruited from generally poor but aspiring occupational groups, such as schoolmasters, solicitor's clerks or the sons of Nonconformist ministers, journalists lacked the collective traditions of most other groups of workers. T. A. Davies, the son of a village schoolmaster, and Lascelles Carr, the son of a Wesleyan minister, were both typical examples.[208] The industrialization of newspapers eventually refashioned both social relations and occupational perceptions within journalism, and led to new barriers being erected between 'journalists' and 'reporters', terms which had hitherto been largely synonymous. But the forms of collective action that were subsequently developed emerged directly from a reappraisal of the journalists' old and always ambiguous relationship with the printers.

Job and wage-rate comparisons between reporters and printers had long been matters of dispute. Journalists who could assure employers that they were also 'able to work at case' had, as has been shown, been common in the early and mid-nineteenth century. The advent of type-setting machines compelled journalist-compositors to become specialists in one or the other. Long after this occupational separation had been completed, however, journalists continued to envy the earnings of printers. Journalists as 'professionals' clearly felt that their work was of a higher order, but this did not prevent them from being jealous of the benefits won by the unionized printers with whom they worked in such close proximity. In 1910, for example, reporters who worked seven days a week were paid less than linotype operators who worked only for six,[209] and this despite the fact that in the rituals of the newspaper office, journalists and the 'literary staff' were clearly regarded with greater respect than the compositors. At the funeral in January 1888 of David Duncan, the founding proprietor of the *South Wales Daily News*, the office hierarchy was clearly and carefully maintained in the order of the procession. After the Duncan family walked the employees of the paper in the following order of importance: the 'literary staff' of senior journalists, the district reporters and, finally, the staffs of the commercial and printing departments.[210]

Unlike the printers, journalists were slow to recognize the advantages of trade unionism, and many continued to feel that combination was inappropriate for journalists given their overwhelmingly individualistic and professional approach to their work.[211] The early activists of the Institute of Journalists, founded in 1884 as the National Association of Journalists, were disappointed to discover that journalists were notoriously difficult to organize. It was not until August 1907 that the NUJ was registered as a trade union and began to exert effective collective pressure on newspaper editors and proprietors. Its founding members in Cardiff were Max A. Wright, John Smurthwaite and T. A. Davies, and H. Hopkins was elected first representative of the South Wales and Monmouthshire District to the National Executive.[212] Territorially, the south Wales branch was the largest in Britain, and included the six counties of south Wales, Monmouthshire, and the city of Hereford. In the early years of growth, local branches were formed to recruit new members in Merthyr, Aberdare, Pontypool, Newbridge and Builth Wells.[213] By 1911 T. A. Davies found that the staff of the *South Wales Daily News* was solidly unionized, but in spite of this wages remained in 1916 at pre-war levels even though linage had by that time all but disappeared. Davies and his colleagues found it increasingly difficult to survive on a 'bare office wage', and a whispering campaign threatening strike action won recognition for the union. Encouraged, the NUJ pressed for and won a five shillings a week pay increase, which brought Davies's weekly pay to £3. In 1918, further increases were obtained of one pound a week for employees with five years service, and ten shillings for those with a shorter period of service. The NUJ also began to organize social occasions to wean journalists away from the paternalism of their employers and to foster a sense of occupational and social solidarity among journalists of various grades and different newspapers.[214]

By 1914, journalism had undergone an enormous transformation in its methods, its organization and its social function since its origins in the late seventeenth century. A newspaper industry had been fashioned out of the unlikely material of scattered religious print-shops, and journalism as an occupation had been restructured to meet the needs of a rapidly changing industrial society. These two broader contexts, the changing structure of the newspaper industry and the nexus of political and religious influence, conditioned the ways in which journalists in Wales became significant, and at times leading, social actors.

2 *Production and distribution*

The making of a newspaper industry in Wales commenced and, in many of its most important respects, was completed during the nineteenth century. Legislation, technology and markets each served to condition the direction and the accelerating but uneven pace of this process, and the history of the industrialization of the press in Wales is punctuated by moments that signalled far-reaching changes in both the structure and style of journalism. The most visible corollaries of industrialization were the formulation of new managerial structures, the increasing dependence on income derived from advertising, the emergence of a skilled, well-organized and mobile printing labour force, and an extension of the newspaper-reading market.

Management

The commercialization of the press was effectively impeded until the middle of the nineteenth century by the continued imposition of the Stamp Acts. Introduced in 1712, these taxes on newspapers were increased steadily throughout the eighteenth century and again in 1819. The 'taxes on knowledge' were, especially between 1819 and 1836, serious obstacles to the growth of the press which more than doubled the cover price of newspapers, and newspapers that in 1832 cost threepence a copy to produce were legally required to pass on to buyers an additional duty of fourpence per issue.[1] The first papers to break into a mass market in Britain did so in the first half of the 1830s as illegal, 'unstamped' journals that normally retailed for a penny or twopence a copy. Even after the reduction of the Stamp duty to a penny in 1836, following which the unstamped press suffered a sudden and terminal decline, legal newspapers continued to face very serious difficulties. In December 1837 Josiah Thomas Jones explained to his readers that the remaining cost of the Stamp had rendered the *Merthyr and Cardiff Chronicle* uneconomic and that he was left with no alternative but to discontinue the title. Jones also objected to the indignity of having to 'send to the Inquisition House in London for the decorative red sign' of the Stamp.[2] The uneven distribution of Stamped sheets of newsprint, particularly for papers distant from London, also acted as a brake on growth. The *South Wales Reporter* complained on 4 March 1837 that the late arrival of the Stamps had lost the publishers £70 worth of advertisements. Failure to acquire the requisite number of Stamps in due time could prevent a newspaper from meeting its intended print-run or oblige it to cancel the publication of an entire edition. *Cylchgrawn Rhyddid* of Caernarfon did not issue a fifth number as expected in January 1841 precisely because its editor had not been sent his quota of Stamped sheets of newsprint in time to meet the printing deadline. The point was made repeatedly in this journal that the freedom in the title also fundamentally involved the freedom to publish. The erratic nature of the supply of legal newsprint in Wales disrupted subscription and advertising arrangements and could deal a devastating blow to recently established papers that were struggling to extend their circulations.[3] Taxation adversely affected both successful and low-circulation newspapers, though in different ways. In the former, the need to purchase individually Stamped sheets prevented the development of the much more rapid web-printing of newspapers from continuous rolls of paper, and thus slowed down the adoption of new printing technology in general. The latter, low-circulation newspapers, including many of the Welsh-language ones, felt particularly disadvantaged by the relatively high level of taxation compared with their proportionately low income from sales and advertisements. The artist Hugh Hughes, publisher of *Y Papyr Newydd Cymraeg*, attributed the increase of the price of his paper to threepence in 1836 to its failure to compete economically with 'English newspapers', which, he surmised, paid the same paper duty, yet 'sell, or expect to sell, as much as ten times as we can ever expect to sell in Wales'.[4]

Avoiding payment of the Stamp was difficult, and incurred risks of prosecution which increased after the reduction of duty in 1836. Occasionally, papers were printed on unstamped newsprint but carried a notice to the effect that the Stamp Office would be duly informed and remunerated when circumstances allowed.[5] Others sought to by-pass the law by publishing monthly periodicals, which were exempt from duty, instead of weekly newspapers. But for some editors the loss of influence thus incurred was too high a price to pay for tax evasion, and the almost totemic importance of weekly production was repeatedly emphasized. In 1835 Hugh Hughes argued ferociously against the reissuing of the weekly *Y Papyr Newydd Cymraeg* as a monthly periodical retitled *Y Diwygiwr Gogleddol* on the grounds that only a weekly newspaper could attain the ambitious political targets set by its founder.[6] A third, more radical, means of avoiding the Stamp was to publish offshore. Attempts to avoid payment of the tax took many inventive forms, including publishing almanacks printed in Trefriw from 1805 under a false Dublin imprint, and publishing regular papers on different days of the week.[7] Free of British taxes, but free also to use the Royal Mail to send newspapers without cost to the mainland, offshore islands attracted the attention of many publishers of radical periodicals. *Cronicl Cymru* was published weekly in Jersey in 1847, and in July of the following year *Yr Amserau Wythnosol*, owned by John Lloyd of Mold and printed by Robert Fargher, began to appear in Douglas on the Isle of Man. The passing of the Postage on Newspapers (Channel Islands) Act in August 1848 eventually withdrew the privilege of free postage from these islands and compelled the mainland newspapers printed there to close or to return to their places of origin. Lloyd's *Amserau* reappeared in Liverpool in September 1848.[8]

The removal of the duty on newspaper advertisements in 1853, and the abolition of the Stamp duty in 1855 and the paper duty in 1862, ended the legal and political insecurities of the era of the Stamp Acts and created new opportunities for the press throughout Britain. New pressures, however, were soon brought to bear on newspapers in the liberalized market that began in the 1850s. Freed from fiscal constraints, the publishers of newspapers remained subject to controls that included libel and censorship, restrictions of the supply of newsprint, and price competition that began in earnest after 1836 and intensified further after 1855.[9] In a wry comment on the new dispensation made in his opening address to *Y Tyst Cymreig* in June 1867, William Rees remarked that 'We in the Newspapers now live under the domination of the penny'.[10] This was no longer a reference to the much resented additional penny duty, but to the full cover price at which newspapers were increasingly obliged to retail simply in order to remain competitive.

The 'domination of the penny' over the weeklies, and within a short while also that of the halfpenny over the dailies, led inexorably towards the professionalization of newspaper management. The need for competent and innovative business leadership initially added yet another dimension to the work of the already stretched newspaper editor. By the 1880s it was relatively common for a local newspaper to consist of an editor-manager who supervised the work of one sub-editor, a chief reporter, one other reporter and a junior reporter, and evidence suggests that for many weekly papers this structure survived well into the twentieth century.[11] For some weeklies, and for all the dailies, this arrangement placed too heavy a burden on executive editors and a division of labour was effected between editors and full-time business managers.

The appointment of business managers also signalled a shift in style and ethos in newspapers. In 1892 W. J. Parry, a Director of the Welsh National Press Co., expressed the view that the appointment of a business manager would not only enable the company to avoid the repetition of costly commercial and political errors, but would also lend a new dynamism and sense of direction to the entire venture. Seeking to persuade David Lloyd George of the efficacy of such an arrangement, he argued that the company 'must have a *stronger* man, a more *energetic* man, a better *business* man than we have in the company now, or the whole thing will go to the wall'. The person he had in mind, he confided, was Beriah Gwynfe Evans, then working as a journalist in Cardiff. Evans, Parry thought, would 'make the thing a success, or *kill* himself in trying. . . . He is a born journalist, a man of great tact, energy and business capacity; and an organiser without his equal in Wales'. Business efficiency, Parry concluded, was the only means of ensuring the survival of a Radical Liberal chain of weekly newspapers, the success of which should be their 'only aim'.[12] The following year, 'with Beriah [Gwynfe Evans] at the head, and M. Ellis Owen looking after the agents, the reporters and the finance', Parry privately informed Lloyd George that he felt 'quite confident' about the future prospects of the company.[13]

By the close of the nineteenth century, business managers were persons capable of exerting considerable influence in Welsh newspapers. In May 1890, William Roderick Haylings was brought in from Cond Brothers in Birmingham to help manage the *South Wales*

Gazette by its proprietor J. C .Durant, and two years later he and a partner were able to purchase both the printing business and the copyright to the paper.[14] They were also well remunerated for their work. The salary of the managing director of the *Western Mail* was increased to £20 a week in July 1895, with additional commission on any profits made in the course of the year. By 1929, Sir William Davies, a director of the same company, was paid £2,000 a year plus a director's fee of £250. In north Wales, the managing director of the *North Wales Chronicle*, K. W. Douglas, was in 1885 paid £340 a year.[15] On other, less successful weeklies, managers were paid substantially lower sums. One applicant for the post of secretary and manager of a Welsh-language newspaper in Liverpool in 1902 asked for a 'salary to commence at fifty shillings per week'.[16]

A thorough knowledge of all aspects of journalism and printing work was regarded as a prerequisite for the post of a newspaper manager. Robert Gordon, a 34-year-old assistant book-keeper and outside sales traveller for the *Bolton Chronicle*, emphasized in his application for the managership of one Welsh newspaper that he had served a full apprenticeship as a printer and was 'competent in every branch of jobbing and newspaper work . . . I have a thorough knowledge of any department – comping, advertising and publishing', and added for good measure that he was an abstainer and 'an active Christian worker in the Baptist denomination'.[17] Thomas Hughes's application for the same post made very similar points, adding that he was a native of Liverpool and a 'Welshman, with practical knowledge of the News Dept of the printing profession'. His previous work included being 'the Liverpool correspondent of a Welsh Weekly Newspaper, and . . . a wide experience as a Welsh writer', and he had 'been brought up to the printing trade, and had a knowledge of the News Department of the same'.[18] Other applicants also mentioned the catholicity of their experience in support of their applications.[19]

The emergence of the manager-editor, or the manager as a separate post within the administrative structure of a newspaper enterprise, was a response to the increasing complexity of running a newspaper as a business. The limitations of amateur production were made starkly clear by the failure rate and infant mortality of so many newspaper ventures during the nineteenth and early twentieth centuries. If success, increasingly and necessarily defined in commercial terms, was now regarded as the 'only aim', and as journalism became more of a full-time, professional occupation, it was essential that the many legal, financial and administrative obstacles that stood in the way of a paper's survival and growth needed to be negotiated skilfully and effectively. In this period of rapid change in newspaper production, managers were compelled to pay particular attention firstly to maximizing income from advertising, and, secondly, to supervising both the introduction of new technology and the workers by whom it was operated.

Advertising

After 1855, advertising was the single most important source of revenue for many, though not by any means all, Welsh newspapers. One journalist conceded that:

> . . . the extension of British journalism has been the result, largely, of cheapness and of ability to obtain news in increasing quantity, and, in some respects, with greater accuracy – always with increasing speed. This was made possible only by a constant growth of revenue from advertisements.[20]

Furthermore, A. J. Lee attributed the 'Golden Age' of British journalism in the second half of the nineteenth century to the political independence conferred by advertising and the emergence of a commercial press. In Wales, however, the commercialization of the press occurred unevenly. Advertisers were relatively scarce, and, as the manager of *The Times* remarked in 1884, 'advertisers are attracted by the classes of readers rather than by their numbers'.[21] In much of Wales, there were neither the classes nor the numbers. Income from advertising, nevertheless, remained a matter of critical importance. The publishers of *Y Dywysogaeth* reported in 1870 that a combination of advertising income and donations was essential for its survival as a weekly paper. With newsprint bills of twenty-five shillings per thousand sheets, each 5,000 print-run cost £15 to produce. Income from sales of around 3,000 copies yielded only £12.10*s*., leaving a shortfall of £2.10*s*. which could only be recouped by advertising and 'the help of friends'. The economics of Welsh weekly newspapers had changed very little by the beginning of the early twentieth century, when it was estimated that sales on a circulation of 5,000 raised only £14 whereas advertisements yielded at least £23.[22]

Payment for placing advertisements in Welsh newspapers was normally made in advance. In 1877 a four-inch space in a weekly paper for a three month period cost somewhere in the region of £2, for which the advertiser was also sent free copies of the paper.[23] In this way, *Y Genedl*, for example, raised in excess of £1,100 in advertising revenue in 1890, whilst its stablemates the *Observer* and *Y Werin*, the latter only recently launched, raised nearly £600 and £15 respectively. The corresponding sums in six months ending June 1891 were of the order of £550, £300 and £200.[24] In the same period, the *North Wales Chronicle* and *Gwalia* raised £1,700 and £500 respectively through advertising.[25] *Gwalia* attemped to increase its volume of advertisements by extending its circulation to south Wales. There, the paper's secretary in 1884:

> . . . proposed to publish *Gwalia* under another name, but in fact practically the same, devoting one or two pages to South Wales local news only. If it was called 'The South Wales Standard' or some name giving it a South Wales look, we think we could get the South Wales advertisers as we now do the North Wales ones'.

A south Wales agent was subsequently appointed to canvass for advertisements.[26]

Advertising agencies were established to meet the new demand during the second half of the nineteenth century. According to a contemporary account these agencies were divided into two groups: reputable companies such as Mitchell's, White's, Algar's, Street's and Barker's, and others who were 'men of glib tongue and active habits' who took orders for a series of advertisements for small sums and were repaid by high commissions from the newspapers who employed them. Around 1860 a new system was introduced that further complicated the relationship between provincial newspapers and London advertisers. Some metropolitan writers offered provincial papers a comprehensive service that involved contributing leader columns and 'London Letters' in return for a column of advertising space. This they offered to fill with advertisements of various kinds which they undertook to collect, set up in print, and forward in the form of stereotype blocks. The practice was widely adopted in the 1860s and 1870s, but declined thereafter as it was found to depress advertising prices to such an extent that it lowered the net advertising income of provincial newspapers.[27]

Advertising agencies, however, continued to exert a powerful influence over a paper's format and occasionally even its content. In January 1890 A. E. Jones of *Gwalia* signed a contract with T. B. Browne, a London advertising agent, which agreed to a number of detailed stipulations. Trade advertisements were to be paid for by the newspaper at the rate of £25 per column per annum, and these were to be inserted in all editions of all issues of the paper, and were to include the approved illustrations on pages decided by the advertisers. A minimum of a £100 worth of business was to be guaranteed in each contract year, all sums payable quarterly, less 15 per cent commission, with additional bonus commissions on payments over £100 and £150. All advertisements were 'to enjoy the utmost display allowed in single and double columns (blocks or otherwise) the same as permitted to other Advertisers'. Finally, it was agreed that all advertisements were to be translated into Welsh, set in the *Gwalia*'s own type and inserted below the pictorial blocks provided by the agency.[28]

Local advertising agencies were also established at this time, including, for example, the Colwyn Bay and District Advertising and Bill Posting Co. Ltd., which was registered under the terms of the 1862 Companies Act in June 1898.[29] Newspapers also advertised their own titles in other papers, in local trade directories and, further afield, in the London Newspaper Directories. *Y Celt*, for example, made arrangements for notices of its contents to be inserted in *Y Genedl Gymreig*, *Tyst a'r Dydd*, and *Baner ac Amserau Cymru*, and in 1881 J. Hemming paid five shillings to have the *Glamorgan Gazette* advertised in May's *Directory*.[30] Adopting a different publicity strategy, the *Caernarvon and Denbigh Herald* was charged a rent of ten shillings a year for pinning its posters on a noticeboard on the town wall facing Castle Square in Caernarfon. The administrators of the Vaynol Estate were reluctant to permit the paper to advertise in this way and the *Herald*'s proprietor, Frederick Coplestone was told firmly by the Vaynol land agent, N. P. Stewart, that he had to 'bear in mind that these things are far from ornamental to a property. In fact they are an eyesore'.[31]

Advertisements were canvassed, directly or through agencies, because they were essential for the survival of newspapers. Of two early Welsh newspapers, the *Cambrian* succeeded because it filled up to 40 per cent of its column space with advertisements, whereas *Seren Gomer* did not because it failed to sell advertising space to English businesses.[32] Many Welsh-language newspapers were desperately eager to attract English advertisements, and *Y Papyr Newydd Cymraeg*, the first Welsh-language weekly to start after the stamp reduction of 1836, assured potential advertisers that 'every advertisement, when required, will be given in English, accompanied by an explanation in Welsh'. This policy was justified on the grounds that English-language newspapers 'received enough in advertising to cover their weekly losses',[33] whereas there were few Welsh-language advertisers who could help sustain the Welsh-language press. In fact, there were comparatively few lucrative advertising accounts to be found anywhere in Wales, in either language. The extractive and heavy manufacturing industries that dominated the economy did not need to advertise their commodities in newspapers, and the relative scarcity of this vital resource stymied the competition between titles by rendering those that were out of favour, even temporarily, with advertisers, vulnerable to financial collapse. The *Merthyr and Cardiff Chronicle* failed in 1837, according to its editor, W. E. Jones (Cawrdaf), because:

> . . . the character of the two towns whose organ we profess to be – and the fact of all patronage [is] in the hands of our opponents. [We] had little to hope from the usual source of profit – advertisements [and] therefore mainly depended on our circulation.

Attempts to avoid such a calamity by broadening the geographical range of both the readership and the advertisers only served to raise fresh difficulties. After the failure of the *Merthyr and Cardiff Chronicle* its editor and publisher planned a new weekly paper, the *Chronicle*, whose Wales-wide circulation would draw on a far wider range of advertisers. Irregular postal deliveries, poor roads and the large area over which the circulation would extend, however, seriously reduced the profit margins of the new paper, and the price of expansion proved to be intolerably high.[34]

Compelled to look elsewhere for advertisers, many newspapers relied more on notices of denominational and public events than on commercial advertisements, but the one exception was the growth of medical advertising. J. O. Jones, editor of the left-wing *Merthyr Times*, expressed in 1895 the not unreasonable view that, given the absence of other forms of advertising:

> Some of the best friends of the press are the much reviled manufacturers of patent medicines. In an indirect way, at least, these people are doing great service to their country. If their pills and mixtures are not beneficial physically, their advertisements enable the press to do much good intellectually.[35]

This type of advertising, arranged in the main by agencies, was only marginally profitable, and could be safely eschewed by the metropolitan quality papers, which, with some exceptions such as Labouchere's *Daily News*, usually refused to print display advertisements of general branded goods.[36] In urban areas, commercial advertising was more plentiful, but competition was often keen between titles. In an attempt to entice local shopkeepers to overcome their distaste of his radical politics, J. T. Morgan, proprietor and editor of the Merthyr weekly, the *Workman's Advocate*, charged half the advertising rates of its rival, the *Merthyr Express*, though to little effect. Like J. O. Jones's *Merthyr Times* two decades later, the vast majority of Morgan's advertising was in the form of medicinal potions from London-based firms. Local advertising was minimal.[37]

Advertisements of dubious legality also found their way into the columns of low-circulation papers that faced financial difficulty. *Adsain* was fined heavily in 1911 after the Home Secretary drew attention to the fact that the paper was illegally advertising lotteries from continental European countries. Whereas the papers that had cultivated a sound advertising base could afford to refuse such material,[38] others could not, and the financial vulnerability which afflicted so many of these newspapers in Wales rendered them particularly sensitive to changes in the economic climate. In the weekly press, the sudden decline in the number of advertisements from London-based companies during the First World War compelled Frederick Coplestone, owner of the *Herald* papers in Caernarfon, to cut staff in both editorial and printing departments. But the dailies also moved to the commercial rhythms of London.[39] In the 1920s the *Western Mail* was so dependent on London-based advertisers that the paper's managing director spent one day a week in the capital where, he explained 'about half our advertising revenue comes from [and] where we have hundreds of very big customers'.[40]

Advertising opportunities were complicated by religion and politics as well as by the vagaries of commerce. Ethical issues were raised by the nature of certain advertised commodities which led some editors to resist the temptation to accept some kinds of material. In August 1891 the directors of *Y Tyst a'r Dydd* agreed that their printer, Joseph Williams of Merthyr, could, without consulting them, refuse to print any advertisement which he judged to be contrary to 'the character of the paper'.[41] The first issue of *Ye Brython Cymreig* in January of the following year informed its readers that it would be easy for them to fill their pages with items advertising medicines, the occult, money-lenders and so forth, but that they had taken an editorial decision 'to stand or fall by not doing so'.[42] It was also said of Thomas Gee that, 'resisting all temptations, [he had] to the satisfaction of his readers, whatever may be said of his balance sheet, practically restricted advertisments on almost all occasions to the outside four pages of his paper'.[43] The radical press took a similar view, and the *Merthyr Star* in its first issue on 12 February 1859 announced that no woodcuts would be admitted for inclusion, and that 'discreditable Advertisements will be altogether excluded'.

The Anglican paper, *Y Gloch*, also gave notice that they intended to scrutinize not only their own advertisements but also those of other newspapers, on the grounds that most forms of advertising were 'damaging to the morals and religion' of the readers.[44] The fear of offending the religious sentiments of the readership with the wrong type of advertising prompted editors to be particularly vigilant in their selection, even when it ran counter to their own financial interests to do so. J. H. Jones, editor of the Liverpool weekly, *Y Brython*, pointedly referred to this difficulty in 1913, remarking that, in consequence, English-language Liberal papers enjoyed an unfair commercial advantage over papers like his own.[45]

Religious and political loyalties also affected the distribution of advertising. Nonconformist manufacturers and retailers were expected to subsidise their respective denominational journals by placing advertisements exclusively in those papers, and, conversely, the general religious and political editorial line of a newspaper might also affect whether or not advertisers bought space in them. In the libel case brought by Mr Pritchard against the Welsh National Newspaper Co. Ltd. in December 1888, counsel for the *Genedl* newspaper alleged that the plaintiff, a leading Bangor Conservative, had been,

> . . . influenced by his political opinions and the feelings excited by the said contest [a municipal election in which he had been opposed by *Y Genedl* and] preferred giving advertisements to newspapers connected with the Conservative Party and newspapers other than those of the Defendants.

Though the newspaper lost the case, it was demonstrated that Pritchard had spent twice as much on advertisment space in the Conservative *North Wales Chronicle* as in its Liberal rival, *Y Genedl*.[46]

Technology and labour

An equally demanding task for newspaper management was the supervision of printing. The relationship between journalism and the printing trade, as has been shown, had always been close, but the division of labour that occurred as a consequence of the industrialization of the press restructured the occupation of printer as well as that of the journalist. The two occupations, however, remained equally essential components of the production of newspapers. Early newspapers had in the main been managed and edited by printers, but those that were not offshoots of printing businesses, or were established by journalists outside the printing trade, still required access to printing plant. This was most easily done by reaching agreements with commercial printers. In 1857, the editor of *Seren Gomer*, William Roberts (Nefydd), paid one such contract printer £20 for printing two thousand copies of his paper.[47] By 1882, the cost of printing a similar print-run of *Y Dyddiadur Wesleyaidd* had risen to £29.[48] Contract printers were able to negotiate favourable arrangements which included a guaranteed print-run plus a proportion of the advertising revenue. In an enquiry regarding the printing of *Y Llan* in August 1901, the editor stipulated that he was prepared to guarantee a circulation of five thousand copies and the prompt payment of all bills and a percentage of the advertisement income.[49] By 1901 the cost of printing commercially an eight-page weekly paper consisting of three pages of advertisements and five pages of editorial had fallen to £15.10*s*. per edition of five thousand copies.[50] Printing rates were relatively cheaper at the turn of the century than they were in the mid-1850s in part as a result of economies of scale made possible by the introduction of new technology and changed work practices. The newspapers best able to take advantage of these developments were those that possessed the facilities to print on their own plant, and to combine journalism with lucrative general or 'jobbing' work.

Methods of printing newspapers changed greatly in Britain during the course of the nineteenth century. Rotary presses had been introduced into the offices of *The Times* in 1814, but the difficulty of placing type on a curved surface remained until a stereo plate that bent to the shape of a curved casting-box was first patented in France in 1845. By the 1860s, freed from the constraints of Stamped newsprint, improved reel-fed web rotary machines could print up to 10,000 complete eight-paged newspapers an hour.[51] Developments in Wales did not lag far behind those in other parts of Britain. The Stanhope machine, worked by two men, and which averaged 150 sheets per hour, was replaced in 1833 at the office of the *Carmarthen Journal* by the faster Columbian press. Napier machines, introduced at the *Hereford Times* at the time of the paper's launch in 1830, were still used to print the *Welshman* until 1851, and the *Silurian* until 1852. A Cowper Steam Press was installed at the *Cambrian* in Swansea in May 1853, which produced one thousand sheets per hour and which may have been the first steam press in use in Wales.[52] Similar machines were subsequently introduced at the printing offices of the *Star of Gwent* in 1856, which remained the only steam printing office in Newport until 1873, and the *Swansea Journal* in 1861.[53] Thomas Gee's acquisition in September 1869 of a new cylinder machine, powered by two steam engines, confirms that although Wales was a decade or so behind England in the introduction of steam presses and platten machines, the most advanced Welsh printing technology followed closely the pattern set by English print-shops.[54] The introduction of the new Hoe Rotary drastically reduced printing times, and by printing at a rate of 250 copies per minute, it could complete in forty-five minutes what had previously taken twelve hours.[55]

Before full advantage could be taken of new printing machines it was necessary to increase the speed with which type was set. Typesetting machines were not in use in Wales before 1870, and prior to that it was not unusual for printing offices to keep only a small stock of type, which was set slowly by hand. The outer pages, containing standing advertisements, articles and earlier news, were printed first and the type was then broken up and redistributed for use in preparing the later news and advertisements on the inner pages.[56] This process was laborious and time-consuming, but by the 1870s 'cold metal' Hattersley and Kastenbein composing machines were being used in south Wales which dramatically accelerated composition: the *Pembrokeshire Herald*, for example, bought a Hattersley machine in 1877. In general, however, mechanized typesetting made relatively slow progress in Wales, and Hattersley machines, originally patented in 1857, were still being used by the *South Wales Daily News* as late as 1915.[57]

Hot metal technology developed gradually in the 1880s, and entered large-scale production in 1890. Linotypes were self-contained hot metal machines that produced self-justifying copy with type selected by keyboard from matrices stored in a magazine at the top. Alloy type was dropped into place, then returned to the magazine to be melted and recast. By 1899 some six thousand of these machines were in use in Britain.[58] Linotypes were introduced into the *Star of Gwent* offices in October 1894 where they were worked on so-called 'stab (collectively bargained established rates) by unionized compositors.[59] At Gee's office all type was set by hand until the second half of the 1890s when a linotype machine was acquired for newspaper work.[60] Linotype machines were hired as well as bought, and in 1904 the *North Wales Chronicle* arranged to hire for one year one Duplex Linotype composing machine, insured for £600.[61]

New printing and typesetting machines, however, were notoriously prone to technical failures, especially, and most exasperatingly, in the weeks following installation. The editor of the weekly *Y Meddwl* apologized to his readers in the second issue (September 1879) that the launch issue had not been sent to the great majority of the subscribers until the following week because the recently acquired printing press had broken down after printing only two thousand copies.[62] The third issue of *Gwalia* in 1881 was also seriously delayed thanks to 'difficulties with the new printing machinery'.[63] Such difficulties were so common that rival newspapers agreed to share each other's machines in the event of a breakdown. The co-operative arrangements reached for example by the *Cambrian News* and the *Aberystwyth Observer*, however, did not always work. The editor of *Ye Brython Cymreig* in Lampeter suffered a machine breakdown during the printing of the first issue of his paper in January 1892 but was refused help by the printers of a rival newspaper in the town. Outraged by such 'shabby and immoral' treatment, help was sought elsewhere and eventually found at the office of the *Carmarthen Journal*.[64]

Despite such obstacles, it was generally agreed that it was preferable for a newspaper to run its own printing plant rather than to contract work out to commercial printers. The acquisition of plant usually involved the purchase of an ailing but well-stocked title, although prices in the late nineteenth century varied enormously. In 1878, the entire plant of the *Wrexham Guardian* was offered for sale for only £600, but a decade later the owner of the *Montgomeryshire Express* was offered £3,500 for the paper and the accompanying printing business.[65] The uneveness of the market is well illustrated by William Mansel's purchase in 1891 of the copyright of the *Swansea Journal* for £150, and the assets, by auction, for only £325, whereas the plant and goodwill of the parent Cambrian Newspaper Company, proprietors and printers of the *Cambrian*, was valued in 1899 at £5,300.[66] Another means of acquiring plant was through the private purchase of an established printing firm. In 1891 the Welsh National Newspaper Company made arrangements to buy out its principal printer, and re-engage his staff as direct employees of the company. The 'value-added' deal involved the purchase of certain additional items, principally new printing and folding machines. Illustrations of the new machines were printed in prominent positions in *Y Genedl* in June 1892 to ensure that the readers fully appreciated the sophistication and modernity of the paper which this arrangement had made possible.[67]

New printing technology altered the scale of the enterprise by making newspapers cheaper to produce but more expensive to launch. In the 1830s, printing constituted a relatively small proportion of the costs incurred in launching a newspaper. In July 1837, setting up the *Merthyr and Cardiff Chronicle* cost

£268 which included the printing of twenty-four weekly issues, folding and franking, the printing of 450 publicity notices, 1,200 prospectuses, 1,500 bill heads and a hundred advertisement cards.[68] In one thirteen-week period in the same year, the cost of Stamps and paper amounted to a third of the production costs of the *South Wales Reporter*, out of total printing bill of £224. Travelling expenses and canvassing accounted for a further 11 per cent, and prospectuses and advertising a further 6 per cent.[69] By the 1880s, the cost structure of newspapers had changed dramatically. Paper was relatively cheaper and newspapers received a better return on advertising revenue, but far larger sums were necessary to launch new papers, for the daily press this reached between thirty and fifty thousand pounds simply for plant and the larger buildings that were required to house it. Following the fire that destroyed the plant and building of the *Western Mail* in 1893, bonds for £50,000 were issued to cover the cost of a new fire-proof building in St. Mary Street and, for insurance, 'a second Newspaper Office [in Tudor Street] completely equipped with machinery, plant and type, where in case of another fire or a breakdown from any other cause, the co's newspapers could be produced at an hour's notice.'

By April 1895, the *Western Mail* comprised leasehold properties worth over £48,000, plant and machinery worth £24,000 excluding Linotype machines which by themselves were worth over £5,000, and assets totalling more than £112,000.[70] Compared with this level of investment and return, the resources of even the most successful weeklies began to look rather pallid. John Gibson's expansion of the *Cambrian News*, also in 1895, which involved the building of new printing offices, won him little more than, 'bare food and clothes and a shortened existence through lack of rest. I have incurred a fresh debt of four thousand pounds and am working hard and living hard in order to pay it off.'[71]

Once acquired, however, printing machines were used for purposes other than the production of newspapers. Josiah Thomas Jones, publisher of the *Merthyr and Cardiff Chronicle*, had previously earned his living by printing lists of voters, election addresses, County Court subpoenas and ballads.[72] Such practices continued throughout the nineteenth century, and by 1889 the average net receipts of the *Montgomeryshire Express* and its jobbing section over the previous thirteen years was estimated to be worth £530 a year.[73] In 1892, only a year after purchasing new printing machines for their newspapers, the Welsh National Newspaper Company tendered for a complete jobbing plant, which included Wharfedale double demy typesetting machines and gas or steam powered Columbian and Albion presses.[74] This jobbing section of their enterprise was used to print commercially such miscellaneous items as lists of voters, election addresses, county council notices, addresses to literary societies and, later, periodicals and books.[75] Others sought new jobbing markets in the flourishing world of friendly societies, social clubs and trade unions. In 1865, William Roberts (Nefydd) printed circulars and club rule books for the Abertillery lodge of the national iron-workers' union, whilst in the early 1870s J. T. Morgan, publisher and editor of the *Workman's Advocate* in Merthyr, was the 'sole supplier of documents' to the National United Association of Enginemen, Firemen and Fitters. Morgan advertised also to 'lodge secretaries and others' that in addition to newspaper publishing and providing stationery, his office was:

> . . . fitted up with every appliance for the execution of every description of printing. Forms, bills, cards, circulars, programmes required for eisteddfodau, literary meetings, penny readings, entertainments, concerts, lectures, societies etc. etc., together with the binding of books.[76]

The increasing capital costs of printing machinery in the late nineteenth century, however, tended to encourage specialization rather than diversity, and jobbing remained a more important component of the smaller presses. Some other forms of printing, such as books in the Brython Press in Liverpool, were effectively subsidised by the income derived from newspaper publishing.[77]

The growing sophistication of printing technology led also to the emergence of a new skilled labour force. Numbers of printers in Wales and Monmouthshire rose from 343 in 1851 to 700 twenty years later, well over half of which, being under twenty years of age, were most likely still apprentices. By 1891 this number had grown to over 2,000, only 3 per cent of whom were women. In 1901 there were over 500 printers in Cardiff alone, with a further 200 each in Caernarfon and Denbigh, 170 in Swansea and 130 in Carmarthen. Not only had the numbers grown, but the social status of printers had also been transformed. In the early nineteenth century printers, journalists and ministers inhabited the same moral world: John James, who opened Aberystwyth's first printing establishment in Bridge Street in May 1809, was a Baptist minister, and William Roberts (Nefydd), another Baptist minister, was also an author and an educationalist.[78] Printers regarded themselves as members of a 'respectable' and 'honourable' trade, and adhered to an appropriate code of conduct. Those who did not were duly, and publicly, chastized. David Evans, a 'wild and reckless fellow' and son of the proprietor and publisher of the *Carmarthen Journal*, disappeared from Carmarthen in 1823 to the evident relief of his colleagues.[79] The honour of the trade grew partly from the rigours of an extended apprenticeship into 'the Art and Mystery of a Printer'. Normally bound for a period of seven years, apprentices were made to obey a stringent set of rules governing their general behaviour, which included the avoidance of 'taverns, Inns, or Alehouses' and 'cards, Dice, Tables, or any other unlawful Game', and abstinence from sexual relations. Wages at the end of the eighteenth century were one and sixpence a week in the first year, rising to four and sixpence by the seventh year.[80] By 1887, these rates had risen only to two shillings in the first year to ten shillings in the seventh.[81] In the following year, apprentices at the same office were paid an overtime rate of a penny an hour in the first year and threepence in the seventh.[82]

Following the completion of the apprenticeship, working conditions for journeymen printers could be harsh. Sporadic high unemployment and short contracts were common. In November 1880, for example, D. J. Rosser, a printer from Swansea, was offered work on the *Glamorgan Gazette* at twenty four shillings a week, but only for the six weeks before Christmas.[83] Working hours, particularly in newspaper work, were irregular, and night work was normal on the daily papers. Between 1810 and 1872 printers normally worked a sixty-hour week, with varying amounts of compulsory overtime. A nine-hour day and a fifty-four-hour week was secured in 1872, but in many offices where the printing unions were weak or non-existent, compulsory overtime frequently increased the weekly hours to levels significantly above those stipulated by this agreement.[84] Even in the 1880s, a sixty-five to seventy-hour week was common in the printing offices of Hughes and Son in Oswestry, though another union agreement reduced these hours to forty-eight per week in 1897.[85] Printers also objected to the industrial time-disciplines that were being introduced into their trade, and Cardiff printers in 1913 protested vigorously against 'the new style of time sheets and clock time-recorders'.[86] The working environment was unpleasant and badly ventilated, particularly in gas-lit offices in which, according to one survey in the mid-1840s, the air was the most polluted of any workshops in Britain. Consequently, printing in the mid-nineteenth century suffered from one of the highest mortality rates of any of the artisan trades. The death rate from consumption among printers, for example, was twice the national average, and in 1883 it was estimated that the life expectancy of a British printer did not much exceed forty-one.[87]

Juvenile and unskilled labour was common. Boys were employed ostensibly as apprentices to feed machines and turn over pages, but could be dismissed once they were old enough to qualify for higher pay.[88] In composition, piece-work was normal practice throughout the nineteenth century. Units of production in Wales were small. In its centenary year in 1910, the *Carmarthen Journal* printing office employed three overseers (aged between thirty-eight and forty-two), two lino operators, a machinist, a compositor, two apprentices as well as an errand boy. This was typical of the compactness of most enterprises outside Cardiff, although there were exceptions. Thomas Gee, for example, employed fifteen compositors in the early 1890s, most of whom worked on Gee's newspapers.[89]

Printers, however, were traditionally mobile workers. George Jenkin Jacobs, a master printer born in 1837 on a farm in Whitland, Pembrokeshire, was apprenticed for seven years at the *Y Diwigiwr* office in Llanelli at the age of twelve. Subsequently he worked for the *Cardiff and Merthyr Guardian* in Cardiff in 1857, and the following year was to be found in Aberdare, working on Josiah Thomas Jones's *Gwron Cymreig* and *Y Gweithiwr*. In 1859 he had returned to the *Y Diwigiwr* office in Llanelli to help to launch a new quarterly magazine, *Y Beirniad*. In 1865, we find him in Merthyr working as a compositor on Peter Williams's *Merthyr Telegraph*, from where he moved to the Newport offices of the *Star of Gwent*. By 1868 he was back again in Merthyr employed on Rees Lewis's *Y Fellten*, and in 1870 had moved to Rhymney, where he published his own weekly newspaper, the *Tredegar Telegraph*, and where in due course, he expanded his printing works, and printed also the *Tredegar Guardian* and the *Monmouthshire Guardian*.[90] Jacob's career pattern was not untypical, but such mobility could either be the result of the opportunities offered by high labour demand in the printing industry, or of the pressures imposed by low demand in an overstocked job market. For much of the nineteenth century, however, there were too many rather than too few printers, and from the 1840s the Typographical Association offered financial inducements to its members in Wales to emigrate to England or Scotland to seek better paid and more secure employment.[91] Such tramping relief schemes were susceptible to fraud and abuse, and were strongly opposed by sections of the Association until their abolition in 1913. Thereafter, unemployed members who sought work elsewhere were paid only their railway fares.[92]

Printers' wages varied widely within and between printing establishments, and in general Welsh printers paid their staffs substantially less than the London rates.[93] Competition between titles eager to hold down production costs acted as a brake on the rising cost of labour in the later nineteenth century, and John Duncan significantly defended the payment of low wages on the *South Wales Daily News* by referring to the precedent set by its rival, the *Western Mail*.[94] In 1850, the weekly earnings of compositors in Newport and Cardiff averaged between twenty-one and twenty-four shillings,[95] but in Dolgellau in 1899 newspaper printers were still being paid only between four and eighteen shillings a week.[96] The growth of trade unionism among printers gradually reversed these generally low wage rates. The introduction of so-called 'stab or 'established' rates of pay was initially uneven, but eventually ensured that wages were roughly comparable in different offices, at least within the same region. Branches of the printers' union fixed their own 'stab minimum rates and maximum hours for the various jobbing, weekly news, evening and morning papers sections, and offices that refused to conform to these standards were designated 'unfair houses' in which union members were instructed not to work.[97]

The unionization of the printing trade in Wales followed closely the British pattern. A Northern Union of printers was formed in 1830, which by the early 1840s included affiliated branches in

Cardiff, Merthyr Tydfil and Monmouth,[98] but a Typographical Society, established in Swansea in 1842, appears to have been little more than a local benevolent and friendly society.[99] The National Typographical Association (NTA), formed in 1844, was, through its South Western Union, the first to attempt to extend its organization across the whole of Wales and Monmouthshire.[100] Its progress, however, was slow, and by July 1846 the NTA comprised only three branches and a membership of no more than three hundred in the entire South Western District.[101] In an effort to revive the union, the Provincial Typographical Association (PTA) was formed in June 1849. This new central body served initially as an umbrella organization, uniting many small local printers' societies such as that which had been active in Cardiff in 1845–6.[102]

The worst obstacles faced by the new union in Wales were the proliferation of printers and the free availability to employers of unskilled boy labour. An early response was to adopt a policy of apprentice restriction, explained and justified in an 'Address to the Printers of Wales' issued in 1841. The document regretted that, 'there are at present a vast number of printers more than the wants of the community require; the consequence of which is, that many have but partial, and many more no employment.' The 'superabundance of hands' depressed wage rates and encouraged 'ratting' in non-unionized 'unfair houses'.[103] Apprenticeship restrictions allowed the union to exercise a degree of control over the supply of labour, though the objection raised in 1845 by the Newport branch to the introduction of a new printer unless he was able to produce 'satisfactory proof of his servitude' appears to have been a very isolated event.[104] Entrance fees to union branches were high. Admission to the Cardiff branch in June 1846 cost £4, although if a member moved from one regional section of the union to another the fee might be paid by the Executive of the old association. By 1913, when the Typographical Association had established a firmer hold on the printing industry in Wales, admission fees and subscriptions in Aberdare, Cardiff, Merthyr, Rhondda and Swansea had been fixed to 'stab rates – sevenpence if the printer was earning twenty-five shillings or under or a shilling if in receipt of £2 or more a week.[105] In another early form of restrictive practice, the PTA hoped to stabilize the labour market by seeking to minimize the turn-over rate of members working in the more volatile sectors of the trade, especially in new newspaper enterprises. In 1852, for example, the union strongly objected to the establishment of Henry Mullock's free-sheet, the *Monthly Advertiser* (later the *Newport Advertiser*), and denied its printers the right to establish their own 'office', or sub-branch, until the paper had demonstrated its viability by continuing publication for an uninterrupted period of twelve months. The new printing staff were informed that they were eligible for enrolment into the PTA as individual members attached to an associated office only after the Executive had conducted the usual 'full enquiries' into their past working records.[106]

Despite a measure of agreement among printers regarding the general principles and modes of operation of the trade union, the PTA's early history in Wales was troubled by conflict between the Cardiff branch and its regional Executive. In September 1851 the Cardiff members were criticized by the Executive of the Midland Board for their 'shameful conduct' in refusing to acknowledge communications from the Executive and, more seriously, for neglecting to submit membership subscriptions. An inquiry held to investigate the management of the branch led to its dissolution, but a new branch was established in October 1851 by a Mr Clarke, who successfully arranged for it to be admitted to the PTA.[107] The negotiated peace did not last long, and by December 1851 the Cardiff branch was found guilty of defying the union's leadership and rules by unilaterally initiating strike action at the offices of the *Silurian* newspaper, in response to what they termed 'supposed encroachment' by non-unionized printers.

Despite these difficulties, the PTA remained a united trade union throughout the manifestly difficult years of the early 1850s. Popular political considerations may have helped to sustain this cohesion. In 1852, all branches of the Midland Board of the union were instructed to organize petitions condemning the 'Taxes on Knowledge', and to provide active support for the Parliamentary campaign then being conducted by Milner Gibson, C. D. Collet and other prominent free-trade liberals to repeal the remaining Stamp Duty on newspapers. But the PTA's principal function was not to organize politically, but to obtain the highest wages and the best conditions possible for their members, and this naturally involved both collective bargaining with employers and organizing strike action supported by union funds. Such action was undertaken even in the earliest years of the PTA's existence in Wales. In May 1850, for example, printers at the offices of the *Principality*, who were earning twenty-one shillings a week instead of 'the proper amount' of twenty-four shillings, were instructed by the PTA to take strike action against their employer. In June, four printers obeyed the call and, led by their foreman, went on strike 'in accordance with the instructions of the Executive' which entitled each to receive strike pay of £5.[108]

The spread of trade unionism among Welsh printers in the 1850s and 1860s was a painfully slow and difficult process. A branch of the Midland Board was established in Holywell in March 1852,[109] but others were reluctant to follow their example. One printer remarked sadly at the end of the 1850s that the PTA was 'at best . . . but the champion of a trampled creed'.[110] It remained so in north Wales until the early twentieth century, when, in December 1917, the Printers' Society of North Wales and the Border Counties was formed. Before that there were only two branches of the Typographical Association in the north, one in Wrexham, founded in October 1862, and the other in Caernarfon, which began to recruit members in March 1891. When the PTA met for its annual national conference in Manchester in 1873, the only Welsh delegates were those representing branches in Cardiff, Merthyr and Wrexham.[111]

Of these three original branches, Cardiff was the most dynamic. Its missionary zeal was applauded as exemplary by the PTA Executive, and evidently met with a measure of success nearer to home. The founding principle of the Cardiff branch was to restrict competition from lower-paid labour in outlying districts, and to prevent as far as possible the flow into Cardiff of surplus printers from these surrounding areas. To achieve these ends, officers of the Cardiff branch travelled extensively through the print-shops of south Wales, held public meetings, distributed agitational union literature, and began gradually to build sufficient support to establish local sections of the union outside Cardiff.[112]

In April 1874, as a direct consequence of such activity, a group of seventeen printers in Carmarthen applied for membership to the Cardiff branch, and an unspecified number of other printers in Swansea expressed their wish to form their own branch of the PTA.[113] Sustaining the morale and commitment of the new members, however, proved to be difficult. A PTA branch was formed in Aberdare in the spring of 1875 around a nucleus of eleven enthusiastic union members from neighbouring Merthyr. These Merthyr activists, however, found it increasingly difficult to attend union meetings, and during the first year the indigenous membership of the Aberdare branch declined sharply.[114]

The ease with which journeymen printers could set up businesses of their own remained a key problem for the PTA, and it was readily acknowledged that small employers, rather than the larger companies, were the real 'bane of the Association'. There were a few exceptions. Two small employers, both of whom had previously been members of the Merthyr branch, publicly 'expressed their warm approval of the object' of the union, and informed the local branch that they wished to become honorary members. As an act of goodwill, they offered a 5s. a week increase to their own printers, raising wages to thirty shillings for a nominal sixty-hour week, although it was grudgingly admitted that 'in no instance was the number worked'. One of them was J. T. Morgan, printer, publisher and editor of the *Workman's Advocate*, whose application for membership was granted by the Executive Committee in July 1875.[115] Guidelines regarding such applications from employers to become honorary members of the union were incorporated in branch rules, and in 1921 the Oswestry Typographical Association confirmed the policy that 'any member entering into business on his own account as a letterpress printer may be placed on the "recognized" list, provided he conducts his business in conformity with Association and Branch rules'.[116]

Not every employer was so accommodating to the demands of the organized printers. The old problem of 'an excess of apprentices' at the office of the *Welshman* in Carmarthen led the PTA in 1875 to declare the office closed to its members. An application by the proprietor to have the office re-opened was rejected by the union's Executive in June 1875 on the grounds that ten apprentices were still at work at the plant, accompanied by only six or seven journeymen. Three of the compositors were willing to join the branch, but as they were under an agreement with the paper for only twelve months, their admission was not recommended. The Executive then resolved to maintain their boycott of the office until all the existing engagements had expired, when it was hoped that the proprietor might possibly have had sufficient adverse experience of non-society labour, 'as it was reported they were already dissatisfied with it', and the office might be 're-opened on honourable conditions'. The Carmarthen branch also promised to extend its activities to the neighbouring towns of Tenby, Haverfordwest and Pembroke, from where 'men now employed on the *Welshman* office came, in avowed ignorance of the existence of any dispute or the existence of the Carmarthen branch'.[117]

In 1877, the PTA was reorganized as the Typographical Association (TA), which incorporated the older tramping Relief Association. But the new organization continued to deal with old difficulties. In August 1887, the TA National Executive was called in to settle a dispute in the offices of the *Western Mail*, caused, once again, by what the union regarded to be the excessive use of boy labour. 'The objectionable fifth boy' in this case was, as the deputation found,

> . . . the son of the managing sub-editor, Mr Parker, who was at one time on one of the Manchester papers. He has other sons journeymen printers, and no friend of the branch, or of the society . . . he talked in his usual loud style, and strongly denounced our apprentice rule.[118]

Unlike the *Western Mail*, the *South Wales Daily News* was not opened to TA members until November 1889, when an agreement between the union and the owners enabled Duncan, the proprietor of the *South Wales Daily News*, to recognize the TA and to accept its local branch rules. The branch in return undertook to admit all the employees of the south Wales printing works at nominal entrance fees, as well as allowing them to participate in the management of the branch business without undergoing the normal twelve months' probation period. A *South Wales Daily News* printer was also elected by the branch to the Cardiff Trades Council. Pointedly, no apology was made to the employers for the 1875 strike which had originally soured relations between the Duncans and the PTA.[119] The TA was aware of the political pressures operating on newspaper proprietors and editors, such as those of the Conservative *Western Mail* and the Liberal *South Wales Daily News*, but had learnt from experience that Liberal and Radical employers were seldom more likely to be sympathetic to the demands of printers than Conservative ones. In a celebrated case, the Anglican newspaper *Y Llan a'r Dywysogaeth* exposed the hypocrisy of *Y Genedl*'s Radical management, who agitated for better wages for agricultural workers while underpaying their own printers. The outraged editor of *Y Genedl* issued a writ claiming £500 damages against his Tory rival, but then withdrew amid a welter of embarassed counter allegations. The editor of *Y Llan* reported triumphantly that 'this demonstrated clearly who were the real friends of the workers'.[120]

The TA in Wales grew most rapidly in the 1890s, in line with the simultaneous acceleration of the pace of the industrialization of newspaper production. Forty members met in Newport in August 1891 to establish a new branch, and in the same year at least as many were founding members of the TA branch in Caernarfon.[121] Growth was accompanied by intensified industrial conflict, and the TA engaged in bouts of tough bargaining with employers in Aberdare and Carmarthen in the spring of 1893, during which, according to one observer, 'extreme measures had to be taken by the printers to press their respective cases'.[122]

From the mid-1890s, however, the machinery of collective bargaining was placed on a more formal, if no less acrimonious, footing. The organization of newspaper proprietors, the Newspaper Society, founded in 1836, had long refused to negotiate with the TA, but in 1894 a new owners' body, the Linotype Users' Association, was formed specifically to open negotiations with the union, and in 1896 it made the first national agreement in the newspaper and printing industry. This body was followed in rapid succession by a number of regional associations, including the Lancashire Newspaper Society in 1904, which later became known as the Northern Federation of Newspaper Owners, and, later still, as the Newspaper Federation. In 1906, the Fleet Street proprietors began to secede from this new body and formed, in 1909, the Federation of Southern Newspaper Owners. In Wales, two societies were formed, the Shropshire and North Wales Newspaper Owners' Association in 1913, and the South Wales and Monmouthshire Association of Newspaper Proprietors in 1926. Both Welsh associations were affiliated to the Midland Federation of Newspaper Owners, but held separate meetings. In 1916, the Newspaper Society was finally reconstituted, and began the process of amalgamating the many regional owners' associations. By the early 1920s, the Newspaper Society had become the only national organization of newspaper proprietors in England and Wales with full authority to negotiate with the Typographical Association.[123]

Proprietors of Welsh newspapers were to play leading roles in the early organization of the revived Newspaper Society. Proprietors of three major Welsh newspapers in turn served as Presidents of the Society, namely J. K. Douglas of the *North Wales Chronicle* in 1871, David Duncan of the *South Wales Daily News* in 1902, and Robert J. Webber of the *Western Mail* in 1926.[124] Among the officers of the Society's National Council in 1936 were Sir Robert Webber of the *Western Mail* (also a member of the Standing Labour Committee), and G. E. Dibdin of the Newport-based *South Wales Argus* (also on the Advertising Committee). Frank Webber of the *Western Mail* and W. R. Southey of the *Merthyr Express* were also present as Substitute Councillors. W.H.Webb, an employee of the *Western Mail*, was Chairman of the Society's Pension Fund. By this time, eighty-two owners of daily and weekly newspapers in Wales and Monmouthshire were represented by the Newspaper Society, though only eight of them were owners of Welsh-language publications.[125]

As its name implied, the main purpose of the Linotype Users' Association was to allow owners to present a united front when challenging the growing clamour of printers' demands over the introduction of hot metal typesetting machinery. From the 1890s, new technology became as important a negotiating issue in the industry as apprenticeship had been in the preceding fifty years. The TA called a strike in Caernarfon in 1893 after the two newspaper managements there had refused to accept the compositors' demands for equal treatment with printers in Bangor and other newspaper offices in north Wales.[126] Conflict over the use of new typesetting machines also broke out in the offices of the *Western Mail* in October 1894. Here, the efforts of the TA to obtain an interview with the *Western Mail* management had been fruitless. The TA deputation complained in their report to the Executive that Lascelles Carr had treated them:

> . . . to a homily on the future of the composing machine, and the unwise course we were pursuing in attempting to hamper their development by unnecessary precautions. He protested against any proposals to increase wages at a time when trade was falling, and was reminded that we had so far no such proposals but that we were there to discuss with him the rules and the prices for the

> Linotype machines, and to listen to any objections he might have to any of them. His reply was that they had invested £6000 in these machines and expected them to be worked honestly.

The matter was not satisfactorily resolved, and five years later the problem of the appropriate 'stab rates for linotype work again disrupted the printing of the *Western Mail*. Characteristically, the TA once more complained of Carr's offensive pugnacity. 'Strong language', they admitted, 'was indulged in'.[127] A union deputation was also sent in 1898 to intervene in a dispute at the *South Wales Daily News* over Duncan's imposition of 'unacceptable' pay and working practices on the paper's newly acquired Hattersley composing machines.[128]

Despite the difficulties posed by apprenticeships, the growth of employers' organizations and the introduction of new technology, the TA in Wales continued to gather strength. The first annual conference of the south Wales branches was held in 1899, and by 1914 branches in north Wales were also beginning to flourish. The union however was not growing as rapidly as some had hoped. A correspondent to *Cymru Fydd* complained in 1895 that:

> Generally speaking, industrial organisation in Wales is in a most unsatisfactory condition. Few classes of workmen need the help of combination more than the Welsh printers. As compared with their English brethren, their wages are miserably small and their hours of work are oppressively long. Yet, although the English Typographical Association has made special efforts to extend its system to Wales, it has met with but imperfect success, at least in the northern part of the Principality.[129]

Branches continued to be plagued by internal conflicts. In Merthyr in 1894, for example, the branch refused to pay their half-yearly returns to the National Treasurer, and a TA representative in south Wales admitted to being mystified by this 'singular state of affairs' and regretted the 'belligerent attitude' of the Merthyr members. The following year, the Aberdare branch secretary absconded with the quarter's membership subscriptions. Anxious that they should remain members of the union, the Aberdare printers asked the TA to take steps to trace and to prosecute the missing secretary.[130] A more serious danger that accompanied union membership was the threat of victimization. In 1895, T. M. Livingstone of Cardiff was awarded compensation by the Executive Committee of the

TA on the grounds 'that he had been victimised in consequence of the prominent part he had taken in the recent movement for an advance of wages'.[131]

Some employers, albeit by the 1890s a decreasing minority, continued to identify with the aspirations of working printers. J. O. Jones, editor of the *Merthyr Times* from 1895 to 1897, explained that, on his paper at least, printers had no fear of being underpaid, cheated by new machines or victimized for union activities:

> Here's a fact which all Trade Unionists should bear in mind: the *Merthyr Times* office is the only Society Printing Office in the district. What does this mean? It means that the men are paid union wages for working union number of hours, and that the office does not swarm with apprentices. No sweating allowed in any shape or form. Here you will get the very best printing at moderate charges, and you will know that the men who do the work are honourably treated.

This attempt to run an enlightened newspaper, in accordance with its editor's ILP sympathies, was cruelly short-lived.[132]

Periodic membership drives further strengthened the TA in Wales. In 1901, ten new members joined the Merthyr branch, and permission was granted to 'open the books for six weeks in order that applicants might be admitted at the minimum entrance fee, normally £5'.[133] There were also successes in recognition talks, and by 1901 all employers in Aberdare recognized the union, and previously closed offices were opened, including, surprisingly, Jenkin Howells' *Aberdare Times* and *Tarian y Gweithiwr*.[134] Also in 1901, members in Pontypridd sought and obtained permission from the TA to put before the Aberdare employers a claim for improved pay and working conditions. Within two months they had won a minimum wage of 28*s*., with the promise of an additional shilling after six months, for a 52-hour week. The TA described their success as having 'exceeded the most sanguine expectations'. Improvements in overtime pay were also conceded by the employers, which, in some offices, meant pay increases of six or seven shillings a week.[135]

As in the 1850s, the TA in the late Victorian and Edwardian periods engaged in a variety of forms of political action. In 1898, solidarity was expressed with striking Welsh miners, and, with the permission of the TA's Executive, the Cardiff branch donated £24 to the miners' strike fund.[136] In 1913, the Cardiff branch also proposed that the TA nationally should establish in the British printing trade a trade-union label or imprint similar to the one then in use in North America.[137]

On the eve of the First World War, few newspapers in Wales had avoided the wheels of commerce or the industrialization of their modes of production and labour relations. Newspaper managers, journalists and printers all belonged to occupations that had been transformed by the political and economic changes that had occurred in Welsh society in the preceding century. This changed society had also made possible a reading public, and it is to the creation of a market for journalism in nineteenth- and early twentieth-century Wales that we now turn.

Markets

The reading of newspapers and periodicals had by the end of the nineteenth century become a deeply engrained social habit that cut across class, language and regional differences. From the Crawshays of Cyfarthfa Castle, who subscribed in the 1850s to the *Swansea Herald* and the *Cambrian* as well as to the London papers, to the young John Griffith (Y Gohebydd), who as a child in Barmouth in the 1830s would wait up each month, sometimes until midnight, for the arrival of 'the big waggon' from Dolgellau that carried the freshly printed copies of *Y Dysgedydd*, the press had seeped into every corner of society.[138] In 1861 a Caernarfonshire farmer proudly announced that he would permit himself to read only the Bible and *Yr Herald Cymraeg*; and Owen Jones (Meudwy Mon) from Anglesey thought it sufficiently important to note in his diary in 1872 his decision to subscribe to *Y Goleuad*.[139] The size of the actual reading public is difficult to measure, but the evidence of such individual readers testify to the existence in nineteenth-century Wales of a widely dispersed and growing market for periodical publications. The expansion of this market was a complex process that occurred as a result of a combination of changing demographic and economic circumstances, increasing levels of literacy, improved communications and the evolution of new patterns of consumption.

The extent of the market cannot accurately be measured by the number and range of the periodicals that were produced, although it is likely that the proliferation of new titles deluded many nineteenth-century publishers into believing that a far larger demand existed than was actually the case. Few could now doubt that the early enthusiasm of editors and publishers led to the outstripping of demand by supply. As we have seen, financial collapse and bitter disappointment was all too often the result of over-optimism. But producers of what was then still a relatively young medium had had few opportunities to learn about the vagaries of commercial markets, and, in any case, many of them were driven as much by non-commercial religious, ethical or political motivations as by a desire to profit by their enterprise. The passion to publish received a further stimulus by events that were visibly transforming Welsh society.

The population of Wales and Monmouthshire increased from about 400,000 at the end of the eighteenth century to just under 700,000 in 1811, rising to over two million in 1901. A 38 per cent increase between 1861 and 1891 was followed by another leap of 20 per cent between 1901 and 1911, when the population rose to nearly two and a half million. The population of Glamorgan rose at the staggering rate of between 25 and 35 per cent each decade between 1841 and 1911. The growth of the towns was even more marked. Cardiff grew from a village of 1,800 in 1801 to a bustling 33,000 in 1861, and by 1901 had reached over 164,000. Merthyr expanded from 11,000 in 1811 to 58,000 in 1891 and to over 80,000 in 1911. Swansea doubled in size between 1861 and 1891. Ffestiniog grew from a thousand or so in 1821 to eleven and a half thousand by 1901, and Caernarfon from just under six thousand in 1821 to over ten thousand in 1881.

Such overall population growth, and the urbanization that characterized it, were the twin forces that made possible a viable and relatively stable newspaper market in Wales. Demographic change enabled a modern newspaper industry, gradually at first, to grow out of the volatile environment of small-circulation, sectarian monthlies and weeklies. But population growth alone did not determine the parameters of the market. Social class was also an important consideration as the more settled forms of mass, commercial journalism that emerged after the mid-1850s, and which came to dominate the field in the 1890s, explicitly targeted the proletarian as well as the commercial sectors of the shifting demography of Wales. Whereas in 1851 the editor of *Seren Cymru* could complain that the main obstacle to the growth of the press in Wales was the absence of a middle class,[140] from the 1860s newspapers were increasingly turning to the relatively recently formed, and hitherto inadequately tapped, industrial working-class market. William Harris launched the first newspaper in the Monmouthshire valleys, the *Tredegar Iron Times*, in 1865, and John Astle announced in November 1880 that the *South Wales Echo* would be aimed principally at 'the working-men, who so long have been left out in the cold by journals claiming popular support'.[141] In the following year, the *Pontypridd Chronicle and Workmen's News* was launched in response to industrial growth and rising population in the vicinity of Pontypridd. 'Literary progress has not kept pace with the industrial prosperity,' the editor explained without a hint of irony, 'and it is to aid in this necessary advance that the *Pontypridd Chronicle* is established'.[142] A decade later, the editor of the *Glamorgan Free Press* was equally forthright in his assessment of the possibilities of the new working-class market for his paper in the industrialized Rhondda, where 'many towns and villages have sprung up as with the touch of a magic wand. Hence the reason for the establishment of the *Glamorgan Free Press*'.[143] In Abertillery, Arthur Tilney launched the *Western Valleys News* in 1887, and the following year, with backing of J. C. Durant, the ex-Radical MP, started the *South Wales Gazette*, whilst in Newport in 1867, Thomas Williams launched *Y Glorian*, and only five years later publishers in the town were sufficiently confident to launch the first daily paper in Monmouthshire, the *South Wales Evening Telegram*.

Language was an important determinant of the market for newspapers and periodicals. The relative strengths of the Welsh and English languages in Wales before the first language census was undertaken in 1891 are unclear, though it was estimated that in Cardiganshire in the mid-1840s only three thousand of a population of nearly 69,000 spoke any English.[144] In 1891, 54.4 per cent of the population of Wales spoke Welsh, some 30 per cent monolingually, though the latter is almost certainly an exaggerated figure which resulted from misunderstandings in the returns. By 1901, however, 93.7 per cent of the population of Merionethshire spoke both Welsh and English, as did 43 per cent of the population of Glamorgan. With the two exceptions of Monmouth (13%) and Radnor (5.8%), percentages of those bilingual in Welsh and

English were no less than 34.4 per cent in any county, and stood at more that 80 per cent in five counties in north and west Wales.[145] But even these high proportions were not felt to be sufficient by some journalists to sustain a stable Welsh-language press. Kilsby Jones, at one time a contributor to Ieuan Gwynedd's *Y Gymraes*, urged the Welsh to learn English and publicly expressed doubts regarding the ability of a Welsh-language press to remain profitable without a target population of over a million.[146]

The growth in literacy was another precondition for the expansion of newspapers and periodicals, but literacy levels are difficult to determine with any degree of accuracy. The development of educational provision gives an indication of popular literacy, but no more. Vavasor Powell's state-run Puritan schools in the period 1653 to 1660 had sought to provide basic literacy skills, and the work was continued later in the seventeenth century by the Welsh Trust led by Thomas George, and, from 1701, by the Charity School movement organized by the SPCK. The Circulating School movement associated with Griffith Jones, Llanddowror, and Madam Bevan made a significant contribution to Welsh education, and Thomas Charles, Bala, was instrumental in establishing the Sunday schools that, hand in hand with the growth of Calvinistic Methodism, were to sweep through Wales from 1800. The non-denominational British and Foreign School Society and the Anglican-dominated National Society, established in 1808 and 1811 respectively, were to have a decisive impact on literacy levels in nineteenth-century Wales. The first National School opened in Flintshire in 1811 and the Society made rapid progress throughout Wales thereafter. The British and Foreign Schools were initially far less successful, and by 1843 only two had been opened in north Wales. The furious controversy that followed the publication of the Reports of the Commissioners of Inquiry into the State of Education in Wales in 1847, however, placed the issue of schooling in Wales at the centre of both political and religious debate. Works schools, associated with many of the major industrial enterprises, developed slowly until the 1840s, after which their growth accelerated until there were 109 such schools in Wales by 1870. In the five years before the passing of the 1870 Education Act, some 51,000 pupils were attending a combination of National, British and Works schools in industrial south Wales. The voluntaryist principle that underpinned these schools was gradually abandoned, particularly by the Nonconformists, and pressure for a state-run, non-denominational education system eventually led to the enactment in 1870 of new legislation. Forster's Act, though bitterly resented by those who had expected a fully integrated, non-denominational system in Britain, provided local School Boards with powers to build new schools and the authority to compel children to attend them. The 1870 Act was further consolidated by the Welsh Intermediate and Technical Education Act of 1889, which led to the opening of over a hundred intermediate 'county' schools in Wales, thirteen years before secondary education was reorganized in England. It is clear, however, that 1870 did not mark a watershed in the history of Welsh literacy, and that long before the Board Schools appeared the voluntary sector, particularly the British and Foreign Schools, had provided the people of Wales with the ability to read the popular press, and for some also the skills to write for it.[147]

The economic, demographic and educational preconditions that obtained in Wales, at least from mid-century, had enabled a consumer market for popular journalism to grow, if not yet to flourish. The proliferation of titles, in both Welsh and English languages, that were produced to meet this demand was impressive. Mitchell's *Newspaper Press Directory*, launched in 1846, provides a general, though by no means precise, impression of the scale of newspaper production during the second half of the nineteenth century:

Sample year	*Total no. of titles*	*Total no. in Glamorgan*	*Daily newspapers*
1846	10	1	–
1861	37	9	–
1876	69	17	2
1891	101	28	4

(Totals include chain local editions)

These figures indicate that an increase of the order of 173 per cent occurred in the number of newspaper titles published in Wales between 1861 and 1891. The period of most rapid growth started in the 1870s and continued until the First World War. It was reported in 1881 that of sixty-five newspapers then extant in Wales, no less than twenty-five had been established in the previous decade. By 1911 the figure had risen to 136 titles.

The growth in the number of new titles was accompanied by a general increase in circulation. One observer in 1893 remarked on the change that had occurred in the market for newspapers since the 1850s. Then 'newspaper readers were to be counted only by thousands; today the difficulty would be to discover by the thousand those who do not read'.[148] For a variety of reasons, precise circulation figures are difficult to confirm with any degree of confidence. Firstly, the multiple reading of individual copies of newspapers vastly increased the actual circulations, by a factor of seven or eight in the countryside, and upwards of thirty in the towns. Secondly, circulation figures provided by editors, managers or proprietors of newspapers are notoriously inaccurate, more often inserted to impress advertisers than to inform the readers. Thirdly, the government-published Stamp Returns are inaccurate guides to the real circulations of newspapers, although R. D. Rees has ably shown that such Returns are a more reliable guide to circulations of newspapers in Wales than they are to those in London, largely because in Wales surplus Stamps were more difficult to dispose of by sale to other papers. Rees records how in 1833 the *Welshman* purchased more Stamps than it needed, and subsequently attempted to sell the unused Stamps to the *Cambrian* and to the *Carmarthen Journal* before being exposed by the latter for what were described as 'disingenuous and dirty expedients to deceive advertisers'.[149]

Stamp Returns, when supported by manuscript and other evidence of a more accurate if less ordered kind, demonstrate a trend towards larger readerships for certain titles. The claim by the publisher of *Y Papyr Newydd Cymraeg* to have reached a weekly sale of nine hundred in 1836 sounds high, but not unreasonably so, and neither does the circulation of the *Western Vindicator*, which appears to have mustered a sale of between three and four hundred in Merthyr alone in 1840. Hugh Jones of Llangollen was said by C. D. Collet to have sold 2,300 copies a fortnight of *Yr Yspiwr* until the 1836 Act forced him to Stamp it and turn it into a monthly. The resultant reduction of its circulation to an unprofitable six hundred a month led inevitably to the paper's discontinuation. Collet, a leading protagonist of the campaign against the 'Taxes on Knowledge' and secretary of the Newspaper Stamp Abolition

Committee, used Jones's case to good effect in his history of the campaign, published in 1899. By 1854, the *Monmouthshire Merlin* was selling just over two thousand copies a week, while the *Swansea Herald*, the *Cardiff and Merthyr Guardian*, the *Cambrian* and the *Star of Gwent* each sold between a thousand and fifteen hundred copies a week. By 1863, the latter, under Thomas Williams's ownership, had increased its circulation to eleven and a half thousand copies a week.[150]

The size of the readership is difficult to estimate, but in 1870 it was thought that some 81,000 copies of Welsh-language newspapers were circulating in Wales each week, and in 1886, Beriah Gwynfe Evans reported that some 120,000 Welsh-language newspapers were being printed each week, and not a single title sold fewer than 1,500 copies a week. The circulation figures of individual titles tend to confirm these no doubt generous national estimates. *Tarian y Gweithiwr*, for example, reached 15,000 a week in the mid-1880s, and the joint circulations of *Y Genedl Gymreig*, *Y Werin* and the *North Wales Observer* reached 20,000 in December 1889, and 22,078 per week in the six months to July 1892. The geographical distribution of newspapers is yet more difficult to determine, but Joseph Williams's notebooks reveal that of its circulation of 2,250 a week in the summer of 1893, 1,798 copies of *Y Tyst a'r Dydd* were sold in south Wales, 319 in north Wales and 133 were posted to various destinations in England.[151] The targeting of the readership involved close scrutiny of the available means of circulation as well as of the papers' contents. Daniel Rees, for example, edited *Yr Herald Cymraeg* with a view to an extensive, national Welsh readership, whereas his *Caernarfon and Denbigh Herald* deliberately targeted a more local market.

The circulation of monthly or quarterly periodicals also increased during the second half of the nineteenth century. In 1841 the publishers of *Y Drysorfa* aimed at a target of 8,000 issues a month, on which they estimated they could make profit of £1,000 a year. In contrast, the English-language journal of the Calvinistic Methodists, the *Monthly Herald*, with a circulation of only two and a half thousand in 1858, failed to become a self-financing venture. The circulation of the Baptist *Seren Gomer* could be counted in the hundreds in the mid-1860s, although by 1895, according to David Lloyd George, it had reached 'a most respectable' circulation of 7,000 per month. The 1880s and 1890s were decades of opportunity for the periodicals as they were for the weeklies, and 5,000 copies of O. M. Edwards's *Cymru* were being printed within a few months of its launch in 1891. According to Beriah Gwynfe Evans's calculations, 150,000 copies of Welsh-language magazines were circulating in the mid-1880s.[152]

The breakthrough into mass circulation of papers published within Wales was made by the daily newspapers. The *Western Mail*, founded in 1869, and the *South Wales Daily News*, in 1872, both spawned halfpenny evening newspapers in the late 1880s and early 1890s. If, as the *Printer's Register* held, a population of at least 50,000 was necessary to support a daily paper, that point was first exceeded in Cardiff in 1871, albeit following a census boundary change. Beginning with a circulation of some 6,000 in 1869, the *Western Mail* had reached over 12,000 by 1873. It is significant, however, that the circulation of its stablemate, the *Weekly Mail*, reached 13,000 in the same year. At least until the 1880s in Cardiff, and until much later in other parts of Wales, the weekly press remained buoyant largely because of its lower price, but also because entrenched reading habits continued to favour the less frequent newspaper. By the end of the 1880s that pattern was beginning to change, as the weeklies became increasingly aware of their vulnerability in the face of competition from the dailies. The editor of the mid-week *Cardiff Argus* assured his readers in the first issue of the paper in May 1888 that 'the aim will be not to reproduce anything which has been previously published, and it will therefore form a weekly addition to the daily papers'.[153]

Supplying the market was at first difficult and expensive, but methods of distributing newspapers improved as a result of legislation, better transport facilities and the development of a network of retail outlets and public institutions. Early newspapers were distributed by 'newsmen', agents who toured the areas of circulation collecting advertisements and replies. During the Napoleonic Wars, the newsman of the *Gloucester Journal* would also read aloud from the steps of the Beaufort Arms in Chepstow the latest news of the war.[154] An equally direct means of distributing newspapers locally was to sell them on the streets. John Thomas Morgan advertised in February 1874 for 'several sharp, active boys' to sell his weekly newspaper in Merthyr and Dowlais, and in the 1880s the streets of Cardiff resounded to the competing calls of young newspaper sellers. One inhabitant expressed his disapproval in vivid terms:

> 'Pity the sorrows' of every unfortunate resident in the main streets of Cardiff since the advent of the halfpenny 'Speshuls' – or evening papers. The entire lung power of our juvenile population seems to be requisitioned every afternoon and evening to scream these delightful (?) depositories of 'Latest Telegrams' and 'Horrible Murders' in the ears of the public, from the shrillest alto to the excruciating falsetto baritone of the ragged boy who has caught a cold by sleeping the previous night in the open air . . .[155]

The *Western Mail* put their boys in uniform to distinguish them from 'the rabble' employed by its competitors, though to little avail. In Caernarfon too in the 1880s, copies of *Y Genedl Gymreig*, *Y Werin*, *Yr Herald Cymraeg* and *Gwalia* were being hawked about the streets by, among others, Twm the Crier, 'a blind old man of gentlemanly appearance'.[156] Such work was casual and poorly paid, and, even in the 1920s, boys in Cardiff received only threepence a dozen for street sales.[157] As early as 1864, however, R. J. Derfel had criticized the Welsh press, and the Welsh-language press in particular, of not being sufficiently aggressive in the methods they adopted for selling their publications. Newspapers, he argued should be boldly and widely publicized. Should this problem be overcome, and he acknowledged that to a certain extent the problem was a cultural one, he forsaw that a sustainable Welsh-language daily newspaper might in the near future be a practicable possibility. The readership existed, Derfel concluded, but it had not yet been sufficiently canvassed and organized.[158]

Selling newspapers to customers further afield than the streets of the town where the paper was printed required a more sophisticated distribution system. Roads had improved since the Association for the Improvement of Roads in Wales started its work in 1789, and by the first decade of the nineteenth century there were a number of good mail routes available for the distribution of newspapers and periodicals. But the pattern was uneven. Merthyr, Dowlais and Tredegar had a good service to Cardiff five days a week from 1804, and a daily service from 1821, but Merthyr had no link with Brecon until 1823 and Carmarthen had no daily mail to Cardigan until 1836. A mail service between Merthyr and Neath was started in 1834, and was extended to Swansea in 1835, but was discontinued in 1836 because of the poor state of the roads. Payment of the Stamp Duty entitled papers to free carriage by the mails, but in Wales the mails only travelled along a limited number of routes. Effective distribution thus required editors to make their own very precise arrangements for delivery to subscribers scattered through small villages, farms and cottages in the Welsh countryside which depended on the often unreliable co-operation of shop- and inn-keepers, farmers and ministers. The loss, theft and damage of bundles of newspapers were hazards that editors and their subscribers were compelled to regard as normal risks of delivery. Under these circumstances, papers printed in cross-road towns, such as Brecon and Carmarthen, or towns on important mail routes, such as Bangor, received and disseminated news far more rapidly than did those in more isolated settlements.[159]

So dependent were editors on the availability of the post that they set the frequency and the timing of their publications to suit its rhythms. Thus the *North Wales Gazette* came out on Thursdays instead of Tuesdays in February 1808:

> Tuesday being no post day from London was the first inducement for us fixing that as our day of publication – but finding by experience, and the strong representations of our friends, that from that circumstance no post proceeds from this quarter, so as to enable them to receive the North Wales Gazette in even a reasonable time . . .[160]

But if the pulse of publication and distribution was largely determined by physical conditions and the frequency of the postal services, they were also negotiated locally by editors and readers. In 1829, Hugh Jones (Erfyl) complained that the irregular delivery of *Y Gwyliedydd* was inexcusable 'in the present state of conveyances through every part of the country'. Thanks to the improved road system, he argued, it no longer mattered where a paper was printed. His optimism was premature. In 1836, a reader of *Y Papyr Newydd Cymraeg* from Llansanffraid, Conwy, remarked that, although the paper was carried free of charge by the post, it remained difficult to transport copies to outlying districts. Consequently, newspaper readers in the village, being situated three miles from the nearest Post Office, paid an additional penny for each English newspaper that was delivered to them, although Hugh Roberts, the local postmaster, agreed as a sign of his 'genuine patriotism' to deliver Welsh newspapers to the village for a halfpenny.[161]

Despite such difficulties, the postal subscription was a relatively safe way for the editor to conduct business. Sale was guaranteed for a minimum print-run on a quarterly or even annual basis, the loyalty of a well-defined readership was reasonably assured and, in the less accessible rural areas, clear and long-term lines of distribution could be established. The responsibilty for arranging subscription networks in the localities devolved onto voluntary or appointed subscription agents. Robert Evans of Trefriw, for example, distributed 148 copies of *Y Gwladgarwr* in his village in 1833, collecting £3.14*s*. for the publishers. Among his subscribers were six publicans, three shoemakers, two smiths, two glovers, a milliner, a nailer, a druggist, a saddler and a carpenter.[162] Another network was built by the publisher of *Y Papyr Newydd Cymraeg* in October 1836 by paying threepence to each agent for each new name added to the paper's subscription list. It was essential, however, that the information of the agents was accurate on the day of printing in order to avoid either the production of too many or too few copies. The most important advantage of distribution by postal subscription through organized networks was that it enabled small circulation newspapers to prevent wastage and thus to cut their costs by printing precisely the number that would be sold.[163]

A number of such networks were established in the 1830s. Subscribers to the *Merthyr and Cardiff Reporter* in 1836 could be found not only in Cardiff and Merthyr, but as far afield as Brynaman, Brecon, Newport, Llanelli, Swansea and Llandovery. They included John Frost, the Chartist mayor of Newport, and individuals who ranged from miners, stonemasons, joiners, shoemakers and tailors to ministers, ironmongers, works overseers and shopkeepers.[164] By 1839, similar distribution arrangements had been made by *Tarian Rhyddid*.[165] Local agents, though drawn from a variety of occupational groups, were often people who enjoyed a certain status in their communities. The agents for the periodicals *Y Ffenestr*, *Y Cerddor* and *Y Gerddorfa* in Llanrhystud in the mid-1870s, for example, were the brothers David and John Lewis (Eos Glan Wyre), both well-known singers,[166] and the early agents of the *Carmarthen Express*, which claimed a thousand subscribers at its launch in 1874, included stationers, grocers, chemists, builders, drapers, a Post Office keeper and numerous individuals trading from private adresses.[167] By 1899, the Welsh National Press Ltd. claimed to have 1,600 agents in Wales and in 'all the large towns of England'.[168] In addition to supplying a well-honed distribution system, agents formed a valuable support network for journalists.

A memorial collection for the editor and essayist Evan Jones (Ieuan Gwynedd) in April 1852 was organized by the concerted action of local agents who served a variety of Welsh-language newspapers across Wales.[169] The newspaper distribution networks compromised what Raymond Williams termed 'cultural formations', loose but complex organizations of interlinking groups of like-minded individuals from different areas and occupations which could also be mobilized for more aggressively political and religious purposes.

Local agents distributed the bulk, but not the entirety, of the circulation of many of the Welsh weeklies. A thousand copies of *Y Celt* were distributed each week in the early 1880s by local agents, but a smaller number was sent directly by post to individual subscribers and institutions. Volunteers remained the most important distributors of the religious papers long after the more commercial papers had evolved alternative systems, and twice as many chapels than newsagents distributed copies of *Y Celt* in the 1880s. The use of chapels as a distribution system for newspapers was useful for publishers, but could cause controversy within congregations. Some regarded the practice as an affront to their own Sabbatarianism, but despite such protests one minister in Tredegar in 1842 organized the Sunday distribution of *Cylchgrawn Rhyddid*, *Seren Gomer*, *Yr Athraw*, *Y Dirwestydd* and *Y Bedyddiwr*.[170] The Welsh-language denominational newspapers also kept in close touch with each other. *Y Celt*, for example, sent free copies each week to *Y Dydd* in Dolgellau, *Y Tyst a'r Dydd* in Merthyr, *Y Llan* in Wrexham, and three Welsh newspapers in the USA, *Y Drych* in Utica, *Y Wasg* in Pittsburg and *Y Cenhadwr Americanaidd* in Rensen, New York.[171] Lloyd George's *Udgorn Rhyddid* was also distributed in the USA from January 1888.[172] The *Western Mail* employed other methods of extending its subscription readership, including offering free accident insurance, on condition that a copy of the paper was in the possession of the reader at the time of the incident. For a subscriber, however, insurance would be automatic, and details of the insurance scheme were accompanied by prominent subscription forms.[173]

Distribution by individual subscription ensured that a substantial proportion of newspapers were read privately, at home. But, as with other political and cultural activities, the practice of reading newspapers, whether in the private or public spheres, was structured by gender. Children and adolescents were often familiar with the papers and their contents, but women who worked outside as well as inside the home had fewer opportunities to read newspapers, and fewer still to correspond with their editors. That working-class women were regarded by publishers as an important segment of the readership is clear from their advertisments, particularly for female domestic servants, and from the 'Women's Columns' and supplements that appeared in increasingly large numbers towards the end of the century. It is certain that both women and children had better access to the press in the home than in some of the other places where newspapers circulated, such as coffee houses, taverns, clubs and reading rooms which, though by no means exclusively male, were rarely attended by working women.[174] Children's periodicals proved to be a spectacular commercial success, as Thomas Levi found when he brought out *Trysorfa y Plant* in 1862. It appealed to children across the denominational boundaries, and its circulation soon reached 44,000 a month. The income from this one publication was sufficient to pay the entire production costs of both *Y Drysorfa* and *Y Traethodydd*.[175] In January 1891, O. M. Edwards began to publish an equally successful non-denominational children's magazine, *Cymru'r Plant*. But if home and school were the key access points to the children's market, periodical publications for adults, in the period prior to the emergence of the mass press, relied more heavily on other public and institutional avenues of distribution.

Public institutions had from the beginning been important sources of income for newspapers. The first Welsh weekly, the Swansea-based *Cambrian*, was, according to a Home Office informer, received by three coffee houses in London, including the Jacobin 'Chapter and George's'. In rural Wales, however, it was in taverns rather than coffee houses that newspapers were most commonly found, portions of which were read aloud for the benefit of the illiterate, a practice that survived until at least the 1870s.[176] Significantly, some 40 per cent of the circulation of the *Merthyr and Cardiff Reporter* in 1836 was distributed to public houses. Newspapers attracted customers to public houses, as landlords were only too well aware, but pressure was increasingly brought to bear during the course of the century to open newsrooms and reading rooms as a means of 'drawing visitors from the public house, breaking the evening and keeping them sober . . .'[177]

Small lending libraries had circulated books and pamphlets in Wales since the early eighteenth century. A lending library was operating in Carmarthen in 1708, and W. Cox's Circulating Library was active in Aberystwyth in 1815. These provided the earliest models for the collective distribution of periodicals and, later, newspapers. In 1823, the Holywell Reading Society circulated, in addition to its list of books, copies of the *Annual Register*, the *British Critic*, the *Monthly Review*, *Pamphleteer* and the *Quarterly Review*, and a newsroom established by Samuel Holland in 1842 in Pen Cei, Porthmadog, supplied, in 1848, for an annual subscription of ten shillings, a wide range of newspapers and periodicals, as did the Reading Room that the Abercarn Scientific Institution leased rent free from the Abercarn Colliery Company. Others were in operation in St Asaph and Holyhead in the 1840s, and Bethesda, Carmarthen and Briton Ferry in the 1850s.[178] Cardiff was the first town in Wales to adapt the Public Libraries Act of 1855, and in 1862 combined and expanded its voluntary library and reading room. By the 1880s, reading rooms, many attached to free libraries, had also been opened in Aberystwyth, Newport, Swansea, Wrexham and Bangor, in which 'newspapers were freely supplied'.[179] The Aberystwyth Public Free Library and Reading Room kept a list of eleven daily newspapers, sixteen weeklies and three monthlies, which in 1883–4 amounted to nearly half (£23) of their expenditure on books (£51).[180] The demand for newspapers was so great in reading rooms that new, more stringent rules of behaviour were introduced. The managing committee of the Llansteffan Reading Room resolved in 1888 that no user in future would 'be entitled to retain any newspaper or periodical for more than 10 minutes after it has been bespoken by any other member wishing to read it'.[181]

Mechanics' Institutes, such as the one in Milford Haven that spent nearly £12 on newspapers and periodicals in 1884, or the one in Narberth that local people fought to keep open in September of the same year, were also places where newspapers were read. Many, however, as a correspondent for the *Morning Chronicle* discovered in 1850, were 'comfortless and dreary' places, attended 'not by mechanics and labourers, as would be inferred from the name, but by clerks, shopmen, and others, who have already made material progress in the rudimentary branches of learning'.[182] A writer in the *Westminster Review* in 1857 regretted that the average Mechanics' Institute had degenerated into 'a middle class lounge',[183] but by the early twentieth century, the workmen's institute libraries, particularly in the villages of the south Wales coalfield, were important centres for working-class newspaper reading. In 1912, for example, the Parc and Dare Institute Library in Treorchy took in nine daily newspapers, thirty weeklies (including seven Welsh weeklies) and thirteen monthlies (two in Welsh).[184]

Control of reading rooms was highly contested, and not only by philanthropists. In 1909, George Eyre Evans launched a fund to establish a new, secular reading room in Penparcau, Aberystwyth, with the slogan 'No public house, no policeman in village!' Others were organized by the churches, such as the Bangor Reading Society which met in the 1850s in an Independent Chapel. These societies, along with the efforts of individual ministers, were integral to the distribution networks of the denominational papers. Thirty per cent of the distributors of the Baptist *Seren Gomer* in 1864 were Baptist Ministers, although others included colliers, quarrymen, tailors, chandlers, ironworkers, saddlers, grocers, chemists, booksellers and (five) publicans.[185]

Political organizations were also involved in the distribution of newspapers. The Aberystwyth Junior Radical Club in the 1880s bought a variety of newspapers and periodicals,[186] as did many other Liberal Clubs in Wales. The North Wales Liberal Federation, for instance, purchased and circulated offprinted articles and pamphlets from *Yr Herald Cymraeg* and other papers to their members and supporters, as well as to public libraries and Liberal Clubs.[187] In 1892, the *South Wales Radical*, edited by R. N. Hall, secretary of the South Wales Liberal Federation, was aimed primarily at an institutional political readership that included:

> . . . secretaries of Liberal Associations, Women's Liberal Associations, Liberal Clubs, Radical Organisations, Labour Societies, Trade Unions, Fabian Society branches, Disestablishment Committees, Nonconformist Unions, Anti-Tithe Societies, 'Young Wales' Societies, and Irish League Branches.[188]

Trade unions were particularly active newspaper distributors. In November 1873 John Thomas Morgan of the *Workman's Advocate* addressed the General Association of Smiths and Strikers at their annual conference at Neath on the subject of the importance of a labour press. The conference unanimously resolved to recommend that its lodges should 'encourage the circulation of the *Workman's Advocate* as much as possible, and that each lodge in this Union undertake the sale of at least one dozen copies.' By the end of 1873, Morgan had gained similar support from the miners, the ironworkers and from the trade societies of the tinplate workers, enginemen and stokers. Individual agents, however, were victimized for carrying out this resolution in their workplaces. One complained that he had been sacked by his employers for 'attempting to increase the circulation of the *Workman's Advocate*, and for being prominent in the union'. Morgan regretted that this had not been the first instance of such victimization.[189] Half a century later, *Y Dinesydd* continued to rely on the initiative of individual trade-union supporters to extend its circulation. Two Ffestiniog quarrymen, Hugh Lloyd and Ivor Thomas, arranged an advertising campaign for the paper in the mid-1920s,[190] while representatives of the Transport and General Workers' Union (TGWU) and the National Union of Railwaymen (NUR) respectively took charge of the paper's distribution in the Wrexham, Glyn Ceiriog and Bala areas. In Wrexham, J.W.Williams of the TGWU even tracked down 'the only Labour newsagent in the town' and sent his name and address to a grateful editor of *Y Dinesydd*.[191] Not all trade unions, however, subscribed to copies of radical or socialist newspapers, and in December 1879, the Rhosllannerchrugog branch of the Miners' Association subscribed instead to the *Colliery Guardian*. Other groups of workers collectively subscribed to a variety of different newspapers. In the Croesor slate mine in 1902 fifteen copies of three periodicals, and a wide range of newspapers, were delivered to the miners' barracks.[192] Others responsible for the distribution of newspapers included such voluntary associations as the Good Templars, whose quasi-masonic lodges, which flourished in Wales between 1873 and 1914, supervised the circulation of the *Good Templars' Advocate* and *Y Temlydd Cymreig*.[193]

The relative significance of such distribution methods declined as newspaper reading became more of an individual than a collective practice, and as commercial distribution through bookstalls and newsagents increasingly came to dominate the volume sales market in the growing urban and industrial society of the later nineteenth and early twentieth centuries. This process marked a quantitative and a qualitative shift from a 'closed' market, which depended on the loyalties of particular voluntary social networks, to an 'open' one, which relied far more on retail outlets. The numbers of those who declared their occupations to the Census as 'newspaper agents or newsroom keepers' increased from twenty-six in 1861 to forty-six in 1871, and leapt from 108 in 1881 to 180 in 1891. Booksellers had long been important distributors of newspapers and journals in towns and larger villages. Mr White's bookshop in Merthyr in 1849 sold copies of thirty-one periodicals, by far the most popular being the only Welsh-language journal, the penny paper *Yr Eglwysydd*. Another Merthyr bookseller confirmed that 'if the cheap publications were in Welsh the sale would be enormous'.[194] In the first week of January, 1863, a bookseller in Ystalyfera received for sale one daily newspaper (the *Leader*), and ten weeklies, both Welsh and English, from north and south Wales, including *Baner ac Amserau Cymru*, which by 1892 had agents in all the counties of Wales except Radnor and Pembroke.[195] Distributors were necessarily sensitive to their local markets. Hugh Evans built up and sustained a regular clientele of 350 readers of Welsh periodicals in Liverpool in the early 1890s, and supplied them with a choice of a dozen titles,[196] but the demand even within Wales was highly volatile. A newsagent in Tylorstown reluctantly discontinued the sale of *Y Deyrnas* in 1919 on the grounds that 'the customers are all gone back to the North'.[197]

An uneasy relationship existed between newspaper publishers and their commercial distributors. Substantial discounts and commissions were normally demanded by commercial agencies despite the evident poverty of many of the titles, and distributors were often exasperatingly slow in paying for their newspapers. In December 1820, T. Jenkins of the *Cambrian* informed his agents that, thanks to the 'heavy duties on Newspapers' credit was impossible and the prompt payment of all bills was a condition of the paper's survival.[198] The difficulties which Jenkins faced continued to worry publishers throughout the remainder of the century. In 1851, the publishers of *Seren Cymru* reiterated the policy that no 'sale or return' arrangement was possible, the ratio between sales to agents and the total print-run being too small to allow such privileges.[199] Newspapers operating on tight profit margins offered commissions to agents only when prompt payment was guaranteed. In 1878 Hemming of the *Glamorgan Gazette* offered a Mr Austie, a Llantrisant watchmaker, 25 per cent commission if monthly settlements were paid without delay. Papers were delivered to the agents by train in prepaid parcels, but unsold copies could be returned to the publishers only during the first three months of the contract.[200] Newsagents, however, were notorious for their failure to comply with such agreed terms, and requests, appeals and threats to agents were common occurrences. David Williams of *Seren Gomer* instructed Joseph Jones in December 1843 to pursue an indebted agent 'by fair means – or else *law*', and in the early 1850s Ieuan Gwynedd sharply upbraided his distributors with the warning that 'if a hundred copies are ordered, then a hundred have to be paid for, not eighty'.[201] In 1888 the editor of *Y Gwyliedydd* complained that virtually all his agents were late in making their payments,[202] the consequences of which for the economy of any newspaper could be serious, even fatal. *Y Gweithiwr Cymreig* in its valedictory number in September 1889 significantly blamed its demise jointly on Welsh religious sectarianism and 'difficulties with the distributors'.[203]

But these were minor difficulties, occupational hazards that could be endured or negotiated, compared with the immense opportunities that were opened up for the press in the 1850s. Rapid population growth, urbanization, the repeal of the 'Taxes on Knowledge', the introduction of improved printing technology and the commercialization of production all provided key contexts for the development of the press in Wales, but the single most important contribution to the growth of a mass newspaper market was made by the railways. By 1844 there were four railway companies operating in Wales, the Taff Vale, the South Wales, the Bridgend and the Duffryn companies. Six months later another three had been registered, extending north to Brecon, and west to Swansea and Aberystwyth.[204] Fourteen railways had been completed by 1850, and in the twenty years that followed the rail network grew to connect the major towns and villages with each other and with the major urban centres of England. In the north, the Chester to Holyhead line was completed in 1850, and, principally through the efforts of David Davies, Llandinam, the railway from Oswestry was extended to Newtown in 1861, reaching Machynlleth in 1862 and Aberystwyth in 1864. The Cambrian Coast line was opened in 1867, linking mid- and north-west Wales. Trains reached Pembroke and Tenby in 1863, and Aberystwyth from Pencader in

1867. In south Wales, by 1850, the South Wales Railway had been linked to the Great Western Railway via Gloucester, and trains were running on the Swansea to Chepstow line.

The growth of railways, far more than the improvement of roads, transformed the relationship between the press and its market. It improved the collection of news, and simultaneously hastened and reduced, relatively, the cost of distribution. On the other hand, the railways also opened 'neglected Wales'[205] as a market for the English press, thus changing decisively the competitive balance of Welsh journalism. Most editors were quick to grasp the advantages of the trains. In September 1858 the *North Wales Chronicle*, seizing the opportunity to use the new railway to extend its catchment area, issued the following notice:

> The construction of the railway from Rhyl to St Asaph and Denbigh, having more closely allied the counties of Denbigh and Flint with those of Caernarvon and Anglesey, the Proprietor of the *North Wales Chronicle* has pleasure in announcing that it is his intention to avail himself of the facilities thus offered for paying increased attention to the business of those counties.[206]

The editor then charged his brother, William Martin, as 'Special Agent and Reporter' based in St Asaph, with the responsibility for gathering news and attracting local advertising.

Railways as a means of distributing newspapers, despite their speed and the general efficiency of their uniformed army of staff, were not without their problems. Newspaper publishers could grow so accustomed to the manifest advantages of the trains that they neglected those readers in outlying areas who, in earlier times, had formed the backbone of subscriptions and voluntary distribution networks that had made possible the survival of so many small circulation papers. *Tarian y Gweithiwr* met this challenge by producing a slimmed down version of their weekly paper, without advertisements, for transmission by post to those subscribers who did not live close enough to railway stations to collect the full paper.[207] Negotiations regarding terms of carriage could also prove difficult. John Gibson complained that the Cambrian Railway Company 'always want two shillings for eightpence', but by 1893 the *North Wales Chronicle* had negotiated two separate rates for carriage, the 'ordinary', in which the railway company accepted ordinary liability for the newspapers carried, and 'reduced liability', where the paper relieved the carriers of 'all liability for loss, damage, misdelivery, delay or detention'.[208]

Railway travel also brought larger numbers of tourists to Wales, facilitating the emergence of a new, albeit seasonal, readership. The *Llandrindod Wells Chronicle and Visitors' Directory* was started in August 1876 as a proselytizing journal for the town's tourist trade, and eleven years later John Gibson in Aberystwyth started a similar summer season newspaper, the *Cambrian Bay Visitor*, a paper that contained, on the editor's own admission, 'neither news nor articles'.[209] Long train journeys themselves created a demand for cheap reading matter, a demand that was satisfied above all by the station bookstalls.

W. H. Smith and Son opened bookstalls in railway stations in Wales from the early 1860s, in Neath in December 1861, Merthyr in October 1863, New Milford in February 1865, and in other stations virtually as soon as they opened. The value of sales of newspapers and periodicals from these outlets increased from £3,000 from eight bookstalls in 1867 (comprising a third of the total bookstall income), to nearly £40,000 from forty-four outlets in 1895, and rising to £74,000 in 1930–31, £42,000 of which came from twenty-two outlets in south Wales, and the remainder from twenty-one bookstalls in north and mid Wales. Newspapers to the value of more than £10,000 were sold on the Cambrian Coast line alone in 1925–6, although W. H. Smith's contract with this line was to expire in the following year. By 1931 there were in Wales five W. H. Smith wholesale houses, and thirty-nine 'B' or principal bookshops that drew supplies through the London Head Office, most of which had under their control one or more sub-branches located at the same or neighbouring stations.[210]

W. H. Smith and Son, more than any other single agency, transformed the newspaper market in Wales. Not only did it make special arrangements to be the sole distributors of some titles, such as the *Cardiff Hansard* from December 1882, but it also became a partner in certain Welsh publishing ventures. *Y Meddwl* in 1879, for example, was published jointly by the Cambrian Publishing Company and W. H. Smith and Son, and was sold by the latter 'in every Railway Bookstall in Wales'.[211] It also allowed Welsh newspapers to be transported and sold in English cities.[212] The main traffic, however, was in the other direction.

The market for newspapers in Wales had at no time been confined solely to those titles edited, printed and published within its borders. Papers published in London, Manchester, Liverpool and elsewhere had long circulated in Wales, and as early as the the 1800s Charles Broster had acknowledged that the major competitor for his fledgeling *North Wales Chronicle* was the *Liverpool Mercury*, a paper which even then enjoyed a wide circulation in Denbighshire and Flint.[213] But the coming of the railways, with their network of station bookstalls, considerably increased the volume of imported titles. Arnot Reid claimed in 1886 that 'when we go further from the seat of Government . . . and where the local paper grows larger and better in the ratio of distance, then the sale of London papers becomes quite exceptional'.[214] After the 1850s, the circulation of London papers in Wales may have been small, but it was hardly 'exceptional'. By 1852, *The Times* could reach Carmarthen from London on the evening of the day of publication, and London news could be read directly long before the editors of the local weeklies had had the opportunity to copy its main stories into their own columns. This may have served to persuade local editors to pay greater attention to local matters and to reduce the London news to summaries and comment.[215]

The demand for non-Welsh newspapers was satisfied also by titles produced in towns near the Welsh border, from the *Western Vindicator* in the early 1840s to the *Gloucester Journal*, the *Bristol Chronicle* and the *Liverpool Daily Post*. Some, including the *Manchester Guardian* and the two Liverpool dailies, employed Welsh correspondents and printed special columns devoted to Welsh matter.[216] In the early nineteenth century, London papers also offered such inducements as engravings, Derby tickets and prizes.[217] The English Sunday papers, particularly the *News of the World*, *Reynolds's Newspaper* and *Lloyd's Weekly Newspaper*, attracted a growing readership, and paved the way for a mass newspaper reading public in Wales.[218]

These and other English newspapers and journals were circulating freely, and in increasing numbers, throughout Wales in the nineteenth century. The Porthmadog newsroom in 1849 stocked, in addition to such Welsh titles as the *Caernarvon Herald*, *Y Traethodydd* and *Y Dysgedydd*, copies of *The Times*, the *Shipping Gazette*, the *Illustrated News*, *Punch*, the *Liverpool Mercury*, the *Mark Lane Express*, the *Quarterly Review*, and *Chambers' Journal*.

The Reading Room in the Abercarn Scientific Institution in 1850 had placed a regular order for two daily and eight weekly metropolitan and provincial newspapers, and seven periodicals, including *Chambers' Journal*, *Hogg's Instructor*, *Bentley's Miscellany*, the *Edinburgh Review*, the *Westminster Review*, the *Foreign Quarterly*, and the *Eclectic Review*. In 1850, the Wilkins' bookshop in Merthyr sold a selection of fifteen newspapers and journals, including 189 copies of the *News of the World*, sixty copies of *Reynolds's Miscellany*, thirty-six copies of *Reynolds's Political Instructor*, twenty-four *Lloyd's Miscellany* and, even at this late date, twelve copies of the Chartist *Northern Star*. In Bethesda in 1855, the local reading room subscribed to *The Times*, the *Liverpool Mercury*, and the *News of the World* in addition to a selection of the north Wales weeklies, and in the Llŷn peninsula in 1870, the *Liverpool Mercury* was the most widely read daily newspaper.[219] The religious leaders also kept up with the latest denominational news in the English religious press. In 1873, a Calvinistic Methodist minister normally bought the *Daily News* in addition to the denominational journal, *Y Goleuad*, 'so as not to be ignorant of the affairs of the world', and the Revd J. Davies, Cardiff, duly noted in his diary each week that he had 'read the *Nonconformist*', then edited by Edward Miall.[220] The publishers of the *British Workman* in 1860 even went to the lengths of translating the entire contents of the paper into Welsh in order to attract monoglot Welsh readers. The exercise was not repeated.[221]

The growth of the English press in Wales was not without its critics. In 1876, a writer in *Y Diwygiwr* complained that too many English newspapers were circulating in Wales, and warned that dire consequences for the morality of the Welsh would follow if their numbers and their influence were not reduced.[222] The writer would no doubt have been delighted by the decision taken by the Aberystwyth Junior Radical Club in October 1888 to remove the satirical paper, *Ally Sloper*, from their subscription list, but less pleased to find that three years later they resolved to discontinue *Baner ac Amserau Cymru* in favour of *Reynolds's Newspaper*.[223] However, the political advantages of utilizing the English papers were quickly grasped by the Welsh political parties, and William Hawkins Tilston, secretary of Cymru Fydd, noted with enthusiasm in December 1889 that 'as the Manchester papers circulate largely in the Northern localities it will be a very effective way of bringing our questions before the public'.[224] The following year, the North Wales Liberal Federation circulated copies of the *Christian World* and the *Manchester Guardian* to each member of their Executive Committee.[225] The political value of the English press intensified in the early twentieth century, particularly perhaps for the Left. The Marxian Club in Blaenclydach received from the Twentieth Century Press in Clerkenwell Green, London, copies of such papers as *Class War*, the *Clarion*, *Justice* and *SDP News*.[226]

The distribution methods of the socialist press were, in essence, no different from those of most of the equally under-resourced religious weeklies. They depended, above all, on networks of partisan volunteers and sympathetic institutions, which had been the normal pattern of distribution of the majority of weekly newspapers in Wales in the early and mid-nineteenth century. But the railways revolutionized these systems as abruptly and as decisively as the new printing and composing machines had broken the bonds between printers and journalists. The simultaneous industrialization and commercialization of the production and distribution of newspapers polarized the press into identifiable mainstream and marginal categories, or those operating in the 'open', and those in the 'closed', markets. Ironically, the same processes that had led to the industrialization of Welsh journalism, and to the enlargement and democratization of its market, would also, in time, reduce its diversity and blunt its radical edge.

3 *Ownership and patronage*

Tensions that developed within the newspaper industry have been shown to have been important determinants of the form and content of newspapers. But journalists, business managers, printers and distributors necessarily operated within a broader set of social relations, and other, external, agencies also exerted an influence over the press. This influence took two forms. On the one hand, economic liberalization stimulated the growth of a commercial press, one that was subject to the demands of advertisers and investors as much as to those of readers, whilst on the other, non-commercial pressures remained sufficiently strong to complicate the operation of the free market. In the former, the changing nature of ownership, from the individual to the collective, was an essential feature of expansion, but for the latter, where economic uncertainty was unavoidable, ownership was less important than systems of patronage in determining the shape of the press. The survival of such titles depended not so much on advertising and shareholding as on subsidies, occasional gifts, loans or other services, forms of patronage whose existence acknowledged that the press was not an ordinary business, but one which conferred a privileged voice in the control and distribution of that most important ideological commodity, information. For the contesting forces that were consciously re-shaping Welsh society in the nineteenth century, the press was too important an instrument of change to be left to the mercy of the free market. Consequently, external intervention in the work of editors and journalists assumed a multitude of forms, ranging from direct ownership to the more subtle manipulation of influence and obligation.

The pattern of ownership

The industrialization of the press in Wales occurred during, and was structured by, a transformation in its pattern of ownership. Types of ownership varied widely, and included individuals, families, partnerships, co-operatives and commercial or joint-stock companies. Printers were both the first journalists and the earliest newspaper owners. The importance of Thomas Gee, John Gibson, John Duncan and William Davies has already been mentioned, but there were many less talented, or less fortunate, but equally enterprising printers who launched their own titles. This, as has been shown, was neither difficult nor expensive. Much of the non-local news was obtainable from news agencies for little more than a few pounds a month, and the remainder of the paper could be filled by readers' letters and local reports, many sent in by voluntary correspondents. That the simplicity was in very many cases deceptive, and that severe difficulties often faced those who tried to maintain such papers in an over-supplied market for any length of time, even after the abolition of the Stamp Duty in 1855, has also been noted. But there can be no doubt that running a newspaper was an attractive proposition for those who had the means and the small initial capital necessary to start production, and printer-proprietors were common in Wales as elsewhere throughout the nineteenth century. John Evans owned and printed *Seren Gomer* and the *Carmarthen Journal* in the 1820s and John Williams and David Rees were both the printers and the proprietors of the *Cambrian* in 1851. *Cyfaill y Werin*, published in Newcastle Emlyn in 1861, was, like so many other low-circulation papers, printed by its owner, in this case D. M. Jenkins.[1] In the following decade, John Mills, with his partners Lynch and Davies, who had previously been printers in the *Gwladgarwr* office, announced the opening of their own printing office in Aberdare at which their co-operatively owned newspaper *Tarian y Gweithiwr* was edited, printed and published.[2]

So common an occurrence was it for printers to start newspapers, often for no better reason than to attract local advertisement revenue, that both journalists and journeymen printers complained that the proliferation of small businesses was one of the main reasons for their low wages and poor prospects. Many printers, one historian has noted, 'knew little about journalism and less of the value of good journalistic service.' Newspapers were brought out with the intention of covering areas which could not possibly sustain them if fair salaries were paid. In many cases, the printer with a small business 'was not a good newspaperman and kept his paper going by grim administration, economic shifts and dodges' and, significantly, often 'with the help of a political subsidy'.[3] The vulnerability of this sector to commercial and political pressures is an issue to which we shall return.

The proportion of titles owned by individuals or families declined as economic circumstances increasingly began to favour joint-stock companies that collectively could command greater resources. One 'Old Journalist' argued that in 1839 it was possible to launch a newspaper 'without credit or cash',[4] but even if this had ever been true in Wales, it was perfectly clear by the 1850s, and even more so by the 1890s, that newspapers required abundant quantities of both. Newspaper companies in Wales were as old as the press, the *Cambrian* having been started by a group of Swansea businessmen who, in 1803, had raised capital by floating £125 shares. These directors then appointed a Worcester printer, Thomas Jenkins, to be the new paper's editor, printer and publisher.[5] The backers of the *Carmarthen Journal* also raised the necessary pre-launch capital of £2,500 by issuing a hundred one pound shares, but henceforth 'determined to remain exclusive, and to keep a close watch on the manner in which the newspaper was conducted'.[6]

Company ownership and a dependence on capital raised by issuing shares, however, could prove dangerous. Josiah Thomas Jones formed a company and raised £175 through a £5 share issue in 1836 to keep afloat the *Merthyr and Cardiff Reporter*,[7] but the stability and financial security he believed he had achieved soon turned out to have been illusory. Firstly, the directors of the paper, subsequently renamed the *South Wales Reporter*, demonstrated their power in April 1837 by deciding to dismiss the editor, Mr Adderley, the sole registered proprietor, on the grounds that he had 'neglected and otherwise misconducted himself in the editing and Reporting' of the paper. The two reasons for Adderley's summary dismissal appear to have been his adherence to the Tory principles he had previously adumbrated in the *Gazette and Guardian*, and his imprisonment for debt in 1837.[8] Furthermore, it was revealed in the following year that of the forty or more registered shareholders, only nine had paid in full, another nine had paid half their shares 'and the rest paid not a farthing'. Some seven or eight had promised to give the amount of one share as a gift towards establishing the paper, which amounted to £7 a week for a thirteen-week print-run of a thousand copies per edition, but only two of them had done so. Moreover, having removed the editor, the directors 'soon afterwards dropped the paper and left [Jones] in the lurch' with an unpaid bill for the purchase of 'two hundred and fifty types and a press for the purpose of printing the paper'. The managing committee in this case were 'all men of property', though the majority belonged to the lower echelons of the local middle class, and included a draper, a grocer, two freeholders, two innkeepers and a smith and ironfounder, all from Merthyr. Of the £340 which Josiah Thomas Jones had spent on the launching of the weekly paper, only £125 was recovered.[9]

Generally, however, newspaper shareholders and company directors tended to be relatively wealthy and influential local people. The subscribers of the Cambrian Newspaper Co. Ltd. at the time of its launch in October 1890, included the manager of a tinplate and smelter works, a director of the Glamorgan Banking Co. Ltd., a shipowner, a solicitor, a manager of a copper works, a journalist and a mining engineer. The last three were also directors of the new company.[10]

Changes in individual ownership occurred frequently in order to clear debts incurred in the publication of a paper. L. Jones, proprietor and editor of *Y Punch Cymraeg* in Liverpool, offered in June 1864 to sell his satirical paper to John Ceiriog Hughes for £130, £110 of which were outstanding debts.[11] In December 1880 Howel Walters Williams took William Mansel into partnership of the *Cambrian* 'in consideration of his paying off debt and costs' of £310. Williams, however, relinquished control of the paper in December 1891 leaving new debts of just under £100, half of them bad.[12]

The risk of incurring debts and losses, and the increasing costs of newspaper production, further encouraged the establishment of limited liability companies. In 1899, the chain which included the *Cambrian Daily Leader, The Herald of Wales, The Neath Gazette* and the *Mid-Glamorgan Herald* was acquired by the Cambria Daily Leader Co. Ltd. for just under £34,000, a sum which included £18,000 for the freehold property, £10,000 for copyright and goodwill and £5,000 for plant and type. Few individual journalists or printers could afford such sums, but a combination of local chartered accountants and solicitors enabled the papers' managers and senior journalists to raise the required capital to continue the business.[13] Company ownership, however, was no guarantor of success. The Merthyr Telegraph Printing Co., registered with the Board of Trade in March 1907, and with a nominal capital of

£2,500 divided into £1 shares, included among its first directors a confectioner, a contractor and a solicitor. In April 1912, however, the company went into liquidation and was wound up in September of the following year.[14]

Ownership of some of the independent monthly and quarterly journals operated on rather different principles. The relationships between the proprietors and editors of such periodicals as *Y Traethodydd* were far closer in technical and financial terms than they were on the more commercial newspapers. Early attempts to extend shareholding in *Y Traethodydd* were innovatory, but unsuccessful. The founder, Lewis Edwards, suggested that the first two editors should send prospectuses and 'addresses' to two hundred trusted individuals requesting each of them to sign up four subscribers. Thus, in a short period of time, the journal would be underwritten by a thousand shareholders. 'Every pound we lay out now' in pre-launch publicity, he argued, 'will bring in ten pounds'. Lewis Edwards's optimism was not well-placed, and the burden of cost fell on Thomas Gee, Roger Edwards and Lewis Edwards himself.[15] The Revd Daniel Rowlands took up the editorship of the *Traethodydd* in December 1864, and at the end of the following year took a share of the ownership by paying the owner, Revd Roger Edwards, 15 per cent of the net profits of the publication for four consecutive years, in lieu of which Edwards was to become sole proprietor of the journal. In 1865, *Y Traethodydd* yielded a profit of £70, which was subsequently shared between Roger Edwards (£7.10s.), Daniel Rowlands (£13) and twenty-five contributors. Profits rose from £80 in 1866 to £100 two years later, when Rowlands was able to pay himself a salary of £43. His income from the journal remained at between £40 and £50 per year until profits were hit sharply in 1884. By 1887, income from the journal had fallen to only £25 a year.[16]

The ownership of the copyright to titles could also be a source of contention. Some owners were reluctant to part with a good title, even if the paper itself was no longer extant. Robert Isaac Jones (Alltud Eifion), for example, refused to sell the copyright of the title of his defunct newspaper *Y Brython*, even for a 'reasonable amount', to the owners of a new paper who were eager to trade under the old name. The problem was eventually solved by employing the ingenious device of replacing the Welsh definite article '*Y*' with the archaic English form '*Ye*', and the editor of the new *Ye Brython*

Cymreig devoted considerable space on his first front page to the etymology of the little word which had enabled him mischievously to publish under such an 'excellent title'.[17]

The ownership of both newspapers and periodicals in Wales was a shifting and precarious business, but, in general, the pattern of ownership conformed to that which had developed elsewhere in Britain in the late nineteenth century, and which was characterized by a growing concentration of ownership in the hands of fewer companies and the gradual disappearance of the individual editor or printer proprietor. In Wales, however, this process was modified by the continuing, and in some instances intensifying, pressure exerted on the press by religious and political institutions.

The religious press

It was reported at the Church Congress, at its meeting in Swansea in 1879, that, '. . . the native press is almost entirely in the hands of the Dissenters'.[18] In 1894, there were over 800,000 adherents of Nonconformist Protestant denominations in Wales, comprising 47 per cent of a population of just under 1.8 million. The largest denominations were the Congregationalists, (278,981 adherents), and the Calvinistic Methodists (268,415), followed by the Baptists (215,868) and the Wesleyans (69,093).[19] These denominations were strong in both rural and urban areas, and in March 1861 there were thirty Nonconformist chapels in Merthyr alone.[20] Nonconformist groups were divided not only by doctrinal differences, but also by styles of organization and even social class. The Calvinistic Methodists were politically the most powerful, and already by 1840 had 115 ministers in Wales and Monmouthshire.[21] In 1890, R. H. Morgan and O. M. Edwards could declare confidently, if controversially, that:

> The Celt is naturally Calvinistic, for Calvinism is but fatalism regenerated . . . it forms the basis of all Welsh thought . . . it is the law which perfects liberty, the sadness which is inseparable from true mirth. . . . Wales of the future will be the Wales of the Calvinistic Methodists.[22]

Making and re-making this Calvinist Wales, however, required the establishment of strong religious institutions. How these were to be built was a matter of some debate. They were not, emphatically, to be constructed by the normal, secular ways of the existing capitalist order, and Thomas Rees denied forcefully in 1883 that chapels, for example, were or should be built by companies of shareholders 'as railways are constructed', and that the imputation that they were was, he angrily claimed, 'a monstrous fabrication . . . invented by some Church man'.[23]

Among the acknowledged means of building and maintaining the denominational loyalty of the congregation was the weekly newspaper and the monthly or quarterly journal. The production of this kind of partisan journalism also was the subject of debate, particularly as the press as a whole, including its methods of distribution, became more commercially oriented towards the end of the century. *Y Goleuad* was started in Caernarfon in October 1869 to extend the influence of the Calvinistic Methodists and to maintain the network of ministers, laymen and congregations throughout Wales and beyond. It was, however, privately owned by the printer and journalist John Davies. A devoted Calvinistic Methodist, his religious and political enthusiasms were deeply scored on the paper, and made it particularly attractive to other members of the denomination. By 1872, however, Davies had been obliged for financial reasons to abandon *Y Goleuad*, and the business was purchased by D. W. Davies, who installed the Revd Evan Jones as editor. This and subsequent changes of ownership were conducted in such a way as to ensure that the sympathies, and the readership, of the paper were not disturbed. It was, then, from the start, a private venture, but one which maintained a special relationship with the leadership of the Calvinistic Methodists. Significantly, however, one leading member of the connection admitted in 1902 that should any obstacles prevent the publication of the paper, then the denomination itself would take it over directly 'as its own property'. The *Goleuad* was, he argued, indispensable to the efficient running of the various activities of the church, and, whatever the cost, the denomination should not countenance its discontinuation.[24] The title of *Y Goleuad* was eventually purchased by the governing body of the Calvinistic Methodists in July 1914, and five years later the connection also bought the building and plant of the Welsh National Newspaper Co. in Caernarfon.[25]

Before 1914, however, the denominational leadership consistently refused to involve itself in the risks and difficulties of producing, funding and distributing their own newspaper. Attempts to launch a paper under the direct control of the church leadership were rejected during intense discussions on the issue in May 1892 by, among others, Thomas Charles Edwards.[26] A decade later, efforts made in January 1902 to bring out a special edition of *Y Goleuad* in Liverpool were over-ruled by the General Meeting, whereupon it was decided by a group of Calvinistic Methodists in that city to proceed to launch a weekly newspaper of their own. The committee consisted mainly of ministers under the chairmanship of William Jones. Modelled on the *British Weekly* in terms of format, it was further argued that for it to succeed 'it must be of high standard and [pursue] a strong and clear policy or mission'. The organizers of the proposed paper emphasized four desiderata. The first was the need to attract an able and educated editor. Secondly, a good sub-editor and staff who were able to report, translate and so forth would need to be recruited. Thirdly, an energetic book-keeper and advertisement canvasser was deemed to be essential, and finally an office would need to be found in a central location.[27] No paper was produced, despite the evident professionalism of the venture, although another group of Calvinistic Methodists in south Wales, led initially by John Pugh and motivated by the American evangelist Dwight L. Moody's description of Cardiff in 1891 as 'Wales's Chicago', successfully launched the *Christian Standard* in June 1890.[28]

The Independents were prolific publishers of newspapers and journals. *Y Dysgedydd* magazine was started in 1821 by Cadwaladr Jones of Dolgellau, profits from which were used to provide financial support to retired ministers. *Yr Efangylydd* was established as a denominational magazine in Llandovery in 1831 at a cost of £500, but was criticized in 1835, the year in which it ceased to appear, for having given 'out an uncertain sound, insulted our principles by ridicule, favoured Toryism, and cried up Churchism in a saucy and impertinent manner'. It was retitled *Yr Haul*, and was soon to become one of the leading Tory and Anglican polemical journals in Wales under the skilful and infuriating editorship of David Owen (Brutus). The Independents established in the same year, under the editorship of David Rees (Y Cynhyrfwr) of Llanelli, a new paper to 'counteract the evil influence of the *Efangylydd*', under the title *Y Diwygiwr*.[29] By 1902, ten papers were published by the denomination, *Y Dysgedydd, Dysgedydd y Plant, Y Diwygiwr, Y Tyst, Y Celt, Tywysydd y*

Plant, Y Cronicl, Y Cronicl Cenhadol, Y Cenad Hedd, and *Y Dydd*.[30] From an early date, Independent ministers used the joint-stock method of financing and administering their press. The Welsh Newspaper Company Ltd., with two hundred £5 shares, was established in Liverpool in June 1867 to publish *Y Tyst Cymreig*. Chaired by Revd William Rees (Gwilym Hiraethog), seven of the twelve provisional directors were Independent ministers. Its first treasurer, Ebenezer Rees, was employed by the North and South Wales Bank, Liverpool, and the first fourteen overseers included at least four printers and five stationers and booksellers.[31]

Successive attempts were made to tighten shareholders' control over editorial policy. One shareholder argued in 1891 for the creation of a managing committee, composed of company shareholders, to which a balance sheet should regularly be submitted for approval. Furthermore, he advised that this committee should also 'act as a kind of directorate' for the paper. Shareholders, he argued, felt that at present 'too much power is given to the Editorial Staff'.[32] Increasing control over editorial matters by shareholders in effect was a means of extending ministerial control over the paper's contents and style, since in 1893 fifteen of the paper's eighteen registered proprietors were congregational ministers.[33] However, there is little evidence to show that detailed editorial decisions were taken on a regular basis by the owners of *Y Tyst*. On the contrary, the arrangement seems to have been one of employing an editor – in the early 1890s it was Dr J. Thomas, for about £100 a year – or, as was the case in 1893, renting the title out to Joseph Williams for £70 a year, and leaving him 'to make the best of it'.[34]

Following an internal dispute in 1880, a dissident group of Independents launched a rival Celt Newspaper Company. Seeking to raise a capital sum of £2,000 through the sale of £1 shares, it attracted support mainly from poorer members of the congregations. Only four of the 103 early shareholders held shares worth two or more pounds, thirty-eight held one share only and a further fifty one held shares worth only four shillings each.[35] Nonetheless, the Celt Newspaper Company succeeded in launching the weekly newspaper *Y Celt* in 1881. Among its seven initial subscribers, four were Independent Ministers, whilst others included a draper, a retired schoolmaster and a colliery proprietor, each holding between five and ten shares.[36] As was the case with all denominational newspapers, managers and editors were grateful for contributions from individuals or sympathetic groups. *Y Celt*, for example, obtained a grant of £15 from the Dr Williams Trust towards publication costs for the six months between September 1891 and March 1892.[37]

Among the Baptists also, the relationship between the denomination and the editors or owners was indirect. In 1851, the copyright of *Seren Gomer* was owned by twenty-eight Baptist ministers, who were, the editor explained, essential links between the paper and its readers.[38] Thomas Price was concerned in 1864 that the seven titles then associated with the Baptists were not being circulated effectively or aggressively enough, advocating, against the strong Sabbatarianism of the age, the sale of newspapers on Sundays. The circulation of *Seren Gomer* had fallen to 700 that year, and another publication, *Y Bedyddiwr*, published by John Jones, Llangollen, was discontinued in 1843. Support for infant baptism in this paper led other Baptists to start *Y Gwir Fedyddiwr* in 1842 to pursue a more orthodox policy. *Seren Cymru*, a privately owned paper of Baptist persuasion, was in 1880 the subject of a takeover bid by the newly formed Seren Cymru Publishing Company. One of its directors, John Jones, Felinfoel, along with J. Rhys Morgan of Llanelli, subsequently became the paper's editor. Claiming a circulation of 5,000 copies a week, it nonetheless attracted a great deal of criticism from local Baptist Associations, some of whom wished the paper to become the formal property of the denomination.[39] The Wesleyans also raised money and retained control over their publications by issuing shares. In 1877 a quarter of the shareholders of the Gwalia Printing Company were Wesleyan ministers, while another 14 per cent were quarrymen. Farmers and grocers comprised 8 per cent each. The average shareholder held only three shares.[40]

The Anglican Church, notwithstanding its firm belief that 'the heart of Wales, in spite of all its Dissent, still warms to the Church',[41] encountered difficulties and strong competition in the newspaper market. When in 1830 Evan Evans (Ieuan Glan Geirionydd) proposed to establish a new Welsh Anglican periodical along the lines of the *Saturday Magazine* he approached the Welsh bishops for patronage and funding, but *Y Gwladgarwr* which he edited from 1833 to 1836 was a financial disaster. In *Yr Haul* and its vitriolic editor, David Owen (Brutus), the Established Church in Wales had found its most incisive and effective advocate, but from the 1860s the Anglican press met with less success. In 1877 a gravamen presented to the Archbishop of Canterbury by the Dean of Bangor and fourteen other leading Welsh Anglicans indicated that the Church in Wales had suffered heavy losses thanks to Nonconformist dominance of the press, and the Church journals' neglect of the working class had only served to increase their hostility to the principles of the Established Church. The Archbishop was urged to instruct the Welsh bishops to pay closer attention to this problem, and to engage more emphatically with Nonconformity by establishing a propagandist Anglican press.[42] Four years later, *Y Llan* was launched in Wrexham under the vigorous editorship of the Revd Ellis Roberts (Elis Wyn o Wyrfai), and the following year incorporated *Y Dywysogaeth* and *Amddiffynydd yr Eglwys*, established in 1870 and 1873 respectively. His efforts, however, were publicly dismissed by Anglican evangelists in 1889. *Y Llan*, they argued, was 'a decided failure' which lacked the crusading spirit necessary to 'meet the assaults of the enemy's Press', and this despite the subsidies given to the paper by the Church Defence Institution from 1886 in return for the publication of Welsh Church Defence material supplied by the Institution. The entire Anglican press, they concluded, was seriously in need of being 'overhauled'.[43] In 1898 the Welsh Church Press and Printing Co. Ltd. was launched at the Caxton Hall, Lampeter, with a nominal capital of £6,000 issued in £1 shares. These were taken up by 843 shareholders, and the company was registered 18 March 1898. It survived until September 1919.[44] A rival Angican paper, *Y Gloch*, failed to attract the support of Welsh Anglican ministers,[45] and, in general, the unwillingness of the Church hierarchy to fund popular evangelical Anglican journalism proved to be a strong disincentive to the production of such publications.[46] Ecumenical publications fared no better, although a *Church of England Catholic Chronicle and Monastic Times* was edited by Fr Ignatius of Lanthony Abbey, near Abergavenny, between 1883 and 1885.

Welsh Catholicism remained relatively weak throughout the nineteenth century, but began to develop its own press in the early twentieth century. The *Welsh Catholic Herald* was launched in Cardiff in 1902, and survived until its incorporation into the *Catholic Herald* in July 1934, by which time a *Welsh Catholic Times* had also been launched (in November 1931). Attempts to convert north Wales to Catholicism were from 1900 led primarily by two Breton priests, Fathers Trébaol and Mérour, and in 1910 the former began to publish *Cennad Catholig Cymru* in Llanrwst.

Many Christian pressure groups, charities and missionary societies published or circulated their papers in nineteenth-century Wales. The Salvation Army, to take one example, was active in Merthyr, Dowlais, Aberdare, Newport and Cardiff by 1879, and the *War Cry* was a familiar sight in the streets and public houses of these towns. The first Welsh-language group was formed in Caernarfon in 1886, and their paper *Y Gad-lef* first appeared in April of the following year. It was incorporated into the *War Cry* in 1890 and discontinued two years later.

The political press

Overlapping with the religious press, but in many respects also separable from it, the political press made a distinctive contribution to the shape of journalism in Wales. Like many in the religious denominations, however, politicians both national and local expressed deep reservations regarding the wisdom of direct party ownership. This was particularly, though not exclusively, true of the Conservatives. Lord Lowther had complained in 1831 that it was no easy matter to establish a British Tory newspaper, particularly a daily, and estimated the launching cost at between £30,000 and £40,000. Naturally, he added, many were prepared to volunteer to take over the management of such papers and to be 'employed to spend the Tory Money.' But the sums required were not easily raised, nor was it desirable that a political party should do so. Rather it should, he argued, be 'a matter of trade' and not of party subsidy. What the party needed above all else, he argued, was an enterprising 'tradesman to embark his own capital in the concern'.[47] 'Tory Money' however, continued to be invested in sympathetic journalism during and after the 1830s, and in 1832–3, immediately after the Tory defeats of 1830–2, the Carlton Club was said to have awarded Alaric Watts of the *Standard* £10,000 to spend on the development of Tory newspapers outside London.[48] Yet, as Croker complained in April 1834, the Tory press 'seemed to be asleep. People were lamenting that the Party had no newspapers, or rather, that the two they did have were left unsupported'.[49] In the changed circumstances of the the post-1855 period, however,

Arthur Murphy could argue that a political party was in a far better position to fund the political press than individual proprietors. 'Few individuals' he reasoned in 1874,

> . . . can afford to spend the necessary sums without looking to the profit. But a party can. An individual may not be able to spend any portion of his income in propagating his political principles. But a party can. And a tithe of the sum spent on electioneering would suffice to establish journals that would render half of it unnecessary.[50]

The argument linking journalism and propaganda, and the control of the press with the achievement or retention of political power, which Murphy and others explicitly made in the 1860s and 1870s, was a powerful and persuasive one. Nonetheless, the general pattern regarding political ownership of the press in the nineteenth century was one where journalists sought closer financial ties with political parties, but the parties themselves preferred others to undertake the work for the lowest possible cost to themselves.

An important aspect of the debate about political funding and ownership was the issue of extending sympathetic party papers beyond London. The need to reach and influence new audiences became an urgent necessity after the Reform Act of 1867, but the desire to establish successful Tory newspapers outside London remained strong in the 1890s, when Sidney J. Low, editor of the *St James' Gazette*, urged Tories 'to emulate the remarkable financial, social, and commercial triumphs achieved by the Radical organs of the "new journalism".' Low's chief concern, it seems, was to ensure that the Conservative Party could rely on dependable local newspapers outside the south of England which might enable it 'to get into power by the votes of the remoter portions of the United Kingdom where the London papers are hardly read at all'.[51] Thus the two issues of party subsidy and the extension of a Conservative press into areas outside London and the south of England preoccupied the Conservatives from an early date. Their implications were not lost on Conservatives in Wales who sought to put into practice their party's wish to establish sympathetic newspapers. However, it was not the Conservative party itself that was responsible for creating a supportive press in Wales, but rather the work of printers and journalists who also happened to be Conservatives.

In north Wales, the Tory press can be traced back to Broster's *North Wales Gazette* of January 1808, which was subsequently retitled the *North Wales Chronicle* following its purchase in 1826 by John Brown. Regional rivals, such as the *Caernarvon Advertiser*, 'a Loyal and Constitutional Newspaper', printed from January 1822 at the Cymmrodorion Press by James Hulme,[52] were less successful, and the *Chronicle* remained throughout the nineteenth century the most important Tory newspaper in north Wales. In 1850, the paper was bought by the proprietor of the *Liverpool Mail*, and following his death ten years later, it was sold to John Kenmuir Douglas. W. M. Martin, the deceased owner's brother, left the paper to establish the *North Wales Advertiser and Vale of Clwyd Gazette* after 'feeling the want of a medium to represent the Clerical, Landed and Commercial Interests of the Counties of Flint, Denbigh, Merioneth and Montgomeryshire in a truly Conservative spirit'.[53]

The interests of the Conservative party strongly motivated both John Kenmuir Douglas and his brother Kenmuir Whitworth Douglas. The latter owned and published *Llais y Wlad*, a halfpenny weekly which began life as a Tory electioneering sheet in February 1874, but which continued for a decade. The Douglas brothers also owned two local editions of the Bangor-based parent paper, the *Llandudno Chronicle* and *Cronicl Cymru*.[54] In 1885, the ownership of the paper passed into the hands of the North Wales Chronicle Company, among whose shareholders could be counted some of the most senior Conservative politicians, industrialists and landowners of north Wales. Sir Hugh John Ellis-Nanney, the unsuccessful opponent of David Lloyd George in the Caernarfon Boroughs by-election in 1890, held shares to the value of £2,000, and George William Duff Assheton-Smith of Vaynol Park had invested £2,500 in the company by May 1890.[55] Lord Penrhyn disclosed to the Royal Commission on Land in 1894 that he also was a shareholder in the North Wales Chronicle Company, and that he 'most undoubtedly assisted the Conservative press in Wales'.[56]

But the Conservatives were not always so successful, even when local support was forthcoming from wealthy supporters. The North Wales Constitutional Press Company Ltd., which owned and published the *Wrexham Guardian*, launched soon after the election of 1868, was declared bankrupt in May 1873. A hurried attempt to rescue the company was organized by leading

Conservatives in the area, and in July 1874, Sir Watkyn Wynn was persuaded to subscribe £200 a year for two years to enable the company to continue to bring out the weekly Conservative paper. George Thomas Kenyon, a director who had already invested over £1,000 in the venture,[57] volunteered to lead the company out of its difficulties. The directors were confident that the paper could 'be carried on for £400 a year for two years and at the end of that time it ought to be a good property so that Mr Kenyon has every chance of not coming out a loser'.[58] A year later, however, the paper was still in financial trouble. Faced with the imminent prospect of paying off the mortgage taken out on the original plant, the worried directors tried to ensure that 'some steps should be taken to bring the matter before the shareholders and the Conservative party. Mr Kenyon must not be a loser and if things are properly managed he won't'.[59] But within three years the arrangement between local dignitaries and the Constitutional Association which had enabled the paper to be published in the interests of the Conservative party since 1869 had signally failed. Kenyon admitted that the paper had been started with too little capital, and had 'only managed to exist for the last nine years by the liberality of a very few Conservatives'. In the four years since 1874 the paper had been subsidized almost entirely by Kenyon and Sir Watkyn Williams Wynn, who between them had donated nearly £3,000, and twenty other sympathizers, including Lord Penrhyn, who had contributed some £16,000. Despite such generosity, the paper could be made neither profitable nor self-financing, and in 1878 £2,000 was needed to pay off all existing debts and an additional subsidy of £300 a year was thought to be necessary to guarantee the paper's survival. As the two leading patrons argued in their joint confidential letter to local Conservative supporters:

> . . . there is no reason why Sir Watkin [*sic*] and Mr Kenyon should be exclusively taxed for the maintenance of a Conservative Organ, the existence of which is a matter of the utmost importance to every Conservative in North Wales, especially at this time when we are rapidly approaching another General Election.

Despairing of any improvement in the paper's fortunes, the plant and title of the *Wrexham Guardian* were sold in August 1878 to a private newspaper proprietor from Dover, F. K. Edward Roe, for £600 and the clearing of a debt of more than £1,600.[60] It remained a Conservative newspaper into the twentieth century. Ironically, within five years of the collapse of the North Wales Constitutional Press Co., Stafford Northcote toured Wales 'urging Conservatives to do more to develop their own press',[61] and in the early summer of 1892 it was rumoured in political circles that certain north Wales Conservatives, including Sir John Puleston and Issard Davies, were attempting to float a new company in order to publish a Conservative newspaper to counteract the influence of the Liberal papers, particularly *Y Genedl Gymreig*.[62]

In south Wales, the *Merthyr Guardian*, founded in 1832 by William Mallalieu, was by 1839 also facing severe financial difficulties. Thomas Booker informed the Marquess of Bute in November of that year that the paper was 'misplaced at Merthyr if it is to depend on the Conservatives, and it is making a considerable loss which falls heavily on the few protectors of the Conservative interest.' Booker advocated its incorporation with another Tory paper, such as the *Bristol Journal*, 'which would also make it more generally interesting.' The paper's circulation would doubtless improve, and might lead to the establishment of a profit-making Conservative paper in Cardiff 'as an individual enterprise'.[63] On hearing that the publisher of the *Merthyr Guardian* was about to abandon the paper and move to greener pastures in Cardiff, J. Bruce Pryce advised him strongly not to do so without first consulting 'those who had the greatest interest in the result of his move'. He also suggested which journalists should be employed to undertake the task of conducting the 'only Conservative paper' in the Cardiff area.[64] By December 1839, however, the paper was up for sale, and its editor, Snow, was, according to Henry Scale, spending 'his time and talent to little purpose'.[65] By August 1841, the paper was being run by Henry Webber in Cardiff, and in 1865 it passed into the hands of the Cardiff and Merthyr Guardian Newspaper and Printing Co. Ltd. Henry Webber continued the lonely struggle against the dominant Liberal press by publishing the *Cardiff Standard and County Chronicle* from 1865 to 1867.[66] In Monmouthshire in October 1837, the Conservatives launched the *Monmouthshire Beacon* to help publicize their cause in the political contests of the later 1830s.[67]

The *Western Mail* began to extol the Conservative virtues in Cardiff in 1869. Launched in the midst of a local political campaign between the Conservative Marquess of Bute and his Radical cousin,

Colonel Stuart, the paper was heavily funded, as was its predecessor the *Merthyr Guardian*, by the Bute estate. It was estimated that by 1873 Bute had donated, through his solicitors, some £30,000 to the *Western Mail*.[68] As in the 1830s, however, the Bute dynasty still maintained a studied distance from the paper's management. But if Bute's involvement, whether financial or editorial, remained a private matter, the relationship between the paper's management, the Conservative party and Bute remained close. In May 1894 the Conservative Club rented a floor in a new *Western Mail* building in St Mary Street, and following a fire at the paper's offices in 1893, the Bute estate hastened to the rescue by offering the owners of the *Western Mail* prime site land for the erection of temporary buildings for two years for the peppercorn rent of £1 a year.[69] Owned in the 1880s by Daniel Owen, the paper was purchased by the Western Mail Ltd. in February 1896. Among its seven original directors were Daniel and his wife Sarah Owen, George A. Riddell, Lascelles Carr, the paper's editor, and his son Emsley. In 1910, William Davies joined the Board as editor of the *Western Mail*. Riddell and Lascelles Carr were to be the two guiding forces of the paper, and were most responsible for its success as a national Welsh newspaper which began in the mid-1890s.[70] Early attempts at extending the ownership were often unsuccessful, and the proposed arrangement with an evening paper in Newport had to be abandoned in 1892. In January 1896, Riddell was instructed to buy for the new Western Mail Ltd. the goodwill and copyright of the *Evening Express*, and it was able from that time to grow with greater confidence.[71] Other Conservative papers in south Wales included the *Welsh Conservative and Unionist* published in Pontypridd between 1911 and 1916.

The *Western Mail* did not remain for long the only daily paper in the rapidly growing town of Cardiff. In 1872, David D. Duncan, proprietor of the *Cardiff Times*, launched a rival, Liberal paper, the *South Wales Daily News*, though not without a considerable effort. Thomas John Hughes (Adfyfyr) recalled in 1888 that south Wales and Monmouthshire Tories 'and their Whiggish satellites' held 'the supreme sway. They had their fingers in the banks, in the railways and docks, and in every speculation'. The establishment of the Liberal daily involved 'a hand-to-hand conflict' with these interests, and 'Welsh Toryism and Welsh ecclestiasticism tried their utmost to ruin the solvency of Mr David Duncan'.[72] Despite this level of opposition, the *South Wales Daily News* survived as an independent Liberal newspaper until it was finally taken over by the *Western Mail* in 1928. On David Duncan's death in 1888, this paper along with its sister paper, the *South Wales Echo*, passed into the ownership of his three sons, John, David and Alexander Duncan. John Duncan was for ten years a member of the governing body of the Press Association, and was instrumental in establishing the Reuters' News Agency. He was also a Trustee of the Newspaper Society and a Fellow of the Institute of Journalists. He was knighted in 1909, and died in January 1914.[73]

There is no evidence that the Liberal party centrally funded a Welsh newspaper, in the way in which Ostrogorski claimed that the Liberal caucus had done to compete with Joseph Cowen's independent Liberal *Newcastle Chronicle*. Support from central Liberal political funds were scarce, although Joseph Chamberlain, excited by Henry Tobit Evans's attempt to start a Liberal Unionist paper in Wales, advised him in 1887 that the only source of funds from which it would be possible to give him any assistance was the Liberal Unionist Committee in London.[74] Nevertheless, there were numerous attempts by Liberals, for primarily political reasons, to launch, buy or subsidise newspapers, or to control them by other means. The *Welshman*, for example, was started in 1832 by Parliamentary reformers in Carmarthen specifically for the purpose of extending the reform campaign, and the Revd Henry Rowlands willingly parted with £100 in November 1839 to prevent the 'annihilation' of the *Caernarvon Herald* and thus to support the 'liberal interest' in north Wales.[75] Throughout the nineteenth century there was a great deal of discussion in Welsh Liberal circles about the future of the Liberal press.[76] In practical terms, the discussion focused in some areas on the very existence of a Liberal press, and in others on the means whereby factions in the party could extend their control over its editorial policy and content. Two examples, from Montgomeryshire and Caernarfonshire, illustrate the concerns and the methods of local Liberal politicians in relation to the press.

Major Liberal figures in Montgomeryshire, including A. C. Humphreys-Owen and Lord Rendel, had long toyed with the idea of starting a new local Liberal newspaper. In 1885, however, they were finally persuaded that an established Liberal weekly would serve their purposes adequately and at a lower cost. They were informed by local Liberals that the *Montgomeryshire Express*, owned by Messrs Stephens and Edwards and published in Newtown, had 'considerable influence' in the area, and that Stephens, the editor and co-proprietor, was 'an old war horse of the Party' who 'might excite much ill-will if met with competition'.[77] The working alliance between the paper and the local Liberal leadership was disrupted in 1888 by the editor's decision to retire and to sell his newspaper business. Humphreys-Owen, Rendel, Martin Woodall (owner of the *Oswestry Advertiser*), Pryce Jones and Richard Williams (a Newtown solicitor, Rendel's election agent and translator into Welsh of Sir Francis Bacon's *Essays*), moved swiftly to ensure that 'the only Liberal paper in the county' would not be 'going out of Liberal hands'. Woodall and Pryce were in favour of buying the paper and plant from Stephens at a negotiable price of between £2,000 and £3,000.[78] Despite Stephens's 'absurdly exaggerated idea' of the paper's value, Humphreys-Owen conceded that it enjoyed:

> . . . a considerable circulation among the farmers and if it went over [to the Conservatives, it] would have time between now and the election to turn some votes from the class who let their papers do their thinking for them.

He advised Rendel that the best means of ensuring the continued support of the *Montgomeryshire Express* for the Liberals in mid-Wales was to assist a takeover bid by either Woodall or Pryce Jones.[79]

Richard Williams took the view that it would be unwise for the *Montgomeryshire Express*, under new management, to compete with the other local Liberal newspaper, the *Oswestry Advertiser*, and advised that the best way of 'securing friendly co-operation between the *Advertiser* and the *Express* would be to merge the proprietary interests in both'. Ideally, he mused, the *Express* would be edited by the existing, and trustworthy, incumbent of the *Advertiser*'s editorial chair, Fred B. Mason. Williams promised aid in the form of a loan to the *Oswestry Advertiser* to help Woodall defray his expenses. If, on the other hand, as was more likely, the *Express* would continue as an independent undertaking, Williams informed Rendel that he would not wish to become a proprietor, because he 'could not watch or control the property, and because profits had better go to those upon whom the earning of a profit much depend.' Rather, his position would be that of 'a creditor content with a modest interest upon modest security, but able to wind up a failing business. Of course, he added, 'I must be satisfied that the business starts upon financial conditions of a profit earning character.'[80]

Williams's concern for the viability of the proposed enterprise was evidently shared by Rendel and Humphreys-Owen, but such financial and strategic deliberations were overtaken abruptly by unexpected and unwelcome events. Stephens had long since made it known that he would accept 'three hundred pounds less than that the Conservatives should get hold of the Express', and that it was believed that he had directed in his will that the paper 'should be sold for a thousand pounds less rather than it should become a Tory paper', but a new offer, made in April 1889, of £3,500 for the paper and the printing business, prompted a reconsideration. The approach apparently had 'not come directly from the Conservatives', but Stephens expressed concern that if the offer was accepted, 'the paper might get into their hands'.[81]

The Liberal grandees and their supporters did not respond to Stephens's appeal, but Fred Mason, editor of the *Oswestry Advertiser*, seized his opportunity to profit from the party's indecision. He presented to Rendel detailed proposals for the efficient and profitable running of the *Montgomeryshire Express*, and appealed to him for a substantial low-interest loan that would enable Mason not only to edit the *Express* but also to own it. His initiative was disregarded, and in May 1889 Rendel announced instead that the 'purchase of the Express by the Liberal party in the county [was] out of the question' and that 'the sale from what we are told must take place to the Conservatives'.[82] He did concede, however, that it might now be feasible to launch a new Liberal weekly in the town,[83] to which Mason once again responded positively by advising Rendel:

> . . . that a new Liberal paper for Montgomeryshire, circulating also in Radnorshire and Merionethshire, might soon be made to pay. I think too, that with the support of the Liberals of Newtown a general printing business might be established without difficulty as an auxiliary to the paper. The expense of carrying on the paper might be materially lessened by connecting it with the Advertiser, and this, I imagine, might be done without interfering with its editorial independence.[84]

The *Montgomeryshire Express*, however, was bought by Mr Phillips, a Newtown printer, and its subsequent relationship with the mid-Wales Liberals deteriorated rapidly. In June 1893, the secretary of the Montgomeryshire Central Liberal Association openly condemned its new editor for printing what he regarded to be a critical and unfair article on the Association, and voiced strongly his disapproval of the paper.[85] The events in Montgomeryshire in 1889 and 1890 reveal, firstly, the reluctance of politicians, Liberal as well as Conservative, to commit financial resources to newspapers, even in order to safeguard their party interests, and, secondly, the enthusiasm of journalists for precisely that kind of external involvement. Political patronage of the press was a more important means of advancement for journalists than for the politicians.

A second example of Liberal efforts to control the press occurred at much the same time in Caernarfon, and involved the attempted take-over of the *Herald* group of newspapers by the proprietors of *Y Genedl Gymreig*. The objective, however, was not, as in Montgomeryshire, to maintain a Liberal presence against a Conservative one, but rather to extend the factional influence of one brand of Welsh Liberalism at the expense of another. The *Caernarvon Herald* was started in 1831 by William Potter, and was later sold to James Rees. The title and the liberal politics of the earlier paper were adopted by *Yr Herald Cymraeg*, which first appeared in May 1855, timed to take advantage of the repeal of the Stamp Duty, which obtained the Royal Assent on 15 June of that year. John Evans, a schoolmaster and Caernarfonshire Secretary to the Liberal Federation, launched local editions of the paper in Cardiganshire and Merionethshire (in 1879) and Anglesey (in 1881), but went bankrupt in October 1884. The papers were then bought by R. F. Smith and Frederick Coplestone, the latter becoming sole owner in July 1890.[86]

Frederick Coplestone was an English journalist of strong Liberal sympathies. Apprenticed as a journalist on the *Hereford Times* in the late 1860s, he had worked as a reporter on the *Chester Chronicle* before being appointed, while still in his twenties, the founding editor of the *Crewe and Nantwich Chronicle*. He later edited and co-owned the the *Chester Chronicle* until his death in 1932. Coplestone's connection with north Wales developed during frequent mountaineering visits to Snowdonia, and was further cemented following his appointment as the north Wales correspondent of *The Times*. Although his base of operations remained in Chester, Coplestone became a man of some considerable standing in north Welsh political circles. The mayor of Caernarfon attended his funeral in 1932, and a poignant message of sympathy was sent to his widow by David Lloyd George.[87]

Lloyd George had good reason to miss his old friend. In 1901 – 2, Coplestone had instructed the editors of his papers in Wales to take the unfashionable view that the Boer War was unjust, and to support Lloyd George's anti-war campaign. Picton Davies, then editor of the *Herald* papers, strongly disagreed with the policy of his proprietor, but dutifully obeyed his instructions. In consequence, Davies later claimed, the *Herald* lost 'thousands' of the 30,000 readers who had previously been regular buyers of the papers.[88] During the First World War, now with John Jones as editor, Coplestone again gave powerful and sustained support to Lloyd George's Ministry, for which he was rewarded with a CBE. But in the late 1880s, the two men were locked in a long battle over the ownership and control of virtually the entire Liberal press in north-west Wales.

David Lloyd George's interest in journalism in the late 1880s was expressed primarily through his involvement with the management of a group of newspapers in Caernarfon which included *Y Genedl Gymreig*, and, later, *Y Werin* and the *North Wales Observer and Express*. Established in 1877 to further the interests of the Merioneth and Caernarfon Liberals, *Y Genedl Gymreig* grew from an original staff of eleven to twenty-nine within three years,[89] and in 1884, W. J. Parry, a Liberal local politician and businessman, was approached by John Thomas (Eifionydd), founder and editor of *Y Geninen*, with the proposal that a company be formed to take over the management of *Y Genedl Gymreig*, the *North Wales Express* and the *Bangor Observer*. Parry consented on condition that the new company would remain strictly non-denominational, and that all four main denominations would be represented on its Board of Directors. On 9 August 1884, Parry's Welsh National Newspaper Company bought *Y Genedl Gymreig*, and within the week also became proprietors of the *Bangor Observer* and the *North Wales Express*.[90] These papers gave strong support to Lloyd George before and during the by-election of 1890, in which he was narrowly elected for the first time as MP for Caernarfon Boroughs.

Lloyd George well understood the value of newspaper support in the achievement of political ambition. In 1888 he had launched, with D. R. Daniel, a short-lived weekly in Pwllheli, *Udgorn Rhyddid*, and within a year had become involved with the Caernarfon group of journalists based in the offices of *Y Genedl Gymreig*. One Caernarfon journalist said of him that he 'wanted newspapers to be at his call', and that he was chiefly responsible for politicizing the newspapers of the company.[91] Angered by the lack of enthusiasm for his ambitions in the *Herald* papers, and fearing that his candidature at the forthcoming election would thus be endangered, he lobbied strongly for the Welsh National Newspaper Company to buy Frederick Coplestone's newspapers in north Wales, and convert them into actively pro-Lloyd George organs. Meetings with Coplestone and his solicitor to negotiate the terms of the transfer of ownership began in October 1889,[92] and at first progressed very slowly. The imminent prospect of a General Election added a note of urgency to the talks, as W. J. Parry disclosed in a confidential note to Lloyd George in February 1891, 'I feel strongly we should do something before the General Election or the two papers may turn out a curse to the cause. If we amalgamated there would be one voice and a strong voice.'

As well as a strong, unified political voice, the amalgamation of the two newspaper groups would enable Lloyd George and his supporters in the Welsh National Newspaper Company to own and control a daily newspaper in north Wales. *Yr Herald Cymraeg* would appear on Tuesday, the *Observer* on Wednesday, *Y Genedl* on Thursday, the *Caernarvon Herald* on Friday and *Y Werin*, which had been launched by W. J. Parry in 1885, on Saturday. 'In this manner' Parry explained, 'we would have a daily paper except Monday'. Parry and Lloyd George were also thinking along the lines of launching an evening paper, though that idea was reluctantly put to one side because of their fear that the advertisement revenue which accrued to the existing papers might thus be lost.[93] The need for a unified Liberal press in north Wales in the early 1890s was intensified by the emergence of a chain of Conservative newspapers, which included *Gwalia* on Tuesday, the *Llandudno Directory* on Wednesday (and *Cronicl Cymru* also from 1893), *Y Clorianydd* on Thursday (with the addition of *Y Chwarelwr Cymreig* in 1893), and the *North Wales Chronicle*, the parent paper, on Friday.

Negotiations to amalgamate the two Liberal newspaper groups continued from February through to October 1891. Parry's scheme, which came very close to being realized, involved the creation of a new company, consisting of the existing directors of the Welsh National Newspaper Company and Frederick Coplestone. Both the Company and Coplestone would sell their copyrights, plant and jobbing businesses to the new company.[94] Negotiations foundered eventually on Coplestone's insistence on a price of £8,000, a figure, Parry insisted, which made 'the scheme impossible'.[95] By early October, the amalgamation negotiations formally came to an end. Parry expressed his deep disappointment, but closed his final letter on the matter to Lloyd George with the words 'our duty is clear – work away'.[96]

W. J. Parry's scheme to launch a new company remained an attractive proposition as a means of improving the management of the newspapers and of clearing existing debts, which, by late 1891 amounted to £900. The revived organization, Parry assured Lloyd George in November 1891, would enable them to 'bring the Herald to their knees very soon'.[97] One means of securing the future of the new company was to strengthen its links with the Welsh Liberal party, and when the new Welsh National Press Company was formed on 1 January 1892, it included among its directors not only the denominational representatives of the previous company, but also prominent Liberal politicians such as T. E. Ellis (MP for Merionethshire), William Abraham (Mabon, MP for the Rhondda Division), S. T. Evans (MP for Mid Glamorgan), Alfred Thomas (MP for East Glamorgan), David Randell (MP for Gower), Evan Rowland Jones (editor of the *Shipping World*), and David Lloyd George, who served also as the company's solicitor. Shareholders in the previous company were urged to keep their shares in the new enterprise, though it is evident that many did not do so.[98] But the Welsh Liberals were delighted by events in Caernarfon, and T. E. Ellis applauded the work of Parry, Lloyd George and their friends who had, he explained to Lord Rendel, 'saved the *Genedl, North Wales Observer* and *Werin* from inefficiency if not from collapse by buying up the Company and thoroughly reorganising them. They are now doing splendid Liberal work.'[99] Ellis had himself taken out shares in the new venture, and urged Rendel to follow his example.[100] The new company also acquired the copyright of other titles and began to publish such important

Welsh periodicals as *Y Traethodydd* and *Cymru* (previously *Cymru Fydd*).

This then was Lloyd George's appenticeship in newspaper politics. If, as James Magarch has argued, he was the first prime minister to discover Fleet Street, and the first to proceed 'deliberately and cynically to establish his personal ascendancy over the Press', it was in Caernarfon in the late 1880s and the early 1890s that his skills were developed in the manipulation of journalism. The experience gained proved invaluable in later years, and in 1901, with the aid of George Cadbury and his old friend David Edwards, erstwhile manager of the Welsh National Newspaper Company in Caernarfon, Lloyd George bought the *Daily News*, and in 1918 engineered the takeover of the *Daily Chronicle*, which enabled him effectively to control the entire United Newspapers Syndicate.[101]

Unlike the Montgomeryshire Liberals, those in Caernarfon were able to harness political energies to commercial interests. Despite their failure to secure a monopoly over Liberal journalism, which in the event was proved to be unnecessary by Coplestone's enduring loyalty to Lloyd George, they succeeded in maintaining a strong Liberal presence in north Wales which was actively supported by Liberal politicians, locally and nationally. In the mid-1890s, W. J. Parry enjoyed the irony of the north Wales Conservatives' acknowledgement that the Welsh National Press Company had provided them with an ideal model for the ownership and control of the political press.

The political identity of a newspaper, then, was largely dependent on the sympathies of its owners, and a change in ownership could entail an abrupt change in the paper's politics. Such sudden transformations were not unusual among the Welsh weeklies. The *Merthyr Times* was described in 1895 by its editor, J. O. Jones (Ap Ffarmwr), then fresh from W. J. Parry's *Y Werin*, as 'the organ of pronounced Liberalism', but following Jones's departure for Nottingham late the following year, the paper was bought by Edwin Davies and Valentine Watson, the latter a Conservative party agent, who converted the paper into 'a Conservative and Unionist paper' which 'claimed the support of every association which has the cause of the [Conservative] Party at heart'.[102] Equally volatile were the papers associated with Welsh pressure groups, including such temperance journals as *Y Cymedrolydd* and *Y Cerbyd Dirwestol*, both published by Owen Jones in Mold in

1836 and 1837 respectively, and *Y Cantor Dirwestol*, published by temperance societies in Merthyr in 1844.

The emergence of Labour as a political force in Wales also contributed to the changing configuration of the political press. The labour papers of the late nineteenth century claimed a lineage that extended back to the radical bi-lingual paper *Y Gweithiwr/The Worker* of 1834, the Chartist *Udgorn Cymru* and the *Advocate* of 1840, *Cyfaill y Gweithiwr*, edited by John Morris in Ffestiniog in 1854 and the *Merthyr Star* of the 1860s. Other papers aimed at the organized working class included the *Workman's Advocate/Amddiffynydd y Gweithiwr* of 1873–6, *Tarian y Gweithiwr*, started in 1875, Jenkin Howell's *Y Gweithiwr Cymreig* of 1885–9 and the *Industrial World*, the official organ of the Welsh tinplate workers between 1892 and 1898. Socialism also found expression in *Llais Llafur*, run by Ebenezer Rees in Ystalyfera from 1898, and in two monthly papers closely associated with the Independent Labour party, the *Labour Pioneer*, which appeared from March 1900 until November 1902, and the *South Wales Worker*, started in February 1902. The former was published by the Cardiff Trades Council and the Cardiff Socialist Society, whilst the latter, a successor to the *Swansea and District Workers, Journal* (1899–1901), was edited by J. V. Esmond, a teacher, and was issued by the Swansea Socialist Society. It was revived as the *South Wales Worker* in 1913–14 as a continuation of the *Rhondda Socialist Newspaper* of 1911–13. The *Merthyr Pioneer*, also started in 1911, survived until 1922.[103] The *Plebs Magazine*, from 1909 until the First World war, acted as an essential conduit of socialist ideas into industrial south Wales from Ruskin College and the Central Labour College.

By 1906 in north Wales it was possible to detect a 'changing tone', especially in the politics of Gwynedd. From 1904, emphasis began to shift from disestablishment to poverty and unemployment, and as a result radical journalism began to lose the support of many Nonconformist leaders. As in south Wales where *Llais Llafur* had superseded *Tarian y Gweithiwr* as the voice of the Left, so in north Wales the leading Liberal organs of the late nineteenth century, *Y Genedl* and *Y Werin*, were replaced by the *Labour Leader* and, from 1912, a home-grown socialist alternative, *Y Dinesydd Cymreig*.[104] Its origins and seventeen-year history demonstrate the opportunities and the difficulties of producing a popular, socialist, Welsh-language weekly by an autonomous group of printers and local political activists. The *Dinesydd Cymreig* was conceived during a printers' strike that started in Caernarfon on 3 February 1912 involving eight printers from the *Caernarvon and Denbigh Herald*. Despite efforts by the mayor to arbitrate, the employers responded to the strike call by opening all the offices in Caernarfon to non-union labour. The cause of the strike was a workers' demand to raise the minimum wage from 27*s*. 6*d*. to 30*s*., although the average minimum wage in north Wales offices at that time was no more than 24*s*. On the *Caernarvon and Denbigh Herald*, a management representative explained, only one printer was on minimum pay, and others received weekly wages ranging from 30*s*. to £3. Printers, he claimed, were paid more than correspondents or sub-editors. The strike was led by Caernarfon's branch of the PTA, and, most vocally, by its secretary, Peter Angel.[105] Attempts were made to break the strike by importing workers into two newspaper offices, and the fourteen unemployed printers who arrived from London in early February 1912 were 'vigorously hooted' by a large crowd of printers and their supporters. Shortly afterward, each was given a railway ticket and a sovereign by the local PTA branch, although the striking printers did not regard their presence as particularly threatening given their ignorance of Welsh. 'As they are Englishmen', one observed, 'it is apprehended that they will experience much difficulty in setting up Welsh matter, though it is said the "copy" is being carefully prepared for them'.[106] The *Caernarvon and Denbigh Herald* and *Y Genedl* continued publication through the first weeks of the strike largely because of the efforts of managers and apprentices. The strikers were adept at publicizing their case, and drew powerful support from leading local political figures of the Left. David Thomas, Rhostryfan, advised the religious denominations at a public meeting held in defence of the strikers 'not to give their printing work to offices which did not pay a fair wage', while G. H. Roberts, Labour MP for Norwich, remarked, to appreciative laughter, 'I have read leading articles advocating trade unionism in papers published by some of the employers concerned, but, when asked to adopt those principles themselves, they first asked if it was to cost anything.'[107] By the end of February 1912, however, there was no sign of a settlement, and, fearing a long strike, some printers began to leave the town.[108] Their fears were well-founded, and the dispute remained unsettled until July 1924, when the offices of the *Herald* and *Y Genedl* were once again officially recognized by the Typographical Association.[109]

Another group of striking printers, however, responded by remaining in Caernarfon and setting up their own newspaper business. Influenced by the socialist *Daily Citizen* (a 'Club of Young Citizens' had been formed in Llanberis in 1910),[110] John Hugh Williams and two other members of the local PTA launched the first issue of *Y Dinesydd Cymreig* on 8 May 1912 as a twopenny weekly newspaper. A motion was put by members of the quarrymen's union at a May Day meeting in Nantlle that the paper be adopted as the union's official organ, and the suggestion was approved by the union's executive in July 1912.[111] Other trade unions from the NUR to the TGWU lent their active support to the paper in the course of the following two decades, and a Dinesydd Publishing Company was established to oversee the paper's production.

John Hugh Williams, the founding editor, was replaced in 1924, amid some acrimony, by Percy Ogwen Jones, who, as Caernarfonshire's Labour party agent, tied the paper even more firmly to the policies and electoral interests of the Labour party. It was, he explained in June 1926, 'above all else a paper to further Labour party policies'.[112] Iorwerth Peate reluctantly withdrew his support for the paper in 1926, and two years later Kate Roberts demanded the return of her shares.[113] Dependent on a small, if loyal, activist readership, and starved of advertising income, *Y Dinesydd* was discontinued in July 1929, one month after Ramsay Macdonald had formed a Labour government.

The particular political motivation of *Y Dinesydd Cymreig* may have marked a relatively recent development in Welsh journalism, but the origins of the paper lay in a much older desire by printers to assume control over both the production process and editorial policy. Such enterprises had been common in the early nineteenth century, but were becoming increasingly difficult to sustain in the twentieth. The paper also illustrates the dilemma that faced many other politically and religiously committed journals, namely the difficulty of balancing loyalty to a sect or party with the need to satisfy the heterogeneous tastes and expectations of a wider readership and the demands of advertisers and distributors. But the political press in Wales extended beyond those papers that, like *Y Dinesydd Cymreig*, openly declared their party loyalties. By virtue of distributing news and commenting on events, journalists of all kinds actively participated in a general political process. In this sense all newspapers were political agencies that were necessarily and inextricably engaged in the broader task of weaving the social fabric. Journalism articulated and helped to shape society's structure, values and contradictions, but it was also subject to the cross-currents of its influences.

The politics of patronage

Influence over the press was exerted by means other than ownership. Engaged individuals, religious denominations and political parties sought by a variety of means to sustain or change, strengthen or undermine, the editorial policies, contents and formats of newspapers, and the association of such external forces with the press strongly implies that assumptions regarding the social power of journalism went largely unquestioned. Just as advertisers assumed that newspapers were capable of persuading readers to buy their products, religious and political movements also expected a return on their intellectual and financial investments. Arthur Aspinall has shown that it was not uncommon in Britain for influence to be exerted 'over the provincial press by a powerful county family determined to support both its own local political interests and the wider interests of the party to which it was attached.' [114] The bonds that tied such individuals or groups to the editor of a local or regional newspaper spanned the many forms of ownership, through the influence exerted by shareholders or advertisers to selective funding and the disclosure of information. The policies of a privately owned press could still be guided by agendas set by external activists. These might themselves be journalists, even editors, though were more likely to be local MPs, religious leaders, landowners and industrialists. In general, the ideological forces that guided the nineteenth-century press operated through patronage rather than ownership, through a system of close interdependence between editors and their patrons in which editors were almost always the most dependent, on news, funding, advertising and political contacts. Doubtless, politicians and other patrons of the press needed the support of journalists, and were avid readers of their newspapers, but in public they were far more likely to keep them at a distance and to regard them with a degree of suspicion, even contempt. The duality of Victorian attitudes towards journalists was the subject of the following complaint by a newspaper editor in 1839:

> I have frequently attempted to account for the extraordinary pains which are taken by some persons in England to conceal their connection with newspapers and other periodicals. They come, cap in hand, to editors to entreat them to support their views; to obtain the insertion of an article, there is no politeness, even to humility, which they do not shew; and when, in presence of the man whose press they would influence, they are profuse in professions of friendship, yet, in their own circles, they affect to have a profound contempt for the occupation which they follow as amateurs, and would be shocked if they were met arm-in-arm with an editor. This affectation of disdain is not confined to the aristocracy.[115]

This ambivalence was ingrained in popular and political attitudes well into the nineteenth century, and helps to explain why political leaders often wished to conceal their connections with the editors of even their own party newspapers. At the same time, it was also recognized that sympathetic editors could provide useful support for politicians, particularly during elections. Thus Richard Jefferies could observe that the 'solid matter, temperate argument, and genuine work' of the ordinary local newspaper 'in the long run, pay the best. An editor who thus conducts his paper is highly appreciated by the local chiefs of his party, and may even help to contribute to the success of an Administration.'[116] Shifts in public attitudes towards journalists began to occur after 1832, when their value as partisans was reflected, according to R. D. Rees, by their 'inclusion in the list of toasts at political dinners. Each group reserved its praise for the proprietor of the newspaper which wrote in its support.'[117] In a society that remained largely aristocratic in many of its political formations, Rees concluded, it was hardly surprising that journalists should have been regarded 'at best as useful employees or retainers'.[118] Conversely, journalists acknowledged that religion and politics were not only essential ingredients in the nineteenth-century newspaper, but were the key components of its self-image.[119] All journalists conducted their work within this complex web of external social influences, but all were not affected by them in the same way. It is possible to distinguish between three forms of influence, each with very different ramifications: the private, the prescriptive and the negotiated.

The most subtle form of influence was exerted privately and indirectly. In March 1842 the Marquess of Bute asked E. P. Richards 'to hint to the editor of the *Cardiff and Merthyr Guardian* his Lordship's disapproval' of the substance of an article that had appeared in the paper the previous week.[120] Half a century later, Sir Charles Phillips of Picton Castle, Pembrokeshire, expressed his displeasure to Hugh Carleton Tierney, a Carmarthen correspondent to the *Western Mail*, regarding an assessment of the political scene in south-west Wales which had appeared in that paper in February 1889. Tierney apologized for the article, but emphasized that, although the editor of the *Western Mail* normally paid 'a good deal of attention' to his advice, he lived 'too far from Cardiff to prevent mistakes of this kind being occasionally made by the sub-editors who know little or nothing of our district.' He also described how he had communicated the substance of Sir Charles's complaint to the *Western Mail*, suggesting a suitable means whereby the offence that had been caused might be rectified. The procedure was conducted with the utmost discretion, and involved, as Tierney explained, sending a copy of Sir Charles's letter:

> . . . privately to a personal friend of mine who is managing sub-editor, accompanied by a letter of my own in which I told him of your own and Lady Phillips' popularity, of the sacrifices which you had made in promoting the Conservative cause etc. I begged of him to see that a good paragraph was inserted, remedying past injury as far as he could.

Tierney again expressed his sincere regret that Picton Castle 'should have been so badly treated by a paper with which I am more or less connected.'[121]

Few would publicly admit to the prevalence of such private communications between powerful local figures and the editors of newspapers, and public accusations of external interference in editorial affairs were most often met by heated denials. Lord Penrhyn, when questioned on his relationship with the editor of the *North Wales Chronicle* by the Royal Commissioners on Land in the early 1890s, disclaimed all responsibility for editorial decisions, which were, he insisted, a matter for the independent judgement of the editor alone.[122] In private correspondence, however, a rather different picture emerges. In a confidential letter to Humphreys-Owen in October 1879, Lord Rendel observed that, in the reporting of his speeches in the *Montgomeryshire Express*, he had 'noticed an able hand . . . a word softened here and a phrase dropped out there', which he attributed to Humphreys-Owen's influence over the editor. 'It is to you the Editor turns' Rendel explained, 'and I respect him for that. Of what service a first-rate provincial paper can be to the country and how highly repaid.'[123]

Conversely, a press that affirmed its independence of external influences might be 'repaid' not with praise but with criticism and the application of pressure on owners or directors to discipline or dismiss the erring journalists. The editorial view taken by E. Morgan Humphreys towards Welsh Disestablishment in *Y Genedl* was so resented by the Revd Evan Jones and other Calvinist ministers that strenuous efforts were made to unseat him from the editorial chair.[124] In April 1901, a similar campaign succeeded in its aim of dismissing T. R. Roberts from the editorship of the same paper. W. J. Parry's strong objections to the publication of letters in *Y Genedl* by quarrymen who opposed the Penrhyn strike raised for Roberts serious issues concerning press freedom and the guarantees that he had been given regarding editorial independence. In his own defence, he 'insisted upon the freedom of the press' and reminded the directors of the company of his terms of employment:

> When I was appointed two of the conditions were that I should have a perfectly free hand, subject of course to the papers being conducted on democratic lines, and that no individual Director should interfere. Both these conditions have been broken.[125]

Seventeen years later, as the First World War drew to its close, E. Morgan Humpherys was sacked as editor of *Y Goleuad* for having dared to criticize a speech advocating conscription given by Lloyd George at Conway two years previously, and for having allowed letters written by pacifist correspondents to be printed in the paper. Once again leading Nonconformists, such as John Williams, Brynsiencyn, had led the campaign for his dismissal.[126] Privately exerted influence, though subtle in its operation, could prove devastatingly effective in practice.

A second form of influence was applied more directly and prescriptively. In October 1881, shortly following the launch of *Y Llan*, the Dean of Bangor sent detailed editorial instructions to Lewis Jones, described as the paper's sub-editor but in practice responsible for the day-to-day running of the paper. These ground-rules specified that all references to Nonconformity were to be avoided, and under no circumstances was the name of a Nonconformist publication to be mentioned, but rather 'described as a contemporary, and in respectful language'. Furthermore, 'no paragraph in weekly summary, or leading articles' was to be included in the paper 'unless read by a representative of the Committee'.[127] Despite being a trustworthy Anglican evangelist, a loyal member of the Flintshire Constitutional Association and, from 1888, an Associate of the Primrose League,[128] he was subjected to a torrent of criticism in a series of confidential letters from the Church hierarchy. The Dean berated him for introducing 'weak and trashy matter' into the first issue of *Y Llan*, and on subsequent occasions found fault with his reports of religious events, insisting that 'some paraphrase, vague and civil' be employed when referring to other denominations, and his use of translations from other papers and selection of readers' letters.[129]

The prescriptive form of influence, however, was untypical, even exceptional, and few other religious or political bodies either desired or were capable of exerting such direct control over a paper's editorial policy and style. Furthermore, a considerable number of journalists, particularly those in independent or privately owned newspapers, were sufficiently autonomous to accept external influences on far more favourable terms by being able to negotiate the conditions on which patronage was offered. The affairs of John Gibson, owner and editor of the *Cambrian News*, demonstrate the forms such negotiations assumed. In day-to-day matters of detail, Gibson happily printed material sent to him by local Liberal leaders but pointedly did so in a form that he alone determined. Urged by Lord Rendel in 1886 to put the substance of a telegram into a leader column, the editor agreed instead to put it in the form of a letter. 'I write leading articles', Gibson replied firmly to Rendel, 'but never . . . in the shape of speeches'.[130]

At a more general level, the sympathetic coverage of political events, especially elections, involved negotiations of a rather different order between editors and local or national political leaders in which economic rather than political considerations were uppermost. Gibson succinctly articulated the nature of the editors' argument by referring to the consequences of political reporting for his own newspaper. Copies of the *Cambrian News* were sold below their actual value, and while advertisements guarded against losses, Gibson calculated that to cover the expense of producing and distributing the *Cambrian News* he 'ought to sell it at 4s.5d. a copy and sell over 3,000 a week'.[131] The paper actually sold for one penny, and it is doubtful if the circulation could have much exceeded three thousand copies weekly. If the paper was to continue in business, he argued, additional revenue would have to be forthcoming from other sources. Before 1883 and the passing of the Corrupt and Illegal Practices (Prevention) Act, this extra funding had been donated periodically by parliamentary candidates. According to Gibson's account of this arrangement:

> . . . under the old system, if a candidate wanted to contest a constituency in which he was comparatively unknown, he came down as soon as Parliament was dissolved, set all the printers at work, practically took possession of the newspapers for the time being, hired an army of clerks and lecturers and made himself known at a cost of £8,000 or £20,000 as the case might be.[132]

By these means, an ailing newspaper could repay its accumulated debts as well as enable the favoured candidate to assume a high profile in the constituency. After 1883, however, the new law governing the conduct of elections severely reduced a newspaper's income by institutionalizing the election agent and introducing stricter codes regarding election expenses. Furthermore, under the terms of the Act, it was 'quite out of the question to take possession of the newspapers'. Candidates' agents, anxious to work within smaller budgets, required newspapers to tender for the insertion of a reduced number of candidates' addresses. Also, papers were expected to cover election campaigns at their own expense, which in Gibson's case would have entailed hiring more reporters and issuing special editions. Election coverage was thus becoming a prohibitively expensive undertaking, involving 'serious pecuniary loss upon newspapers'. An inevitable consequence of these changes, Gibson warned, was that the local press would lose interest in politics, and even as committed a Liberal as himself could not afford take the financial risks involved in supporting a political party. In 1887, exasperated by the fact that 'services rendered to the Liberal party . . . are requited with brutal neglect', Gibson communicated his anxieties to Lord Rendel:

> . . . I have long since decided that in future elections I shall not go to great expense as I have on previous occasions. I shall not abstain out of any sort of spite, just out of inability to afford the money. An election is loss enough by the general paralysis of business without spending £150 on extra reporting and special editions. What I am driven to do other papers will be driven to do – indeed already have been driven to do. The resolve not to go to expense at election times causes a loss of interest in the question at other times and month after month will go by without the local member's name being mentioned, or without any care being taken to kill false reporting and mistakes.[133]

The implications of this process of depoliticization for the electoral prospects of the Liberal party were, he opined, ominously clear. The problem needed to be addressed urgently by the Liberal party at all levels, and Gibson's approach to Rendel constituted an attempt to persuade the Welsh Liberals to devise a system whereby not only could the costs of political journalism in local newspapers be defrayed, but the balance in the relationship between the press and the party might reach a new state of equilibrium. Gibson proposed that government advertisements, normally published exclusively in the London press, should also be printed in provincial papers, and that local authorities likewise should be compelled to advertise their proceedings, accounts, and so forth, in the local press. He also suggested that the power to place advertisements should be taken away from public auditors and the poor-law districts and given instead to unspecified 'local bodies', by which he presumably meant local town councils. With regard to the Liberal party, Gibson took the view that both the Parliamentary party and the local associations should be 'urged to take interest in their papers' and to send their own items of news to the local press. Finally, a debate within the party should reconsider 'the whole question of newspapers and reporting during contested elections', which would include the possibility of candidates being charged for reports, publicity and all other material at a standard rate per column. Henceforth, he implied, supportive political journalism was a commodity that would have to be paid for.

A Liberal press policy as envisaged by John Gibson was neither enacted nor framed by the Welsh Liberals, and relations between politicians and the press continued in a piecemeal, *ad hoc* fashion. Yet the interdependence between them remained strong: politicians sought influence, newspapers required money. H. A. Latimer, a candidate in the municipal election in Swansea in 1904, pleaded with the proprietor of the *Cambrian*, 'May I make an earnest appeal to you not only to give me your vote but to use all your influence on my behalf',[134] whilst, two years earlier, John Rowlands of Machynlleth had pleaded with Lord Rendel for funds that would enable the *Welsh Gazette* to continue publication on the grounds that the Liberals should have 'reason to know that the publication of the *Welsh Gazette* and its circulation did much to enlist support from the voters from this end of the country, and helped to keep the Liberals in line during the progress of other contests.' In response, Rendel chose to 'depart from [his] general rule regarding newspapers' and offered to help subsidize the paper.[135]

Influence over the press was, in the main, exerted through a continuing process of bargaining, rather than through ownership or prescriptive controls. Patronage was an intrinsically negotiable means of influencing the content of newspapers, and one which operated in a variety of ways. Long-term subsidies were seldom offered to journalists by religious or political bodies, but other forms of patronage by influential local figures were relatively common, principally in the granting of emergency loans, the securing of political legitimacy and in the aid given to the occupational advancement of journalists.

The provision of financial aid in the form of gifts or loans to meet unexpected production and other costs was an important if problematic form of patronage. J. T. Jones, publisher of *Y Gwron Cymreig*, received from a local spirit-merchant and an innkeeper a substantial sum of money to cover the legally required surety against libel, but the unexpected withdrawal of this support in August 1853 threw his paper into a financial crisis.[136] But aid could create difficulties for the giver as well as the receiver. Thomas John Hughes (Adfyfyr) obtained from Lord Rendel between 1889 and 1891 a number of personal loans amounting to more than £100 to enable him to continue to edit *Cymru Fydd*. Despite an undertaking to repay the loans at the 'earliest convenient date',[137] the best Hughes could offer was the free supply of 'a half weekly epitome of movements at home when you are from home'.[138]

Referring to such occurrences, an angry John Gibson informed Rendel that the way he 'had been bled in Wales' often made him feel 'ashamed of the whole business' of Welsh journalism. Patronage through loans was evidently a sore point with Gibson, who had borrowed £400 from David Davies, Llandinam, in order to buy the *Cambrian News*, but had aroused Davies's displeasure by repaying the sum in full some years later. 'He practically sulked with me . . .' Gibson recollected, 'He never forgave me for repaying him. He thought the money was lent to me by some of his opponents in order to repay him. And when I fought him in 1886 he had no doubt about it.'[139]

That wealthy individuals were prepared privately to subsidize the press there can be no doubt, and their readiness to do so repeatedly was clearly an important factor in the survival of many Welsh newspapers. John Rowlands, in a letter to Rendel in October 1902, explained how George Rees, formerly of the *Cambrian News*, was attempting to set up a new paper in mid-Wales to 'uphold Liberal principles and assert Liberal views'. The venture had been endangered, however, by the sudden death of T. E. Ellis, who had given 'great financial and other assistance' to the new paper. Since his death, financing the paper had proved virtually impossible, and the publishers and their Liberal supporters were, naturally, now looking for assistance from Rendel himself. Despite the growth in circulation, Rowlands explained, the high initial cost of purchasing and installing machinery prevented George Rees from improving his stock 'and so reduce current expenses'. Rendel was asked specifically for a one-off but substantial payment which would give the new paper a chance of survival.[140]

Donations made by wealthy supporters to party local associations also found their way into newspapers. Lord Rendel, for example, paid sums of £100 annually to the Montgomeryshire Liberal Association in the 1890s, and also contributed generously to the North Wales Liberal Federation, of which he had been elected president in 1886.[141] In turn, the patronage of the Liberal associations and federations was accorded to sympathetic printers and publishers, and advertisements were judiciously placed in the more supportive papers. Propaganda funds were also made available by such political organizations. In October 1888, the North Wales Federation resolved 'that the immense power of the English and vernacular Liberal Press of Wales should be solicited to carry out . . . all objects of the Council,'[142] and three years later, at the height of the Welsh Disestablishment campaign, the Council further resolved 'that the assistance of all Editors and Proprietors of Liberal Newspapers published in the Principality be enlisted.' The campaign fund comprised between £3,000 and £5,000, a substantial portion of which was earmarked for the purpose of ensuring widespread sympathetic press coverage.[143]

Apart from money, politicians provided newspapers with valuable contacts and publicity. In 1888 T. J. Hughes sent Rendel a bound set of *Cymru Fydd* in the hope that he might be persuaded 'to ask Mr Gladstone to accept them'.[144] In 1891, Ernest Bowen-Rowland, editor of the *Welsh Review*, asked Rendel to perform much the same kind of service: 'If you would so far assist the Review (which only needs advertisements to become the leading magazine of the day) by ordering . . . some copies and giving them to your friends you would do me a great service.'[145] More explicit in seeking publicity, Beriah Gwynfe Evans in 1892 urged T. E. Ellis to persuade more MPs to buy shares in the Welsh National Press Company in order to strengthen the paper's representation in Parliament, to emphasize the national character of the paper, and, perhaps most importantly, to help attract a new 'advertising cliency'.[146] Politicians, however, possessed the ability to promote journalists as well as newspapers, and the social mobility of journalists who had declared their allegiance to a party could be highly dependent on the support of local party grandees. T. J. Hughes, anxious that Beriah Gwynfe Evans, then editor of the *Cardiff Times*, should be appointed an Assistant Charity Commissioner in 1889, wrote privately to Lord Rendel extolling Evans's many virtues and talents and urging him to use his political influence to help Evans attain his ambition. Two decades later, Hughes again appealed to Rendel for support in his own application for a post with the Board of Trade, which, being an experienced journalist, he explained, he was well qualified to undertake.[147] Beriah Gwynfe Evans's pleading letters to T. E. Ellis in 1893, when his despondency with *Y Genedl* reached its neurotic height, reveals in poignant detail the journalist's dependence on the goodwill of politicians for their career advancement:

> I venture to submit for your consideration and that of Lloyd George, that the Liberal Party has at its disposal more than one kind of appointment I am fully qualified to fill, and to which public opinion would clearly endorse my selection. An Inspectorship of Schools, a Poor Law Inspectorship, a Permanent Assistant Commissionership and the like suggest themselves naturally to the mind.[148]

Early in the following year Evans extended his appeal to Lloyd George, imploring him for assistance to obtain a post in the London press:

> I cannot believe but that through Ellis's influence, backed up by the bulk of the Welsh Members who would, I trust, support such an appeal on my behalf, some Government appointment might be secured for me. Failing this, then among your fellow members you might surely find some journalistic work suited to my needs and capacities – Dafydd Dafis would, I think, make no mean gallery descriptive reporter for a London daily.[149]

Evans's dependence on such support was so complete that, when he failed to achieve any of his ambitions, he could blame only his patrons. Lloyd George, who had been 'very much dissatisfied' with the 'fine mess' Evans had made of managing the Welsh National Press Company in 1893,[150] was accused by Evans in 1905 of 'treating him in an unkind and shabby way'.[151]

The mutuality of interests between politicians and ambitious journalists, along with other forms of patronage, ensured that in Wales the 'fourth estate' was of necessity a highly problematic construction. Notions of editorial independence and the freedom of the press were vividly emblazoned on title pages and in the collective self-image of journalists, but they operated within the bounds of larger economic, religious and political constraints over which journalists individually could exert little influence. But while the control of the press through ownership or patronage was fiercely contested, largely in secret, by powerful social forces, issues regarding the ownership, control and influence of the press were also addressed in a wide-ranging public debate that continued throughout the nineteenth century.

4 *Conflict and culture*

The pattern of ownership and control of the press in nineteenth-century Wales, outlined in the previous chapter, was the product of the unequal distribution of resources and of changes in the nature of the readership. But it was also the product of a set of beliefs regarding the kinds of influence that journalism in general exerted on society. These beliefs were often openly scrutinized, but they remained a strong motivating force for journalists and others throughout the period. Newspaper owners, patrons, printers, editors and reporters shared a firmly held view that the cheaply circulated written word lay at the very hub of both civil society and the political world. In particular, they believed that their society was structured in such a way as to ensure that no political strategy, no evangelical campaign, no social movement could make any serious progress unless support from a section of the press had first been secured. Politicians, religious leaders, social reformers, anyone with a message to communicate, agreed that a good press was an essential prerequisite for success. Although journalists were often put under great strain to deliver what was, given their slender resources, often unreasonably expected of them, on the whole they basked in the self-importance they were accorded by their social role.

The usefulness of the press as a channel of communication rested on a widely held assumption that both political and religious messages could be 'sold' by newspapers very much in the way that consumer goods were sold through advertising. Although the intended message was articulated most explicitly in leader columns, it was believed that it was more effectively transmitted in the everyday treatment of news stories, particularly local news, in the selection of readers' letters and in the general application of news values. Journalism communicated with its audience primarily through language, and whatever power the press was assumed to possess stemmed principally from its ability to conjure meanings and evoke sentiments from the skilful manipulation of words. The function of this use of language was very often unashamedly propagandist, a term which, until the 1920s, implied little of its present, more derogatory, meaning. But as a means of educating, enlightening and empowering, the propaganda of journalism was not confined to writing alone. Many journalists were also prominent local or national public figures, whose work involved speaking at public meetings, organizing campaigns, and standing for, and serving in, public office. In addition to being read, journalists were frequently also seen and heard, and in consequence were the subjects of public criticism as well as admiration. By combining writing with other forms of social activism, journalists represented and embodied the social forces that shaped the pattern of authority and dissent, and in so doing ensured that journalism remained a highly controversial issue in the political culture of nineteenth-century Wales.

But in addition to being self-consciously partisan agents on the cutting edge of social conflicts, in a less formal way journalists were also actors in a more consensual process of change in Welsh popular culture. The popularization by the press of literary forms from poetry to the novel, its extending news coverage, its reviews, women's sections and sports pages, engendered an inclusive sense of community that carried with it a sense of nationality. Journalism was thus regarded as being both an agent of conflict and of consensus, and the question of the social influence of the press in the period before 1914 must address both aspects of this duality.

The 'moral machine'

Contemporary nineteenth-century British evaluations of the social power of journalism shared the view that its influence was far-reaching, but differed as to whether it inflamed or quietened passions, or divided or unified communities. In 1824 it was argued that the press was 'the most powerful moral machine in the world, and exercises a greater influence over the manners and opinions of civilized society than the united eloquence of the bar, the senate and the pulpit.'[1] Five years later Thomas Carlyle caustically observed that 'the true Church of England, at this moment, lies in the Editors of its Newspapers.'[2] The identity of the journalist as a social actor was thus well established in contemporary British thought by the time newspapers began to proliferate in Wales. However, the underlying concept of the 'moral machine', and the harnessing of technological change to ideological ends that it implied, was open to differing, even contradictory, interpretations. The communication of news was accorded a lower priority for the *Figaro in Wales* on its launch in 1835, for example, than its declared intention 'to lash the rascals naked through the world'.[3] More generally, Sir Robert Peel had warned of the same decade that, as a consequence of Parliamentary Reform, Britain would be subjected to 'the very worst and vilest species of despotism – the despotism of demagogues; the despotism of journalism . . .'[4]

An alternative view offered in 1824 argued that a liberalized press would lead to 'the suppression of intense and angry political feelings among the labouring population' and to the calming of 'party zeal'.[5] Jeremy Bentham agreed, regarding newspapers as:

> . . . a safety valve as well as a controlling power . . . Experience has shown that newspapers are one of the best means of directing opinion – of quieting feverish movements – of causing the lies and artificial rumours by which the enemies of the State may attempt to carry on their designs to vanish.[6]

The value of journalism in maintaining social control was clearly expressed in 1824: 'Before man can enjoy the blessings of equitable laws he must first be instructed, and before he will lend his aid to establish and protect such institutions, the Press must first teach him their value.'[7]

The anatomy of press influence was considered more closely by Sir E. L. Bulwer, who wryly observed in 1840 that the influence of the press was a subject more declaimed than examined. In his own examination of the issue, he concluded that newspapers were able to influence opinion because not only did they discuss issues, but, crucially, that they published 'the results of systems', such as proceedings at law, convictions before magistrates, abuses in institutions and unfairnesses in taxation. By selecting and bringing such discontents to the public eye, the press acted both as a witness to events and as a counsel in their interpretation.[8]

If, as Bulwer had argued, the power of the press lay essentially in its manipulation of pre-existing social grievances, it follows that much of journalism was inherently oppositional to established authority. Observers from both sides of the political spectrum conceded, with greater or lesser willingness, that this was indeed the case. One Conservative journalist asserted in 1886 that the provincial press was intrinsically Radical because, to survive, it required the support of 'buyers of small means' who were 'of the class that would like to be better off than they are, and to this extent are dissatisfied with institutions that Radical politicians tell them are prejudicial to their prosperity.' The exposure of grievances thus attracted aggrieved readers to the provincial papers, and the political relationship was further cemented by the care Radical leaders took to 'look after their journalists, elect them to their political clubs, and generally make friends of them.'[9] A third theory suggested that some 'dominant opinions' lent themselves more readily than others for circulation in the public arena. Arthur Murphy speculated in 1874 that Liberal ideas could 'more naturally accommodate themselves to the conditions of public discussion,' and could "be made more of" by writers for the public press,' than the more defensive ideas of Conservatism.[10]

The notion of subliminality was also considered as a means of explaining the social influence of the press. A correspondent to the *Printer*, a journal as much exercised by the issue of press freedom as by the technicalities of the printing trade, argued that the printed word exerted 'a secret influence on the understanding' and that 'he that entertains himself with moral or religious treatises will imperceptibly advance in goodness'. Another correspondent, writing in the same periodical, agreed that the press in the mid-1840s was 'operating as one of the most powerful causes in favour of the civilization which tends to the formation of great cities', and regarded the growth of the newspaper press as a natural and necessary corollary to urbanization and industrial development.[11] It was often observed, however, that press influence was uneven and that it affected certain sections of the population more directly and decisively than others. Arnot Reid, writing in 1886, was convinced that workers were more easily swayed by journalists than were the middle class. 'The workman', he explained, '. . . insensibly . . . is moved as the journalist wills', and the provincial press, for each copy sold, enjoyed a larger measure of political power than did the London papers.[12] Sceptics, however, took a different view. The Revd J. R. Breakbridge confessed despairingly in 1845 that in his experience, the moral dimension of the press was generally ignored by the population at large. 'Of all literary efforts' he mused, 'those connected with the periodical press are the most fruitless and evanescent. Of all kinds of influence, that exerted by it is the most doubtful and precarious.'[13] Some forty years later, Lord Rendel, despite his continuing support for Welsh Liberal journalism, admitted privately to similar doubts when he expressed 'surprise' at 'how little hold the Press have on the imagination of the People.'[14]

Those with most to gain from the proposition that the press wielded great power and influence were, the editors and journalists themselves. In addition to attracting advertisers and the patronage of politicians and religious leaders, faith in their own power allowed journalists legitimately to offer to social groups and movements not only a form of internal liaison within communities of belief, but, more importantly, a means of external communication with a wider public. News and comment in the press were directed at larger goals, at the enactment of political and religious principles that would transform society. Thus Roger Edwards held that the duty of the periodical press was to assist the public to discover 'the right way to live', and that the successful journalist was characterized by the excellence of his social leadership.[15] Political commitment was articulated in similar terms: the editor of the Liberal *Carmarthen Express* informed his readers in April 1874 that the 'primary object of the proprietors . . . is a political one, to carry out the work of political education. The political, like the religious, creed, must be constantly repeated for the benefit of the young and unsophisticated.'[16] The editors of *Tarian y Gweithiwr*, who continued in Merthyr in 1875 the radical political tradition they had left behind in their home town of Llanidloes, 'famous for flannel and sedition', and where Paine, Volney and Robert Owen were still being taught at the Sunday School in 1850, were equally ambitious. Their aims were to 'make the worker self-educated in knowledge, personal, social, industrial, political, moral and religious principles', and to 'protect the interests of the south Wales miners against the attacks of the oppressive capitalists of the day.'[17] T. E. Ellis, with other political goals in mind, informed the editor of the *South Wales Star* at an interview in the Reform Club in May 1891 that, 'it is our new writers which are bringing to the minds of the Welsh people that they have a past and are a nation . . . to bring this about, Mr Editor, should be your work.'[18] The editor of *Y Genedl Gymreig* echoed these sentiments by declaring that the principal function of his paper, and of its stable-mates *Y Werin* and the *North Wales Observer*, were to 'defend the interests of Nonconformity, and to teach the principles of Liberalism and Nationalism.'[19]

The firm and publicly announced attachment to a cause thus brought financial and other rewards. Conversely, the papers that attempted to cross political and denominational boundaries, or to rise above sectarian conflicts, did so at considerable risk. *Seren Cymru*, started in 1851, pledged itself to be free of all party or denominational partisanship, and in consequence faced concerted opposition from denominational writers.[20] *Y Winllan*, started in 1847, was edited by ministers of different denominations, alternating each three years. *Y Twr*, in April 1870, attempted to avoid this difficulty by appointing four editors, each representing the four major Nonconformist denominations, the Independents, the Baptists, the Calvinistic Methodists and the Wesleyans, but were less successful than the editors of *Y Genedl Gymreig* who were temporarily able to sublimate inter-denominational rivalry with an appeal to a common Disestablishment political campaign.[21] Even in the 1890s, the launch of a new Nonconformist newspaper could be met by the derision of rival groups, and the publisher of *Ye Brython Cymreig* was characteristically accused by a Calvinstic Methodist minister in Aberystwyth in 1892 of 'spreading poison throughout the land'.[22] Though troublesome, such denominational rivalries were mild compared with the conflicts of the satirical press of the 1830s and 1840s. Jacob Glochydd had brought out the *Figaro in Wales* in Bangor in 1835 and 1836, and his example was followed in the same town in 1843 by Robert Jones and Isaac Harries, publisher and editor respectively of the bilingual satirical paper *Figaro the Second*. In the same year, their rivals L. E. Jones and Edeyrn ab Nudd brought out the *Anti Figaro*, but both papers were closed after costly libel actions, and Isaac Harries was subjected to a public whipping in the streets of Bangor.[23]

Political and religious labels, however, could be misleading. John Gibson noted with alarm in 1887 how 'the Tories all over the country [were] making very free use of Liberal newspapers' by means of press releases, particularly those issued by the Primrose

League.[24] The editor of the Liberal *Y Cymro*, on the other hand, was outraged by the normally well-informed J. E. Southall's description of his paper as a 'Welsh Socialist' organ. In 1892, articles had appeared in the paper by socialists and Radicals, including R. J. Derfel and J. O. Jones, but the editor considered *Y Cymro* to be more a platform for the religious denominations than a political paper of any description.[25]

In spite of such misunderstandings and difficulties of interpretation, political and religious loyalties were manifestly present in the language of nineteenth-century journalism, as was the rationalist belief that social change could be effected by newspapers through the dissemination of moral principles and useful knowledge. But the persuasive power of the press was drawn also from the activity of journalists as speakers, mobilizers and organizers. Within their readership catchment areas, and frequently beyond them, journalists were household names and leading figures in the local community.[26] Others, no doubt, toiled in obscurity, like Wilfrid Meynell's editor who spent the 'flower of his days in speaking to a public which is and will always be utterly ignorant of his individuality',[27] but in general the press in Wales was renowned for its vivid personalities. As in the north-east of England, the 'vigour and resourcefulness' of an editor with local political clout and a strong political identity augured well for a newspaper, and like dissident journalists everywhere, they were 'simultaneously leaders and chroniclers of their cause'.[28] For such journalists, the press was an opportunity to be everywhere at once, a means of continuing the traditions of what the Irish nationalist John Cornelius O'Callaghan had termed the 'literary agitator'.[29] The politics of editing could thus make for an uncomfortable life as, 'distrusted by his partisans, detested by his political adversaries, harrassed within and assailed from without', the editor tottered 'alike under his own magnificence and the blows of his assailants'. Risking street abuse and even physical assault, journalists participated actively in public affairs, and took sides in local quarrels.[30]

Many journalists performed minor functions in their churches, such as John Evans, proprietor and publisher of *Seren Gomer* and the *Carmarthen Journal*, who was for many years a Deacon and Elder of the Independent Church in Carmarthen,[31] or in local political associations, such as John Gibson, a leading supporter of the Aberystwyth Liberal party.[32] Others were active in pressure groups, such as William Pugh, the radical landlord and founder in 1835 of the *Montgomeryshire Herald*, who was also an active Parliamentary reformer and a local leader of the Society for the Diffusion of Useful Knowledge. Or John O'Dwyer, a reporter and leader writer for the *Monmouthshire Merlin* from 1839 to 1844, who was a leading anti-Chartist, and who was sworn in as a special constable during the riot of 1839.[33] Thomas Stephens, managing director of the *Merthyr Express*, as well as being an antiquary, a literary critic and the owner of a pharmacy, was also High Constable of Merthyr in 1858, and was instrumental in founding the town's public library. William Williams (Caledfryn), editor in turn of *Y Sylwedydd* in 1831, *Tywysog Cymru* from 1832 to 1833, *Y Seren Ogleddol* in 1835, *Yr Adolygydd* in 1839, *Cylchgrawn Rhyddid* in 1840 – 42 and *Yr Amaethydd* in 1845 – 46, was also active in the Anti-Corn Law League, the Peace Society and the Liberation Society.[34] Others served as emigration agents or insurance brokers. In the 1890s, the Aberdare journalist D. M. Richards acted as an agent for the British Workman's Assurance Company, was appointed secretary of the Aberdare and District Grocers' Association, and still found the time and energy to campaign for improved public facilities on the Great Western Railway. Others were closely involved in the local state, particularly the county councils that were established after the Local Government Act of 1888.[35] W. J. Parry, who had acted as the Liberal agent for Caernarfonshire in the 1860s and 1870s, was a founder member both of the North Wales Quarrymen's Union and the National Liberal Club, was elected onto the Caernarfonshire County Council on its formation in 1889 and rose to be its chairman in 1893. He was also an active member of the Welsh Language Society and the National Liberal Federation.[36] Thomas Gee was similarly embroiled in political activity, being the first chairman of the Denbighshire County Council in 1889, and an organizer of the anti-tithe agitation in north Wales.[37] In 1896, Gee was presented with a National Testimonial raised by a committee which included F. E. Hamer of the *Manchester Guardian*: the subscription list read like a roll call of the most prominent Welsh public figures. William Hughes, another journalist trained at the Gee offices in Denbigh, and editor and publisher of *Y Dydd* in Dolgellau, was both a deacon in the

Tabernacle Congregational Church and chair of the Merioneth County Council in 1912 and 1913. He later became an alderman and a JP.[38] Like Gibson, Gee and Parry, Hughes was a leading activist in the north Wales Liberal party. Beriah Gwynfe Evans, assisted by D. R. Daniel, led Lloyd George's election campaign in Caernarfon in 1890, and was a salaried organizer of Cymru Fydd in 1894–5. Evans was active also in denominational affairs, and, as an Independent, was a leading exponent and secretary of the Interdenominational Conference which attempted to re-establish the machinery of co-operation between Welsh Nonconformists after the 1895 election. Other journalists were active supporters of trade unions, notably J. O. Jones (ap Ffarmwr) whose trenchant articles on the condition of the Anglesey farm workers in *Y Werin* from November 1889 led to the establishment of the short-lived Anglesey Agricultural Labourers' Union in June 1890. Five years later, Jones, by then editor of the *Merthyr Times*, chaired the founding meeting of the ILP in Merthyr.[39]

Politicians and political activists also dabbled in journalism almost as a matter of course. T. E. Ellis, for example, wrote frequently and powerfully in both newspapers and periodicals, but declined the post of editor of *Cymru Fydd* in January 1889 on the grounds that his Parliamentary duties were too onerous and time-consuming. Political activists of lesser renown were also eager to further their part-time journalistic ambitions. The use of the press in political campaigns was discussed by the Birmingham branch of Cymru Fydd in November 1897. One member described how he wrote a regular column to *Y Celt*, and the secretary of the branch, a contributor to *Yr Herald Cymraeg*, urged others at the meeting to become correspondents to Welsh newspapers.[40]

Not only were journalists often prominent public figures, but their influence over the affairs of public life *qua* journalists was also acknowledged by their contemporaries. T. M. Jones observed that Roger Edwards's journalism had effectively created a Welsh public opinion on political matters, and the articles of William Rees in *Yr Amserau* in the 1860s on Hungarian politics triggered petitions to Parliament and won him the commendation of Kossuth himself. The other Welsh journalist of genius, Thomas Gee, on the occasion of his eightieth birthday in 1895, was hailed by Lloyd George as 'the Welsh Grand Old Man', whose 'skill and influence has enabled us to win the battle in the constituencies with an ease which is almost incomprehensible.'[41] Further recognition of the value of journalists came from the Cymmrydorion Society, which awarded its first medal in 1884 to William Rees (Gwilym Hiraethog), and candidates for future awards included John Gibson (Perry Winkle), John Griffith (Y Gohebydd), and the London correspondent of *Y Goleuad*. Cymru Fydd branches in London were also named after leading Welsh journalists including 'Hiraethog' (William Rees) in Finsbury and the City, 'Gohebydd' (John Griffith) in Hackney, 'Cynlas' (T. E. Ellis) in Kensington, Paddington and Hammersmith. Significantly, other branches were named after such older national heroes as 'Glyndŵr' and 'Llywelyn'.[42]

It is evident, then, that contemporaries believed that journalists were individuals of power and influence in Welsh political life. Henry Richard summarized this attitude in 1888 in his own tribute to the political journalists of the mid-Victorian period:

> Men of light and leading among the Nonconformist Ministers, instead of regarding politics as something common and unclean, began to teach their countrymen that they were bound by solemn responsibilities to God and man to take their part in the duties of citizenship. New organs of opinion, newspapers, and magazines, were started, through which these men were enabled to address the people.

Richard included in his panoply such journalists as Joseph Harries, David Rees of Llanelli, Samuel Roberts, William Rees, Thomas Gee and Dr John Thomas. It was they above all who, 'began to leaven the public mind, and to give rise to a vague feeling of dissatisfaction, among at least some of the leaders of the people, at the somewhat ignoble position which Wales occupied in our political system.' In the same way, a correspondent to *Cymru Fydd* in November 1890 could announce confidently that '*Y Werin* is now one of the recognised powers of North Wales . . . [it] has a mission, and ability.'[43]

After more than eighty years of weekly journalism in Wales, Liberals, at least, were content that the new forms of communication that had evolved since the first appearance of the *Cambrian* in 1804 were having their desired effects on Welsh society. Journalism and journalists were woven into the social fabric, and for Liberal Nonconformity, the 'recognized power' of the 'moral machine' had reaped rich rewards. But where Nonconformists and Liberals sensed moral elevation, Anglicans and Conservatives could see only venality.

Authority and dissent

The challenge to the Liberal hegemony raised abruptly for the press the question of the uneven distribution of power in Welsh society. Journalism operated inescapably within the social patterns of authority and dissent, and the self-perceptions of journalists, and criticisms of their work, turned essentially on where they were deemed to be located in the shifting sets of power relations. The issue of the political influence of the press was regarded largely in terms of the capacity of individual journalists or titles to defend or to disturb the political balance of forces at any given moment.

Fears that the press was a dangerous and intrusive new phenomenon that could subvert as well as maintain social and political order prevailed among many observers throughout the nineteenth century. The prospective editor of the *Oswestry Herald* in 1820 sought to establish his 'constitutional' credentials by denouncing 'the grossness of that popularity which is acquired by participating in the revolutionary clamour of the demagogue and of the disaffected' which he observed in other newspapers.[44] The revolutionary potential of newspapers was also criticized by a Bala Anglican in 1830:

> I am glad to tell you that the *Cymro*, that revolutionary Welsh periodical is dead, and peace, I say be to its memory. It would be no loss if the *Seren* were to get to rise no more and if a few more of the same tendency were to share the same fate – we should then have the Principality more peacable and less disposed to revolution . . .[45]

Such sentiments were most evident at times of social tension, in particular in the 1830s and 1840s, and again in the late 1880s and 1890s.

Political journalism derived from a tradition of criticism, satire and dissent that had developed in the form of ballads and pamphlets. Richard Williams (Dic Dywyll), who sang his ballads with one finger in the corner of one of his sightless eyes, was attributed with delaying the introduction of the workhouse in

Merthyr for twenty years, so successful was his 'Song on the effect of the new law, or The Workhouse'.[46] Pamphleteers like Thomas Roberts, Llwyn'rhydol, a goldsmith who was a founder of the Cymreigyddion in 1796, President of the Gwyneddigion in 1800 and 1808, and a frequent contributor to both the Welsh- and English-language press, published *Cwyn yn erbyn Gorthrymder* (Complaint against Oppression), a satire against the tithe, in London in 1798; and at the end of the nineteenth century, Robert Ambrose Jones (Emrys ap Iwan), influenced by Pascal and Paul-Louis Courier, continued to employ the pamphlet to excellent effect.[47]

Political partisanship had thus long been a feature of Welsh journalism. The *Cambrian* and the *Carmarthen Journal* had clashed noisily over the issue of the Reform of Parliament in 1832, as the *Pembrokeshire Herald* and *Cylchgrawn Rhyddid* were to do over the campaign for the repeal of the Corn Laws in the early 1840s. Chartism brought the press firmly into the political arena, and in so doing alarmed the authorities, particularly in south Wales. *Y Gweithiwr/The Workman* was first published in Merthyr Tydfil in April 1834 as a bilingual unstamped newspaper priced a penny halfpenny per copy, printed in Brecon. Its fourth issue contained articles, in Welsh, on trade unionism, and, in English, on the Corn Laws and the transportation of the Tolpuddle Martyrs. Henry Hetheringtom opened an agency for the *Poor Man's Guardian* in Newport, and in the autumn of 1830 sixteen persons were imprisoned in Usk for selling or offering for sale unstamped publications. Carmarthen and Swansea were also part of his catchment area for the sale of the *Guardian*, the *Destructive*, the *Republican* and the *Radical*.[48] On 7 December 1839, four Newport magistrates wrote to the Secretary of State for Home Affairs, the Marquess of Normanby, recommending the immediate suppression of unstamped seditious papers circulating in south Wales, especially Henry Vincent's *Western Vindicator*. The following year, in October 1840, the Marquess of Bute urged Normanby to 'direct these unstamped newspapers to be prosecuted under the Stamp Act . . .', adding 'But for the publication of the two papers, the *Udgorn* and the *Advocate*, I think very little would be heard of Chartism in this district'. J. Bruce Pryce of Duffryn agreed that 'three-quarters of the Chartist mischief' in the district was caused by the *Western Vindicator*.[49]

Newspapers, along with beerhouses, were frequently cited in such correspondence as being causes of social disorder. Under the Stamp Acts, the conventional response to the radical unstamped papers was to to take legal action, often resulting in imprisonment, against publishers, editors and distributors of unstamped papers. Accordingly, the authorities in south Wales in 1839 sought the necessary legal evidence to prosecute journalists and printers. In December of that year Henry Scale reported privately to the Marquess of Bute that ball cartridges for use by Chartist insurgents were smuggled from London into the Newport office of *Yr Udgorn* 'in a box marked "TYPE" '. Published by David John, Junior, George Town, and Morgan Williams, Merthyr, *Yr Udgorn* was a 4d. stamped paper, carrying translations from the *Northern Star*, and extensive reports from the Chartist convention at which Morgan Williams had been the south Wales representative. These papers were the cause of so much concern in 1841 that Bute urgently petitioned the Clerk of the Magistrates of Merthyr to provide him with translations of the Welsh articles. A close examination of the papers' contents convinced Bute that many of the articles were 'borrowed' from the *Northern Star*. Anxiously he recalled that 'many members' of the *Northern Star* had visited Merthyr in July 1840 'with very bad effects', and made enquiries locally as to the circulation of the *Northern Star* and the *Udgorn/Advocate* in Merthyr and the surrounding district, 'and what is known as to the way in which those papers, or the circulation of them, is maintained.'[50] Bute was clearly aware that these papers were the public face of a movement. The Revd E. Jenkins, Minister of Dowlais, warned his congregation in 1840 not to attend Chartist meetings nor to read 'their inflammatory publications – publications that speak as highly of Tom Paine as they do of Jesus Christ! Publications as full of poison to mind and soul, as the Bible is full of grace and mercy! Read your Bibles!'[51]

Further west, Thomas Campbell Foster reported the Rebecca Riots for *The Times*, and again the authorities were concerned by the effects of such sympathetic reportage. As David Williams noted, the county magistrates and the gentry 'challenged the accuracy of his facts and deplored his ideas'. They also believed that 'his articles had helped to foment discord in Wales'.[52] Victimization of *Udgorn* sellers began in July 1842, and three months later the paper's press committee of shareholders went into emergency session to plan the paper's survival through the political repression. They announced that future editions would be fortnightly or even monthly, but their reports of the arrest of Chartist leaders in Leeds and Manchester were among the last they were to print before the paper's abrupt closure.[53]

The decline of Chartism after 1842, and of Rebecca after 1843, took the edge off the campaign that had been organized by the authorities in Wales against the press. But from the 1850s to the 1870s, the beginning of the 'Augustan Age' of British journalism, Welsh journalism remained politically articulate, even aggressively so. On issues such as education, Welsh and British politics, Parliamentary reform, the Welsh language, religion, the Crimean and American Civil Wars and the economy, Welsh journalists found plenty to say. Some papers, notably *Yr Oes* and the *Merthyr Star* continued in the 1850s and 1860s to manifest the Chartist legacy. But the 1855 repeal of the Stamp Act and the 1867 Reform Act disrupted the pattern of the press, and the explosive mixture of the Disestablishment campaign and the land agitation in north Wales recreated the tensions of the 1840s and brought journalism and journalists once again to the centre stage of Welsh political conflict.

The growing strength of Nonconformity was the catalyst for change. After the trials of the 1840s, Nonconformists slowly felt their way towards a new ideal of political representation. The denominational magazines gave way, as mediums of popular instruction, to newspapers like *Yr Amserau* in 1843 and *Y Cronicl* in 1845, which emphasized the futility of depending on the Whigs for deliverance, and urging their readers to organize themselves politically so that they may 'return men of their own class' to Parliament.[54] The campaign reached a climax, but not its end, in the General Election of 1868.

The Established Church in Wales was sufficiently concerned by these developments to set up a commission of enquiry to report on the structure and the influence of the Nonconformist press. The committee, representing the four dioceses, and chaired by the Dean of Bangor, Henry T. Edwards, submitted their report in 1879. It recommended wide-ranging measures to counteract the baneful influence of the Nonconformist papers, and admonished the Church for failing to realize the 'significance of the changes that have occurred in the last twenty years' and advocated the 'making use of the modern weapons by which alone it is possible to reach effectively the minds of the people'. The report concluded as follows:

> We find that within the last thirty years a new force has come into operation in Wales, and is powerfully influencing the thought and character of the Welsh people. It is of importance that the Church should not be indifferent to the direction of that force . . . It cannot be doubted that the . . . minds of a very large number of people are greatly influenced by the teaching of these organs. What are the principles which are thus being sown broadcast throughout Wales? We find that a very large majority of these organs persistently recommend to the acceptance of the Welsh people, extreme and one sided principles . . .

Finally, the report recommended that a new company be set up, with a capital of £20,000, called the Welsh Church Press Co., to launch two newspapers, one in north the other in south Wales, to 'advocate Constitutional principles'.[55]

An underlying cause for concern for the Dean and his committee was the way in which Nonconformist journalism dovetailed with political Liberalism. Rightly, they surmised that the demand for the Disestablishment of the Church was intimately related to the broader movement to mobilize a Liberal constituency and, by extension, to imply for some an attack on the very principle of the tithe, and on the political power of landlords. But the notion of a radical press involved more than the Nonconformist weeklies. From the 1870s, local leaders of the Conservative party were quick to acknowledge the prevalence of avowedly Liberal local newspapers, and were keenly aware of their electoral significance.

Political developments in Wales by the 1860s had acquired a decidedly Liberal form. Of Wales's twenty-nine MPs in 1852, only eleven were Liberal, but by 1857 Liberals had gained a majority which they held for the remainder of the century. In the 1868 election, Wales voted for twenty-two Liberals and eight Conservatives, and the 1880 election was even more decisive: twenty-eight Liberals, only two Conservatives.[56] Under such circumstances, explicitly Conservative newspapers were on the whole difficult to sustain. The *Western Mail* in Cardiff and the *North Wales Chronicle* were important exceptions, but elsewhere Tory journalists had a very tough time of it, particularly if they worked in the Welsh-language press. *Y Dywysogaeth* ('A General Weekly Newspaper Advocating Constitutional Principles') admitted on 5 February 1870 that it was 'not easy to row against the tide', but efforts were made to resist the Liberal hegemony in the press. *Gwalia* was started on 3 August 1881 to support 'the defenders of the dignity and honour of the British Crown', and *Y Gwirionedd* was launched in Rhyl on 6 November 1885 with an appeal to the 'old Conservative and loyalist nation of Wales'. It ceased publication exactly a month later, after four issues. Yet evidence remained that a market existed for a Tory press in Wales. Walter Yeldham, private secretary to the Liberal Unionist Marquess of Hartington, reported in his diary in September 1887 that in Anglesey at least 'the townsmen are all conservative – it is the farm labourers and tenant farmers who are Gladstonian, and whom it is hard to get at', largely because of a 'regular systematic crusade' conducted on the platform and in the press. It was in the countryside, he discovered, that 'disloyalty and sedition' were rife.[57]

In response to the Liberal hold over so much of the provincial press, *Blackwood's Edinburgh Magazine* in 1880 had advocated a thorough reorganization of the provincial Conservative press, and, in October 1883, Sir Stafford Northcote had advised members of the Caernarfonshire and Anglesey Conservative Association to pay close attention to the local Liberal newspapers, 'to promote the circulation of your own papers, and to watch and see what the language and mischief of the other papers are, and try in any way you can to counteract it.'[58] In some instances, Conservative newspapers were launched to meet the challenge. A prospectus for one such paper, the *Wrexham Guardian*, recalled how 'In the year 1869 and immediately after the General Election, it was felt by the Conservative Party that it would be most advantageous for their interests to start a Conservative newspaper at Wrexham, to battle, to some extent, with the many Liberal organs in that part of the Principality' and the growing power of 'English and Welsh radical papers, against which we have a hard battle to fight.'[59]

From the 1870s, the Established Church and the local Tories organized their forces to combat what they regarded to be the growing threat of a Radical Nonconformist and Liberal press. But, without the Stamp Acts, they were obliged to respond to the challenge posed by radical journalists in relatively new ways. In the 1880s and 1890s, in Wales at least, Conservatives and clerics were beginning to feel their way towards a response which was adequate and permanent. This campaign against the radical press reached its peak in the late 1880s and early 1890s, understandably perhaps, in the heat of the agrarian anti-tithe agitation.

The decade spanning the mid-1880s to the mid-1890s was a turbulent period in rural Wales. A long-standing campaign for the Disestablishment of the Church, spearheaded by the Liberation Society, combined with renewed agitation against the tithe from the onset of agricultural depression in the mid-1880s. Increasingly, the tithe was regarded as being an unfair and unevenly applied form of taxation, particularly in the poorer tenant farming areas, and an affront to the religious and national sensibilities of a predominantly Welsh-speaking and Nonconformist population. Disturbances commenced in Clwyd in August 1886. Many observers noted that links with the Irish land campaign were very much in evidence. Michael Davitt, whose 'plan of campaign' in Ireland caused considerable alarm, spoke at meetings in north Wales in early 1886, including at one in Ffestiniog in February where he shared a platform with Michael D. Jones and David Lloyd George. Anti-Tithe Leagues were formed in many rural counties, merging in 1887 with Thomas Gee's Land League. This organization demanded an immediate reduction of 25 per cent in all tithes, and firm guarantees regarding tenant security of tenure. Among the worst incidents were those which occurred in Llangwm, Denbighshire on 25 and 27 May 1887, and in Mochdre, Caernarfonshire on 15 June of the same year. In the latter instance, the Riot Act was read and violent clashes broke out between police and villagers.

The agitation was from its inception highly charged with political significance. In the rhetoric of its leaders, the campaign against the tithes signified a popular revolt against landlordism and an alien Church, and provided further evidence of the need to pursue a political policy of Welsh Home Rule. In actuality, the political divisions which the agitation exposed were complex, even unexpected. The Liberals were divided, and the Liberation Society was ambivalent, even hostile. Some landowners, reluctant to be tarred with the brush of an unpopular tithe, distanced themselves from the more outspoken defenders of the status quo.

The affair was covered extensively by the press, especially in north Wales. The events of 1886 were reported by the eighteen-year-old Thomas Artemus Jones for the *Denbighshire Free Press*, and at great length in the newspapers of the *Herald* group, *Baner ac Amserau Cymru* and the papers of the Welsh National Newspaper Company.[60] Feelings in Liberal Nonconformist north Wales ran high at this time, and there appears to have been little room for debate, or dissent. Dr E. Pan Jones reported with evident satisfaction that when an editor of the Caernarfon Conservative weekly *Gwalia* tried to intervene in a discussion about land nationalization at a public meeting, 'in ten minutes the crowd threatened to pitch him into the river, and he skedaddled and left the place.'[61] For the proprietors of these newspapers, there was a hidden agenda to the reporting of the tithe agitation. In April 1891, Lloyd George remarked in a letter to T. E. Ellis, that the anti-tithe years had been a 'glorious struggle for Wales. Wales practically monopolized the attention of the House for fully three weeks. To my mind, that is the great fact of the Tithe Bill opposition.'[62] The relationship between local political leaders and editors was often advisory, in which one would confer with the other regarding the best course of action in a particular situation. In December 1887, T. E. Ellis, privately criticized the dearth of features in *Y Goleuad*, and advised the editor to publish a greater number of analytical pieces which could be of value to the farmers and their Liberal leaders in the tithe war. If the tithe war broke out in a parish, Ellis explained, 'it would be an immense advantage if promptly a reliable article [were published] on the relative strength of Nonconformity and Churchism and their respective history and circumstance in that parish.'[63] News, for the agitators of Cymru Fydd, was a weapon in the struggle for political control, and journalists were above all intelligence gatherers for a cause.[64] Political careers were in the making, and a new generation of Welsh leaders took maximum advantage of the conflict. It was out of these struggles that Young Wales and the Cymru Fydd movement emerged, and a new Parliamentary leadership of Welsh Liberals took shape.

These Welsh Liberals conducted their campaign, essentially a bid for power, in public meetings, through the denominational networks and above all through the press. The *Church Times* of 27 February 1891 had warned the Government of the danger of perpetuating in Wales 'the rule of the preacher-journalist'. Certainly, Thomas Gee, proprietor of *Baner ac Amserau Cymru*, Calvinistic Methodist Minister and spiritual leader of the anti-tithe agitation and exponent of other radical movements, including, briefly, republicanism, was a key figure. But other papers were also engaged in the propaganda war, most prominently *Y Genedl Gymreig*, the *North Wales Express and Observer, Y Werin* and *Udgorn Rhyddid*. It was in papers such as these, Nonconformist but assiduously non-denominational and espousing a radical and explicitly Welsh Liberalism, that the case against Conservatism, landlords and the Church was being articulated and publicized. It was not long before the opposition began to organize its fragmented forces and to formulate its own response. Alarmed by the disturbances and by the political agitation which accompanied them, a group of north Wales landowners met in December 1886 to form the North Wales Property Defence Association (PDA) under the founding chairmanship of the formidable Lord Penrhyn. Soon thereafter a similar organization was set up in the south, the Landowners' Association of South Wales and Monmouthshire, with similar objectives. The essence of their argument was that the tithe was a form of private property, which occupiers of rented farms were obliged to pay. Theirs was a stand of total and principled opposition to the Land League, but their meetings and publications suggest that their main target was what they termed the Welsh Radical Press. Like the Church and the Conservative party before them, these men now acknowledged that such newspapers as *Y Faner*, *Y Genedl* and the *Observer* constituted a form of political organization that needed to be challenged.

In a confidential circular sent out to members, dated 11 November 1887, the PDA's secretary, Caernarfon solicitor George H. M. Owen, spelled out the problem:

> For some time the Welsh Radical press has contained dangerous and insidious teachings and doctrines, but within the last few months these publications have contained such violent and exaggerated statements that the above association has determined to refute them and to shew to the country what is the real truth respecting landlordism in Wales . . .[65]

The first front of the counter attack was to be publicity and propaganda, calculated to expose the radical journalists as either charlatans or revolutionaries. But their main difficulty was the fact that much, indeed virtually all, of this journalism was written in the Welsh language. To be exposed, it had first to be read and translated. But in an important sense, the fact that it was in Welsh at all was considered to be evidence of its duplicity. The language had had a bad press in recent years. In September 1866, a *Times* leader had asserted that 'The Welsh language is the curse of Wales', and said of the Welsh, 'their antiquated and semibarbarous language . . . shrouds them in darkness . . . For all practical purposes Welsh is a dead language'. In 1867, H. L. Spring had described the language as 'a sort of freemasonry to delude the strangers', and in the late 1880s, Stanley Leighton, writing in *Punch*, argued robustly that Welsh was by that time pre-eminently the language of the 'professional agitator'.[66]

The PDA's concern regarding the Welsh-language press was emphasized in a brief and confidential policy document, entitled 'Remarks on the Welsh Press', published in 1888, which outlined in greater detail its objections to the radical press, and described its chosen method of combating its influence. As in south Wales half a century earlier, in the age of the Scotch Cattle and the Chartists, Welsh again was regarded as 'the language of conspiracy and sedition':

> It is most important at the present time that serious attention should be called to the dangerous and insidious teachings of the Welsh press, that is the papers published in the Welsh language. The majority of these papers are, and have been, for a long time poisoning the minds of the ignorant Welsh people with the most Revolutionary, Socialistic, and Communistic doctrines it is possible to imagine, often written not only in most violent, but even in profane, language; often as revolutionary and disloyal as anything in the Irish press, and rather more communistic, exciting the people against all those who possess any kind of property, and inflaming their worst passions by all sorts of exaggerated misstatements, such as that 300 years ago all the land belonged to the people, and that they have been robbed of it by the landowners; that the landowners have stolen the common lands from the people; that in the seventeenth century every man had his bit of land; and so on with innumerable other gross misstatements of a nature calculated to inflame the ignorant, and to incite them to hatred of the landowners, and altogether of what has been called the 'classes'.

The fact that much of this material was written and published in Welsh worried them greatly. The document continues:

> Unfortunately, these extreme papers are the only literature nineteen-twentieths of the Welsh people ever read, and the only instruction in the topics of the day they ever receive; and owing to the unfortunate difficulty of the language, their mendacious assertions and communistic teachings practically pass uncontradicted or exposed, for, unfortunately, the only persons who can effectively speak or write in the Welsh language are the violent and unprincipled agitators by whom the people are now almost entirely led, many of them being dissenting ministers, proprietors or editors of newspapers.

Then it turns its attention specifically to the tithe agitation.

> The result of all this is, that a class hatred and war against property is being stirred up, which, if not promptly coped with and counteracted, will, at a much earlier date than is now apparent, land us in Wales in a similar state of things to what has, unfortunately, existed in Ireland for some time; and there can be no doubt that the anti-tithe agitation has been entirely incited by, and is the direct outcome of, the language of the Welsh press.

An equally sinister dimension was the emphasis on Home Rule and on a Welsh nationalism.

> The Welsh press are also advocating and getting up a cry for a species of Home Rule for Wales, and the entire exclusion of all Englishmen from all official appointments . . . Indeed, it seems intended to revive, if possible, the long buried cry of 'Wales for the Welsh', and in other ways to follow the example of the Irish Nationalists.[67]

To demonstrate the truth of these statements would require a very close reading of a great many newspapers, especially editorial columns, local reports and readers' letters. Interestingly, this is precisely what the PDA tried to do. At the end of the pamphlet, two specific recommendations were made. Firstly, that a permanent watchdog, termed a 'central committee', should sit in London, arrange to have translations made of the offending items of Welsh journalism, and see to it that they were published in the London 'and other English papers', and more generally to 'act as a committee of safety for the protection of landowners . . .

in the present grave crisis'. Secondly, that local sub-committees should be set up to select items for translation, arrange for translations to be published in the local English-language papers, before transmission to the central committee in London. In other words, the PDA's principal task was the surveillance of the Welsh newspaper press.

The London committee went swiftly to work. On 27 September 1887 an article appeared in *The Times* which described the difficulties faced by the landowners in the most graphic terms. Ostensibly, it was in the form of a general article about the attractions of the county of Caernarfon, but its comments on the Welsh press were unmistakably pointed:

> Greatest . . . of all influences, is that of the vernacular press, which by dint of the fact that it is usually unnoticed out of Wales, is in a peculiarly strong position for evil. Elsewhere revolutionary schemes must be formulated in secrecy, and can only venture into the full light of publicity when their strength is established. In Wales, on the other hand, any scheme may be suggested with the utmost frankness. The newspapers printed in the vernacular are very numerous; they circulate almost exclusively among the working classes; they abound in libels and in violent suggestions; they make the most startling proposals in the fullest confidence, secure in the ignorance of the Welsh language which prevails in high places . . . Men are alarmed at the language used in the Indian native journals which can be read by Englishmen; they cry out, and most justly, against the violence and the frank brutality of the Irish newspapers; they have remained hitherto in blissful ignorance of the fact that within 200 miles of London are published newspapers at least as bold and virulent as those of Calcutta or of Dublin . . . In the Welsh press agitators have at their absolute disposal a weapon of the most effectual and dangerous character.

The PDA's man at *The Times*, and the author of this article, was James Edmund Vincent, grandson of the Dean of Bangor. Born in Bethesda, educated at Winchester and Oxford, and barrister on the North Wales Circuit, Vincent had joined the staff of *The Times* in 1886. By the following year, he was also secretary of the Landowners' Association of South Wales and Monmouthshire, and an adviser to Lord Penrhyn and the PDA.[68]

The comparison made by Vincent between the Welsh and the Indian press was a considered one. M. M. Bhownaggree was to write in 1897 of the relationship between Indian nationalism and journalists that the Indian vernacular press could act either 'as a safety valve or as an edged tool of seditious enclaves'. He was in no doubt that at that time, the latter was the case. In the same year, an article on Indian Journalism in *Blackwood's Magazine* argued, along lines very simliar to those of Vincent that 'the noisy patriots have it all their own way: they blow the trumpet, harangue the community, denounce every department in turn . . . In addition to pure fabrications and inventions, they deal largely in misrepresentations and distortions', and warned that 'if India is not to become unmanageable, we ought to deal with the native press as we deal with smallpox and other diseases.'[69]

On Boxing Day 1887, the preliminary results of the PDA's survey of the Welsh papers, thought to be sufficiently damning, were published in another article in *The Times*, again penned by J. E. Vincent. Seeking 'to place English readers in such a position as may enable them to appreciate the character and the strength of the influence exercised by the Welsh vernacular Press upon the people of Wales', the author explained his intention to 'let Welsh journalism be judged out of its own mouth'. Discussing a dozen or so extracts from *Y Faner*, *Y Werin* and *Y Genedl*, which though torn out of context, all served to confirm the worst fears of the PDA, the author explained to his readers that:

> The growth of journalism, and of vernacular journalism in particular, in the Principality has of late years been little short of phenomenal . . . The fact is that vernacular journalism and the Bible form, roughly speaking, the entire literary pabulum of the people. Books do indeed exist in increasing but not as yet in great numbers; and journalism is the favourite field of the Welsh writer; hence comes its prosperity, herein lies its strength. Our present concern is with journals of undoubted power.

In April 1888, Sir John Puleston took up the theme and spoke at length at a Conservative party conference in Caernarfon in support of a resolution which condemned the activities and 'misrepresentations of the Welsh Radical Press' and argued in favour of taking firm steps 'to counteract it'. In the following year it was noted that John Owen had been appointed to the Deanery of St Asaph 'with the special view of keeping an eye on the Welsh Radical vernacular press, and to defend the interests of the Church from misrepresentations therein.' A. Griffith-Boscawen also took up Vincent's theme in the English press, warning in the *National Review* in 1893 that 'for the average Englishman, Ireland is bad enough, and yet there is a certain attractiveness, even about Irish disorder; but Wales, with its unknown tongue, its impossible names, and its apparently complete absence of vowels, seems an intolerable theme.'[70] In the 1880s and through much of the 1890s, political and religious leaders in north Wales were preoccupied with the presumed dangers of a radical press which, by all accounts had not suffered the terminal decline brought about by the industrialization and commercialization of the newspaper press.

Vincent's importance lay not only in his supportive articles in *The Times*, but in his organizational abilities. These talents were abundantly displayed in the sessions of the Royal Commission on Land in Wales which sat from May 1893 until 1895, and reported in 1896. It is clear from the minutes of evidence that Vincent is present in many of the interviews, feeding questions and giving advice and information to members of the PDA who were interviewed. It emerges quite clearly from the evidence of Penrhyn and others that the principal objective of the translation exercise was to identify those papers against which libel action could be taken, and strenuous efforts were made in the course of the Commission by Lord Kenyon, Vincent and others to get Gee in particular to admit to having libelled in his papers various landowners and land agents. As Kenyon tartly observed, 'As Mr Gee has studied the aristocracy, perhaps the aristocracy must study Mr Gee.'[71] Finally, Lord Penrhyn produced the evidence collected by the PDA in the form of twenty-seven translated extracts from Welsh newspapers. The cumulative effect of these articles, Penrhyn argued, would prove conclusively that 'the agitation upon the Welsh Land Question was unreal in origin, and had not its source in any genuine sense of grievance on the part of the agricultural community.' 'This agitation', he continued, 'was deliberately fomented by journalistic sensational writings, with the object of creating a feeling in the country which would tend to the advantage of the proprietors of the vernacular press, and to the detriment of the Church and landowners of Wales.' Lloyd George, with characteristic eloquence, retorted that it was the landowners, not the journalists, who were responsible for the agrarian discontent.[72]

But the dangers of libel action threatened by the PDA action was not lost on the editors of the Welsh Liberal papers. In June 1891, for example, the editor of *Y Celt* wrote to one of his correspondents thus:

> If we publish your letter we will place you and ourselves in the dangers of libel law. The Tories in this district have men appointed to look over the Welsh newspapers in search of a chance to bring them before a court of law. This is one of the weapons they use these days to prevent freedom of opinion.[73]

Penrhyn did eventually bring a case against the *Clarion* after they printed an article by W. J. Parry entitled 'The Crime of Bethesda' on 13 July 1901. The editor of the *Clarion* publicly apologized to Penrhyn on 27 July 1901, but Parry refused to do so. Parry was defended by his old friend David Lloyd George, in a case heard in London in 1903.[74]

The relative sophistication of the PDA's monitoring campaign did create difficulties for the Welsh Liberal press, but other, more direct means of expressing disapproval of newspapers had long been practiced. The editor of the *Monmouthshire Merlin* was threatened by an anonymous 'Swing' letter in 1831 for its support of the Duke of Beaufort; and in Chepstow on bonfire night in 1893 a copy of *Skits*, a gossip weekly published by Tom Barfoot, a Newport bookmaker, and a guy representing *The South Wales Argus*, condemned as a 'Radical Print', were publicly burned by a crowd of Conservatives. The *Western Mail* offices in Cardiff were also attacked by an enraged crowd during a riot in October 1886.[75]

The influence of the press may then be seen to have been a matter of some concern in Wales throughout the nineteenth century, but particularly so in times of social or political conflict. It is difficult to measure the extent of the influence of the Liberal press on its readers in general, but the anxieties and manoeuvreing of rival religious and political forces indicate that the effects of the press on leadership groups was considerable. Efforts made by such groups to control the press, and to impose their own hegemony, created a distinctive politics within which journalism was itself the main focus of contention, and which revealed a number of commonly held contemporary assumptions about the ideological forces that conditioned Victorian society. One involved attitudes to the power of writing. Social and political conflicts were also fought in the public arenas of print, literally wars of words, and in these conflicts, texts and their readings were paramount. Another, seen most clearly in the PDA documents, concerned a presumed hierarchy of political discourses. One, at the lower level, was defined as closed, remote, backward-looking, disruptive and Welsh; the other, at the higher level, being open, cosmopolitan, progressive, stabilizing and English. The former was to be combated by being transformed, literally translated, into the latter. Thus the purpose of the monitoring exercise of the PDA was to expose to the scrutiny of respectable, middle-class, metropolitan and English-speaking opinion the supposedly subversive agenda of a species of Liberal Nonconformity so that the messages they believed had been concealed in the language might be decoded.

In general, the press was widely regarded as a key component in social conflict. It became so, firstly, because it was able to draw clear lines of demarcation between conflicting groups. This enabled the leaderships of various movements to use the press as the most immediate form of mass communication at their disposal to test reactions and publicize policies. In addition, at least in the period before 1914, the press was regarded as an instrument for maintaining a degree of cohesion within religious, political or language communities. Increasingly, in the twentieth century, as the structures of these communities began to loosen, the press was to perform very different social functions.

The contours of culture

The remit of nineteenth-century journalists extended far beyond the limited compass of party or religious politics. It embraced an enormous diversity of human interests and concerns, and the presence of a flourishing journalism both conditioned and defined, intellectually and materially, the shape of the culture within which it functioned. If culture may be conceived of historically as a map of an ever-changing landscape, the press may serve as an indicator of the map's moving contour lines. The study of the press allows us to gauge the relative strengths of cultural forces at any one time, and to follow their relative movements over a longer period. It follows that the richness of this culture should not be sought merely in the contents of individual papers, but rather in the ways in which they interrelated, in the tensions that were generated between them, and in the welter of simultaneity that was the experience of the contemporary reader. By regarding the press as a total medium of communication, rather than as the disaggregated sum of its constituent parts, the supposed influences of individual titles or journalists are subordinated to the larger question of how press and society interacted. The press was not, after all, simply a collection of newspapers and magazines, but, far more significantly, a highly problematic social phenomenon whose social effects were widely discussed by contemporaries. Journalism, as nineteenth-century observers knew only too well, helped both to generate social divisions and to foster feelings of community. In the structuring of this complex culture, diversity and schism were sustained by language and religion, while, at the same time, a more inclusive sense of community was engendered through the dissemination of a popular literature and a growing consciousness of Wales as a nation.

The journalism of Wales was divided most starkly along lines of language. Attempts at reaching the two linguistic markets by means of bilingual journalism had long been a feature of the Welsh press. From its inception in January 1808 the *North Wales Gazette* had included a Welsh-language column of news, a practice continued and extended in the 1890s by the more successful south Wales papers, including the *South Wales Star*, the *South Wales Daily News*, the *Western Mail* and the *South Wales Echo*. In the latter two 'Gwyliedydd' and 'Adolygydd' provided regular reviews in English of the contents of the Welsh newspapers. Other editors were more wary. J. Hemming of the *Glamorgan Gazette* announced that he was 'not confident about the venture of introducing Welsh' into his paper, and doubted 'whether the quality of the articles supplied by various Welsh writers [was] worth the trouble of their production.'[76] The more comprehensively bilingual papers, such as *Y Gweithwr/The Workman*, the *Cambrian/Y Freinlen Gymroaidd*, or *Amddiffynydd y Gweithiwr/Workman's Advocate*, which comprised distinct sections in Welsh and English failed to compete with their mono-lingual rivals. A correspondent complained to the latter in 1874 that half his weekly newspaper was useless to him since he did not read Welsh. Bilingual journalism presented political as well as commercial difficulties. Although a bilingual policy was 'inscribed on the banner of Young Wales', O. M. Edwards in November 1889 opposed the simultaneous publication of *Cymru Fydd* and *Young Wales* and expressed the view that the movement would be better served by a single Welsh-language paper, edited preferably by David Lloyd George or Daniel Lleufer Thomas. 'I believe' Edwards repeated in April 1891, 'and have believed from the start, that it was a great mistake to make *Cymru Fydd* into a bilingual paper.'[77]

Thus a minority or token bilingualism, where a column or two of Welsh-language matter was included in otherwise monolingual English newspapers, was common throughout the nineteenth and twentieth centuries, whereas a more thorough use of both languages, though attempted on numerous occasions, met with remarkably little success. Low rates of bilingual literacy, commercial constraints and political objections were clearly obstacles to the growth of a bilingual press, but an even more compelling reason for its failure was that the two languages contained two very different sets of cultural signs and moral values. The difference between Welsh and English was not simply a matter of language but of politics, religion, culture, and with the emergence of language domains, of place.

Signs of difference may be seen in the choice of titles, which to some extent reveals certain assumptions made by newspaper editors and publishers about their expected readerships. Early Welsh-language titles often paid tribute to English newspapers, *Yr Amserau*, for example was intended to imply some of the prestige of *The Times*, but others expressed inclusive sentiments of nationhood (*Y Genedl Gymreig*), patriotism (*Y Gwladgarwr*) and a sense of belonging to a people (*Y Werin*). English-language titles, however, more often stressed the up-to-dateness of their news with titles that referred to the post, the mail, the telegraph or the telephone. There were of course exceptions, and older newspaper titles such as *Herald* or *Chronicle* were used in both languages.

More pertinently, differences between the two languages were expressed in the economic inequality of the two journalisms. In 1836, the publisher of *Y Papyr Newydd Cymraeg* admitted that he did not believe that Welsh speakers would or could ever pay more than threepence a week for a newspaper, even if that paper was as 'large as a ship's sail'. He proposed that the Stamp for Welsh-language newspapers ought to be reduced from one penny to a halfpenny, but added sardonically that it was unlikely that the authorities in London would agree. The most likely outcome, he predicted rather gloomily, was that some publishers of Welsh newspapers would continue for a little while to produce small, expensive papers, which would attract fewer and fewer readers. In time, sufficient numbers of this potential readership would have learnt English to be attracted to the larger, cheaper publications, and Welsh language journalism would finally cease. Both David Owen of *Yr Haul* and his foe, David Rees of *Y Diwygiwr*, agreed that, ultimately, there was little long-term hope for the Welsh language.[78] Pessimism was deeply ingrained in Welsh-language journalism in the 1830s and 1840s, but the shock of the Royal Commission Report on Education in Wales of 1847 brought about the necessary passion and assertiveness that were necessary to propel Welsh as a public language into the late nineteenth century.

The consequences of the report, which legitimately identified numerous inadequacies in educational provision in Wales, were twofold. Firstly, it led to a storm of protest in England about the continued existence of Welsh. *Fraser's Magazine* interpreted the report in a manner that proposed that the Welsh language presented 'an impassable barrier to the reception of new ideas', shutting the Welsh off from 'all communication with the world of thought beyond them'. The Welsh-language press served only to intensify this separation: 'Neighbours to the most enlightened and enterprising nation on the face of the globe, it dooms them to a state of comparative ignorance and mental torpor.'[79] Such responses, of course, rested on a range of attitudes to the Welsh language itself and its social and cultural significance, which preceded the publication of the report and continued for decades afterwards. *Blackwood's*, for example, advised its readers in 1848 of 'the three qualifications for properly pronouncing the Welsh language: a cold in the head, a knot in the tongue, and a husk of barley in the throat.'[80] More seriously, the language was regarded as a barrier to the integration of Wales into the broader development of an industrial and imperial Britain. Following the publication of a Welsh translation of *Chambers's Information for the People* by Robert Edwards, Pwllheli, in 1848, *Chambers's Edinburgh Journal* pronounced 'that any necessity should have existed for the translation, is exceedingly to be lamented . . . That until the middle of the Nineteenth Century the Celtic tongue . . . should be employed as a vernacular, is matter not less of surprise than of national discredit. Who has been to blame for this scandal . . . ?'[81] But a more generous view also prevailed. One English observer in 1848 remarked that Welsh-language periodicals were the means by 'which all that goes on in England may be known in Wales'.[82] It was an easy mistake to make, but no less misleading for that. In fact, much of the reporting of English news was done from a distinctively, and often narrowly, Welsh denominational or political perspective.[83]

The second response occurred within Wales, where it took two forms. One was to deny vehemently the implications that Wales was marginalized and rendered immoral by its attachment to the language. The other was to turn the argument on its head and celebrate the difference, rejoicing in the language barrier that separated Welsh Wales from the rest of the English-speaking world. Both had their effects on the conduct of journalism. Writing of the late 1850s, David Davies endeavoured to dispel the view that Welsh journalism was a hotbed of sedition. The Welsh popular mind, he said, was in 'a transition state' as 'the increasing influence of the Welsh press encroaches on that of the pulpit and gradually undermines the pre-eminence it once enjoyed as the enlightener of ignorance.' The mid-Victorian equilibrium of Wales was unassailable since,

> . . . places of public amusement in Wales are few, and the range of social entertainment very limited. The theatre and the racecourse find little favour in the eyes of the Welsh people. Games and holidays have become well-nigh obsolete. Little remains besides the village and town fairs and the festivities of a wedding. Add to this the favourable circumstance, that, to the best of my knowledge, there is not in the Welsh language a single infidel publication, either original or translated.[84]

John Williams, in his appropriately entitled polemic, *A Defence of the Welsh People Against Misinterpretation of their English Critics* of 1869, argued that, contrary to the view expressed in *The Times*, there was less law-breaking in north-west Wales than in the more Anglicized areas, and that 'popular tumults, sedition, or rebellion (or indeed even strikes) are seldom or ever heard of there.' The Rebecca disturbances of 1843, he claimed, were 'a most childish and insignificant affair', and the Chartist riots of 1839 were 'evidently of English inspiration, and confined almost exclusively in their operations to Monmouthshire, a county of England.' The Welsh press, he concluded, was 'as free as it has ever been from the deadly venom of infidelity, popery, sedition &c.'[85] This distancing of Welsh opinion from the radicalism of the 1830s and 1840s was endemic in the journalism of the mid- and late-Victorian period.

Others conceded that there was much in the Welsh press that was regrettable, but sought at the same time to distinguish between good and bad English-language journalism. Reviewing the recently published volume, *The Power of the Press*, a correspondent to *Seren Cymru* in October 1851 admitted that he would be perfectly happy if such journals as the *Nonconformist*, the *British Banner* or the *Standard of Freedom* were available to Welsh readers, but was delighted that such papers as the *Weekly Dispatch*, the *Sunday Times* or *Lloyd's* were not. These papers, he argued, were angels of destruction that poisoned the morals of the English, whereas the Welsh press did 'not encourage atheism in Wales. This is a country of Bibles and sermons.'[86] In Wales, Lloyd George praised the *Western Mail* and attacked the Liberal *South Wales Daily News* not in terms of their respective politics, but of their news values. The former, he explained 'did not make such herculean efforts as the *News* to rummage all the gutters of Europe for reports of filthy and scandalous police and law cases . . . is it to be wondered at that the *Mail*, Tory and Church organ as it is, is preferred by thousands of staunch Liberals and ardent Nonconformists?'[87] Beriah Gwynfe Evans's fictional Dafydd Dafis disagreed, wishing that the entire 'lie machine' of the *Western Mail* had been destroyed in the fire of 1893. The Welsh-language papers were, he remarked, 'healthier' than the English ones since they did not 'give the Royal Wedding to their readers for breakfast, lunch, dinner and supper, day in day out as do the English papers.'[88] The clearest exposition of this line of argument appeared in the pages of *Y Diwygiwr* in 1874. A correspondent, stung by further reports in *The Times* of Welsh immorality, replied that the English press was responsible for 'sowing the seeds of atheism and free thought', and that he was relieved that the Welsh language acted as an obstacle to the dissemination of such papers, and the ideas that they contained.[89]

John Herbert Jones regarded his work as a journalist for *Yr Herald Cymraeg* and *Y Cymro* in Liverpool to be 'the defence of the civilization and culture of Wales in the face of the large cities.' Others sought to strengthen the Welsh language itself. John Williams (Ab Ithel), for instance, planned in 1859 a new 'patriotic society' based on the organizational model of the Conservative Land Society, whose members comprised 'a fraternity bound to teach the Welsh language to their households, to secure Welsh services in their parish churches, and to introduce Welsh into their schools as the essential basis of education.'[90] The emphasis on the Welsh language created a euphoric climate in Welsh periodical publishing, and explains partially at least the exaggerated and unsustainable ambitions which led to the failure of so many new titles. The first issue of *John Jones*, bought out in Nantlle, Caernarfonshire, in 1878 by the Revd E. Gurnos Jones, reportedly sold five thousand copies. The editor, evidently surprised by his early success, celebrated 'in a way inappropriate for a minister' and did not return home in time to set up the second issue. No further numbers appeared. The history of the Welsh-language press is littered with such failures. *Y Gweithiwr* in 1878 lasted for two issues, and in 1883 *Y Wyntyll*, printed on pink paper, survived for only fifteen issues.[91]

Two further developments affected the Welsh-language press. The first was the growing importance of Wales as an economic region and a dynamic political entity. Welsh Liberalism in the 1890s was an increasingly important Parliamentary grouping, and political journalism in both the languages of Wales reflected this sense of growing confidence and power. Secondly, technical developments in production, news collection, editing and distribution led to the emergence of a popular press from the 1850s, and the growing diversity of the market seriously compromised the idea that the language could for ever be kept under the hegemonic control of Liberal Nonconformity. Modernization brought both opportunities and challenges to those who had hitherto dominated the Welsh-language press, and their responses to the New Journalism were correspondingly mixed. A third element in the changed situation was a shift in English attitudes towards Wales, signalled above all by Matthew Arnold, and by Gladstone's addresses at the Eisteddfod in Mold in 1873 and again in Wrexham in 1888. In response to Gladstone's observations of 1873, *The Times* was obliged grudgingly and incomprehendingly to admit that 'the tongue of Aneurin and Taliesyn is the vehicle of active political and religious controversy in the nineteenth-century.'[92] This was accompanied in Wales by a renewed enthusiasm for, and pride in, the Welsh language, and a growing insistence that it should slough off the imposed image of 'celtic mists' and be admitted as a modern European language. Among the pioneers of this revival were Robert Ambrose Jones, O. M. Edwards, Beriah Gwynfe Evans and the Welsh Language Society. The new, confident mood led Evans to insist that the language should no longer be 'a national embarrassment', and that it should be used in a variety of official and public arenas.[93]

Political parties were also sensitive to the language issue. J. T. D. Llewelyn, a Conservative party candidate in the Cardiff election of 1886, advised his supporters in October of that year that 'it would be necessary for the candidate for South Glamorgan to be thoroughly acquainted with the Welsh language. There was a deal for him to do with the miners in the Rhondda Valley, and also amongst the agricultural labourers, and they would only vote for the candidate who could make himself known in their own language.' The following day, Llewelyn 'advocated the immediate establishment of a Welsh [language] newspaper as an indispensable adjunct to the Conservative propaganda.' The editor of the *Western Mail* disagreed.

> The Welsh miner or steel-worker, or the man engaged in the tin-plate trade, knows well enough that to pursue his business intelligently, that is to say, profitably, he must look to other sources of information and advice than those which are provided him by the vernacular press... The rubbishy reading of the miscellaneous type afforded him by the native newspaper would never compensate for the absence of piping-hot intelligence and comment – commercial, political, social, and religious – which is regularly served up to him . . . by the English daily press.[94]

The paper took a similar view of the efforts of the Anglican Church to sustain a Welsh-language press in the mid-1890s. Whilst congratulating *Y Llan* for increasing its circulation by 1,500 a week in November 1894, an editorial argued that *Yr Haul* was a failure since 'cultured Churchmen prefer English to Welsh, and the brilliant editor wastes his strength on the desert air'.[95] Liberals, particularly in the north, were more supportive of the language,[96] but even there, many were eager to emulate developments in the English press. In 1884, T. E. Ellis congratulated the editor of *Y Goleuad* for introducing a bold new format, and added 'I am glad you are keeping your eye on the *Pall Mall Gazette* which is far and away the most dashing of the journals.' The *Pall Mall Gazette* was then at the forefront of the New Journalism, and a little over a year later the *Western Mail* could without irony describe *Y Goleuad* as 'the *Spectator* of Wales'.[97]

But the modernization of the Welsh press was regarded with troubled apprehension by many. In 1894, Abraham Roberts expressed the common concern that newspapers in both English and Welsh languages were equally guilty of feeding their readers an unhealthy diet, and had abandoned their primary purposes, which were to provide a 'pure and substantial' fare.[98] But even in 1900 it could be said that the Welsh-language press remained 'pure' in the sense that,

> . . . they agree in eschewing news about horse-racing and in devoting but little of their space to games of any kind. They are chary in their accounts of divorce cases and indecent assaults, but they are rather more accessible to accounts of murder and tales of horror. They are more literary than English papers of the like standing, and they are always open to poets and versifiers. . . They may be said to be on the whole Puritan in tone.[99]

W. Eilir Evans asked rhetorically in 1907 'Who would turn to a Welsh paper for an account of the Derby, or the Oxford and Cambridge boat race?' They seldom concerned themselves with 'sport, football, the theatre, and horse racing', and their readers, he declared, took pride in the fact that 'the Welsh press is free from the lewdness and irreligion that mar a section of the English press.'[100] In a more positive vein, J. H. Jones, editor of *Y Brython*, argued in 1913 that Welsh journalism was a highly distinctive genre that offered to its readership a different kind of journalism to that of the English papers. 'We believe in the Literary Gospel,' he explained, 'and do our best to thunder it every week.' There was for him no case for translating and copying English papers when the Welsh press could provide something that was not catered for in 'the *Daily Lie* from London or the *Evening Hoax* from Liverpool.'[101]

Welsh-language journalism was thus regarded not only as a distinctive genre, but also as an effective cultural barrier that isolated Welsh-speaking Wales from the debilitating effects of 'English' values. Recent studies have also lent support to the notion of the distinctiveness of Welsh-language journalism in the nineteenth century. D. Tecwyn Lloyd has argued that the Welsh-language press was culturally unique, and was wholly different in style and content to the journalism that evolved in the rest of Britain. The development of 'a new vocabulary of political and educational controversy', Lloyd has argued, enabled writers and readers in Wales to comment on and to understand national and world events in a specifically Welsh way.[102] The distinctive characteristics of Welsh-language journalism in the nineteenth century were the products of two simultaneous sets of pressures. The first involved the near hegemony of religious institutions over the financing, production and distribution of a substantial proportion of Welsh-language newspapers. In turn, control over the means of communication enabled the institutions of Welsh Nonconformity to influence the political and cultural discourses that were reproduced publicly in the Welsh language. Paradoxically, this material and doctrinal influence both sustained the weeklies in the mid to late nineteenth century and served to weaken them in competition with the English Sundays and dailies in the free market of the early twentieth century. But the other pressure was poverty. For most of the nineteth century it was a poor press, operating on slender resources for a small and relatively poor readership, and under the circumstances it is perhaps not surprising that a cultural virtue was made of economic necessity. The increasing complexity and cost of newspaper production, and the attractions of a fuller menu in the English papers, particularly after the introduction of the techniques and style of the New Journalism in the 1890s, effectively undermined the readership of the Welsh-language papers, especially, though not exclusively, in the urban and industrial areas.

Religion, however, cut across the language barrier and dissected Welsh journalism in an altogether different way. In religious journalism the target of criticism or of outrage was as much the organs of other denominations as those other denominations themselves. The religious papers, and the forces which they mobilized, likened themselves to scattered armies engaged in a bloodless holy war against apostasy. On the one hand, religious leaders held that 'the newspaper, in all its varieties of information and exposition, is a great and unbreakable link in the chain which binds together the Church and the world.'[103] On the other, it enabled communities of belief to distinguish themselves from others, often in the most heated, intemperate forms. The most sustained case of religious conflict of this kind occurred between 1835 and 1865, when the maverick Anglican, David Owen (Brutus) launched in *Yr Haul* repeated attacks on Welsh Nonconformist values as embodied above all by David Rees (Y Cynhyrfwr), editor of the Independent paper, *Y Diwygiwr*. Owen, originally a Baptist whose vitriolic brand of conservative Anglicanism came to fruition only after a flirtation with Llŷn Unitarianism and a long association with the Independents, paradoxically led Rees, an ordained Congregational minister of radical persuasion, to articulate, over a period of thirty years, some of the clearest and most revealing arguments in the defence of Nonconformity. Characterized by the sharpness of the invective and the cleverness of the satire, the feud lasted virtually the whole of their adult lives, and was finally brought to an end only when Brutus relinquished his editorship of *Yr Haul* in the year preceeding his death in 1866. Only then did Rees allow himself to return in kind, and in his farewell address to his readers in December 1865 he finally identified his chief antagonist. The origins of the conflict between Owen and Rees, however, can be found as much in journalism as in religion, since Rees's initiation of *Y Diwygiwr* in 1835 was, at the insistence of the Carmarthenshire Independents, a direct consequence of Brutus's increasing conservatism in *Yr Haul*'s predecessor, the erstwhile Radical paper *Yr Efangylydd*. It was a slight Brutus was not to forget. The gain for evangelical Anglicanism, however, was inestimable, and many saw in Brutus an exemplary journalist, one whose spirit was again to be recalled at the launching of the evangelical Anglican paper *Y Gloch a'r Amserau Eglwysig* in May 1898.[104]

Journalism set its own momentum, which often accounted for the proliferation of titles in areas where there were too few readers and advertisers commercially to sustain them. Hostility between journalists was the prime motivation for the launch of the Radical Independent the *Principality* in 1847. In explaining the reasons for establishing the new paper, the Revd J. Lewis,

Henllan, recalled the bitterness of the attacks made agaist his denomination by the *Welshman* in the early and mid-1840s: 'Not one newspaper in the Principality has been more hostile to us than this one has been. We well remember its behaviour during the Rebecca riots, it overflowed with spite and insult about our manhood and our religion, insulting our nation and our principles.' Edited at first by the gifted Ieuan Gwynedd, the *Principality* in turn aroused the hostility not only of the south Wales Tories, but also of the Unitarians (notably Josiah Thomas Jones) and the Methodists. Its circulation did not exceed 1,600, and the title was discontinued in 1850.

Religious tensions also aroused local animosities. Carmarthen in the 1890s was a bitterly divided journalistic community, with five newspapers (the *Welshman*, the *Reporter*, *Y Brython*, *Seren Gomer* and the *Carmarthen Journal*) and correspondents for the two main south Wales dailies, J. R. Bland of the *South Wales Daily News* and Eliss Hughes of the *Western Mail*. These seven journalists conducted a virtual civil war against one another. T. C. Tierney, editor of the *Welshman*, his nephew Maguire of the *Reporter* and Bland were Catholics, but relations between Maguire and his uncle were poisonous. They snubbed each other in public and attacked each other in their papers. Eliss Hughes was an Anglican and Henry Tobit Evans, editor and publisher of *Y Brython Cymreig* and the *Carmarthen Journal* was a Quaker.[105]

The diversity of the religious press was in this sense self-perpetuating, with papers dividing like amoebae in the heat of sectarian and personal infighting. But controversy could also generate a demand for newspapers. John Thomas (Eifionydd), editor of *Y Gwyliedydd*, grasped perfectly the advantages of religious controversy as a means of increasing the sale of his paper;[106] and public controversy, encouraged by editors, was a valuable form of self-advertisement, and was practiced by most county and town newspapers particularly in letters columns. Criticisms of the press were often forcefully expressed in these columns, and one correspondent to *Y Byd Cymreig* in February 1862 complained that the paper's London Letter was 'trash', and that another of its correspondents wrote nothing but nonsense.[107] Controversy and criticism thus prevailed within and between titles, and no doubt the seriousness of such criticisms, and the equally vehement defence of the same titles in prose and rhyme, were fuelled by the conviction that journalism mattered, that it was a powerful medium that could affect everyday life. Discussion regarding the powers of the press were not confined to newspaper columns, moreover. In 1894, the Corwen Debating Society considered whether the pulpit or the press wielded the greater influence in society. On a division, the votes were evenly cast, and the chairman gave his casting vote in favour of the press. Significantly, the terms of the debate were governed by the assumption that pulpit and press were mutually incompatible forms of communication.[108]

But the vindictiveness with which disagreements between journalists were conducted in newspaper columns caused widespread concern. The *Glamorgan Free Press*, in its first issue in May 1891, made a point of being non-sectarian, and added that 'sectarianism undermines our national constitution: it is the cancer that seeks to consume the very vitals of the Kymry.'[109] E. Morgan Humphreys echoed the sentiment with the view that denominational journalism in the nineteenth century had led to a 'withering of the Welsh mind', and was a dangerously destabilizing and destructive force. W. Lewis Jones, a Cymru Fydd stalwart, was appalled by the aggressive style of *Y Werin*, a staunch supporter of his cause. 'This is not the way to elevate Wales', he complained, 'this is not the way to achieve the ambitions of Cymru Fydd.' R. E. Prothero, in a spirited defence of the Anglican Church in Wales, noted that it was 'with disgust that the extravagance of the vernacular press is regarded by many moderate Nonconformists in Wales, whose religious earnestness has not been perverted by political passion,' and complained of 'the widening gap between the spiritual and secular elements in Welsh Nonconformity.'[110]

Rooted in existing social and cultural tensions, the press exacerbated those divisions, and, as the Anglican cleric the Revd John Jenkins argued in 1895, acted as a lever to inflame the passions already latent in the population. Jenkins appealed to journalists to moderate their bickering, and to adopt *audi alterum partem* as their professional maxim. Across the border in England, itself no stranger to press conflict, the infighting was regarded with a mixture of wonder and contempt. The Gloucestershire weekly newspaper the *Forester* referred in September 1874 to the 'sensational scribbling' and the 'wild pipings' that were the implied to be the stock in trade of correspondents in 'the hilly regions of Taffyland'.[111]

The significance accorded by Anglicans to the press in the growth of Nonconformity cannot be overemphasized, but their allegations that journalists deliberately engineered social movements and fomented disorder were far more difficult to substantiate than those regarding the use of intemperate language, which, ultimately, could be tested in law. The example of the 1904–5 Nonconformist religious revival, however, provides an insight into the interrelationship between the press and the instigators of an evangelical movement that spread with remarkable, some might have said terrifying, speed throughout Wales. The press contributed to this process broadly in two ways. Firstly, R. Tudur Jones has rightly drawn attention to the fact that the revival was the first popular event in Wales to be covered comprehensively from start to finish by a daily press. The *Western Mail* and the *South Wales Daily News* paid particular attention to the sermons and pronouncements of one of its leaders, and thus turned Evan Roberts, who was more a product of the movement than its originator, into the first Welsh media creation. One revivalist in 1904 added a new verse to his prayers, 'Blessed is the *Western Mail*', and the Baptists of east Glamorgan passed a resolution to thank the two daily papers for their support. Secondly, reports of revivalist meetings carried in the daily and weekly papers, especially in *Y Goleuad*, sparked off events in other areas and extended the reach of the revivalist leaders, along established lines of distribution, into the remotest parts of the country. Reports of the interest taken elsewhere further legitimized the movement. W. T. Stead applied the techniques of the New Journalism to his interviews with Evan Roberts, which were serialized in the *Daily News* before being published as *The Rising in the West* in 1905, and reports of the revival were printed in newspapers as far afield as the *Michigan Christian Herald*, which devoted a whole front page to the charismatic Evan Roberts, and *L'Eglise Libre* in Paris. In a retrospective account of the rise and fall of the revival, J. Evans Owen of Llanberis acidly remarked in 1907 that, 'the newspapers had a larger share than any other agency in kindling and spreading the fire; possibly also they must in part bear the disgrace of corrupting it.'[112]

But if the press was fractured along lines of language and religion, at another level it also fostered a more inclusive cultural consensus. Newspapers in both English and Welsh provided an accessible forum for creative writing in prose and verse, set new styles and fashions in fiction, and extended the readership of popular literature. In England, the definition of journalism as a form of street literature in which concepts of authorship were largely disregarded ended in the 1850s, and by 1880 Wilfrid Meynell was easily able to distinguish between literature and journalism. The former, he observed, involved, 'broadly the writing of books, magazines, and reviews, and journalism the writing for newspapers. These are distinct in the talents, character, aims, and remunerations which they imply.'[113] Journalists, it was also claimed, were drawn to newspapers and reviews because they had failed in literature, a view confirmed by H. D. Traill, writing in *Macmillan's Magazine* in October 1884: 'the style of the newspaper-writer is monotonous, cumbersome, conventional . . . a newspaper is one huge repository of the vices which writers should avoid, and so a widely circulating medium of literary demoralisation . . .'[114] Distinctions between journalism and literature in nineteenth-century Wales, however, were far from being this clear. The *Caernarvon Advertiser*, was established by the Cymmrodorion Press in January 1822 to reflect and to participate in what it termed the 'present revival of Cambrian literature'. Demand for such a popular literature remained high throughout the century, and the weekly, and later daily, newspapers were ready to maintain the supply. As late as 1892, T. E. Ellis noted with pride how *Y Goleuad* had 'of late grown so *literary* in taste and tone',[115] and in February 1896, the *Western Mail* launched a monthly literary supplement. An important dimension of this literary provision, and one of the most noticeable attributes of the newspaper in Wales, was the poetry column.

For much of the nineteenth century, poetry remained a lively form of popular writing. David Thomas (Dafydd Ddu Eryri), weaver, teacher and representative of the Gwyneddigion Society in Caernarfonshire, published a translation of Alexander Pope's 'Vital Spark of Heavenly Flame' in the first issue of the *North Wales Gazette* on 5 January 1808, and for the remainder of the century, and beyond, newspapers were important outlets for the poetically talented as well as for the not so gifted. Poetry columns often had their own editors, some of whom were poets of repute, such as David Watkin Jones (Dafydd Morgannwg) in *Tarian y Gweithiwr* between 1875 and 1878, or Thomas Essile Davies (Dewi Wyn o Esyllt) in the *Weekly Mail.* Verses covered both moral questions and more immediate political or social events. Rowland Williams (Hwfa Môn) published poems attacking Napoleon III and in defence of Prussia in *Yr Herald Cymraeg* in 1870, and protest verses against the immigration of rural labourers from Cardiganshire into the iron and coal industries of Merthyr and Dowlais appeared in Welsh in the *Workman's Advocate* in 1873 and 1874. The poetry columns continued to provide a form of patronage to plebeian writers well into the twentieth century. Huw Menai, from Gilfach Goch and a miner in the Cambrian Combine, was unknown until he 'timidly sent some specimens of his verse to the editor of the *South Wales News*'. The poems were duly published, and, emboldened by the experience, Menai began to publish more widely in the *South Wales News*, the *Western Mail* and the *Welsh Outlook*.[116]

Music and song also found space in newspapers. *Seren Cymru*, like many other papers, had its succession of specialist music editors, including for many years J. Parry (Bardd Alaw), from London. Some publications were entirely devoted to musical journalism, including for example David Hughes's *Y Perorydd Cysegredig* (1843) and *Yr Athraw Cerddorol* (1851), John Roberts's *Y Cerddor Cymreig* of 1861–5, and *Cronicl y Cerddor*, published by M. O. Jones and edited by D. Emlyn Evans from 1879 to 1883. The connection between the press and *eisteddfodau* was also strong, both in terms of the coverage of cultural events in both the English- and Welsh-language papers, and also in terms of the involvement of personnel. William Williams (Carw Coch), a Unitarian who built the Stag Inn in Trecynon in 1837 and held *eisteddfodau* there from 1841, was a contributor to the Chartist *Udgorn Cymru* and founder of *Y Gwladgarwr* in 1857.[117]

The serialization of novels in newspapers in Wales began at a relatively early date. In 1842, Henry Vincent's Chartist *National Vindicator*, which circulated in south and west Wales, carried 'The Levellers. A tale Written expressly for the National Vindicator', and in 1861 William Aubrey launched *Y Nofelydd a chydymaith y teulu* in Anglesey. Roger Edwards was almost certainly the originator of the serial novel in the Welsh-language newspaper press, with 'Y Tri Brawd a'u Teuluoedd' in *Y Drysorfa* published in instalments between February 1866 and February 1867. *Y Dydd* also carried serialized stories (for example, 'Ned y Poacher') in the late 1860s, and the first issue of *Y Gweithiwr Cymreig* carried the opening chapter of a novel by Beriah Gwynfe Evans. In 1880 Daniel Owen's *Rhys Lewis* appeared monthly in *Y Drysorfa*, and a young reader in Caernarfon was thrilled by the experience of reading *in Welsh* about 'a man with a two-barrelled gun'. In a town where boat racing and football were regarded as sins by the chapel leaders, and where attending a performance of *Macbeth* in a Liverpool theatre was met by a stern reprimand, *Rhys Lewis* was put on the stage and tolerated, largely, it was reasoned, because it had been legitimated by Roger Edwards, eminent cleric and editor of *Y Drysorfa*. Daniel Owen also published *Y Dreflan* in serial form in the same journal in 1879 and 1880, and his *Profedigaethau Enoc Huws* was serialised in *Y Cymro* in 1890. Previously, Owen had gained newspaper writing experience by translating the American novel *Ten Nights in a Bar* for the fortnightly journal *Charles o'r Bala*, then edited by Nathaniel Cynhafal Jones. Also in the 1890s, the prolific Beriah Gwynfe Evans wrote stories for the papers of the Welsh National Press Company in Caernarfon, including most prominently *Y Werin*. In its Christmas issue in 1892, this paper published a collection of short stories by Beriah Gwynfe Evans, Llew Llwyfo, J. R. Pritchard, J. Arthur Price, J. O. Jones (ap Ffarmwr), Ellis Owen, E. Lloyd Williams and J. H. Roberts. Remuneration for authors was not high. R. J. Rowlands sold the sole copyright of his novel 'Dyrysu Dau Fywyd' to the Welsh National Press Company in Caernarfon for £3. Welsh-language novels were also published in American newspapers. David Lloyd Davies (Dewi Glan Peryddon), who first published his *englynion* in *Yr Amserau* when he was sixteen, became an editor of the 'Lloffion Difyrus' column in *Y Wasg Americanaidd*, and his novel *Ceinwen Morgan* was published serially in *Y Drych* in Utica.[118]

In January 1895 a series of articles was started by Allen Upward in the *Merthyr Times*. Upward stood as a Labour candidate in Merthyr in the 1895 election, but polled disastrously (659 votes against D. A. Thomas's 9,250). He left the area soon afterwards to rejoin the literary life in London, where, the editor of the *Merthyr Times* mused, 'he appears to be making splendid headway . . . as a writer of fiction' and found it ironic that 'this sturdy Cardiff democrat has transferred his affections from the sons of toil to the titled nobles and the august grandees of the Royal Courts of Europe. The erstwhile Labour candidate delights in writing about kings and queens. . .'[119] Another Welsh author who took his talents elsewhere was Owen Rhoscomyl, author of *The Jewel of Ynys Galon* and *Battlement and Tower*, hailed by J. O. Jones as a 'Welsh Walter Scott' whose romances served to 'deepen awareness of Welsh nationality'. Eulogized by the *Saturday Review* and the *Daily Mail*, Rhoscomyl's work was, Jones complained, ignored by the Welsh press. The origins of the Welsh novel can thus be found in the newspaper and periodical press, and serialized stories remained an important dimension until the early twentieth century.[120]

The serialization of English-language fiction become a well organized and profitable industry after William Frederick Tillotson of the *Bolton Evening News* began to commission and sell *feuilletons* to newspapers in 1873.[121] The *Glamorgan Gazette* was one of many papers in Wales which employed the services of such fiction syndicates from the 1870s. Hemming in March 1878, after some bargaining, paid Tillotson's £7.10*s*. for the right to publish *Sophie Crewe*, but warned that it was an experiment and he would continue to buy only at cheaper rates owing to the high cost of producing the paper in a period of depressed trade and the consequent scarcity of advertisements. Hemming, however, continued to buy from Tillotson for some time, his only stipulation being that he would not accept anything that Tillotson would also sell to the Cardiff papers. 'We must have a novelty' wrote Hemming, who did not confine his search for fiction to Tillotson's, and in September 1879 agreed to pay William Andrews of Hull four guineas for a 'Historic Romance Sketches' series, again on the proviso that the '"copy" is supplied to our paper only, as far as Glamorgan is concerned'. The paper also published fiction syndicated by Cassell, Potter and Galpin of London, including *A Living Legacy* provided on stereo.[122] The commercial significance of popular fiction was not lost on newspaper managements. The Welsh-language press was at something of a loss when it came to meet this kind of competition, but improvised as usual. Not to be outdone by the new market created above all by Tillotson's, *Y Genedl* arranged the translation of Charles Reade's novel *Never Too Late To Mend* and published it in Welsh as *Gwell Hwyr Na Hwyrach* in December 1890. Annie Harriet Hughes (Gwyneth Vaughan), herself a prolific writer of Welsh novels for newspapers, also translated into Welsh the works of Henry Drummond. Anne Adalisa Puddicombe (Allen Raine), of Newcastle Emlyn, published her novel *Ynysoer*, which had won a prize at the Caernarfon Eisteddfod in 1894, serially in the *North Wales Observer*, and *Neither Store-house nor Barn* in the *Cardiff Times*. This literary environment attracted and encouraged many aspiring writers and novelists. Howard Spring, perhaps best known for his novel *Fame is the Spur!*, began his writing career as a newspaper man in Cardiff before the First World War, and learnt shorthand and other essential journalistic and literary skills at university evening classes paid for by the editor of the *South Wales Daily News*.[123]

Reviews in newspapers and magazines of poetry, fiction, theatre, choral and orchestral music, opera and the music hall not only brought cultural events to the attention of a larger audience, but also produced some excellent writing in both Welsh and English. Articles by Dr William Davies (Hen Wyliedydd), a shoemaker who became known as one of Wales's finest literary critics for his reviews in *Yr Eurgrawn*, or Joseph Parry, on orchestral music in the *Western Mail*, were widely read at a time when, in many parts of the country, books and concerts were not easily accessible.[124]

The didactic function of the popular press was evident in Wales throughout the nineteenth century. One aspect that deserves greater attention was the role it was made to play in the process of changing and consolidating the standard of written Welsh. A debate on Welsh grammar had surfaced in the periodicals of the Gwyneddigion and the Cymreigyddion in London in the 1800s, and Joseph Davies, founder of *Y Brud a Sylwydd* in 1828, extended the range of his journalism by coining new Welsh words.[125] In response to these developments, R. Williams remarked in the *Quarterly Review* in September 1849 that an influx of fresh thought was expanding the language 'which is evidently growing and enriched daily by the formation of self-evolved words, especially as denote abstraction and generalization.' Thomas Edwards (Caerfallwch), in his English-Welsh dictionary of 1850 devised new scientific terms and introduced such neologisms as *pwyllgor* – 'committee', and William Williams (Caledfryn) in his Welsh grammar of the following year included a section on writing for the press.[126] At the Porthmadog Eisteddfod of 1851 *Seren Cymru* started a series in response to an appeal made there to improve the quality of Welsh letters. The writers who responded with tips and examples of good practice included John Jones (Tegid), William Williams (Caledfryn), Thomas Edwards (Caerfallwch), Silvan Evans and Evan Jones (Ieuan Gwynedd). Later in the century writers and journalists chose to model themselves on the early pressmen: in 1852 Josiah Thomas Jones, in the first issue of *Y Gwron Gymreig*, remarked that the writing style would be as close to that of the old *Seren Gomer* as possible, while in 1886 Ab Ithel in *Y Goleuad* could say that it was in the writings of Roger Edwards that the purest examples of nineteenth-century Welsh were to be found.[127] Dialect writing in Welsh also found favour in readers' letters and, famously, in William Rees's series, 'Llythyrau Hen Ffarmwr', in *Yr Amserau* from December 1846, and in William Williams's less well known 'Llythyrau Bachan Ifanc' in *Tarian y Gweithiwr* in the 1890s. Both series helped substantially to increase the circulations of their respective newspapers.

But by the end of the century there was great unease regarding the kind of language that appeared in the press. Although such writers as J. W. Jones (Andronicus), for whom Welsh was a second language, could still be admired for their racy and idiomatic Welsh, others were being criticized for their increasingly 'pompous Anglicized style'.[128] In their review of the Welsh press of 1900, John Rhys and David Brynmor-Jones reported that 'the shoddy Welsh which prevails in many of the newspapers published in Welsh' was actively undermining 'the supremacy of literary Welsh'. They reserved particular criticism for the practice of translating features and news items from the English-language press, frequently carried out by translators who were all too often 'wofully [sic] restricted in the matter of vocabulary.' More serious still, such translations introduced 'foreign idioms' which many found necessary to translate back into English to understand what was being written. In conclusion, they regretted that 'the tendency of journalism generally, with the hurry and scramble attendant on its periodicity, [was] in the direction of inaccuracy of language and a loose application of its terms.'[129]

The irony of a press that was ostensibly attempting to improve and consolidate standards of writing being held responsible for the deterioration of those same standards can be explained largely in terms of the use in journalism of differential registers. These may be found within individual newspapers, as well as between newspapers of the same or different languages. Editorial commentaries and articles of theological or political analysis often employed more elaborate sentence structures and vocabulary than were to be found in local reports or readers' letters. The reading of a nineteenth-century newspaper thus required constant readjustment as the reader passed from one register to another. The controversy over the use of language in journalism is explicable only when the variety of writing that was found in the press is taken into account.

The newspaper as a vehicle for education continued throughout the nineteenth century. 'Vyvyan' published a series 'On the Popular Superstitions and Customs of Wales' in the *National Vindicator* in August and September 1841, while Henry Richard's series on 'The Social and Political Condition of Wales', first published in the *Morning and Evening Star* in 1865 and 1866, was reprinted in both English and Welsh in a number of papers in Wales. William Jones (Bleddyn) wrote a series on folklore in Caernarfonshire in *Y Brython* in 1862 which were translated and republished in English in 1899.[130] Essay competitions were also popular, many being of a religious nature and requiring considerable biblical knowledge and critical dexterity, and the *Western Mail* in 1894 offered £10 prizes for scientific inventions.[131] Articles on the Welsh abroad, particularly in the USA and Australia, and letters from emigrants to these countries, were frequently printed, and no doubt helped to maintain the flow of emigrant labour from Wales. Welsh foremen or superintendents of mines or mills in north America recruited labour to 'fill the best jobs by writing to a newspaper back home'.[132] A series on 'Welsh Life in Liverpool', published in *Y Cymro* in 1890, also drew attention to Welsh life and opportunities outside Wales.[133]

Letters and other voluntary contributions provide further evidence of the readers' involvement with the press. Lord Penrhyn had informed the Royal Commissioners on Land in 1894 that

'Wales is a land where the people are particularly addicted to sending anonymous letters...', and the weekly papers in both languages attracted a large amount of such correspondence, much of it printed pseudonomously.[134] Many were no doubt used by editors as cheap space-fillers, and often they were subjected to extensive correcting and editing, but they covered a very wide range of subjects and were on occasion critical of a paper's content. Dialogues between correspondents were often sustained over several issues and across a number of different newspapers. Such correspondence provides the clearest indication that the reading of newspapers was a creative process that could add to or alter intended meanings, and in turn produce a vast amount of new, unsolicited writing.

The nature of the readership, as evidenced by such correspondence, was overwhelmingly plebeian. This was openly acknowledged, though the conclusions drawn from it varied. *Y Rhedegydd* in February 1879, replying to an assault on the Nonconformist press by the *Western Mail*, insisted that the Welsh-language press was carried out in a skilful and effective manner, largely because it addressed a working class readership. John Davies (Gwyneddon), in contrast, inferred precisely the opposite when, in *Y Traethodydd* in 1884, he argued that the ill-mannered nature of the Welsh press was due to the fact that 'the working class reads these papers, and makes up most of their correspondents.' Either way, these conflicting responses demonstrate how mistaken a commentator in the *National Review* was when in 1893 he wrote that 'there is one thing we cannot expect the working classe to provide for themselves, and that is their amusements.'[135] The overriding assumption of newspaper editors in Wales was that workers wanted to be educated rather than entertained, in the words of E. L. Bulwer in 1840, what the worker at the loom wanted was '"Advice to the Operatives – full report of the debate on the Property Tax – Letter from an emigrant in New South Wales". That's what I call news.' This, as Bulwer anticipated, would empower the worker by providing a sense of unity and purpose.[136] Thus, in addition to providing the normal service of a job advertiser and labour exchange, *Y Chwarelwr* in 1876 explained that its main function was to 'enable the working class to see their particular interests *vis à vis* other classes in the state', and *Amddiffynydd y Gweithiwr* in 1874 proudly proclaimed that 'Our paper . . . has been started by workers, it is edited by workers, and workers are its chief correspondents.' In the first issue of the *Glamorgan Free Press* in May 1891, a correspondent hoped that 'workers will have access to its columns to discuss freely their rights and grievances.'[137]

In addition to engendering a commonality of interest in terms of occupation and class, the press also contributed to the process of building and maintaining communities of locality and of belief. The sense of belonging to a place or to a group was articulated by both the local and the sectarian press by means of detailed coverage of events, and features that included biographies and portraits of community leaders. In this respect, the press acted as a social integrator that fostered a sense of belonging and which encouraged participation in municipal, party or denominational affairs. But in a wider sense, in the 'mass ceremony' of buying, reading and discussing the press, and of writing for it, journalism was a tangible representation of 'imagined communities' beyond the confines of the locality or the sect.[138] In 1846, W. J. Fox sensed that 'the press is an open place where any one may bring counsel for his fellows . . . and its tendency . . . is at least to make them one great society.'[139] The normative integration into a broader society in Wales was effected through the affirmation of collective social values in the cultural as well as the political contents of the press.[140] Journalists in both Welsh- and English-language newspapers and periodicals explicitly and increasingly sought to frame their analyses of contemporary events within the concept of Welsh nationhood. In 1888, Thomas John Hughes attributed the emergence of the Young Wales movement largely to the work of sympathetic journalism:

> It is superfluous to speak of the Welsh press and its work for Disestablishment; the *Baner* and the *Goleuad*, the *Dydd* and the *Tyst*, *Tarian y Gweithiwr*, *Seren*, *Herald* and *Genedl*, are of us, and have been with us. They have stimulated expression of the political culture which the older of them helped to create. But we have also had English Liberal journals circulating in Wales, and the service they have rendered to Welsh Disestablishment deserves special recognition. The *Daily News* (London), *South Wales Daily News* and *Weekly News*, *Liverpool Post* and *Liverpool Mercury*, the *Oswestry Advertiser*, the *Caernarvon Herald*, the *Cambrian*

> *News*, the Wrexham and Carmarthen weeklies, and many more English Radical newspapers published in Wales, have substantially assisted the Principality to speak its deep-seated conviction in English... The English Liberal Press in Wales has not made Wales less national; it has fortified our nationality, and at the same time enlarged Welsh vision.[141]

In 1907, J. Evans Owen also made the connection between the new nationalism and the press: 'New Wales – the Wales of the People ... is the product of religious revivals, and the spirit of Liberalism and the Welsh newspapers are her progeny [which are] strengthening the ties of our nationality.' W. Eilir Evans similarly felt 'the Nation's pulse' in the columns of the Welsh newspapers,[142] and J. H. Jones of *Y Brython* remarked in 1913 that he and Cemlyn, editor of the Welsh-language section of the *Western Mail*, were the true defenders of the nation.[143]

The press in Wales grew in status as well as in size from the end of the eighteenth century until the beginning of the First World War, and, at its height, during the second half of the nineteenth century, journalism had become an intrinsic part of political, religious and cultural life. The product itself, particularly the weekly newspaper, developed in the midst of this process a distinctive form that either combined news, comment, instruction and entertainment within the one format, or else moved swiftly and seemingly effortlessly from one format to another. *Y Brython*, for example, began life in June 1858 as a weekly local newspaper with literary leanings and by January 1860 had been transformed into a monthly literary journal. Sudden shifts in style of this kind illustrate both the possibilities of mid-nineteenth century journalism, and also its limitations. They strongly suggest that the technological and financial bases of these small publishing enterprises were sufficiently flexible to allow editors to search for new readerships, but they also imply that there existed a structural divide between journalists and their audiences, and that however pliant journalists were prepared to be, they continuously ran the risk that their imagined readerships simply did not exist.[144] From the journalists' point of view, then, the press did provide an indicator of public taste, but only in a very contingent sense. Some interests doubtless remained under-represented, whilst others were demonstrably over-represented. But if the proportions of the cultural map of nineteenth-century Wales that was projected by the distribution of the press are distorted, and some of the features of the landscape are enlarged while others are reduced, the press remained very much *of* its society. Text and context interacted at many levels, fundamentally through the use of language. Language is not a passive social phenomenon, but an active power that has the capacity to alter social realities. The coming of cheap print in Wales intensified attempts to control the public use of language, and, by so doing, to dominate the society itself.[145] Contestation over the social use and influence of language in turn rendered the press an object of criticism both for its content and its form. Concern regarding the powers of the press and its tendencies towards exclusive partisanship, however, were balanced by the inclusive sense of community that the press engendered, and the intellectual excitement fostered by the creative tension between text and reader added its own distinctive dimension to Welsh political and popular culture in both languages. In the twentieth century, however, as both press and society changed, much of this energy was either to be lost or channelled in new directions.

5 *Traditions and transformations*

The modern press since 1914 has undergone major changes in style and structure, but its development has in a number of ways been conditioned by the formative experiences of nineteenth-century journalism. There have been strong elements of both change and continuity in the reconstruction of the newspaper industry in the twentieth century, and in the new patterning of the press in the wake of the concentration of ownership, changes in the readership, and competition from the new film and broadcasting media that occurred during and after the First World War. The Victorian press, which in some of its aspects was sufficiently diverse and challenging to create political anxieties in both Wales and London, reached its height at the turn of the century, but the process of change that was to transform journalism in the early twentieth century had by this time already started to accelerate. Between the 1890s and the outbreak of the Second World War, the diversity of ownership which had characterized Victorian newspapers was dramatically curtailed. There was first a sudden increase then an equally sudden decrease in the numbers of titles on the market, and there followed a steady increase in the circulations of the surviving dailies. These developments brought Wales abruptly into line with the general pattern of the British press, and in so doing it became less of an indigenous press and more of an extension of English and international media empires. By 1940, the increased activity that characterized the period 1890 to 1920 had slowed to such an extent that, in the key centres of publication, the number of titles had been reduced to their 1880 levels. In that year there had been four newspapers in Caernarfon (two of them in Welsh), five in Swansea and six in Cardiff. In 1930 these numbers stood at seven in Caernarfon (five of them in Welsh), nine in Swansea and eight in Cardiff. A decade later the numbers had fallen to four in Caernarfon (three in Welsh), five in Swansea (two in Welsh) and six in Cardiff. An explanation of this trend must consider the changes that occurred in the inter-war years and the condition of journalism in the changed circumstances of post-war Wales. Transformations in the structure and style of the press between the mid-nineteenth and the mid-twentieth centuries are starkly visible, but there is also abundant evidence of the survival of the press traditions of the nineteenth century in the twentieth, even in the midst of the competing new media of radio and television. The balance between tradition and transformation is a shifting one, but its study makes possible an appreciation of the extent to which the conflicts and negotiations of the past continue to condition the structures of the present.

The press in twentieth-century Wales

By 1914 the technological innovations that had made the expansion of the press in the 1880s and 1890s possible had reached their maturity. One of the consequences of the late nineteenth-century revolutions in printing, news gathering and distribution that was most often remarked upon by contemporaries was the transformation of the press from a moral to a commercial machine, a process which at first had encouraged, then disappointed and finally endangered the smaller provincial weeklies whilst at the same time providing huge new opportunities for the urban dailies. Cover prices were lowered as the larger circulation publishers took advantage of economies of scale and increased advertising revenues to undercut their competitors on the open market, and caused further the shrinkage of the 'closed' market that had sustained so many of the smaller scale papers of the previous century. The growth of professionalism, managerialism, advertising, printing technology, and of the buying and selling of news as a commodity, described in the previous chapters, had created a very different kind of newspaper industry. The first major test of the strength and resilience of this new industry came with the outbreak of the First World War.

In the emergency conditions of war, newspapers were regarded by the British authorities as essential instruments of propaganda, particularly in the work of boosting and maintaining public morale. The press was by this time no stranger to the peculiar demands made of it by wartime conditions, and journalists knew well that there were both dangers and opportunities in such circumstances. The Crimean War of 1853–6 had provided much of the impetus for the early success of papers like *Yr Herald Cymraeg* that had emerged with the removal of the Stamp Act in 1855. But journalists were also aware that the war had marked the beginning of military censorship in the modern press. In 1856 a series of reports was published in John Delaney's *Times* by William Howard Russell and Thomas Chenery on the conditions endured by the British forces. These reports so disturbed readers and politicians at home, and implied such ferocious criticisms of Lord Raglan's leadership and the general mismanagement of the war that they helped to bring down a government. From that time, new rules of engagement were drawn up for reporters in the field, and one of the main functions of wartime journalism was to assist in the national mobilization of the British people in support of government. In 1889, an Official Secrets Act had threatened further to complicate the relationship between government and press. Its 'public interest' clause, however, was never tested in court, and no prosecutions were brought following the premature leak of the Report of the Welsh Church Commission in 1910. The pressure to conform to the pro-war mood of 1914 was as overwhelming in Wales as it was elsewhere in Britain, as even the most progressive of the liberal and nationalist journalists and publishers turned their talents to support the war effort.

Broadly speaking, there were three responses to the outbreak of war in 1914: uncritical support, principled opposition, and initial reluctance that very shortly was transformed into patriotic enthusiasm. On the first day of the war, the *Western Mail* printed a cartoon, 'The Call of Patriotism', depicting Dame Wales blowing her patriotic horn. 'Welshmen!', read the text, 'In the hours of danger our Navy asks for coal. It shall not ask in vain. We will show the world that the blast of my horn, resounding in the hills of Wales, can be responded to by men as patriotic as any the world can boast!' The decision by the South Wales Miners' Federation to advise their members not to forgo the summer holidays by opening the pits for war production lent additional poignancy to the Dame's appeal to national pride, and in the years that followed numerous references were to be made to the participation in the war of the 'Loyal Sons of Wales'.[1] Support for the war was by no means confined to the *Western Mail* nor to the English-language press. *Welsh Outlook* and O. M. Edwards's

Cymru, along with the denominational weeklies *Y Tyst* and *Y Goleuad*, also strongly supported the government, although the latter, under the editorship of E. Morgan Humphreys, did so rather more critically than most.

Among opponents of the war were *Seren Gomer* and *Y Gwleidydd Newydd*. Thomas Rees's *Y Deyrnas* was started in Barmouth in October 1916 by a group of Welsh intellectuals that included T. Gwynn Jones and T. H. Parry-Williams specifically in order to campaign against the war. It was distributed throughout Wales, and its organizers maintained close links with the ILP and the No Conscription Fellowship, but its circulation of some two and a half thousand did not mount much of a challenge to the dominant pro-war sentiments of the majority of titles that circulated in Wales in the war years.[2] Explicitly anti-war newspapers met with little favour, and among those that collapsed in the new environment may be included the *Daily Citizen*, which ceased publication in London in March 1915 and in Manchester three months later.

Liberal newspapers whose editors were either initially ambivalent about the war, or even hostile to it, faced crises of conscience and credibility at the onset of war, but many changed allegiances rapidly during its early weeks or months. The *Daily News*, despite A. G. Gardiner's anti-Russian instincts, was soon converted from neutrality to a pro-British position, and in Wales a similar process was also underway. Frederick Coplestone's *Herald* group of papers in Caernarfon, for example, advocated the standard Liberal anti-war arguments on 4 August 1914, arguing that 'the Tory Party is the party of the arms manufacturers, and they are the only ones who will make their fortunes through blood-letting.' On 11 August, however, the *Herald* papers printed Lloyd George's 'Appeal to Wales', and by 18 August Coplestone had acquired a 'special telegraph service' to improve his paper's war coverage. By 13 October, the papers openly supported Lloyd George and the war's 'defence of small nations'. Enlistment notices appeared from 8 December 1914, and the transition was complete with the first heavily jingoistic pro-war leader on 22 December. Coplestone remained a staunch defender of Lloyd George (who according to Lord Beaverbrook, enjoyed 'a good press as a shopkeeper likes a good customer')[3] throughout the war and in the election that followed in 1918. In these and other Liberal papers in Wales,

Lloyd George was given strong support over his break with the *Daily News* over the issue of conscription, and more generally in his criticisms of Asquith's leadership particularly following the Dardanelles Expedition.

Materially, it was thought that the war offered opportunities for the daily press to regain the Victorian pre-eminence within Wales that was being lost to the London papers. The *Western Mail* advised its readers in September 1914 that, unlike their London competitors, they could publish and distribute official announcements and other news at shorter notice. The weekly version of the paper, they suggested, was perfect for sending to 'friends abroad'.[4] In practice, however, the weekly and daily press in Wales faced severe difficulties as the war progressed. Paper rationing, introduced as a result of the shortage of imported newsprint, gas shortages and the scarcity of metal, led, according to one Welsh journalist, to the most difficult years that newspapers had ever experienced – 'it was no wonder that so many journals ceased publication.'[5] Reductions in the number of pages and price increases saved many papers from bankruptcy, whilst others, like the *Daily Herald*, were obliged to switch to weekly publication following a catastrophic fall in advertisement income. But weekly papers were also very vulnerable. Fred Hodson of the *Western Mail* warned his staff early in the war that if papers were to go to the wall, the weeklies would go first. The country, he predicted, 'cannot live without daily papers, however long the war will last.'[6]

War also led to pressure being exerted on editors and publishers to conform to the pro-war consensus through the control of content. Defence of the Realm Acts were passed between August 1914 and March the following year, and in 1914 a Press Bureau, headed by Sir Stanley Buckmaster, was established in order to provide the government with a means of channelling and co-ordinating war news. A Foreign Office News Department was also established. A number of newspaper editors, including Lord Riddell of the *Western Mail*, protested vigorously against the new state powers over information embodied in the new press departments, but others were more sanguine. Within the first fortnight of the war, the editor of the *Merthyr Express* declared his support for the new state policy by advocating that 'the control and censorship of war news by the government is a great boon for the public . . . It will prevent the publication of flesh-creeping, jumpy despatches . . . All news not authenticated by the Press Bureau must be accepted with the traditional grain of salt.'[7] Editors began to receive Defence Notices from 1915, listing security-sensitive issues that required the advice of the censors before publication, which introduced a further, though self-regulating, element of news control in the British press.

In this changed climate, the Sunday papers generally sold well, particularly those with high pictorial content. The absence of a Welsh Sunday paper led to an increased demand for imported Sunday papers, and the *News of the World*, with its close connection with the *Western Mail*, increased substantially its market share in south Wales. It was also during the course of the war that the growing popularity of the Sunday papers began seriously to erode Nonconformist Sabbatarian opposition to their publication and distribution. The war had intensified public interest in news in general, and in political journalism in particular, but the demand for newspapers increased just as economic pressures created difficulties in their production. An assessment of newspaper readerships published in 1931 concluded that 'the universal habit of newspaper reading . . . dates from the war . . . Only a proportion of the population previously regarded newspapers as a necessity. They were a luxury . . . making no very urgent demand upon the attention of democracy.'[8] The war turned newspapers into essential commodities, at home and at the front. The Revd Tom Nefyn poignantly recollected how the soldiers in his company received, read and passed on to other readers their newspapers in the trenches of France in 1915: *Yr Udgorn* for those from Pwllheli, *Yr Herald* and *Dinesydd* for soldiers from elsewhere in Gwynedd and the *Weekly News* for those from Dyffryn Conwy.[9]

The end of the war in 1918, however, did not bring much improvement to the newspaper industry in Wales. Shortages of imported newsprint continued, with the subsequent inevitable increases in prices. *The Times*, for example, raised its cover price to threepence in March 1918. Higher prices in turn affected pre-war patterns of newspaper consumption within different social classes. Throughout Britain, the effect of the war was to accelerate the process of concentrating the ownership of the press, and provincial journalism in particular entered a period of decline. By 1919 the British provincial press faced serious difficulties, largely as a result of the combination of the loss of advertisment revenue to the national dailies, and rapidly increasing production costs. By expanding their regional editions, many metropolitan papers seized on the opportunity to utilize their considerable advantages in terms of production costs and methods, and access to information, to compete more directly with the provincial newspapers. Thus the provincial dailies in particular were obliged to acknowledge, and, if they could, respond to, competition from papers that possessed vastly superior financial and journalistic resources.[10] Faced with falling incomes and spiralling costs, many provincial papers throughout Britiain were either closed or were reorganized as chain editions. Furthermore, it was clear to many local editors that after the war their papers had lost much of their former value as party political organs. The changed political conditions brought about by the war, and the divisions within the Liberal party, subjected Liberal journalists to what Stephen Koss termed a 'numbing perplexity that split their directorates and muddled their editorial views'. This 'atmospheric change' in the condition of post-war journalism could most clearly be seen in the new pattern of concentrated ownership, so much so that by the election of 1918 Gardiner could observe that 'a dinner table for six will seat all the men who control nine-tenths of the Press opinion of the country'. These men, Northcliffe, Rothermere, Beaverbrook, Riddell, Dalziel and Hulton, comprised what Stephen Koss referred to as 'Lloyd George's Press Agency . . . his bodyguard'.[11]

In local journalism, Liberals like Morrell were eager to maintain in the twentieth century the political supremacy won in the provinces in the nineteenth. Even if leading articles in the 1920s were judged to be less influential than they had been in the pre-war period, he argued that the 'tone' remained of 'enormous political value'. At this time, however, the Liberal press was being trained not so much on the traditional Conservative enemy, but on the emerging Labour Party that threatened to usurp their entrenched supremacy in the industrial constituencies. In the new post-war political world, the style of political journalism had changed decisively. Much of the coverage of Wales in the national press was reduced to the affairs of David Lloyd George. Asquith complained in June 1921 that the *Daily News* gave more 'space and prominence to some remarks made in Welsh by Lloyd

George to a lot of Calvinist parsons,' than to his own speeches.[12] Grey of Falloden acknowledged the new political style of the newspapers, and admitted sadly that 'as to politics I am not the sort of person that is wanted now . . . Lloyd George is the modern type, suited to an age of telephones and moving pictures and modern journalism.'[13]

The ownership of newspapers had been changing for some time before 1920. In 1913 Robert Donald, then President of the Institute of Journalists, noted with regret the ending, in the previous twenty years, of the old proprietorial system. 'Instead of individual ownership', he complained, 'we have corporations, public and private.'[14] In 1893 no newspaper corporation was listed on the London Stock Exchange, but by 1913 twelve large newspaper-owning companies, and twenty-six newspaper limited liability companies were registered. The growth of advertising in the Edwardian period, which signalled a renewal of capital investment in the industry, had contributed substantially to this process. Profits from advertising accelerated in the years following the end of the First World War, and in 1928 Associated Newspapers made more than £3 million from newspaper advertising alone. By the end of the 1920s it was clear that the press had become 'a vast mechanism for making profits'.[15]

In Wales in the 1920s, the number of titles, which had increased steadily since 1855, began to decline sharply.

Year	*English-language titles*	*Welsh-language titles*
1914	119	20
1920	131	21
1930	116	18
1940	112	14
1950	105	9
1960	101	8

(Source: Mitchell's and Benn's *Press Directories*, 1914–1960)

The forty years between 1920 and 1960 witnessed a net decrease of thirty titles, eighteen of them disappearing in the 1920s alone, and a further twelve in the 1940s, both immediate post-war periods. The proportion of Welsh-language titles fell from 17 per cent in 1914 to 8 per cent in 1960. By 1920 a large number of provincial papers were up for sale, and one observer predicted that the majority would be bought either by more successful local rivals or by local politicians. Profit margins in local newspapers were too narrow to attract the interest of businessmen, and increased production costs put them effectively out of the reach of most working journalists. Consequently, titles either disappeared or became the properties of a declining number of owners.

The inter-war concentration of ownership in Wales followed closely the broader British pattern. By 1918 the Welsh coalowner, D. A. Thomas, Viscount Rhondda, had acquired control, 'financially though not politically', of the *Western Mail*. He also owned the *South Wales Journal of Commerce*, *Y Faner,* the *North Wales Times, Y Tyst*, *Y Darian,* the *Cambrian News*, the *Merthyr Express* and the five editions of the *Pontypridd Observer*. Control had been acquired over these previously independent papers through the purchase of their companies, namely Gee and Son., Cambrian News Ltd, South Wales Printing and Publishing Co. Ltd, H. W. Southey and Son, The Tarian Printing and Publishing Co., and the family businesses of P. S. Phillips and J. Williams. These titles were then purchased by Henry Seymour Berry, and formed part of a huge empire that extended from Wales to cover the whole of Britain and to compete with the most powerful of the inter-war press barons. Henry Berry, the eldest of three brothers, was born in 1877, the son of a Merthyr estate agent. In 1916, on D. A. Thomas's appointment to the Lloyd George War Cabinet, Henry Berry effectively took command of his entire business, which included the vast Cambrian Combine coal operation. In 1924, the Berry Llewelyn-Rhondda group was described as 'the most powerful capitalist combination in the South Wales coalfield', whose interests extended like 'red threads through the mesh of capitalism in South Wales as in a tangled skein, [and] it is impossible to say where they begin and where they end.'[16] Among these interests were, of course, the press. From D. A. Thomas and Henry Berry (later Lord Buckland of Bwlch), these papers passed on to Henry Berry's two younger brothers, William Ewart Berry, ennobled as Lord Camrose in 1929, and Gomer Berry, ennobled as Viscount Kemsley in 1936, whose business partnership lasted until 1937. William Ewart Berry started his journalistic career in 1893 as a fourteen-year-old apprentice with the *Merthyr Tydfil Times*. He left Wales for London in 1898, and, with Gomer Berry, established the immensely profitable *Advertising World* in 1902. By 1915, they had acquired the *Sunday Times*, and in 1924 bought from Lord Rothermore the *Daily Dispatch*, the *Sporting and Evening Chronicle*, and the *Empire News*, through their holding company, Allied Newspapers Ltd. One direct response to the rapid expansion of the Berry empire into the provincial press was the establishment in 1928 of Rothermere's Northcliffe Newpapers Ltd., but despite this competition, the Berry brothers went on to buy the *Financial Times*, the *Daily Graphic* and the Cassell publishing business.

In 1928 William Ewart and Gomer Berry turned their attentions to Wales and bought the Liberal newspapers of the Duncan family, comprising the *South Wales Daily News*, the *South Wales Echo* and the *Cardiff Times*, and incorporated them into the Conservative *Western Mail*. The economic logic of the takeover was clear, since the *Western Mail* was easily the leading morning paper while the *South Wales Daily News* was a steady loser. Conversely, Duncan's *Echo* was far more successful than the Berrys's *Evening Express*. The Berry brothers reasoned that the south Wales market could sustain one morning paper and one evening paper but not two of each.[17] But the political implications of the takeover were also obvious, at least to the purchasers, who saw it as a means of driving 'another nail in the coffin of the Liberals'.[18]

The ownership of newspapers in Wales had never been so concentrated, and the takeovers of the 1920s inaugurated a period of intense competition for the large and industrial south Wales market. Rothermere's purchase of two Swansea newspapers, the Liberal *Cambria Daily Leader* and the Conservative *South Wales Daily Post*, both in 1929, intensified the conflict between the two giant companies, Northcliffe Newspapers and the Berrys's Allied Newspapers, who were by now also competing in virtually every city in the United Kingdom.[19] The *Post* had been established as a rival to the much older *Leader*, and had at one stage been subsidised by Lord Melchett when, as Sir Alfred Mond, he sat as a Swansea MP. At the end of the 1920s the Berry brothers controlled twenty-six daily and Sunday papers and the assets of Amalgamated Press, whilst Lord Rothermere controlled fourteen, with interests in another three. A truce was finally called in the early 1930s, and Northcliffe Newspapers was liquidated in 1932 following a mutual agreement with the Berry brothers that effectively carved Britain up into newspaper monopolies. In

Wales the terms of the agreement stipulated that Rothermere would stay out of Cardiff, whilst the Berrys recognized south-west Wales as a Rothermere 'fiefdom'.[20] The conflict over ownership was accompanied by a circulation war, the methods of which raised for some contemporary observers 'very curious problems in newspaper ethics'. These included the offers of free insurance, first made by Northcliffe, prize competitions, lotteries, 'guessing competitions' and 'coupon competitions', and various stunts. Owners' reluctance to increase prices in this period of intense competition for market share meant that newspapers became even more heavily dependent on advertising revenues.[21]

The agreement between the Northcliffe and Allied companies in 1932 consolidated the control of the two media empires in Wales, and strengthened the links between the major Welsh dailies and other British publishing firms. Western Mail Ltd., formed in 1896 and with a capital of £196,000 in 1928, thus had strong links not only with the Berry Group through Lords Buckland and Riddell, both of whom were directors of the *News of the World*, but also, again through Riddell, with George Newness Ltd, and C. Arthur Pearson Ltd. By 1936 the Berry Group owned four British national papers and forty-nine provincial newspapers that included the *Western Mail*, the *South Wales Evening Express*, the *Weekly Mail* and the *Cardiff Times*,[22] whereas the Daily Mail and Daily Mirror Group owned the *South Wales Daily Post* and the *Cambria Daily Leader*. In January 1937, the Berry newspaper empire was divided, Camrose taking the Amalgamated Press, with a capital of £6.2 million, and fifty-eight weekly papers, twenty-one monthlies and a controlling interest in the *Financial Times* and the *Daily Telegraph*; and Kemsley taking Allied Newspapers, which he renamed Kemsley Newspapers in 1943, and the *Sunday Times*. The latter, including all its Welsh holdings, was sold to Roy Thomson in 1958.

Another group of three brothers, the Cardiff-born Cudlipps, also emerged from the world of Welsh journalism in the 1920s to leave a lasting mark on the British press, the three editing competing Fleet Street national papers in the 1930s. Percy Cudlipp began as a reporter on the *South Wales Echo*, and moved to Manchester before taking over as editor of the *Evening Standard* in 1933 and editorial manager of the *Daily Herald* between 1940 and 1953. He was also the founding editor of the *New Scientist* in 1956. Reginald Cudlipp, apprenticed on the *Penarth Herald*, rose to be a sub-editor on the *Western Mail* before transferring to the *News of the World* in 1938, and Hugh Cudlipp, followed the same route from Cardiff via Manchester to be editor of the *Sunday Pictorial* (now the *Sunday Mirror*) in 1937, at the age of twenty-four. He was later chairman of the Mirror Group, and succeeded Cecil King as chairman of the world's largest publishing business, the International Publishing Corporation. Known as the 'Prince of the Tabloids', he was made a life peer in 1974. Michael John Cudlipp, Percy Cudlipp's son, was born in Kent but trained at his father's old paper, the *South Wales Echo* in Cardiff, where he worked as a trainee reporter, feature writer, gossip columnist and sub-editor from 1953 to 1957. Following the same route through Manchester to London, he was appointed deputy editor of *The Times* in 1967, and became chief editor of the London Broadcasting Corporation Co. in 1973.[23]

The concentration of ownership in Wales mirrored developments elsewhere in Britain, and other mergers in the 1930s included the amalgamation of the *Daily Chronicle* with the *Daily Citizen* in 1930. The political implications of this process was not lost on contemporaries, but in London the increase in the power of the Conservative dailies was matched to some extent at least by the relative success of the liberal and left-wing weeklies: Kingsley Martin for example referred to the 1930s as 'the great age of the weeklies'. There were some such developments in Wales, though in general terms the press in the inter-war years saw a consolidation of the power of the Conservative owners.[24] Competition continued to cut into the profit margins of the weeklies, and drove out many of the struggling papers. In north Wales, ambitious plans to turn *Y Genedl Gymreig* into a national newspaper were frustrated, and the papers of the *Genedl* group were incorporated into the *Herald* company in 1932. In 1937 it was estimated that nearly 20 per cent of newspapers were operating at a deficit.[25]

Fears were expressed from the 1920s onwards that the new pattern of ownership was changing the political balance of south Wales. Sir Alfred Robbins warned in 1928 that 'if newspaper enterprises were concentrated in very few hands – and the shrinkage through combination has of late been very striking – an independent vehicle for the expression of opinion would cease to exist', and pressed the need for a 'widely centred Press'.[26] Jane Soames declared even more explicitly in 1936 her belief that 'If you know who owns the Press, you will know also what to expect from it . . . the Press only prints what its owners permit.'[27] In Wales, however, the picture was far from clear, and there is evidence that politicians from all parties were exercised by the consequences of a process of political 'de-control' in the new commercial dispensation. One unsuccessful Tory candidate at an election in Swansea West attributed his poor showing to the fact that the Rothermere papers had summarily abandoned him in favour of the Liberal candidate, and Camrose lamented the passing of the older methods of political control when he reported to Baldwin that he had no doubt that had his brother Buckland, who died in 1928, been alive, the electoral results 'would have been different in at least three seats in South Wales'.[28]

Alternatives to the dailies and the surviving weeklies did exist, and, in relative terms, flourished in the inter-war period. Many of these new productions were brought out by the institutions of the Welsh Left, and they coincided with a period of growth for the socialist press throughout Britain. The *Herald* resumed daily publication on 31 March 1919, and the belief that peace meant a return to pre-war practices and partisanship in the press was particularly strong in Labour and trade union circles. The communist *Daily Worker* circulated from 1930, with George Thomas of Treherbert acting as its south Wales correspondent, and contained an occasional Welsh page.[29] But a wealth of locally produced socialist papers also appeared, most notably from the trade unions. The miners' union produced two official journals, the *Colliery Workers' Magazine* from 1923 to 1927, and the *Miners' Monthly*, a revived South Wales Miners' Federation newsletter which lasted from 1934 until 1939. In addition, important unofficial organs, following the tradition of such pamphlets as *The Miners' Next Step* of 1912, included pit papers such as the *Bedwas Rebel* in the early 1920s, and the *Cwmtillery Searchlight*, associated with the Minority Movement in the mid-1930s. The *South Wales Miner* ran from 1933 to 1935, and was edited and produced by Arthur Horner and others in the miners' Rank and File Movement. Like many papers of its kind in the nineteenth as well as the twentieth centuries, it was continually in financial difficulty. Horner even counted the words so as to be sure to be able to afford the printing. Much of the distribution also devolved on the one individual, and Horner recalled that '. . . when the paper arrived, I used to parcel it up, take it to the stations to be sent to the lodges all over the coalfields. We had a circulation of about three thousand . . . but it was read by nearly half the active trade unionists in the area, and I think it had a lot to do with my victory when I came to stand for the Presidency.'[30] The Labour party continued its presence in the post-war Welsh press with *Y Dinesydd Cymreig*, which remained extant until 1929, and, in south Wales, with such papers as the *Rhondda Clarion* in the mid-1930s. The Communist party also produced its own press in Wales, most notably the Rhondda *Vanguard*, started in 1935 and reaching a circulation of some eight thousand.[31]

Relations between the labour movement and the Welsh daily press were strained. Reporters told of being threatened by Maerdy miners, where they were regarded with hostility as outsiders. The *South Wales Daily News* famously referred to Maerdy as 'Little Moscow', and both it and the *Western Mail* were banned from the Maerdy Institute during the General Strike of 1926 on the grounds that they were printed by scab labour, and local newsagents were asked not to distribute them.[32] In May 1926 Aneurin Bevan delivered a mock funeral oration at the public burning of several dozen copies of the *Western Mail* on a hillside in Waunpond, between Ebbw Vale and Tredegar.[33] In May 1927, A. J. Cook denounced the newspapers of south Wales as 'the dirtiest and the most vile press in the country.' Two years later, and incensed by the police baton charge on the miners and the subsequent house searches at Nine Mile Point, Bevan blamed the 'criminal lying of the South Wales press'. If anyone was to be charged for the violence, Bevan argued, it should have been the editor of the *Western Mail*. In the mid-1930s, the *Western Mail* continued to blame industrial unrest on 'red plots', secret societies and paid agitators.[34]

A revived nationalist press also came into being in the inter-war period. In Aberystwyth the student paper *Y Wawr*, edited by Ambrose Bebb, was banned by the college authorities as a result of its editor's attacks on the British state. Shortly later, nationalists briefly adopted the Breton *Breiz Atao* as their official journal, which included a Welsh-language column edited by Bebb. Mainstream nationalism, however, continued to be expressed principally in *Y Genhinen* and *Y Faner*, the latter edited in Aberystwyth by Edward Prosser Rhys, (a founder member of the nationalist party), from 1923 until his death in 1945. D. Hywel Davies, the historian of the nationalist movement, regards this as evidence that early nationalism was exclusively Welsh-speaking. In June 1926, less than a year after the founding of the nationalist party, the new monthly *Y Ddraig Goch* was launched, though the English-language *Welsh Nationalist* was not started until 1932.[35]

Other political movements depended on a press produced outside Wales. There was some fascist activity in Cardiff, Swansea, Pontypridd, Merthyr, Aberdare, Tonypandy and elsewhere in the 1920s, and although some of the Rothermere papers lent their support to Sir Oswald Mosley in the mid-1930s, and such party papers as the *Blackshirt*, the *Fascist*, the *Patriot* or the *New Witness* were distributed by fascist supporters, there is little evidence to suggest that either the New Party or the British Union of Fascists produced their own papers in Wales.[36]

It would be misleading to suggest that all alternative newspapers and periodicals were explicitly political in character. A new cultural press also appeared during the 1930s, including John Eilian's *Y Ford Gron* from 1930 to 1935, *Wales*, edited by Keidrych Rhys, from the summer of 1937 to the outbreak of the Second World War (a second series followed between July 1943 and October 1949), the *Welsh Review*, edited by Gwyn Jones from February 1939 to the winter of 1948, and *Heddiw*, produced by Aneirin ap Talfan from 1936 to 1942. Nor should amateur productions be neglected. The tradition of children's journalism, started by the denominational journals in the mid-nineteenth century was continued nationally by O. M. Edwards's *Cymru'r Plant* and locally by such publications as *Y Crwt*, written and produced by the children of Llanfrothen primary school between 1922 and 1926 under the guidance of the headmaster, novelist, dramatist and film-maker John Ellis Williams.[37]

But such Welsh-produced papers of the inter-war years were, in market terms, overshadowed by the dailies and mainstream weeklies, and differences between the alternative and mainstream press was greater than at any time in the previous century. One aspect of this separation was the continuing professionalization of journalism. Partially in recognition of this fact, journalists' salaries nearly trebled between 1914 and 1928, but the disparity between pay levels in London and the provinces also increased and was the cause of much resentment.[38] Adequate training also became a prerequisite for work in journalism, and R. D. Blumenfeld, chairman of the *Daily Express*, announced in 1929 that, 'You can no more present to the world a first-class all round journalist without long and careful training, than you can expect to find a great painter, or musician or physician who has had no previous experience.'[39] New schools of journalism were established, including a two-year diploma in journalism at London University, a Premier School of Journalism in the Adelphi, and in 1919 Lord Northcliffe, along with Lords Dalziel, Riddell, Beaverbrook, Harmsworth and the first Director, Max Pemberton, founded the London School of Journalism. A Society of Women Journalists was established in January 1923, with its journal the *Woman Journalist* displaying its devotion to 'Patriotism and Progress'. Members of the council included Viscountess Rhondda and Viscountess Northcliffe, and the society was subsidised by, among others, Lord Riddell and Sir William Berry. A 'women's news service' was also established by the society, but its attempts to reconcile the National Union of Journalists and the Institute of Journalists failed. However, it did serve to highlight the role of women in journalism, though there remained few equivalents in Wales of such major Irish journalists as Susan Carpenter or Charlotte O'Connor Eccles.[40] But the self-image of journalism from the 1930s originated as much in Hollywood as in the training schools. Dylan Thomas, who had joined the *South Wales Daily Post* after leaving school in July 1931, later recalled how as a cub reporter he had 'tried to slouch like a newshawk, even when he was attending a meeting of the Gorseinon Buffalos . . .'[41] Further training initiatives were undertaken by the National Council for the Training of Journalists, set up in 1952 by the Guild of British Newspaper Editors, the NUJ and the IOJ to provide both vocational and academic education, and by University College, Cardiff, which began its journalism course in October 1970 under the founding directorship of Tom Hopkinson. A similar initiative, based on the Cardiff course, was launched by City University, London, in 1976.

During the inter-war years the press in Wales had undergone very considerable changes in terms of its ownership, the diversity of its titles, and its circulation. The coming of the motor van and the further improvement of the road network had further facilitated its distribution, and at the same time enabled newspapers from England, particularly from London, to penetrate further the Welsh market. The new technological and social environment inaugurated by the First World War and consolidated in the 1920s and 1930s led inexorably to a very different kind of newspaper industry in the post-war world. The events of 1939 to 1945, and their longer term consequences, brought their own particular pressures to bear on the Welsh press which distorted further the pattern of ownership and control that had evolved during the previous century. The most immediate danger came from German aerial bombardment of newspaper offices and their printing departments. Twice in 1941 Luftwaffe bombing prevented the production of the *Western Mail* and the *South Wales Echo* in Cardiff and the *South Wales Evening Post* in Swansea, and led to all three papers being transferred for printing purposes to the offices of the *South Wales Evening Argus* in Newport, thus briefly bringing the entire Welsh daily press into production under one roof. On March 3 1941, unexploded bombs were discovered around the *Western Mail* offices, and the presses were run slowly throughout the night to avoid vibration. During this wartime emergency, reporters of the *Western Mail* and the *Echo* made their headquarters in the offices of the Rugby Football Club in the Cardiff Arms Park, while the advertising staff made do with an air-raid shelter.[42]

But attacks by enemy aircraft were not the only problem with which the wartime press had to contend. Censorship was introduced to cover all forms of communication by the Emergency Powers (Defence) Act of 1940, and a Regional Office of the Chief Press Censor was immediately established in Cardiff. The call-up into the armed forces caused a serious depletion of the ranks of both reporting and printing staff, and given the priorities of war production, the replacement of printing plant became virtually impossible to secure. But the greatest difficulty faced by newspapers was the supply of newsprint. The Control of Paper Order 16 stipulated that no new newspaper or periodical could be printed, and its terms restricted the publication of existing newspapers to their pre-1940 frequency and prohibited the production of posters to advertise newspapers. Furthermore, Paper Order 36, issued in November 1941, controlled precisely the amount of paper a newspaper could consume. As a result of these Orders, the total British consumption of newsprint at the height of the war was reduced to only 20.33 per cent of the pre-war figure.[43] One consequence of this was a sharp reduction in commercial display advertising, and a switch to small advertisements, which led to the further diminution of newspaper revenues.[44]

Paper shortages remained acute for some time after the end of the war in 1945, and as late as 1948 new Paper Control Regulations limited paper supply for new newspapers and journals to a 'printers' quota' of eight hundredweight for each four-month period, which effectively pegged their maximum circulations at around four thousand copies per month. Paid advertisements, furthermore, were not allowed to exceed 20 per cent of the total printing space of any newspaper.[45] Moreover, the cost of newsprint trebled between 1939 and 1962. The consequences of the war for the Welsh newspaper industry had become clear by 1948, by which time the numbers of both morning and evening daily papers had been halved since 1921, morning papers from two to one, and evening dailies from four to two. The number of weekly titles in Wales (excluding Monmouthshire) had also been reduced from 106 in 1921 to 95 in 1937 and to 88 in 1947. The reduction in the number of titles between 1921 and 1947 of 16.9 per cent compared well with the English figure of 23.2 per cent, though rather less well with the Scottish figure of 15.3 per cent.[46]

However, despite the war, and the resulting newsprint shortages and staff losses, there remained in Wales a newspaper press that was reported by the Royal Commission on the Press in 1949 to be 'still very numerous and of great variety'. Local weekly newspapers were still being published in fifty-five provincial towns, and R. T. Jenkins could observe of Caernarfon in 1955 that 'smells of paper and ink still rise to the nostrils'.[47] Newspaper circulations in general increased substantially during and after the war. In Britain as a whole, the daily sales of provincial morning papers rose from 1.7 million copies at the outbreak of the war in 1939 to 3.3 million in June 1947, and the circulations of provincial evening papers rose from 5.2 million to 7.2 million in the same period. By 1947, it was estimated that one hundred thousand copies of British national dailies were being sent to Cardiff for distribution in south Wales.[48]

The relative circulations of British national newspapers, Welsh dailies and weeklies and Welsh-language papers can be seen in microcosm in the town of Tregaron, Cardiganshire, (population in 1951, 5,450) in 1946. Virtually every home in Tregaron received at least one daily newspaper from a wide range of titles on offer in the town's two newsagents, whilst in the farms and cottages of the outlying areas reading habits tended to favour the weeklies. The range of papers supplied by the newsagents were as follows:

Dailies	*Copies sold*	*Weeklies*	*Copies sold*
Western Mail	139	Welsh Gazette	347
Daily Mirror	58	Cambrian News	14
News Chronicle	46	Weekly Mail	21
Daily Express	40	John Bull	39
Daily Mail	19	Radio Times	108
Daily Telegraph	8	Listener	3
Daily Sketch	6	Y Cymro	30
Times	3	Y Faner	9

The newsagents also sold in addition to these a further 264 copies of women's journals, nine religious titles (nineteen copies in English and 105 in Welsh), 106 trade journals, sixty children's papers, twenty-eight Sunday newspapers, and thirty-five copies of other miscellaneous titles.

The Tregaron survey reveals two apparent anomalies in the pattern of consumption. The first was that, in an overwhelmingly Welsh-speaking town, the reading of Welsh-language periodicals was almost entirely confined to the religious press, and the second was the popularity in a Liberal town, birthplace of Henry Richard, of the Conservative papers, particularly the *Western Mail* and *John Bull*. Emrys Jones, the social anthropologist who conducted the survey, surmised that 'the politics of the *Western Mail* has little interest to the people of Tregaron, and even its news is criticized', but its advantage was that it contained good coverage of Welsh news. The popularity of *John Bull* was explained simply in terms of the insurance policies which the paper had issued before the war, and which were kept carefully by its readers and on which claims were not infrequently made. This provided, Jones concluded, 'the supreme example of the lack of correlation between the political views of the purchaser and those of the paper'. But the range of periodical reading was, Jones found, a relatively recent phenomenon in Tregaron, which to a substantial extent had replaced the previously more prevalent practice of reading Welsh-language books.[49]

The preference for local or regional newspapers over national ones remained strong for a considerable period after 1946. In February 1959, for example, the Newspaper Society's Regional Readership Survey among housewives in Wales revealed the continuing dominance of local newspapers.

Area	*any local paper (%)*	*local evening (%)*	*local weekly (%)*	*local morning (%)*
Glamorgan and Monmouth	81	53	45	13
North Wales	88	17	84	19
Central and west Wales	87	20	84	30

The proportion of those reading local newspapers was higher than that of the nine national morning newspapers combined. Of these, the *Daily Mirror* led with 29 per cent followed by the *Daily Express* with 25 per cent, but these were the only two national morning newspapers that were more popular than the regional morning newspapers. In geographical terms, an average of about one Welsh housewife in six was found to have read a local morning newspaper the day before the interview, and in central and south Wales the corresponding figure was almost one in three. In all rural areas almost one in four housewives was found to have read a local morning newspaper. In terms of social class, 40 per cent of AB housewives read local morning papers, and 28 per cent of housewives in C. Only one national newspaper, the *Daily Express*, with a C1 class coverage of 29 per cent, exceeded this figure.[50] As late as 1977 it was found that in Wales and south west England 45 per cent of adults read a local weekly, 30 per cent an evening paper and 13 per cent a regional morning newspaper.[51]

The continuing popularity of local weekly newspapers can partially at least be attributed to the availability of a wide range of local papers. Unlike the nineteenth century, however, many of these had by the middle of the twentieth century been amalgamated into newspaper groups or chains, and were owned, produced and distributed by a small group of companies. The South Wales Weekly Argus Ltd., for example, produced an evening as well as a weekly version of their newspaper, and the latter was published in twelve local editions, each of which contained some pages carrying news of the district in which it circulated. All the editions, however, were produced in one office by the same editorial and production staff that produced the evening paper.[52]

The substitution of chain editions for independent local newspapers disguised the overall reduction in the diversity of the press. Some independent family businesses, and even some individual editor-proprietors, continued to exist, but increasingly, as the 1949 Royal Commission on the Press discovered, the larger undertakings, including of course the chain papers, were owned 'by big joint-stock companies'.[53] Some of these had already created local, or 'simple', monopolies. Kemsley, for example, which by 1943 was the largest newspaper owner in Britain, had long since owned the two Cardiff dailies, and in so doing had gained control over half of the daily newspapers published in Wales in 1949. Camrose, owner of the *Daily Telegraph*, also had interests in the *Merthyr Express* and the *Pontypridd Observer*.[54] By the early 1960s, the landscape had changed yet again. Thomson Scottish Associates Ltd., owners of the *Sunday Times*, owned, through Thomson Investment Holdings Ltd., the Western Mail and Echo Ltd., H. W. Southey and Sons Ltd. (*Merthyr Express* and its editions in Aberdare, Rhymney Valley and west Monmouth), the Glamorgan County Times Newspaper and Printing Co Ltd. (publishers of *Glamorgan County Times*, *Rhondda Leader*, *Rhondda Fach Leader* and *Porth Gazette*), the Rhondda Valleys Newspapers Ltd. (publishers of the *Pontypridd Observer* and the *Llantrisant Observer*) and the Celtic Press Ltd.[55]

By the 1960s, five major newspaper groups dominated the Welsh press. In south-east Wales, the South Wales Argus Ltd., a private company established in Newport in 1892 by Sir A. Garrod Thomas with shares owned by individuals unconnected with any other newspaper, though it later became a subsidiary of United Newspapers, published a group of eleven local editions of its Newport-based daily. In Cardiff, Thomson Regional Newspapers Ltd. retained control over the *Western Mail* and local editions of the *South Wales Echo* and expanded its weekly newspaper interests by acquiring five more weeklies in west Wales and in

Mid Glamorgan, where it provided three-quarters of the weekly circulation. In Gwent, however, Thomson's weekly interests were slight compared with those of South Wales Argus.

In south-west Wales, the Swansea Press Ltd., a subsidiary of Associated Newspapers, published the *South Wales Evening Post* and the *Herald of Wales* (which incorporated the *Cambrian*, the first Welsh weekly paper). Associated also extended its weekly interests into Dyfed by the acquisition of the *Carmarthen Journal* in 1966 and the *Llanelli Star* series in 1968. In the rural counties of mid-Wales, Woodall's Newspapers Ltd. were owners of *Y Cymro, the Wrexham Leader, the Montgomeryshire Express, the Flintshire Leader* and the *Radnor Times*. Finally, in north Wales, the North Wales Chronicle Co. Ltd. published, in addition to their main paper, editions of the *Chronicle* in Colwyn Bay, Rhyl and Holyhead, as well as *Y Clorianydd,* the *North Wales Pioneer*, and the *Flintshire Observer*. By the 1970s this company, now known as the North Wales Newspapers Ltd., and in which the Thomas family still held the majority holding, published the *Wrexham Evening Leader* and nine associated weeklies, the *Wrexham Leader*, the *Border Counties Advertiser*, the *County Times*, *Y Cymro*, the *Flintshire Leader*, the *Rhyl Journal*, the *Denbighshire Free Pioneer*, the *Colwyn Bay Pioneer* and the *North Wales Chronicle*. It had increased its share of the weekly circulation in its market area to 17 per cent by 1974, and its turnover in March 1976 was £2 million. These five companies echoed in Wales the dominance that five other newspaper groups had by that time won over the British press.[56]

The findings of the two Royal Commissions on the press in 1962 and 1977 reflect the rapid change in the pattern of ownership that had started after the First World War. In 1962, it was held that the 'concentration of ownership of local weekly newspapers is negligible', whilst fifteen years later it was stated that the 'greatest increase in the concentration of ownership' had occurred in the provincial weekly newspapers. As evidence of the latter, it was shown how the proportion of the total circulation of British newspapers controlled by the largest five companies had increased from 30.3 per cent in 1961 to 54.4 per cent in 1974, and the largest ten companies from 46.3 per cent to 74.2 per cent in the same period.

The consequences for editorial freedom of such a pattern of

ownership was also a matter of dispute. In 1947, Kemsley dismissed the idea that editors were being subjected to undue influence by proprietors, and acknowledged that his contacts with provincial papers were not as close as they were with his London papers. Proprietorial interference in editorial policies was, he argued, unnecessary since his editors were all 'men with similar ideas to [his] own and it is quite unnecessary to tell them of [his] views on a subject.' 'They know our policy,' he added, 'and they are free.' The Commissioners agreed that the concentration of ownership was 'not so great as to prejudice the free expression of opinion or the accurate presentation of news or be contrary to the best interests of the public.' Yet they readily acknowledged that there were 'inherent dangers' in local monopolies. Roy Thomson, pursuing a slightly different line of argument to that of Kemsley, argued in the same year that there were strong practical restraints on the abuse of multiple ownership, and that 'it would be bad business' to run newspapers in any other way. Consequently, most of the major proprietors 'allowed their editors a considerable degree of independence and latitude.' In 1953, a General Council of the Press, recommended by the Royal Commission of 1949, was finally established to monitor such issues. But the concentration of ownership also affected the structure of the industry itself. In evidence given by the South Wales Argus Ltd. to the 1949 Royal Commission the case was put forward that economic pressures would further diminish the diversity of ownership. One of the major threats to the survival of the industry in Wales, it was argued, was the difficulty of attracting good journalists as a result of competition from similar professions. Competing salaries in particular put 'another nail in the coffin of small papers'.[57]

Shifts in the balance of ownership thus led to considerable soul-searching and debate within the newspaper industry itself, but there is little evidence to suggest that the reading public was concerned or even aware of such developments. In the United Kingdom in 1977 only 27 per cent of a survey sample correctly identified their paper as being a Thomson-owned title, and only one in seven of those questioned about a local weekly owned by a group with national newspaper interests was able to identify correctly who owned it.[58]

One of the more visible consequences of the changing pattern of ownership, however, was the shift away from the weeklies towards the dailies. The difficulties in which weekly newspapers found themselves were clearly illustrated in the case of the Thomson weekly, the *Cardiff and South Wales Times*, that folded in May 1957. During its final years, advertising revenue fell by 10 per cent and production costs increased by 22 per cent, whilst the circulation remained static at 21,500 a week. Advertisers increasingly switched their accounts to the more attractive dailies, and the higher costs were incurred principally by increasing demands for higher pay from production staffs, all of whom were employed primarily on the printing of the Company's daily newspapers and only on a contract basis for the printing of the weekly. The paper made a loss of £4,900 in 1955, increasing to £8,250 in the following year, and its closure, without redundancies, was estimated to have saved Thomson £8,000 a year.[59] Such commercial decisions were taken by many other publishers during the 1960s, and the number of companies in Wales that published weekly papers only fell from forty-seven in 1961 to twenty in 1974. This was reflected also in the changing geography of the printing trade. By 1977, of the 183 printing establishments in Wales only twenty-eight possessed newspaper printing facilities, and even the *Western Mail* experienced difficulties in recruiting trained printing staff. In 1962 the paper was short of three compositors, five linotype operators and five stereotypers.[60] The estimated circulations of the surviving weekly newspapers in Wales increased from 680,000 in 1961 to 611,000 in 1974, but as a proportion of the total newspaper circulation, sales of the weeklies were virtually halved in the same period, falling from 52.2 per cent in 1961 to 29 per cent in 1974.[61]

The daily newspapers, on the other hand, continued to expand, with the two Thomson papers in the lead. The *South Wales Echo*, an evening paper with a circulation of 151,000 in 1961, had raised its cover price from from 2*d*. to 3*d*. in June 1956, but neither the *South Wales Argus* nor the *Swansea Evening Post* did the same. As a result, *Echo* sales fell by 15 per cent in one year, and only half of the losses were recovered in the following four years.[62] The *Western Mail*, a morning paper with a circulation of 102,000, raised its price gradually from one penny in January 1951 to 3*d*. in March 1961, but though sales fell off in 1952, its circulation increased from 82,322 in 1951 to 104,198 ten years later.[63] The Swansea-based *South Wales Evening Post*, owned by the Daily Mail and General Trust Ltd., followed with a circulation in 1961 of 72,000, and the *South Wales Argus*, also an evening paper, came fourth in the league-table with a circulation in 1961 of 51,000. Profits in these papers remained constant throughout this period, despite rising costs, thanks to the increased volume of advertising.[64]

A strong case may be made also to include the *Liverpool Daily Post* as a fifth Welsh daily. It maintained a strong circulation in north Wales, despite a more expensive cover price, and provided a good Welsh news service with eight reporters in Wales. J. R. Spencer explained in 1962 that, in common with many of their readers, the staff of the *Liverpool Daily Post* looked 'upon Liverpool as the capital of north Wales. A fair proportion of the population of Liverpool is Welsh or has Welsh ancestry. Also the people of Wales have their own weekly shopping day in Liverpool. The idea that it is the capital of north Wales is a tradition.'[65] A sixth daily, the *Wrexham Evening Leader*, was established in 1974 with a circulation of some 13,000.

Sunday newspapers were not so successful. The Kemsley-owned and Manchester-based *Empire News* started its first Cardiff-printed edition as 'Wales' Own Sunday Paper: Printed in Wales for Wales' on 3 October 1954. The first ever Sunday newspaper in Wales, it began well with a glittering array of writers. Columns were contributed by Jack Jones and, in Welsh, by Saunders Lewis, and an opening series on Welsh nationality ('Should Wales Be Free?') was initiated by Megan Lloyd George and followed by Jim Griffiths and Gwynfor Evans. It contained excellent film coverage and a lively television column, but it died suddenly in 1959 following a take-over by the *News of the World*, which had 'no plans to launch a new Sunday paper for Wales with the cost situation so problematical.'[66] Although Welsh sabbatarianism and the hostility of some of the denominational papers had played their part in the collapse of the *Empire News*, Lord Thomson insisted that it had been killed above all by economics. 'It was a strange time, indeed,' he remarked, 'in which a newspaper with a circulation of almost a million and a half could not pay its way. That was what labour and paper costs and television had done to another Kemsley paper.'[67]

Sulyn, the first Welsh-language Sunday newspaper, was launched on 17 October 1982, and survived for fourteen issues before being discontinued in January 1983. Edited in Caernarfon and printed in Welshpool, and targeted primarily at readers in Gwynedd, the paper began with a print run of 10,000 and a small staff of eleven, comprising four journalists, one illustrator, two advertising sellers, and three administrative workers. Criticized for its vernacular, *Sulyn* contained a refreshingly alternative view of the functions of the Welsh media.[68] Seven years later, on 5 March 1989, Thomson launched their own *Wales on Sunday* in Cardiff, partly in recognition of Wales's 'over-dependence on the London Press.'

Free newspapers, such as the *Leader* series in north Wales, also appeared, particularly in the 1980s, but the most remarkable development of that decade was the growth of community newspapers, especially the Welsh-language *papurau bro* which by 1990 flourished with some fifty-three titles and an estimated joint circulation of some 70,000. In many respects, the *papurau bro* continued the traditions of local nineteenth-century journalism, and had important precedents in, for example, *Seren y Mynydd*, established in 1895 by O. M. Edwards to serve Llanuwchllyn and neighbouring villages. Other publications, such as the weekly news magazine *Golwg*, have taken advantage of desk-top publishing technology to reduce production costs. The diversity of ownership that was lost in the newspaper press has thus been maintained in the magazines and other periodicals, of which there were forty-four separate titles in the Welsh language alone in 1990. The Welsh Arts Council continued to provide much coveted financial assistance to some titles, whilst others, such as *Rebecca* and *Arcade*, did not survive the early 1980s. *Y Faner*, once the leading Welsh-language newspaper, was itself discontinued in 1992. The production of periodical literature has always been a difficult and risky undertaking, but the continuing diversity of titles in post-war Wales does provide ample evidence of the resilience of a tradition of journalism that has survived since the nineteenth century, and that has actively been developed in the twentieth. The urge to publish remains as strong as ever. What has changed in the century since 1890, however, is the balance between the resources and the circulations of the major newspapers on the one hand and the more marginal, in quantitative terms, local papers and periodicals on the other. The imbalance, although often expressed in technological terms, is fundamentally an economic one that has its origins in the uneven pace of the development of Wales in relation to the other regions of the United Kingdom, and also within Wales itself. This uneveness shaped the growth of the Welsh newspaper industry in the nineteenth century, and continued to do so in the twentieth.

The press and the new media

In 1981 D. H. Simpson drew a gloomy picture of a sclerotic newspaper industry in Wales, one which had long abandoned any lingering Victorian pretensions to advance social enlightenment in favour of the vulgar simplicities of the cash nexus.[69] The transition from nineteenth- to late twentieth-century press values, however, did not proceed along such a smooth downward trajectory. In reality, at least since the removal of the Stamp and other duties in the 1850s and early 1860s, newspapers had always been at the mercy of market forces, whereas the traditions of nineteenth-century journalism survived into the twentieth century not only on the margins of the modern media, but also in important ways in its mainstream. Asked in 1977 how journalism compared with other occupations, a high proportion of journalists replied it was better as regards, *inter alia*, the 'value of the work to the community' and the 'opportunity for influencing events', both of which can be regarded as typical Victorian press values.[70] The continuity of press traditions, then, was a complex process. From the early Victorian period onwards, newspaper publishers and journalists were required to satisfy three criteria. The first was to work within an economic framework determined largely by advertisers, the second was to meet the presumed needs of their readers and thus increase or at least maintain circulation figures, and finally to be able to persuade their financial backers that they were capable of exerting a social influence. The journalist's craft developed within these often contradictory criteria and, in this sense at least, the nineteenth-century experience has provided the essential frame of reference for all the variants of modern journalism.

Twentieth-century journalism, however, can be distinguished from its nineteenth-century antecedents in one important respect, namely the emergence, particularly in the inter-war years, of new forms of communication media. Fears were commonly expressed that in the changed circumstances newspapers would 'fade away', and that journalists and readers alike would migrate to other, more immediate and more attractive forms of communication.[71] There can be no doubt that such fears were justified, and that the newspaper press was to be fundamentally changed in the course of its engagement with the new media. However, despite the new techniques and possibilities of cinema, radio and television, there existed a substantial degree of continuity between them and the traditions of print journalism that had preceded them. The historical development of journalism in the nineteenth century had created an audience, and often a highly critical one, for mass forms of communication in Wales, and had also provided the contexts, economic, political and cultural, within which the introduction of the new media could be negotiated.

Cinema emerged from the travelling shows of Walter Haggar in south Wales. Haggar made three or four films a year after 1902, and *The Salmon Poachers*, *The Mirthful Mary* series and the moralistic *Life of Charles Peace* were highly successful in and outside Wales. The distribution rights for these films were held by Gaumont except in south Wales, where they could only be shown by, or with the permission of, Haggar himself.[72] The steady growth of new outlets in the Edwardian period signified the increasing popularity of film entertainment in Wales, and by 1914 the Swansea-based Coutt's Circuit was one of only thirteen circuits throughout Britain with more than ten halls. At the beginning of the First World War, Swansea had nineteen picture theatres, and Cardiff had twenty-one. Both towns were close to the British national average for towns with populations over one hundred thousand.[73]

The growth of cinema was not unproblematic. The same concern was shown towards its possible corrupting influence as had been expressed over the proliferation of cheap newspapers in the nineteenth century. A British Board of Film Censors was established in 1912, and in 1916 the National Council of Public Morals, whose object was the 'Regeneration of the Race – Spiritual, Moral and Physical', was invited to establish a Commission of Enquiry into the social effects of the cinema, particularly on youth.[74] Their report, submitted in 1917, found that children attended the cinema 'more than any other form of public amusement', but that although films exerted a 'profound influence upon the mental and moral outlook of millions of our young people', there was no direct link between cinema and delinquency.[75] The concern was equally deep in Wales. In February 1912, the *Liverpool Daily Post* warned unambiguously of 'Animated Picture's Path to Crime' in a report on the supposed effects of the cinema on a child charged with stealing £2.15*s*. from a shop in Blaenau Ffestiniog. The magistrate explained that he had 'failed to trace anything in her home or surroundings . . . to account for the deed . . . except twice nightly animated pictures which were quite a craze with both children and grown-up persons.'[76] In December 1917, an alliance of Nonconformist denominations in Caernarfon met to try to agree a method of censoring films shown in the town, and thus to reduce 'the evil effects of undesirable cinema films . . . which are injurious to morals and encourage crime.'[77] Despite these attitudes, the popularity of cinema increased throughout the inter-war years, and Wales produced not only avid audiences, but also its own generation of stars. In 1924 Ivor Novello was voted one of Britain's 'favourite film stars' by readers of the *Daily News*. New theatres were opened throughout Wales, and a major new circuit, the Cambria and Border Cinemas, with twelve cinemas, had been established in Wrexham by the end of 1930.[78]

Cinemas competed with newspapers not only as entertainers, but also as disseminators of news. The major international companies, such as Pathé, Gaumont, Eclair and Eclipse, had distributed newsreels in the Edwardian years, but their value increased during the First World War. The 'Whirlpool of War' series revealed the exciting new possibilities, and also the limitations, of film in war reporting, and throughout the war pressure on military commanders increased to allow cameramen as well as journalists to report the war from the front lines of battle. Subsequently, *The Battle of the Somme* was filmed in action by Geoffrey Malins and J. B. McDowell in July 1916 and shown on British cinema screens the following month. The impact of this film was extraordinary, and Lloyd George, who quickly grasped its immense propaganda value, insisted 'that this picture . . . reaches everyone'. One of the more important experiments in film journalism was *The History of the Great War* series, started by Pathé in 1917 as a weekly series of half-reelers dealing with events since 1914.[79] Many of these war newsreels were characterized by an absence of comment, or indeed of any apparent editorial viewpoint.[80] By 1921, there was much talk of 'screen newspapers', and newsreels adopted such newspaper titles as *Pathé Gazette*, *Pathé Weekly Pictorial*, *Topical Budget*, *Gaumont Graphic*. Not surprisingly, the newspaper magnates began to take an interest in the new film industry, and in 1919 Lord Beaverbrook bought shares valued at £400,000 in the Provincial Cinematograph Theatres, one of the first public companies in the British film distribution business, and acquired also substantial holdings in Pathé and other companies.[81]

Drama documentaries like *Y Chwarelwr*, filmed by Sir Ifan ab Owen Edwards and John Ellis Williams in the mid-1930s, marked the extent to which cinema was extending into Welsh-language culture, whilst Donald Alexander's *Eastern Valley* and the Welsh scenes of *Today We Live* by Ralph Bond, both shot in 1937, brought the life of working-class south Wales during the Depression vividly to the attentions of cinema audiences throughout Britain.[82] Later, film was also used as a means of marketing newspapers. In 1947 and 1948, cameraman Geoff Charles and journalist John Roberts Williams shot *Gone to Press*, three publicity films for Woodall's Newspapers, publishers of *Y Cymro*, *Border Counties Advertiser* and the *Montgomeryshire Express*, which used the new technology to advertise newspapers. The same team were responsible for *Tir Na'n Og* and *Yr Etifeddiaeth*, a documentary, financed by Woodall's Newspapers, of life in Penrhyn Llŷn in 1947.

By the mid-1920s, the new media were undoubtedly beginning to challenge the dominance of print, particularly when radio arrived to complement the cinema newsreels. The history of radio in Wales began in 1897 when Marconi and Sir William Preece, the Caernarfon-born Chief Engineer of the Post Office, began to experiment by sending radio signals from Lavernock, near Penarth in Glamorganshire, to the island of Flat Holm. The British Broadcasting Company was established in 1922, and a Cardiff station of the new company was opened in February 1923.

Radio posed two separate challenges to the newspapers. The first concerned the transmission of news. Sir Roderick Jones, speaking for the news agencies to the Sykes Commission, argued that the BBC should neither collect nor arrange news, while Sir James Owen, for the Newspaper Society, insisted that the timing and content of radio news bulletins should be rigorously controlled. Lord Riddell, for the Newspaper Proprietors Association, stressed that the broadcasting of sports results would 'seriously interfere with the sale of newspapers'. Newspapers, it was feared, would become 'stale' by comparison to radio, and Riddell went on to condemn the reporting by radio of Parliamentary debates as an attempt 'to take the bread out of our mouths'.[83]

The second difficulty was that radio began to attract staff, particularly journalists, from the press, or at least to recruit from the same reservoir of writing talent that had sustained the nineteenth- and early twentieth-century newspapers. Local papers had traditionally been regarded as a training ground for journalists wishing to climb the career ladder to the Welsh dailies or the British nationals. The cost for the locals was, of course, high, as they suffered constantly from the loss of their best apprentices and even their editorial and production staffs, but the situation worsened with the coming of radio. Recruitment to the BBC began in Wales in May 1935 when nine posts were advertised in the new Welsh Region. According to the *Daily Herald*, three thousand 'ministers, teachers and bards' applied for the posts.[84] Only two of the successful candidates were journalists, namely W. Hughes Jones, Programme Director, and previously editor of the *Welsh Outlook*, and Sam Jones. Wynford Vaughan Thomas joined the service in the following year, again with little previous experience of journalism. However, experienced print journalists were soon being recruited by the Corporation. Picton Davies graduated in the 1930s from preparing BBC schedules for the *Weekly Mail* to writing radio programme scripts, and Angus McDermid, a third-generation journalist on the *North Wales Chronicle*, made his first broadcast, a football report, in 1949, and joined the BBC in 1957 as a general reporter in the home news section. As a foreign correspondent from 1963, he avoided the censors by filing sensitive reports in Welsh.[85] Many others were to make this transition from newspaper to radio and television journalism. Tommy Eyton Evans, who had risen from an apprentice to be the deputy editor of the *North Wales Weekly News*, started with the BBC as a sports editor in 1958, and in 1985 he acknowledged the debt many in the new media owed to the stepping-stone of the local papers between the 1930s and the 1960s.[86] Increasingly from the 1960s many more came from the universities, and included far larger numbers of women. Others moved freely to and fro between print journalism and the BBC. John Eilian, for example, was apprenticed as a reporter with the *Western Mail* between 1924 and 1927 before taking up the editorship of the *Times of Mesopotamia* in Basra, Iraq, and returning via the *Daily Mail* to establish *Y Ford Gron* in 1930 and *Y Cymro* in 1932. By 1934 he was editor of the *Times of Ceylon* before taking a post with the BBC, following which he supervised the *Herald* papers in Cernarfon[87]. For a young Welsh journalist of talent in the 1930s, the combination of the British Empire and the BBC could make for an eventful career. At an administrative level, Huw Wheldon, grandson of T. J. Wheldon, a Welsh Calvinistic Methodist preacher and Liberal activist, and son of a 'master of inner circles' who worked for Lloyd George's London legal practice, became Director General of the BBC in 1968.[88]

News and current affairs were only very imperfectly covered by radio in the inter-war years. Sporting events such as football and boxing were broadcast, and a number of attempts were made to reflect on Welsh industry and work. In 1935, a twelve-part series, 'Workday World', explored 'the problems confronting industry in Wales', and included a discussion between R. H. S. Crossman and H. A. Marquand on industrial management.[89] In July of the same year, Sam Jones launched the Welsh-language documentary series, 'Diwrnod Gwaith', beginning with a description of a day in the life of a coal miner. In January 1937, the year in which the Welsh Home Service was established, T. Rowland Hughes began his 'Industries of Wales' series, using the outside broadcasting facility of the recording van, and in 1938 the first Welsh National Lecture (by Dr Thomas Jones) was broadcast.[90] But no concerted radio news service existed for the first twenty years of Welsh broadcasting, and there was no news editor even in 1939. A brief 'South Wales News' bulletin, criticized by the Welsh Nationalist party as being 'a précis of the English bulletin', followed the main news from London, and the daily 'Welsh News Bulletin' started on 1 January 1934 was disappointingly shortlived. Commenting on the preponderance of music on the radio, the *North Wales Chronicle* in October 1936 scorned the BBC: 'Ten minutes of news in Welsh and an hour and a half of foxtrots! Is Wales really alive?'. From 1937, news was broadcast four times a week, but there was still no permanent news staff. In February 1939 a 'Radio Newsreel' programme was introduced by J. C. Griffith Jones and E. Morgan Humphreys.[91]

But the most important questions raised by early broadcasting in Wales pertained not so much to its content as to its control. The press had self-consciously sought to generate a sense of nationhood in nineteenth- and early twentieth-century Wales, and the potential of radio, far more than the cinema, to do the same was abundantly clear. John Reith inclined to the view that the Welsh language adequately expressed the cultural distinctiveness of the Welsh, and to some extent Welsh-language broadcasting, transmitted from Daventry from January 1929, ensured that protests against centralization were weaker in Wales than they were in Scotland. With David Lloyd George serving as chairman of the Welsh Religious Advisory Council from March 1932, John Reith could confidently remark that the Welsh language constituted 'a bond of enormous value and importance'.[92] Appropriately, the service opened in north Wales on the evening of 8 November 1935 with an election broadcast by Lloyd George. But the political and cultural dimensions of broadcasting were not to be addressed so easily. In January 1936, C. A. Siepman's *Report on the Regions* advised that sufficient time should be allowed in the introduction of broadcasting in Wales for 'political and racial passions provoked by past controversies' to cool. In the same year a Regional service was introduced, but Wales did not become a full Region until July 1945. John Coatman, Northern Regional Director of the BBC had strongly advised against this in 1944 on the grounds that broadcasters in Wales would be 'driven into politics and twisted and warped away from their primary business of broadcasting as parts of the inclusive nation to which they belong, namely, the British nation.'[93] In a sense, he was right. Undeb Cymru Fydd soon demanded a separate Broadcasting Charter for Wales, and when Welsh Regional Director Alun Oldfield-Davies told Welsh MPs in June 1946 that there was 'not enough talent . . . in Wales to sustain a full continuous programme', there were fierce protests that implied that the BBC was far too dependent on a small group of broadcasters who happened to live close to the Cardiff studios, and did not take advantage of a wealth of talent distributed more widely through the country.[94] In practice, however, radio did play a central role in the post-war cultural renaissance in Wales, and Philip Burton attracted to the BBC such writers as Islwyn Williams, Henry Green, and Robert Gwyn, and broadcast the work of Dylan Thomas and previously lesser known writers like E. Eynon Evans. BBC radio extended its coverage of local areas in 1967 by means of local stations, and the operation of the Bangor studio provides an excellent example of community radio in Wales. In the south also, commercial stations of the Swansea Sound variety achieved considerable success. Relations between radio and the press also remained close at the ownership level, and by 1961 four of the seven directors of the Caernarvon Herald and Associated Newspapers were also directors of Radio Caernarvon Ltd.[95]

The resumption of BBC television in 1946, and its extension to areas outside London and parts of the south-east of England to which it had been confined between 1936 and 1939, did not unduly affect the radio service. Its expense, at around five times the cost of radio per hour to produce, and the proven success of radio during the war, gave television a lower priority. Staffing levels in BBC television stood only at 1,320 at the start of 1954, when only 20 per cent of all British households possessed television sets.[96] The balance between radio and television broadcasting changed abruptly, however, when the BBC monopoly was broken in 1955.

Independent Television (ITV) started on 22 September 1955, and the first ITV consortium was established one year later to serve south Wales and west of England (TWW). Unlike the BBC, independent television made possible a new alignment of the commerical newspaper and broadcasting media. Among the directors of the consortium, headed by Lord Derby, was Sir William Carr, owner and chairman of the *News of the World*, and grandson of the editor and owner of the *Western Mail*, Lascelles Carr. It was estimated that 58 per cent of the population of south Wales read the *News of the World*, and Carr owned 20.5 per cent of the TWW shares. A further 14 per cent were held by the *Liverpool Daily Post*. Virtually all the share capital came from outside Wales. Others on the board included Huw T. Edwards (chairman of the National Council for Wales), Sir Ifan ab Owen Edwards, and a host of other prominent men. TWW opened on 14 January 1958, broadcasting from the new Pontcanna studios in Cardiff. A total of 84,000 sets tuned into TWW at its opening at 4.45p.m., and by 7.15p.m. that figure had risen to 115,000, from a total of 310,000 sets in the TWW region. Pressure within the Independent Television Authority by Jenkin Alban

Davies MP and others in Undeb Cymru Fydd successfully led to the introduction of mandatory Welsh-language programming of at least one hour a week, and Welsh-language broadcasts started in the spring of 1957. By this time, Granada was broadcasting extensively in north Wales. Sets receiving TWW increased from 445,000 in January 1959 to 673,000 in November 1960, and perhaps more than half of these were on the Welsh side of the region.[97]

In September 1962 a new channel, WWN, opened in north and west Wales with Haydn Williams, followed by Eric Thomas, as managing director and Nathan Hughes as general manager. This region proved to be far more difficult to serve than the south, due to its sparser population and its mountainous topography. It was, moreover, largely Welsh speaking. Technological difficulties in transmitting strong signals across Snowdonia, and the overlapping of transmission areas with Granada in the north east and with TWW in the south west, led to soaring costs that put the company in severe financial difficulties in 1963. In January of the following year WWN was taken over by TWW.[98]

TWW lost its franchise to Harlech Television in 1967, and following a moving valedictory by John Betjeman to the old company, HTV came on the air on 4 March 1968. Harlech, like TWW before it, had also summoned powerful support, including such prominent BBC broadcasters as John Morgan and Wynford Vaughan Thomas, actors and performers like Richard Burton, Stanley Baker and Geraint Evans, for whom it was said a Welsh station offered 'a welcome means for the expression of their cultural patriotism.'[99] Also included in the new HTV line-up were poet Alun Llewelyn-Williams, Alun Talfan Davies QC, and Eric Thomas of Woodall's Newspapers.[100]

The newspaper did not disappear as a means of communication in the face of competition from the new media. An accommodation was gradually reached between the old and the new that allowed each medium to concentrate on what it could do best in relation both to the strengths of the other media and the preferences and expectations of the audience. Thus, film, radio and television were able to complement as well as to compete with the newspaper press, and, in terms both of staffing and ownership, the barriers between these media were permeable.

The notion of press traditions overlapping with the new media may be seen, firstly, in the high degree of continuity in the crossover of personnel, which in turn led to a new functional relationship between the press and broadcasting, in which, for example, the press became an important training ground for radio and television journalists, at least in the period before the growth of specialization and graduate entry. Whilst it must be acknowledged that journalism, as David A. Patten has argued, 'as a profession and as a set of standards, has never been independent of the tools used to communicate a given message',[101] it should also be emphasized that the skills of the new media were not developed independently of the existing methods and priorities of newspaper journalism. In any case, the introduction of new technologies of news collection, printing and distribution in newspapers have meant that the press itself became a 'new medium'.

The interconnections between the press and the newer media in the twentieth century also involves the pattern of ownership, and in particular newspaper interests in television companies. The matter was not regarded as an important one by the Pilkington Committee in 1961, but increasing public concern was expressed by an ITA memorandum to the committee in April 1961 which warned 'lest the means of communication should fall into fewer hands than would be consistent with the needs and nature of a free society.'[102] It was also feared that, on the one hand, traditional newspaper partisanship would threaten television's impartiality, and, on the other, that the ITA statutory restraints constituted a threat to traditional press freedoms. Pilkington, however, disagreed, replying that a ban on press participation would 'impede initiative, confine talent, restrict the growth of the energetic and artificially separate two means of communication between which some mutual influence is beneficial', and that in consequence, ownership of television companies by national newspapers was not a 'threat to democracy'. It was, however, decided to recommend that in no television group could press owners become dominant, which in practice meant that no newspaper group could own more than half the voting shares in any television company.

Finally, some of the general assumptions regarding the functions of media in society and political life were also carried over from nineteenth-century newspapers to twentieth-century broadcasting. Among them was the idea that, if employed in the right way, forms of communication could help maintain a sense of nationhood and protect the integrity of the Welsh language. This was reflected in the demand for cultural autonomy through the establishment of the BBC Welsh Region and independent Welsh television companies, the extension of Welsh-language programming from the 1920s, the establishment of BBC Wales in 1964, the creation of Radio Cymru and, above all, in the campaign of civil disobedience that preceded the transmission of the Welsh Fourth Channel, Sianel Pedwar Cymru (S4C), in November 1982.[103] The Welsh language has also raised scheduling difficulties for broadcasters, and the débâcle over S4C itself essentially turned on the most equitable distribution of programming in the two languages. But the balance of Welsh and English languages had also raised acute difficulties for nineteenth-century editors. The Crawford Committee had arrived at much the same conclusion in 1974 as J. T. Morgan had done exactly a century earlier when he divided his bilingual Merthyr weekly into two separate papers, targeted at two distinct language communities.[104]

The irony of the Welsh media, as Jeremy Tunstall observed, is that, unlike that of Scotland, it has had, at least from the 1920s, an overwhelmingly English-oriented press, whereas its television and radio has provided 'a uniquely rich set of regional offerings'.[105] The creativity of these forms of communication produced what Patrick Hannan has termed an 'extended seminar on Welsh life'[106] that allowed 'new kinds of Wales' to be invented,[107] characteristics that were, in the previous century, so closely associated with the newspaper press. Seen in these terms, it can be argued that Welsh journalism did experience a migration from the press to the new media in the course of the twentieth century. The distinctiveness, diversity and local colour that were so characteristic of Victorian newspapers have survived, although in a different form, in aspects of Welsh broadcasting, particularly perhaps in radio. But the media in twentieth-century Wales has witnessed transformation as well as continuity. Broadcasting has created its own structures and codes, and, increasingly, its journalism will need to break free from the traditions of print and to be studied in its own, autonomous terms.

Conclusion

The popular press, for almost two centuries, has been woven into increasingly elaborate patterns in the fabric of Welsh society. This study has searched for the means by which these patterns were produced, and has surveyed their sometimes vivid but often elusive shapes and tones. Regarded for much of the nineteenth century as a brash, disturbing but not wholly unwelcome new presence, journalism was closely associated with the economic, political and cultural processes that were so rapidly changing the shape and character of Welsh society. Demand for a popular press increased with population growth, urbanization and improvements in education, and it was financed largely through advertising, a spin-off of economic expansion. The industrialization of the economy allowed for the growth in skills and the development of new technology that made the production and distribution of newspapers faster and, given the economies of scale, cheaper, while political, religious and cultural institutions subsidized many of its titles and sustained its diversity, often in the teeth of fiercely hostile market pressures.

But while popular journalism was a product of this society, it was also, at the same time, a way of changing it. Belief in the 'power of the press', loudly celebrated both by journalists and their critics, was often a necessary precondition for a newspaper's survival. Nineteenth-century Welsh journalism was targeted primarily at small audiences, and journalists satisfied this fragmented market by producing a huge variety of periodicals aimed at a wide range of identifiable and potential readerships, and the passion and invective that characterized many of these publications signify the extent to which they engaged with and structured issues of public importance. Regional, class, religious and linguistic inequalities with regard to resources certainly existed, but the structure of the press was far less hierarchical in the nineteenth century than it was to become in the twentieth. Developments in broadcasting in the twentieth century, however, did not annihilate earlier forms of journalism, and despite many technological and structural changes in media production and patterns of consumption, the legacy of the nineteenth-century press has continued to provide the categories within which the newer media are conceptualized.

A serious examination of the history of the newspaper press in Wales has to reject the notion that newspapers are inferior to other kinds of texts that are more conventionally regarded as literary. Newspapers not only contained politics and literature both high and low, but, more significantly, as this study has shown, they acted as public faces of the culture. As a consequence of the close, even symbiotic, links between journalists and local, political, religious, occupational and language groups, readers, in the present as in the past, have to address the diversity of the culture and the ways in which self-perceptions, expectations, tastes and desires differ from place to place and over time. Reading a nineteenth-century newspaper in this way involves engaging with elaborate patterns of cultural history that shift and re-align as if seen through a kaleidoscope. But the history of culture extends beyond the columns of newspapers, however pervasive their presence, and the limitations imposed by concentrating primarily on journalism in this respect are palpable. Reconstructing the interconnections between the products of the printing press, in all their forms and modalities, and the communities and institutions that created and consumed them, might tease out further insights into the cultural processes involved in reproducing Welsh society during the past two hundred years.

The newspaper press and the society with which it engaged, text and context, were both transformed in the course of the nineteenth and early twentieth centuries. The styles and purposes of newspapers changed from the audacious amateurism of the early printer-editors to the studied mannerisms of the professional reporters of the New Journalism, and from the denominational bickering of the religious writers to the full-blown virtuous passions of the Gladstonian journalists. This sustained bout of creativity, which was at its most intense between the 1850s and the 1880s, achieved more than the establishment of a new Welsh industry in an age of new Welsh industries. The voices that the press allowed to be heard, and the narratives that they provided, changed the ways in which the outside world was comprehended and, at the same time, enabled a society to speak to itself, and so to begin to define itself. Long before they won the right to participate in a democratic polity, the editors, writers, printers, distributors and readers of newspapers in Wales came as near as any to realizing the possibilities of a democratic culture.

Abbreviations used in the notes

C.M.Arch.	Calvinistic Methodist Archives, National Library of Wales
Clwyd Arch.	Clwyd County Archives
Clwyd Arch. Haw.	Clwyd County Archives (Hawarden)
CPL	Cardiff Public Library
CRO	Companies Registration Office
DWB	*Dictionary of Welsh Biography*
GGLB	Glamorgan Gazette Letter Book
Glam.R.O.	Glamorgan Record Office
Gwyn. Arch. Dol.	Gwynedd County Archives (Dolgellau)
Gwyn. Arch. Caer.	Gwynedd Archives (Caernarfon)
JWBS	*Journal of the Welsh Bibliographical Society*
MRC	Modern Records Centre, University of Warwick
NLW	National Library of Wales, Aberystwyth
NWC	*North Wales Chronicle*
NWLF	North Wales Liberal Federation
PRO	Public Record Office, Kew, London
PTA	Provincial Typographical Association
RCP	Royal Commission on the Press
SPCK	Society for the Propagation of Christian Knowledge
SPL	Swansea Public Library
TA	Typographical Association
UCNW	University College of North Wales, Bangor
WM	*Western Mail*
WRC	BBC Wales Record Centre, Cardiff

Notes

All books published in London, unless otherwise stated.

Preface

1 John Hampden (Ed.), *Anthony Trollope, Novels and Stories* (1948), p.vii.

2 Raymond Williams, *Culture* (1981), p.225. Twenty years earlier, Williams had criticized 'the widespread failure to co-ordinate the history of the press with the economic and social history within which it must necessarily be interpreted', a failure which he argued had serious consequences for the understanding of the functions of the media in the present, Raymond Williams, *The Long Revolution* (1961), p.173.

Introduction

1 Elizabeth L. Eisenstein, *The Printing Revolution in Early Modern Europe* (Cambridge, 1983), p.273. See also Elizabeth L. Eisenstein, *The Printing Press as an Agent of Change*, vols. i and ii, (Cambridge, 1979).

2 Gwyn A. Williams, *When was Wales?*, (Harmondsworth, 1985) p.215.

3 Kenneth O. Morgan, *Wales in British Politics 1868–1922* (Cardiff, 1970), p.9.

4 Ieuan Gwynedd Jones, 'The Dynamics of Politics in Mid- Nineteenth Century Wales', *Explorations and Explanations. Essays in the Social History of Victorian Wales* (Llandysul, 1981), p.294. Boorstin makes a similar observation but in a different context, 'perhaps the most important single change in human consciousness in the last century, and especially in the American consciousness, has been the multiplying of the means and forms of what we call "communications",' Daniel J. Boorstin, *Democracy and its Discontents: Reflections on Everyday America*, (Random House, 1974), p.7.

5 Editorial, 'The Frontiers of Tradition', *British Journalism Review*, vol. i, no. iv, Summer 1990, p.2.

6 'The Fourth Estate', *The Rambler*, vol.iii, pt. xv, Mar. 1849, p.472.

7 Collet D. Collet, *History of the Taxes on Knowledge. Their Origin and Repeal* (1933), p.78.

8 Sir J.F.Stephens, 'Journalism', *Cornhill Magazine*, vol. vi, July 1862.

9 A. Elliott, 'Newspapers, Statesmen, and the Public', *Edinburgh Review*, vol. 185, Jan. 1897, p.215.

10 There is much scope for further research into individual titles, journalists and publishers. The work of Geraint H. Jenkins on late seventeenth- and early eighteenth-century almanackers, Philip Henry Jones on Thomas Gee, and Joanne Cayford on the *Western Mail*, for example, indicate the range of issues that new research could address.

11 G. Osborne Morgan, 'Welsh Nationality', *Contemporary Review*, vol. 53, Jan. 1888, p.91. A similar sense of exclusion obtained in Scotland: 'English periodicals, even when superior as a whole to the northern publications, were almost devoid of interest in Scottish affairs', Mary Elizabeth Craig, *The Scottish Periodical Press 1750–1789* (1931), p.79.

12 T.B.Browne, *The Geography of the Provincial Press* (1891), p.6.

13 Creswick R. Corbitt in *People's Journal, Annals of Progress*, vol. 3, 17 Apr. 1847, p.32. For a more recent formulation of the 'liberal tradition' see La Prensa, *Defence of Freedom* (1952), pp. 203–9.

14 Prospectus, *Caernarvon Advertiser*, 1821, Library of the University College of North Wales (UCNW).

15 The *Silurian* was printed successively in Brecon, Merthyr and Cardiff before being incorporated into the *Monmouthshire Merlin*.

16 'Y Newyddiadur yw cronicl gwareiddiad . . . . Dengys i ni yr unig fyd y gallwn ei weld a'i deimlo', *Y Byd Cymreig*, 9 Hyd. 1862.

17 Claude Morris, *I Bought a Newspaper* (1963), p.54.

18 Corbitt, *People's Journal*, 1847, p.32.

19 Printed letter, Swansea, 12 May 1879, Mansel Coll. 734, Swansea Public Library (SPL).

20 William Haslam Mills, *The Manchester Guardian. A Century of History* (1921), p.3.

Chapter 1

1 Joel H. Wiener, (Ed.), *Innovators and Preachers. The role of the Editor in Victorian England* (Westport, Connecticut, 1985), pp. xii–xiii.

2 C.F. Wingate, *Views and Interviews on Journalism* (New York, 1875), p.327.

3 R.Geraint Gruffydd, *Argraffwyr Cyntaf Cymru. Gwasgau Dirgel y Catholigion Adeg Elisabeth*, (Caerdydd, 1972), pp. 8–11.

4 Geraint H. Jenkins, *Thomas Jones yr Almanaciwr 1648–1713* (Cardiff, 1980), esp. pp.41–71; T.W.Hancock, 'The First Shrewsbury Newspaper', *Bye-gones*, May 1881, p.240; M. Clement, *The SPCK and Wales 1699–1740* (1954), p.47.

5 Isaac Carter's early printing venture was 'a philanthropic gesture' and followed the 'literary and spiritual awakening in South Cardiganshire', Eiluned Rees, *The Welsh Book Trade Before 1820* (Aberystwyth, 1988) pp. xxii–xxiii; *Carmarthen Journal*, 17 July 1912; Dafydd Wyn Wiliam, 'Y Wasg Argraffu ym Modedern, Mon', *Journal of the Welsh Bibliographical Society (JWBS)*, June 1971, vol.x, no.4.; Ifano Jones, *A History of Printers and Printing in Wales to 1810, and of successive and related Printers to 1923* (Cardiff, 1925), pp.218–9; Ivor Waters, *Chepstow Printers and Newspapers* (Chepstow, 1981), p.19.

6 Ivor Waters, *About Chepstow* (Chepstow, 1952), pp. 46–50. See also James Henry Clark, *Reminiscences*, (1908).

7 R.D.Rees, 'A History of South Wales Newspapers to 1855', (Ph.D., University of Reading, 1954), p.124.

8 National Library of Wales, Aberystwyth, (NLW), MS 13475C; Malcolm and Edith Lodwick's *Story of Carmarthen* (revised edition, Carmarthen, 1972) pp. 132–5, is an excellent source of further information about the printer-journalists of Carmarthen. Some fifteen newspapers and magazines were published in the town between the 1760s and the 1960s. See also David J.V. Jones, *Before Rebecca: popular protest in Wales 1793–1835* (1973). Printers and editors regarded themselves as being of roughly equal status, and in the late 1820s, editor David Owen (Brutus), spent his evenings drinking with his friend the printer Samuel Thomas in the Coopers' Arms in Aberystwyth: see (NLW) MS 4296C.

9 *The Dictionary of Welsh Biography Down to 1940* (1959), (*DWB*), p.250.

10 *DWB*, p.617.

11 Philip Henry Jones, 'A nineteenth-century Welsh printer; some aspects of the career of Thomas Gee, 1815–1898', (Unpub. Fellowship of the Library Association, 1977), p.27. Details of early journalists in Wales are scarce, and there is no comparable Welsh source to D. Croal's study of the Scottish press, *Early Recollections of a Journalist 1832–1859* (Edinburgh, 1898).

12 *Caernarvon and Denbigh Herald*, 6 Nov. 1847; Bangor MS 2424, UCNW.

13 John Gibson to Stuart Rendel, 21 Jan. 1887, NLW MS 19450C/167; Gibson to Rendel, 30 Dec. 1895, NLW MS 19450C/189.

14 Gibson to Rendel, 23 Dec. 1887, NLW MS 20571D/240.

15 *Nottingham Evening News*, 23 February 1916. Edwards and George Bernard Shaw stood unsuccessfully as Progressive candidates for the London County Council, but his time with the *Daily News*

was not a happy one. Installed against the better judgement of his advisers by Lloyd George, with whom Edwards had worked during the Disestablishment campaign in Caernarfon in the 1880s, and over whom it was believed by W.T.Stead that he 'had some hold', Edwards was sacked 'with a generous indemnity' in January 1902, S.Koss, *The Rise and Fall of the Political Press in Britain*, vol. i, (1981), pp. 401–4.

16 'Yn y dyddiau hynny byddai aml argraffydd yn troi'n ohebydd os cai gyfle. . .', Picton Davies, *Atgofion Dyn Papur Newydd* (Lerpwl, 1962) p.157. For Watson's reference to W.E.Adams, see Aaron Watson, *A Newspaper Man's Memories* (1925), p.51.

17 J.H.Jones, *O'r Mwg i'r Mynydd* (Lerpwl, 1913), p.30. For his remarks on other editors of *Yr Herald Cymraeg* and the *Caernarvon and Denbigh Herald*, see pp. 31–3.

18 *DWB*, p.236.

19 NLW MS 3366D.

20 Hugh Jones (Erfyl) to Morris Davies, Porthmadog, 26 Nov. 1840, NLW MS 9031E.

21 C.Tawelfryn Thomas, *Cofiant Ieuan Gwynedd* (Dolgellau, 1909), p.255.

22 Bangor MS 2936, UCNW.

23 R.D.Rees, 'A History', p.104.

24 Fred B. Mason to Stuart Rendel, 1 Nov. 1888, NLW MS 19457C/IX619.

25 Mason to Rendel, 17 Nov. 1888, NLW MS 19457C/IX624.

26 £2.10s. was paid in 1884 to Thomas Hughes for editing *Gwalia*, and £4.10s. for Beriah Gwynfe Evans, manager and editor of the Welsh National Press Co., because of his 'exceptionally heavy workload', R.M. Thomas, 'Y Wasg Gyfnodol yn Nhref Caernarfon hyd 1875. Gyda sylw arbennig i argraffwyr a chyhoeddwyr' (MA, University of Wales, 1979) p.236.

27 NLW MS 8842D.

28 J.Miles to W.J.Parry, 21 July 1897, NLW MS 8842D.

29 H.C.Strick, 'British Newspaper Journalism, 1900–1956: a study in industrial relations', (Ph.D., University of London, 1957), p.255.

30 'Golygodd y *Sylwedydd*, cyhoeddiad misol, heb gael dim ond y golled oddiwrtho. Golygodd y *Seren Ogleddol*, heb daliad erioed; a chyn hyny *Tywysog Cymru*. Golygodd *Cylchgrawn Rhyddid* am ddim. Golygodd yr *Amaethydd*, heb gael un rhan o bedair o'r tal a ddylasai gael. Golygodd y *Gwron* am bedair blynedd, a chollodd drwy hyny dros saith bunt a deugain', Thomas Roberts (Scorpion), (Gol.), *Cofiant Caledfryn* (Bala, 1877), p.68.

31 T.J.Hughes to Stuart Rendel, 10 Mar. 1891; Rendel to Hughes, 11 Mar. 1891, NLW MS 19451D/286.

32 Davies, *Atgofion*, p.124.

33 John Oldcastle, (Wilfrid Meynell), *Journals and Journalism: with a guide for literary beginners* (1880), p.73.

34 J.M. Milne, 'The Politics of *Blackwood's*, 1817–1846: a study of the political, economic and social articles in *Blackwood's Magazine* and of selected contributors', (Ph.D., University of Newcastle upon Tyne, 1985), p.405.

35 'Mae Golygydd y Papyr hwn wedi blino mor llwyr ar ei orchwyl, fel y mae yn gobeithio na syrth i'w ran ef byth mwyach gyfarch ei gydwladwyr yn y fath swydd. Y mae yn disgwyl y bydd i eraill gario ymlaen y Cyhoeddiad gyda mwy o ymroad. . . . Nid oes gennym ni, wrth gilio oddiar y chwaraefwrdd cyhoeddus, ond dymuno eu llwyddiant hwy mewn peth difudd, iddynt eu hunain, digysur, a diddiolch', *Y Papyr Newydd Cymraeg,* 8 Mawrth 1837.

36 Richard Jefferies, *Hodge and his Masters* (1890 edition), pp. 263–71.

37 Jefferies, *Hodge*, p.264.

38 Jefferies, *Hodge*, p.267.

39 Jefferies, *Hodge*, pp. 270–1.

40 Rowland Williams to Hugh Jones, 26 May 1829, NLW MS 9031E.

41 12 Mar., 28 Mar., 10 Apr., 22 Oct., 29 Oct., NLW MS 8813D.

42 John Grigg, *The Young Lloyd George*, (1973), p.49.

43 For further details consult Peter F. Carter-Ruck, *Libel and Slander* (1972).

44 F.J. Mansfield, *Sub-editing, A book mainly for young journalists* (1932), pp. 148–92.

45 S.B.Jones to C.E.G.Philipps, 2 August 1884, Picton Castle 3900, NLW.

46 W.J.Parry, *Diary*, 29 May 1889, NLW 8813D; W.J.Parry to D. Edwards, 2 June 1891, NLW MS 882C/475.

47 Gwynedd Archive Service, Caernarfon (Gwyn. Arch. Caer.), XCV/226

48 D. Lloyd George to W.J.Parry, 11 May 1893, NLW MS 8824C.

49 Davies, *Atgofion*, p.114.

50 Gibson to Rendel, 9 Oct. 1893, NLW MS 19450C/1886.

51 *Returns of Applications for his fiat made to Director of Public Prosecutions under Section Three of 42 and 43 Vict. c. 60* (The Newspaper Libel and Registration Act, 1881), (1888), p.4.

52 Lucy Brown has argued that for editors in Victorian Britain in general, 'it was not difficult to collect news and fill columns: the problem lay with its interpretation and control. The newspaper which was in good standing with an authority which had something to tell received a good deal more than the occasional oddment of exclusive information; and conversely the investigative journalist had massive difficulties to surmount. . . . Publicity was actively sought by important

groups and interests', Lucy Brown, *Victorian News and Newspapers* (Oxford, 1985), p.244.

53 E.P. Thompson, *The Making of the English Working Class* (1965), p.151.

54 H. Findlater Bussey, *Sixty Years of Journalism* (1906), p.30.

55 R.D.Rees, 'South Wales and Monmouthshire Newspapers under the Stamp Acts', *Welsh History Review*, vol. 1, no. 3, 1962, p.307.

56 *Y Papyr Newydd Cymraeg*, 22 a 28 Medi 1836.

57 NLW MS 3366D.

58 *Cylchgrawn Rhyddid*, 1 Chwefror 1841.

59 For example a report of Gladstone's visit to Rome in 1888 in *The Daily News* and *The Standard* was reproduced in *Y Gwyliedydd*, 18 Ion. 1888.

60 *Liverpool Daily Post*, 9 January 1904.

61 *Y Gweithiwr Cymreig*, 29 Ion. 1885.

62 *Baner ac Amserau Cymru*, 7 Chwef. 1894. See also 7 March 1894, in which John Griffith (Gohebydd) remarked that 'as a journalist I acknowledge my debt to the *Pall Mall Gazette*...'. See also Richard Griffith, *Cofiant Gohebydd* (Dinbych, 1905); Griffith also travelled in the USA in 1865–6, France in 1867 and Austria in 1873 for Gee's newspapers. In 1875 he recuperated after an illness in Switzerland, a trip paid for by Samuel Morley.

63 For example, *Y Gwyliedydd*, 2 Mai 1888.

64 For example the *Montgomeryshire Express* in 1905, details of articles bought from other papers by J.G.Morris (from 1912 Morris was Welsh Editor of the *Liverpool Daily Post and Mercury*).
Items purchased in January 1905:
Manchester Guardian (14)
Liverpool Courier (8)
South Wales Daily News (5)
Daily Despatch, Manchester (9)
Liverpool Daily Post (10)
Daily Chronicle, London (2)
Morning Leader (2)
Western Mail (5)
Daily Express, London (1)
Standard, London (1)
Source: 'Journalist's Account Book', J.G. Morris, Welshpool, NLW MS 2290B.

65 *Liverpool Daily Post and Mercury*, 3 February 1912.

66 J. Hemming to S. Curtis, Solicitor, Neath, 4 March 1878, Glamorgan Gazette Letter Book, D/DX bd, (GGLB), Glamorgan Record Office, Cardiff (Glam RO).

67 Revd. Ll. Williams (Vicarage, Beaufort, Mon.) to Editor *Y Llan*, 12

July 1888, NLW MA 6402D. Clag Books, introduced by W.T.Stead, were collections of clippings on persons and events which were kept in newspaper office libraries, Brown, *Victorian News*, p. 253.

68 H.Gwalchmai to Hugh Jones, 27 Nov. 1841, NLW MS 9030E.

69 Maurice Milne, 'Survival of the Fittest?', in J. Shattock and Michael Wolff, *The Victorian Periodical Press: Samplings and Soundings* (Leicester/Toronto, 1982), p.215. John Lawrenson and Lionel Barber, *The Price of Truth. The Story of the Reuters Millions*, (Edinburgh, 1985), pp. 36–8.

70 Brown, *Victorian News*, pp. 118–9; also *Printers' Register*, Feb. and June 1873.

71 For which Hemming was charged the sum of 5s. Hemming to Saunders, 12 Feb. 1878, GGLB, Glam RO.

72 Cash Balances, North Wales Chronicle Co. Ltd., 1886, 1887, *NWC1*, Gwyn. Arch. Caer. Other news agencies were started in the 1890s, including Davidson Dalziel's agency, an exponent of American New Journalism but which was in decline by 1896. The rise of Reuters sealed its fate, and that of many others. Local agencies were also established, such as J. Denley Spencer's 'Aberystwyth News Agency', still in existence in 1930, *Willing's Press Guide*, 1915, 1930.

73 'Proceedings of Meeting of Delegates from the Typographical Societies of the United Kingdom and the Continent', 21–3 Oct. 1886, University of Warwick Modern Records Centre (MRC) 39A/5/MISC/2/2, pp. 10–11. For further details on the development of stereo technology, consult Philip Gaskell, *A New Introduction to Bibliography* (Oxford, 1972), p.205.

74 Brown, *Victorian News*, p.116.

75 *Forester*, 17 September 1874.

76 Hemming to Leader and Sons, 7 Jan. 1878, 18 Feb. 1878, 13 May 1878, GGLB, Glam RO.

77 Hemming to Leader, 28 May 1878, GGLB, Glam RO.

78 Hemming to Excelsior Stereotype, Birmingham, 28 Mar. 1879, GGLB, Glam RO

79 Hemming to Manager, National Press Agency, 13 Mar. 1880, GGLB, Glam RO.

80 Hemming to Griffin and Hawkes, Birmingham, 16 Mar. 1880, GGLB, Glam RO.

81 Hemming to Cassell, Potter and Galpin, 7 Feb. 1881, GGLB, Glam RO. The following is a typical weekly order from Hemming:
2 columns, serial tale 'Living Legacy',
1 column Agriculture,
2 columns Epitome of News,
2 cols General News, full heads, including Parliamentary Summary,

Hemming to Cassell, Potter, Galpin, 14 Feb. 1881, GGLB, Glam RO.

82 Hemming to Griffin and Hawkes, 14 June 1881, GGLB, Glam RO.

83 Hemming to Hawkes and Phelps, Birmingham, 15 August 1882, GGLB, Glam RO.

84 *Gwalia*, 8 Chwef. 1882.

85 *Registrar of Joint Stock Companies*, 1846(504) XLIII,55 and 1857–8 (324) LIII,591.

86 Rees, *A History*, p.374.

87 Hemming to Saunders, Central News, 7 Feb. 1878, GGLB, Glam RO.

88 Hemming to Saunders, Central News, 12 Feb. 1878, GGLB, Glam RO.

89 Hemming to Saunders, Central News, 14 Feb. 1878; 'You will therefore put us on the following services in due time', including 'the Service General News and Closing Prices of Cork Butter, Corn in Liverpool and London', Hemming to Manager, Central News, 26 June 1882, GGLB, Glam RO.

90 Hemming to Secretary, Telegraph Department, General Post Office, London, 19 Jan. 1878, GGLB, Glam RO.

91 Hemming to Manager, Central News, 22 Sept. 1882, GGLB, Glam RO.

92 D.R.Daniel. *Diary*, 24 June 1890, D.R.Daniel Coll. 515, NLW.

93 D.R.Daniel, *Diary*, 13 Aug. 1890.

94 *Ye Brython Cymreig*, 1 Ion. 1892. In the United States, the telegraph provided 'the driving force behind the creation of a mass press', James Carey, *Communication as Culture. Essays in Media and Society* (Boston, 1988), p.70.

95 Hemming to H.Cousins, 16 Feb. 1878, GGLB, Glam RO.

96 Fred B. Mason to Stuart Rendel, 4 Apr. 1890, NLW MS 1945D/428.

97 Davies, *Atgofion*, p.112.

98 Davies, *Atgofion*, pp. 112–3.

99 Mansfield, *Sub-Editing*, pp. 2–4; 'It was only as newspapers grew in size and influence, as the shackles of censorship and taxation were removed, and the materials and machinery of production became cheaper, more ample and more efficient, that staffs began to develop'.

100 Brown, *Victorian News*, p.84.

101 NLW MS 3366D.

102 W.Williams to Editor, *Aberdare Times*, 1 Aug. 1863, NLW MS 3366D.

103 Mansfield, *Sub-Editing*, p.8.

104 John Duncan to T.E.Ellis, 17 Oct. 1885, T.E.Ellis MS 368, NLW.

105 The sub-editor at *Lloyd's* fell ill with consumption, and Catling, to his evident surprise, was offered the post. Later, after Blanchard Jerrold's death, Catling was appointed the paper's editor, T. Catling, *My Life's Pilgrimage*, (1911), pp. 85–6.

106 Cash Balance, North Wales Chronicle Co., (NWC1), 1886, Gwyn. Arch. Caer.

107 J.H.Jones to OEO, 6 Feb. 1902 NLW MS 3300D.

108 Mansfield, *Sub-Editing*, p.14.

109 Mansfield, *Sub-Editing*, p.35.

110 Rees, 'South Wales . . . Newspapers', p.307.

111 *Journalist and Newspaper Proprietor*, 6 Nov. 1897.

112 Cardiff Public Library (CPL), MS 3.348.

113 Oldcastle, *Journals*, p.45.

114 For example, 2 Jan. 1863, 'Rees Evans killed at Wern. Reported the accident to the *Leader*', Bookseller's accounts, Ystalyfera, NLW MS 10940A.

115 NLW MS 4613A. David Samuel, Headmaster of the Old Bank Grammar School, Aberystwyth, from 1890 to 1920 wrote articles on a variety of subjects to the following journals: *Aberystwyth Observer, Cambrian News, Cymru, Y Geninen, Y Traethodydd, Wales, Young Wales, Y Goleuad, Welsh Gazette, Monthly Treasury, Y Drysorfa, Yr Ymweledydd Misol, Y Greal, The Nationalist, London Daily News, County Schools Review, Y Brython, Journal of the Welsh Bibliographical Society, Y Beirniad, Y Wawr, Transactions of the Cardiganshire Antiquarian Society, Y Cerddor, Welsh Outlook, Y Darian*. E.Morgan Humphreys obtained freelance income from *Daily News, Traethodydd, Western Mail, Cymru, Y Genedl, Manchester Guardian, Liverpool Daily Post* ('Welsh Notes'), *Newspaper World, Daily Citizen* and *Y Drysorfa*. In 1910 he received £6.8s.11d. for nine articles, but by 1912 could command more than twice that sum for seven articles (Bangor MS 16005).

116 Dyfed Evans, *Bywyd Bob Owen* (Caernarfon, 1977), p.85; NLW MSS 7234–53, 8404.

117 David Davies, *Reminiscences of my Country and People*, (Cardiff, 1925), p.51.

118 S.Gwilly Davies, *Wedi Croesi'r Pedwar-Ugain* (Llandysul, 1967), pp.40–1. See also Jones, *O'r Mwg i'r Mynydd*.

119 *Ironworkers' Journal*, 1 May 1874.

120 R. Iwan Jenkin, Editor, to John Jones (Ivon), 15 Feb. 1892, NLW MS 3291 E/9.

121 Enoch Arnold Bennett, *Journalism for Women. A Practical Guide* (1898), p.24.

122 Oldcastle, *Journals*, p.41.

123 Other prices paid by *Y Traethodydd* in 1865 were as follows:
5 articles, 37 pages, £4.10s.
1 article, 6 pages, £1
1 article, 12 pages, £1.5s., Bangor MS 223, UCNW.

124 NLW MS 10440C/8/9/10.

125 Michael MacDonagh, 'The Bye-Ways of Journalism', *Cornhill Magazine*, New Series, vol. vi, Jan. to June 1899, p.398–9.

126 Hemming to S.W.Henry, Maesteg, 20 Nov. 1877, GGLB, Glam RO.

127 Hemming to Frank Williams, Maesteg, 29 May 1878; Hemming to Gandy, Neath, 19 Jan. 1878, GGLB, Glam RO.

128 Hemming to Gandy, 25 Apr. 1878, GGLB, Glam RO.

129 Sub-Editor, *South Wales Daily News*, to D.M. Richards, 22 Oct. 1892, NLW MS 3293E/12.

130 Kennedy Jones to D.M. Richards, 25 Mar. 1899, NLW MS 3293E/4.

131 William Davies to H.Haydn Jones, 3 Apr. 1905, Sir H.Haydn Jones MS 26, NLW.

132 *Y Gwyliedydd*, 8 Chwef. 1888.

133 Ibid.

134 *Y Dydd*, 5 Mehef. 1868.

135 Hemming to R.Dugmore, Neath, 27 Sept. 1878, GGLB, Glam RO.

136 Davies, *Atgofion*, p.149. This was not as difficult for the editor as the apocryphal activities of a newspaper correspondent in the west of Ireland who, according to Michael MacDonagh, was eventually gaoled for a series of outrages, such as burning hay-ricks and maiming cattle, which he himself committed, and then 'telegraphed the harrowing details to various journals', MacDonagh, 'Bye-Ways of Journalism', p.397.

137 William Roberts (Nefydd), *Diary*, NLW MS 17799A, p.22.

138 John Duncan to T.E.Ellis 14 Aug.1886, T.E.Ellis Coll. 369, NLW.

139 Calculated by Duncan on the basis of two articles by Ellis printed in the *South Wales Daily News*, Mar. 31 and June 10 1886, John Duncan to T.E.Ellis, 8 Sept. 1886, T.E.Ellis Coll. 376, NLW.

140 Carneddog (Richard Griffith), *Gwaith Glaslyn. Detholiad o'i Farddoniaeth a'i Ryddiaeth* (Caernarfon, 1914). His pseudonyms included 'Briglwyd', 'Henafgwr' and 'Llwyd' for the *Nelson*, and 'Arthur', 'Nanmawr', 'Chwarelwr Annibynol' (Independent Quarryman) and 'Un o'r Dosbarth Gweithiol' (One from the Working Class).

141 Evans, *Bob Owen*, passim.

142 Royal Commission on Land in Wales, *Report*, vol. iv, Q.64102, Q.64119.

143 *Y Gweithiwr Cymreig*, 12 Ion. 1888.

144 Ilffe, Henley and Sweet to William Lewis, 27 June 1892, Picton Castle 920, NLW.

145 G.G. Fisher to Sir Charles Phillips, 1 July 1892, Picton Castle 920, NLW making reference to the 1892 General Election.

146 Ilffe, Henley and Sweet to Sir Charles Philipps, 8 July 1892, Picton Castle 920, NLW.

147 Ilffe, Henley and Sweet to Sir Charles Philipps, 15 July 1892, Picton Castle 920, NLW.

148 A. Patchett Martin, 'Robert Lowe as a Journalist', *National Review*, vol. xxii, Sept.–Feb. 1893–4, p. 352.

149 *Minute Book*, North Wales Liberal Federation (NWLF), 1 July 1890, NLW MS 21,171D; NLW MSS 19451D/274, 19451D/286. The New Journalism of the late 1880s and 1890s extended from the United States and London, and introduced lively new formats and styles of writing into newspaper journalism. The most important of these were headlines, bylines, 'scoops' and a more imaginative use of illustrations. Best suited to the larger dailies, the New Journalism was pioneered in Wales by the *Western Mail*.

150 News Editor, *Daily Chronicle*, to D.M. Richards, 20 Feb. 1904, NLW MS 3293E/6.

151 Davies, *Atgofion*, p.101. The news values that developed towards the end of the nineteenth century, particularly in the daily press, have remained largely unchanged: 'news is only news while it is new. 'Worthy, but dull', is one of the most damning indictments you could make about a news report. News should make you suck in your breath and exclaim, sit up, take notice and listen'. Andrew Boyd, *Broadcast Journalism. Techniques of Radio and TV News* (Oxford, 1988), p.4.

152 Lord Kemsley, 'Journalism as a Career', *Welsh Anvil/Yr Einion*, vol.i, Apr. 1949.

153 *Y Dydd*, 5 Mehef. 1868.

154 Davies, *Atgofion*, p.78. Thus Dylan Thomas in his cub reporter's notebook '"Called at British Legion: Nothing. Called at Hospital: One broken leg. Auction at the Metropole. Ring Mr. Beynon *re* Gymanfa Ganu. Lunch: Pint and pasty at the Singleton with Mrs Giles. Bazaar at Bethesda Chapel. Chimney on fire at Tontine Street. Walters Road Sunday School Outing. Rehearsal of the *Mikado* at Skewen" – all front page stuff. . .'. Dylan Thomas, 'Return Journey', in Dylan Thomas, *Miscellany One. Poems, Stories and Broadcasts* (1974), p.108.

155 John Roberts to Dr Lewis Edwards, n.d., NLW MS 9918E. For further biographical details, consult J.E.Jones, *Ieuan Gwyllt, ei fywyd, ei lafur, ei athrylith, ei nodweddion, a'i ddylanwad ar Gymru*, (Treffynnon, 1881).

156 T.M.Jones, *Llenyddiaeth Fy Ngwlad* (Treffynnon, 1893), p.17. According to Philip Henry Jones, this is 'a mine of well-intentioned

misinformation', Philip Henry Jones, '*Yr Amserau*: The First Decade 1843–52', Laurel Brake, Aled Jones and Lionel Madden (Eds.), *Investigating Victorian Journalism* (1990), p.86.

157 Hemming to M.R.Marsden, Cardiff, 1 Jan. 1878, GGLB, Glam RO.

158 Hemming to James Farquhar, Caerleon, 7 Jan. 1878, 10 Jan. 1870, Hemming to Ernest Forrest, 11 Jan. 1879, GGLB, Glam RO.

159 Hemming to H.C.Fraill, Manager, *South Wales Daily Telegram*, Newport, 17 Jan. 1878, GGLB, Glam RO.

160 Davies, *Atgofion*, pp. 78–101.

161 Brown, *Victorian News*, pp. 77–8.

162 An account of these papers and their editors may be found in Sian Rhiannon Williams, '*Y Frythones*: Portread Cyfnodolion Merched y Bedwaredd Ganrif ar Bymtheg o Gymraes yr Oes', *Llafur*, vol.iv, no. i (1984), pp. 43–56.

163 Findlater Bussey, *Sixty Years*, p.30.

164 William Eames, 'Brithgofion Newyddiadurwr', *Y Genhinen*, cyf. xiv, rhif i, Gaeaf 1963–4, pp. 36–7; *Y Dinesydd Cymreig*, 21 Mawrth 1917.

165 Haydn Morgan to Percy Jones, nd, Bangor MS 1219/92. UCNW.

166 David Davies, 'The Journalism of Wales during the Victorian Era', *Young Wales*, 31, 32 Aug. 1897.

167 Brown, *Victorian News*, p.82.

168 He was paid a salary of £30 for the first and second year, £50 for the third year. A fee of one hundred guineas was paid to Douglas for the privilege, NWC 103, Gwyn. Arch. Caer.

169 L.J.Jessop to Revd O. Eilian Owen, 3 Mar. 1902; J.Huss to Revd O. Eilian Owen, 5 Mar. 1902; Patrick McSweeney to Revd O.Eilian Owen, 5 Mar. 1902, NLW MS 3300D.

170 Davies, *Atgofion*, p.106.

171 Cyril Bainbridge, *One Hundred Years of Journalism* (1984), p.123.

172 Davies, *Atgofion*, pp. 84–102.

173 Strick, 'Newspaper Journalism', p.256.

174 Davies, *Atgofion*, p.163.

175 F.J.Mansfield, *Gentlemen, the Press!* (1943), pp. 475–6.

176 Davies, *Atgofion*, p.142. There is a reference to a simlar 'reporters' ring' in Hartley Aspden, *Fifty Years a Journalist* (Clitheroe, 1930), p.21.

177 L.W.Lewis to unknown correspondent, 14 Dec. 1862, NLW MS 5906B.

178 *DWB.*, p.392; Picton Davies, *Atgofion*, p.163.

179 *South Wales Critic*, 22 May 1869.

180 *Y Clorianydd*, 20 Awst 1891.

181 *Caernarvon and Denbigh Herald*, 19 Jan. 1912.

182 *South Wales Daily News*, 21 Aug. 1895.

183 Brown, *Victorian News*, 1985, pp. 150–1; J. Tunstall, *The Westminster Lobby Correspondents* (1970). It would be difficult to reconstruct the history of the secretive workings of the early Lobby, even had the records of the first fifty years not been incinerated by a wartime bomb, Rt. Hon. Margaret Thatcher, Text of a Speech at Parliamentary Lobby's Centenary Lunch, 18 January 1984, repr. in Peter Henessy, *What the Papers Never Said*, (1985), p.156. Henessy decries the undue influence Downing Street has been able to exert over the political agenda of the press through the operation of the Lobby System. John Boon gained access to the 'inner Lobby' only by 'devious routes' in 1886, John Boon, *Victorians, Edwardians and Georgians. The Impressions of a Journalist Extending Over Forty Years* (1928), vol. i, p.64.

184 David Duncan to Sir Edward Reed, 14 Mar. 1892; H.D.Erskine to D.Duncan, 11 May 1892; J.H.Dalziel to D.Duncan, 6 Dec. 1892. See also D.Duncan to T.E.Ellis, 16 Dec. 1892. T.E.Ellis Coll. 378, NLW Griffith, *Cofiant Gohebydd*, passim. Griffiths was awarded a National Testimonial in 1869 'for services to Welsh Journalism', NLW MS 5775B.

185 See for example Thomas Geoffrey Morgan, 'The Welsh Press and Prince Louis Napoleon Boanaparte, 1815–1871', (MA, University of Wales, 1979), p.57. Morgan demonstrates how Welsh coverage of French politics was mediated by its Protestantism, Liberalism, pacifism as well as by the continuing influence of English Gallophobia.

186 For example, *Western Mail (WM)*, 1 to 7 Nov. 1894.

187 Beriah Gwynfe Evans, *Dafydd Dafis. Sef Hunangofiant Ymgeisydd Seneddol*, (Wrexham, 1898).

188 For example the 'Beautiful Britain' series in the *Western Mail*, 1 Nov. 1894. Davies, *Atgofion*, p.87; John Roberts Williams, *O Wythnos i Wythnos* (Caernarfon, 1987), p.10; *Willings Press Guide*, 1915; Simon Thomas, 'Gwaith Geoff Charles', *Barn*, Ion. 1988, p.21. For the production methods of illustrated newspapers, wood engraving, electrotyping and the techniques of 'special artists in war', consult Mason Jackson, *The Pictorial Press. Its Origins and Progress* (1885), pp. 315–354.

189 Brown, *Victorian News*, p.84.

190 Emily Crawford, 'Journalism as a profession for women', *Contemporary Review*, vol 64, Sept. 1893, p.366.

191 Strick, 'Newspaper Journalism', p.252.

192 Bennett, *Journalism for Women*, p.96.

193 Lenore O'Boyle, 'The Image of the Journalist in France, Germany, and England, 1815–1848', *Comparative Studies in Society and History*, x, 1968, p.291.

194 *Printer*, 1 Jan. 1845.

195 Rees, 'South Wales ... Newspapers', p.323.

196 Arthur Murphy, 'The Tory Press', *Contemporary Review*, vol. 23, Apr. 1874, p.823. A good description of the layout of new newspaper offices, with illustrations of the editor's room, reporters' room, and printing room with machinery may be found in *Seventy Years of Progress. A History of the Sheffield Independent from 1819 to 1892* (Sheffield, 1892), passim.

197 W. Hunt, *Then and Now. Fifty Years of Newspaper Work* (Hull, 1887), p.vi.

198 T. Frost, *Reminiscences of a Country Journalist* (1886), p.329.

199 F.J.Mansfield, *The Complete Journalist* (1936), p.373.

200 Mansfield, *Gentlemen*, p.481.

201 Emily Crawford explained the prevalence of low wages in terms of journalism appearing to be 'the easiest of professions, and a rush (being) made towards it for this reason. This leads to overcrowding in the lower branches, and poor and precarious wages', Crawford, 'Journalism ... for women', p.366.

202 Oldcastle, *Journals*, p.45.

203 E.Morgan Humphreys, *Y Wasg Gymraeg* (Caernarfon, 1944), p.7.

204 Cash Balances, North Wales Chronicle Co. Ltd.,1886–1901, NWC1, Gwyn. Arch. Caer.

205 Patrick McSweeney to Revd O.Eilian Owen, 5 Mar. 1902, NLW MS 3300D.

206 Strick, 'Newspaper Journalism', pp.248–54; Mansfield, *Gentlemen*, p.477.

207 Strick, 'Newspaper Journalism', p.248; Mansfield, *Gentlemen*, p.480.

208 Brown, *Victorian News*, p. 76; Mansfield, *Gentlemen*, p.481.

209 Strick, 'Newspaper Journalism', pp. 172, 258–9.

210 *South Wales Daily News*, 19 Jan. 1888.

211 Strick, 'Newspaper Journalism', p.472.

212 Clement J. Bundock, *The National Union of Journalists. A Jubilee History 1907–1957* (Oxford, 1957), pp. 3, 14, 17.

213 Mansfield, *Gentlemen*, p.476.

214 'Dances, smoking concerts and whist drives' were held 'in order not only to bring the members together but to interest their women folk in the affairs of the Union', Mansfield *Gentlemen*, p.479–82. T.A.Davies, NUJ activist, had been apprenticed as a printer at the *Brecon Beacon* office, and at the age of twenty-two was managing editor of the *Brecon County Times*. He was elected onto the National Executive of the union in 1920, and became NUJ President at the Nottingham Conference in 1922. W.E.Pegg, assistant editor of the *Western Mail*, was south Wales treasurer of the NUJ from 1908 to

1936 was also a member of the NUJ National Executive. He was the first member of the Union to receive the dual status of honorary and life membership.

Chapter 2

1 The *Hereford Times*, a weekly paper that circulated in Monmouth, Glamorgan and Brecon, published its production and taxation costs as a protest against 'the taxes on knowledge', *Hereford Times*, 30 June 1832.

2 *Merthyr and Cardiff Chronicle*, 16 Dec. 1837.

3 *Cylchgrawn Rhyddid*, 1 Chwef. 1841.

4 *Y Papyr Newydd Cymraeg*, 5 Hyd. 1836.

5 *Y Papyr Newydd Cymraeg*, 19 Hyd. 1836.

6 *Y Papyr Newydd Cymraeg*, 8 Mawrth 1837.

7 Robert Roberts, publisher of *Cyfaill Glandeg* etc. 1805–37, printed by John Jones, Trefriw, *DWB*, p 877; Rees, 'A History', p.300.

8 Jones, '*Yr Amserau*', pp.91–3.

9 Printers in Aberdare in 1833 bought paper from manufacturers in Liverpool and Wrexham, whilst the manager of the *Glamorgan Gazette* in 1878 purchased his newsprint for a shilling a ream from a paper mill in Salford. Paper supplies were also susceptible to political pressures, particularly at times of national emergencies. In March 1917, for example, the producers of the Caernarfon weekly, *Y Dinesydd Cymreig*, met to discuss the reduction in the size of the paper which would inevitably follow government restrictions on the supply of newsprint, NLW MS 3322D; Hemming to Messrs. Chadwick and Taylor, 10 Jan. 1878, GGLB, Glam RO; *Y Dinesydd Cymreig* 7 Mawrth 1917.

10 *Y Tyst Cymreig*, 29 Mehef.1867.

11 For example, the *Glamorgan Gazette* and the *Carmarthen Journal*; Hemming to Surveyor of Taxes, 10 Sept., 1879, GGLB, Glam RO; NLW MS 7975 B.

12 W.J.Parry to David Lloyd George, 24 Dec. 1891, NLW MS 8816C/318.

13 Parry to Lloyd George, 8 Jan. 1892, NLW MS 8816C/356.

14 Jones, *Printers*, p.278.

15 Meeting of Directors, Western Mail and Echo Ltd., 6 Sept. 1895, Records, vol. 7 and Private Salaries and Fees, April 1929, Records, vol. 39, NLW; Cash Balance, North Wales Chronicle Co., 1885, NWC1, Gwyn. Arch. Caer.

16 J.Raglan to Revd O. Eilian Owen, 4 Mar. 1902, NLW MS 3300D.

17 Robert Gordon to Revd O. Eilian Owen, 4 Mar. 1902, NLW MS 3300D.

18 Thomas Hughes to Revd O. Eilian Owen, 5 Mar. 1902, NLW MS 3300D.

19 Twenty-year-old W.Rathbone Owen, also of Liverpool, stressed that he could write Welsh, and expected to receive a salary of one hundred pounds a year, whilst R.J.Williams, twenty-six, with twelve years' experience of general office work and close connections with Welsh 'social and religious movements', asked for a 'salary of about forty five shillings' a week. W.Rathbone-Owen to Revd O. Eilian Owen, 6 Mar. 1902; R.J.Williams to Revd O. Eilian Owen, 5 Mar. 1902, NLW MS 3300D.

20 J.S.R.Phillips, 'The Growth of Journalism', in A.W.Ward and A.R.Waller (Eds.), *Cambridge History of English Literature*, vol. xiv (Cambridge, 1916), p.175.

21 Brown, *Victorian News*, p.23, draws on the example of the *Bucks Herald*, which in 1848–9 had a mere 220 subscribers, an income from sales of £4 a week, but £13 a week from advertisements, p.15.

22 *Y Dywysogaeth*, 5 Chwef. 1870. Tenders for the printing of a new Welsh newspaper in Liverpool in 1901, T.Amos Hughes to Revd O. Eilian Owen, 4 Oct. 1901, NLW MS 3300D.

23 Hemming to W.E.Vaughan, 23 Nov. 1877, GGLB, Glam RO. Records of advertisement revenue is available for a number of Welsh newspapers, including the *Aberdare Times* from April 1876 to December 1902. The illusionist Professor Dupec paid 3s. 6d. for one insertion on 6 March 1880, papers of Josiah Thomas Jones, N.L.W. MS 3325B, 33256B, 3327C, 3328E. Details of advertisement receipts of *Y Celt* can be found in NLW MS 9598B, folio 128. Scales of advertisement charges for *Glamorgan Free Press* in 1891 may be found in the D.M. Richards Papers, NLW MS 3293E/11.

24 Parry to Lloyd George, 10 Sept. 1891, 18 Sept. 1891, NLW MS 8816C/85.

25 North Wales Chronicle Account Book, NWC 6, Gwyn. Arch. Caer. For an example of block advertising in this paper, see the correspondence of N.P.Stewart to Editor e.g. 13 Apr. 1892, X/Vaynol/2404/187, Gwyn. Arch. Caer.

26 S.B. Jones to C.E.G.Phillips, 2 Aug. 1884, Picton Castle Coll. 3900, NLW MS.

27 'The Advertising Agent', *The Newspaper Press*, 1 Mar. 1871, pp. 64–5.

28 'Pictorials for page 7 across the 5 centre columns (top and bottom) and changeable weekly, the space varying in depth from 8 to 15 inches. The pictures to be surrounded by matter, and no other Adverts. to appear on either page 6 or 7, with the exception of small pars.', T.B.Browne

to A.E.Jones, 4 Jan. 1890, NWC 114; see also Browne to Jones 10 Jan. 1890, NWC 185, Gwyn. Arch. Caer.

29 Report of Registrar of Joint Stock Companies, 1899 (359), lxxxix, 131.

30 R.Williams to S.Roberts, ? June 1878; Joseph Williams to S.Roberts, 21 June 1878; Receipt from Thomas Gee, 25 Mar. 1878, NLW MS 9598B; Hemming to F.May and Co., 19 Dec. 1881.

31 N.P.Stewart to Frederick Coplestone, 14 Dec. 1892 and 16 Dec. 1892, Letter Book, X/Vaynol/2404/664, Gwyn. Arch. Caer.

32 Rees, 'South Wales . . . Newspapers', p.305.

33 *Y Papyr Newydd Cymraeg*, 22 Medi 1836, 5 Hyd. 1836.

34 *Merthyr and Cardiff Chronicle*, 16 Dec. 1837. Formerly the *South Wales Reporter*. The economic difficulties faced by the Welsh press during much of the nineteenth century resembled those of other countries. A contemporary observer of the Indian press remarked that 'the unremunerative character of the native journalism is due, not so much to the lack of buyers of papers, though this is a serious drawback, in a country where one man buys a paper for hundreds to read, but rather to the entire lack of advertisements in a country where most internal commerce is ruled by custom instead of competition', Roper Lethbridge, 'The Vernacular Press of India', *Contemporary Review*, vol. 37, Mar. 1880, p.463.

35 J.O.Jones, 'The National Awakening', *Young Wales*, Dec. 1895, p.280; CPL MS 3.348.

36 Brown, *Victorian News*, p.22.

37 *Workman's Advocate*, 11 Dec. 1874.

38 *Yr Herald Cymraeg*, 28 Tach. 1911.

39 Davies *Atgofion*, p.131.

40 Joint Managing Director to E.Jacobson, 22 Aug. 1928, Western Mail and Echo Records, vol. 33, NLW.

41 *Y Tyst a'r Dydd* papers, NLW MS 8842D.

42 *Ye Brython Cymreig*, 1 January 1892.

43 Beta, 'The Vernacular Press of Wales', *Young Wales*, Feb. 1892.

44 *Y Gloch*, 6 Medi 1898.

45 Jones, *O'r Mwg i'r Mynydd*, pp.125–7.

46 A.I.Pryse MSS 517, NLW. Maurice Milne has said of the north-east of England, 'The placing of advertisements in the Victorian period probably owed as much to personal contact and political sympathy as to precise market analysis', Milne, 'Survival', p.216.

47 The scale of charges in 1857 was as follows: £14.10*s*. for 1,200, £16.5*s*. for 1,500 and £19.15s. for 2,000 copies, Nefydd, *Diary*, 1857, NLW MS 7073A.

48 Papers of W.Williams and Sons, Holywell, printers, D/DM/436/1, Clwyd Arch. Haw.

49 NLW MS 6402D.

50 T.Amos Hughes, Liverpool, to Revd O.Eilian Owen, 4 Oct. 1901, Geo. L. Miller to Revd O. Eilian Owen, 19 Feb. 1902, NLW MS 3300D.

51 Gaskell, *Introduction*, p.263. See also F.J.F.Wilson and D.Grey, *Modern Printing Machinery*, (1888).

52 Rees, 'A History', p.383; *The Hereford Times*, 30 June 1832.

53 Jones, 'Thomas Gee', p.67; Rees, 'A History', p. 383.

54 Jones, 'Thomas Gee', p.68; Jones, *Printers*, p. 253.

55 The new Hoe did not save much on labour, as a stereotyper was still needed, but it radically cut the cost of overtime for machinists, counters and packers, Bangor MS 16009, UCNW.

56 Rees, 'South Wales . . . Newspapers, p.307; Rees 'A History', p.383.

57 Gaskell, *Introduction*, p.274.

58 Gaskell, *Introduction*, p.276.

59 Minutes, Provincial Typographical Association Executive Committee Meeting, 20 Oct. 1894, MS 39A/TA/1/18/1, p.24, MRC.

60 Jones 'Thomas Gee', p.57.

61 North Wales Chronicle MS 129, Gwyn. Arch. Caer.

62 *Y Meddwl*, 27 Sept. 1879.

63 *Gwalia*, 17 Aug. 1881.

64 *Ye Brython Cymreig*, 8 Jan. 1892. The same printer failed to print *Y Celt* in Jan. 1896 due to difficulties with their printing machine, NLW MS 4616B.

65 MS D/KT/22, Clwyd Arch.; Mason to Rendel, 19 Apr.1889, NLW MS 19457C/IX 629.

66 Mansel Coll. 753, and Minutes, Extraordinary General Meeting, Cambrian Newspaper Co. Ltd., Mansel Coll. 769, SPL.

67 Memorandum of Agreement, Welsh National Newspaper Co. Ltd., NLW MS 8843E/5; *Y Genedl Gymreig*, 1 June 1892.

68 NLW MS 3322D.

69 NLW MS 3366D.

70 Minutes, Meeting of Directors, Daniel Owen and Co., 27 Jan. 1892 and Debenture Prospectus, Apr. 1895, Western Mail and Echo Ltd, NLW vol. 7.

71 Gibson to Rendel, 30 Dec. 1895, NLW MS 19450C/189.

72 Jobbing Printer's Account Book, 1832, NLW MS 3329A.

73 Mason to Rendel, 19 Apr. 1889, NLW MS 19457C/IX 629.

74 The complete jobbing plant consisted of the following items, '2 Wharfedale double demy machines with flyers, 2 Foolscap folio treadle machines, 30 inch guillotine, with steam gear, iron standing press, Columbian and Albion presses, iron galley press, 3 iron imposing surfaces, stereo foundry, 8 hp gas/steam engine, folding machine, wire

stitching machine, perforating machine, book and jobbing founts', *Y Werin*, 1 Hyd. 1892.

75 See, for example, receipt of payment for printing by Moriah Literary Society, April 1896, X/Moriah/1341, also XQS/1856/H/120 and X/Poole/796, Gwyn. Arch. Caer. and NLW MS 9598B.

76 NLW MS 7097A; Public Record Office, Kew, (PRO), FS7/5/188; *Workman's Advocate*, 1 Aug. 1874.

77 P. Gaskell, *Introduction*, p.252.

78 NLW MS 4296C.

79 NLW MS 13475C.

80 Apprenticeship Indenture, Thomas Gee, to William Collister and Sons, Chester, 14 Jan. 1796, NLW MS 8319E.

81 Apprenticeship Indenture, Edward Owen Jones, to David Williams, North Wales Chronicle Co., NWC 106; see also NWC 107, 108, 109, 110, 111, Gwyn. Arch. Caer.

82 NWC 108, Gwyn. Arch. Caer.

83 Hemming to D.J.Rosser, 13 November 1880, GGLB, Glam RO.

84 Gaskell, *Introduction*, p.290.

85 T. M. Bassett, *Braslun o Hanes Hughes a'i Fab* (Oswestry, 1946) p.38–9.

86 Quinquennial Meeting of the Provincial Typographical Association (PTA), June 1913, MRC 39A/TA/4/3/8/, p.109.

87 Gaskell, *Introduction*, p.291; Boswell Reid, *Theory and Practice of Ventilation* (c1844) ; Bassett, *Braslun*, p.39.

88 Jones, 'Thomas Gee', p.80.

89 NLW MS 7975B; Gaskell, *Introduction*, p. 292; Jones, 'Thomas Gee', p. 57.

90 Jones, *Printers*, p.282. See also travelling map of the Typographical Association (nd), including routes in Wales with mileages, MRC 39A/TA/4/14/1.

91 Midland Board, Typographical Association, 5 July 1852, MRC 39A/TA/1/1/1.

92 A.E. Musson, *The Typographical Association. Origins and History up to 1949* (Oxford, 1954), pp. 51, 279. So mobile were printers in the nineteenth and early twentieth centuries in Wales that, during periods of expansion in the industry, it became so difficult for such newspapers as *South Wales Gazette* to retain staff that they began a new programme to recruit and train their own printers, Jones, *Printers*, p.278.

93 Rees, 'A History', p.392.

94 Report Book of Deputations, PTA, 23 March 1872, MRC 39A/TA/7/DEP/1.

95 Rees, 'A History', p.391.

96 The printers' wage bill in the office of *Y Dydd* in Dolgellau stood on average at four pounds a week. By August 1935 the number of printers had been reduced from seven to three, and labour costs were no more than they had been at the end of the nineteenth century. Salary Book, *Y Dydd* Office, 1899, Z/M/301/14 and 1932–42, Z/M/115/9, (Gwyn Arch Dol).

97 Musson, *Typographical Association*, p.170.

98 Musson, *Typographical Association*, p.34.

99 Rees, 'A History', p.390. Such developments were not uncommon in the 1840s. Four journeymen and two apprentices at a printing office in Newport, Monmouthshire, established in 1847 an insurance and self-help group. It was not a trade union. 'FirstReport from Newport, Mon.', *People's Journal*, 6 Feb. 1847, p.11.

100 *Printer*, 1 Aug. 1844.

101 Musson, *Typographical Association*, p.62.

102 Bassett, *Braslun*, p.38. The PTA superceded also such organizations as the Newcastle upon Tyne Typographical Mutual Improvement Society, founded October 1846. Its President, Mr Oliver Moore, overseer of the *Newcastle Guardian*, lectured on such subjects as 'the formation of language' and 'the art of printing', *People's Journal*, 17 Apr. 1847, p.32

103 The apprentice problem was worst in Scotland, London and Wales, Musson, *Typographical Association*, pp. 42–4.

104 Minutes of Board Meeting, 8 May 1845, Midland Board PTA, MRC 39A/TA/1/1/1.

105 MRC 39A/TA/1/1/1; MRC 39A/TA/4/7/20 (i).

106 The PTA argued that the paper did not conform to the fifteenth rule of the PTA which stipulated that 'no newspaper shall be entitled to an office until it has been in existence for 12 months', Minutes of the Midland Board PTA, 23 Oct. 1852, 5 July 1852, MRC 39A/TA/1/1/1.

107 Minutes, Midland Board PTA, 16 Sept. 1851, 16 Oct.1851, MRC 39A/TA/1/1/1.

108 Minutes, Midland Board PTA, 21 May 1850, 8 June 1850, 13 June 1850, MRC 39A/TA/1/1/1.

109 Minutes, Midland Board PTA, 30 Dec. 1851, 16 Mar.1852, MRC 39A/TA/1/1/1.

110 *London Press Journal or General Trades' Advocate*, 1 Nov. 1858

111 Bassett, *Braslun*, p.38; MRC 39A/TA/4/3/2/2.

112 Musson, *Typographical Association*, pp. 93, 165.

113 Minutes, Executive Committee PTA, MRC 39A/TA/1/7/1.

114 Report Book of Deputations, PTA, 18 June 1875, MRC 39A/TA/7/DEP/1.

115 Musson, *Typographical Association*, p.82; Report Book of Deputations, PTA, 18 June 1875, MRC 39A/TA/7/DEP/1; Minutes, Executive Committee, PTA, 10 July 1875, MRC 39A/TA/1/7/1.

116 Rules of the Oswestry Typographical Association (1921), MRC 39D/TA/4/6/129/1.

117 Report Book of Deputations, PTA, 19 June 1875, 39A/TA/7/DEP/1.

118 Minutes, PTA, 29 Aug. 1887, MRC 39A/TA/1/13. See a full list of members of the Typographical Association, noting age, date of registration, branch, date of joining, continuous or intermittent membership etc. in 'Register of Members', June 1888, MRC 39A/TA/4/5/1 (ii).

119 Minutes, PTA, Cardiff 25 Nov. 1889, MRC 39A/TA/1/14.

120 *Y Clorianydd*, 13 Awst 1891.

121 Minutes, PTA, Newport, 25 Aug 1891, MRC 39A/TA/1/15. There were at least 44 members in the Caernarfon branch of the PTA in 1891, and a further two had recently left the town to take up work in Liverpool and Wrexham. Ages ranged from 20 to 51, with an average age of 29, (incomplete) 'List of Members of the Caernarvon Branch', 1891, MRC 39B/TA/2/1/5.

122 Minutes, Quinquennial Delegate Meeting, PTA, June 1893, MRC 39A/TA/4/3/8, p.55; E.W.Davies, *The Newspaper Society, 1836–1936* (1936), p.36.

123 A Scottish Daily Newspaper Society was also formed in 1915, E.W.Davies, *Newspaper Society*, pp.18–22.

124 E.W.Davies, *Newspaper Society*, pp. 26–32.

125 These had offices in Llangefni, Caernarfon, Denbigh, Wrexham and Merthyr Tydfil; E.W.Davies, *Newspaper Society*, p.70.

126 Minutes, Quinquennial Delegate Meeting. PTA, June 1893, MRC 39A/TA/4/3/8, p.55.

127 Further details of negotiated settlements with regard to wages, hours etc. may be found in 'Scale of Prices and Regulations for Linotype Composing Machines in the Daily Western Mail offices', Report from Cardiff, PTA, 15 Oct. 1894, 9 Jan. 1899, MRC 39A/TA/1/18/1.

128 Report from Cardiff, PTA, 29 Aug. 1898, MRC 39A/TA/1/21.

129 A Celt, *Cymru Fydd*, Feb. 1895, p.36.

130 Report from Merthyr, PTA, 30 Oct. 1894, MRC 39A/TA/1/18/1; Musson, *Typographical Association*, p.127; Minutes, Executive Committee, PTA, 19 Oct. 1895, 39A/TA/1/18.

131 Minutes, Special Executive Committee, PTA, 14 September 1895, 39A/TA/1/18.

132 *Merthyr Times*, 16 Jan. 1896.

133 Minutes, Executive Committee, PTA, 13 July and 27 July 1901, MRC 39A/TA/1/24.

134 Minutes, Executive Committee, PTA, 30 Nov. 1901, MRC

39A/TA/1/24; updated lists of open and closed offices appeared regularly in *Typographical Circular*.

135 Minutes, Executive Committee, PTA, 23 Feb. 1901, 20 Apr. 1901, MRC 39A/TA/1/24. In 1898 delegates were sent from seven Welsh branches to the union's national conference – Cardiff, Caernarfon, Merthyr, Newport, Pontypridd, Swansea and Wrexham, Minutes, Delegate Meeting, PTA., Liverpool 1898, MRC 39A/TA/4/3/5/3. By June 1913, nine branches sent delegates to the national conference, representing Aberdare, Cardiff, Caernarfon, Llanelli, Merthyr, Newport, Pontypridd, Rhondda Valleys, Swansea, Quinquennial Delegate Meeting June 1913, MRC 39A/TA/4/3/8, p.109.

136 Minutes, PTA Sub-Committee, 4 May 1898, MRC 39A/TA/1/21.

137 Minutes,Typographical Association Conference, June 1913, MRC 39A/TA/4/7/20 (i).

138 Cyfarthfa Papers vol. 5, Nos. 516 and 735, NLW; Griffith, *Gohebydd*, passim.

139 *Yr Herald Cymraeg*, 23 Mai 1955; diary entry for 5 Jan. 1872, Meudwy Mon MS. 2, UCNW; William Davies was drawn towards journalism as a youth in the 1870s by a diet of weekly newspapers that comprised *Y Goleuad*, *Y Faner* and *Y Tyst a'r Dydd*. In later life he became editor of the *Western Mail*, Davies, *Atgofion*, p.157.

140 'Nid yw y ris ganol yn lliosog a dylanwadol yn Nghymru . . . *Diffyg* dosparth canol sydd wedi, ac yn parhau i niweidio addysg yn ein gwlad ni', *Seren Cymru*, 2 Hyd. 1851.

141 *South Wales Echo*, 13 Nov. 1880.

142 *Pontypridd Chronicle and Workman's News*, 15 Jan. 1881.

143 GGLB, Glam RO.

144 R.Williams, 'Methodism in Wales', *Quarterly Review*, vol. 85, Sept. 1849, p.341.

145 *Census of England and Wales*, 1811 to 1891.

146 Vyrnwy Morgan, *Kilsby Jones* (Wrexham, 1897), p.213.

147 The British and Foreign Schools were 'universal, democratic in organization, and brought into being a reading public and a literate nation', Leslie Wynne Evans, *Education in Industrial Wales 1700–1900. A study of the Works Schools System in Wales during the Industrial Revolution* (Cardiff, 1971), pp. 233. See also J.A.Davies, *Education in a Welsh Rural County 1870–1973* (Cardiff, 1973); W. Gareth Evans, *Educational Development in a Victorian Community* (Aberystwyth, 1990); W.Gareth Evans, *The Establishment of Intermediate Education in Carmarthenshire, 1889–1914*, (Aberystwyth, 1980); W.Gareth Evans (Ed.), *Perspectives on a Century of Secondary Education in Wales, 1889–1989* (Aberystwyth, 1990); G.W.Roderick, 'Education, Culture and Industry in Wales in the Nineteenth-Century', *WHR*, 1986–7, pp. 438–52.

148 J. Thackeray Bunce, 'Church and People', *National Review*, vol. xxii, Sept.-Feb. 1893–4, p.388. Other sources generally confirm the Mitchell figures, see Saunders, Otley and Co, *The Newspaper Press of the Present Day* (1860), pp. 95–7; *Y Gwyddoniadur Cymreig*, vol. vii, p.64; *Gwalia*, 3 Awst, 1881; *Y Traethodydd*, xxxix, 1884, pp. 192–3; J.E.Southall, *Bi-lingual Teaching in Welsh Elementary Schools* (1888), evidence of Beriah Gwynfe Evans, Royal Commission on Education, 1886–7, par. 42,567.

149 Rees, 'A History', p 44; A. Aspinall, *Politics and the Press, c.1780–1850* (1949), pp. 24–5; Joel H.Wiener, 'Circulations and the Stamp Tax', J.Don Vann and R. T.VanArsdel, *Victorian Periodicals. A Guide to Research*, vol.i (New York, 1978), pp. 149–74.

150 *Y Papyr Newydd Cymraeg*, 7 Dec. 1836, declared a weekly circulation of 9,000; the *Western Vindicator and Liberator of the West and Wales* enjoyed a 'regular sale in Merthyr of about 300 to 400 weekly', and a year after the Newport riots, 'unstamped periodicals were still being circulated to a considerable extent. . . . *Udgorn Cymru*, and its English translation, *The Advocate*, were the work of the Workingmen's Press and Publication, and were financed locally', C.R.Fay, *Round About Industrial Britain, 1830–1860* (Toronto, 1952), p.77. 'Mr Hugh Jones of Llangollen was in the habit of publishing fortnightly a penny paper called *Yr Ipsyr* (*sic*), of which he used to sell 2,300 copies', before 1836, Collet, *Taxes on Knowledge*, pp. 78–9. See also Jones, *Printers*, pp. 230, 254, and *Stamps Issued to Welsh Newspapers, 1870* (1871). Postal services improved markedly during the first half of the nineteenth century. In 1750 the post from London arrived in Wales twice a week, normally on Tuesdays and Saturdays, and returned on Mondays and Fridays, P. Archer, 'The Post in Wales', *Old Wales*, vol. ii, no. i,1906, p.215.

151 Thomas Williams (*Y Tyst a'r Dydd*) to W.J.Parry, 23 Aug. 1893, NLW MS 8842D. *Y Dywysogaeth*, 5 Chwef. 1870; *Y Chwarelwr* 24, Ion. 1877; '*The Wrexham Guardian* has now a first class circulation of 2000', 24 Jan. 1878, Clwyd Arch., D/KT/22; 300 copies were distributed of the first issue of *Gwalia*, *Gwalia*, 3 Awst 1881; the circulation of *Tarian y Gweithiwr* reached 15,000 a week in the 1880s, *Y Darian*, 29 Ion. 1925. For circulation figures for *Y Genedl Gymreig* group of newspapers, see Southall, *Bi-lingual Teaching*, evidence of Beriah Gwynfe Evans, par. 42,576; W.J.Parry to J.Thomas (Eifionydd), 31 Aug. 1891, NLW MS 8816C/68; W.J.Parry to F.Coplestone, 2 Sept. 1891, and W.J.Parry to D. Lloyd George, 2 Sept. 1891, NLW MS 8816C/74; *Y Werin*, 3 Medi 1892. In contrast, the readership of Welsh-language periodicals in the early 1970s had fallen to under 30,000, K.O. Morgan, *Rebirth of a Nation, Wales 1880–1980* (Cardiff and Oxford, 1981), p.367.

152 *Y Drysorfa* records, 1841, item 15411, and minutes, *Monthly Herald*, 16 Mar. 1858, item 28706 C.M. Arch., Gen. Coll., NLW; 'Rhestr o enwau y personau a dderbyniant neu a ddosbarthant Seren Gomer, Ebrill 1864–Ionawr 1865', NLW MS 7079B; Jones, 'Thomas Gee', p.142; *Merthyr Times*, 28 Nov. 1895; Beriah Gwynfe Evans, *Cymro, Cymru a Chymraeg, yn eu cysylltiad ag addysg, papyr a ddarllenwyd o flaen Cymdeithas Gymdeithasol Gymreig, Lerpwl, Ion. 29 1889* (Liverpool, 1889), p.69.

153 *Cardiff Argus*, 30 May 1888; it was estimated that a population of 50,000 was needed before a daily newspaper could be sustained. The population of Cardiff reached 57,000 in 1871, two years after the launch of the daily *Western Mail*, Brown, *Victorian News*, p.46; *Mitchell's* (1874) for average circulations of the *Western Mail* in 1869, 1870, 1871, 1872, 1873; Francis Hitchman, 'The Penny Press', *Macmillan's Magazine*, Vol. 43, April 1881, p.396.

154 Ivor Waters, *Chepstow Printers and Newspapers* (Chepstow, 1981), p.11.

155 *Workman's Advocate*, 26 Feb. 1874; *South Wales Free Press*, 27 Dec. 1884.

156 T.Hudson-Williams, *Reminiscences of Caernarvon* (Llandysul, 1952), p.14.

157 Bill Twamley, *Cardiff and Me Sixty Years Ago* (Newport, 1984), p.49.

158 R.J.Derfel, 'Papyr Newydd Dyddiol Cymraeg', *Traethodau ac Areithiau* (1864), reprinted in D.Gwenallt Jones (Ed.), *Detholiad o Ryddiaith Gymraeg R.J.Derfel* (Dinbych, 1945), pp. 81–4.

159 Rees, 'A History', pp.158, 307.

160 *North Wales Gazette*, 9 Feb. 1808.

161 Rowland Williams to Hugh Jones (Erfyl), 26 May 1829, NLW MS 9031E; *Y Papyr Newydd Cymraeg*, 28 Medi 1836.

162 Account book of Robert Evans, Trefriw, local distributor of *Y Gwladgarwr*, Jan. to Dec. 1833, NLW MS 9213A.

163 *Y Papyr Newydd Cymraeg*, 5 Hyd. 1836, 22 Medi 1836, 7 Rhag. 1836; Robert Munter, *The History of the Irish Newspaper 1685–1760* (Cambridge, 1967), p.80; Irene Collins, *The Government and the Newspaper Press in France 1814–1881* (Oxford, 1959), p. xi.

164 List of shareholders in the *Merthyr and Cardiff Guardian*, 1836, NLW MS MS 3316A.

165 Subscription list, *Tarian Rhyddid*, 1839, NLW MSMS 10218A, see also MSS 10268A, 7077A, 7079B.

166 Subscription lists, *Y Ffenestr*, *Y Cerddor*, *Y Gerddorfa*, 1874–8, NLW MS 8240A; *Yr Athraw*, 1850, NLW MS 10268A; *Yr Athraw Gerddorol*,1855–1860, NLW MS 10348A.

167 *Carmarthen Express*, 10 Apr. 1874.

168 NLW MS 8843E/8.

169 C. Tawelfryn Thomas, *Cofiant Ieuan Gwynedd* (Dolgellau, 1909), p.239.

170 Siân Rhiannon Williams, 'Rhai agweddau cymdeithasol ar hanes yr iaith Gymraeg yn ardal ddiwydiannol Sir Fynwy yn y bedwaredd ganrif ar bymtheg', (Ph.D., University of Wales, 1985), p.282.

171 Distributors of *Y Celt*, 1881–4, NLW MS15523A.

172 *Udgorn Rhyddid*, 1 Chwef. 1888.

173 *WM*, 2 July 1914.

174 Aspinall, *Politics*, p. 27.

175 For details of the distribution of *Y Drysorfa* consult Bangor MS 223A and *DWB* p.543.

176 Some papers were written in such a way as to be read aloud in public places, see Richard Jeffries, *The Toilers of the Field* (1894), pp. 81 and 100; Aspinall, *Politics*, pp. 28–9; Brown, *Victorian News*, pp. 50–51.

177 W. Odell, Jr., 'Free Libraries and their Workings', *Macmillan's Magazine*, vol. 43, Apr. 1881, p.440.

178 Bob Owen, 'Cymdeithasau darllen gan mlynedd yn ôl', (unpublished MS), NLW MS 16283E, see also NLW MSD/KK/457(13), NLW MS 3322D, NLW MS 333D; Aspinall, *Politics*, p.25; J.Ginswick (Ed.), *Labour and the Poor in England and Wales, 1849–1851, vol. iii, The Mining and Manufacturing Districts of South Wales and North Wales*, (reprinted 1983), pp. 140–3.

179 Chris J. Evans (ed.), *The Book of Cardiff* (Oxford, 1937), p.118; James Hibbert (Ed.), *Notes on Free Public Libraries and Museums* (Preston, 1881).

180 The list was as follows: daily newspapers: *The Times, Standard, Daily Telegraph, Daily News, Liverpool Mercury, Liverpool Courier, Birmingham Daily Post, Manchester Examiner and Times, South Wales Daily News, Western Mail, Shipping Gazette*. Weekly newspapers: *The Graphic, Illustrated London News, Punch, Judy, The Spectator, Literary World, Y Genedl Gymreig, Gwalia, Cambrian News, Aberystwyth Observer, Hereford Times, Midland Counties Herald, The Freemason, Worcester Herald, The Bullionist, Money*. Monthly periodicals: *Nineteenth Century, Harper's Magazine, The English Illustrated Magazine*. See Borough of Aberystwyth, *Annual Report of the Public Free Library and Reading Room Committee, 1883–4* (1884).

181 NLW MS XZ 675 S8 L79.

182 Ginswick, *Labour*, p.141; Statement of Accounts, Milford Haven Mechanics' Institute, Mar. 1884, Picton Castle Coll., MSS 3899, 3900, NLW.

183 'Representative Government – what is it good for?', *Westminster Review*, new ser., vol. xii, Oct. 1857, p.457.

184 Gwynedd Archive Service, teaching pack for *Dragon has Two Tongues*, *Oes y Werin*, 3, p.18; NLW MS 6999B; NLW MS 4296C; Gwyn. Arch. Dol. Z/M/177/1; C.Baggs, 'Well done Cymmer workmen! The Cymmer Collieries Workmen's Library 1893–1920', *Llafur*, Vol. 5, No. 3., 1990.

185 NLW MS 7079B.

186 Minutes, Aberystwyth Junior Radical Club, 1888, NLW MS 5426C.

187 Minutes, NWLF, 15 May 1890, NLW MS 21,171D.

188 Minutes, NWLF, 30 Apr. 1889; *South Wales Radical*, 14 May 1892.

189 *Workman's Advocate*, 29 Nov. 1873, 3 Jan. 1874, 6 Nov. 1874.

190 Hugh Lloyd to Editor of *Y Dinesydd*, 19 Aug. 1925, Bangor MS 1219/85, also 1219/118, UCNW.

191 Bangor MS 1219/34, 35, 45, 126, UCNW.

192 Account Book, Rhosllannerchrugog Miners' Association, 1879, NLW MS 18957C; Evans, *Bob Owen*, p.29.

193 Minutes, Temlwyr Da (Good Templars), Croesor, 19 Feb. 1873, NLW MS 19255B.

194 In 1850 the following sales were recorded at two locations in Merthyr:

White's bookshop:

Title	no. of copies
The Artizan	5
The Mechanic's Magazine	6
The Practical Mechanic's Journal	10
The Builder	6
Family Herald	19
Chamber's Journal	5
Eliza Cook's Journal	2
Art Journal	10
People's Journal	2
Banker's Magazine	2
New Monthly	1
Bentley's	1
Blackwood's Magazine	7
Eglwysydd	150
Churchman's Penny Magazine	50
Church of England Magazine	7
Christian's Penny Magazine	20
Baptist Magazine	11
Juvenile Missionary Magazine	30
Juvenile Missionary Herald (Baptist)	63
Christian Witness (Independent)	15

Child's Companion	55

Wilkins' bookshop:

The Family Herald	360
The London Journal	360
Eliza Cook's Journal	18
The People and Howitt's Journal	18
The Home Circle	18
Reynolds's Miscellany	36
The Domestic Journal	12
The Northern Star	12
The News of the World	189
Dipple's Miscellany	12
The Physician	24
Lloyd's Miscellany	24

Source: Ginswick, *Labour*, p.59. See also the account books of a Bangor bookseller, 1830–40, Bangor MS 782, UCNW, and a Brynmawr grocer, 1843, NLW MS 10292E; distribution arrangements for *South Wales Reporter*, 1838, in NLW MS 3366D, and for *Seren Gomer*, 1851–52, in NLW MS 7078A.

195 Bookseller's account book, Ystalyfera, 1863, NLW MS 10940A; bookseller's account book, Aberystwyth, 1883–88, NLW MS 6999B; account book of *Y Dydd*, 1871–1946, Gwyn. Arch. Dol., Z/M/115/1; *Gwalia*, 3 Awst 1881; Hemming to J. Hill, Chemist, Neath, 22 Dec. 1877, GGLB, Glam RO; distribution of *Y Deyrnas*, 1918, Bala-Bangor MS 28, UCNW; Beta, 'Vernacular Press', pp.38–42.

196 Account book, Hugh Evans, Liverpool, 1887 in C.M.Arch., Gen. Coll., NLW.

197 M. Williams to editor *Y Deyrnas*, 2 Nov. 1919, Bala–Bangor MS 28, UCNW.

198 Letters and accounts, the *Cambrian* Office, 1820, Glam RO MS D/D XCZ 43.

199 *Seren Cymru*, 13 Awst 1851.

200 Hemming to Austin, 11 Apr. 1878, GGLB, Glam RO.

201 Thomas, *Ieuan Gwynedd*, p.189.

202 *Y Gwyliedydd*, 11 Ebrill 1888.

203 *Y Gweithiwr Cymreig*, 26 Medi 1889.

204 *Report of the Registrar of Joint-Stock Companies*, 1846 (504), XLIII, p.55.

205 Articles by T.J.Hughes (Adfyfyr) in *Daily News*, 12 and 27 Oct. 1887, 16 Nov. 1887, quoted in Morgan, *Wales*, p.2.

206 Bangor MS 523/194, UCNW.

207 *Tarian y Gweithiwr*, 13 Medi 1878.

208 Gibson to Rendel, 15 May 1887, NLW MS 19450C/171; NLW MS 4613A; NWC 124, Gwyn. Arch. Caer.

209 *Llandrindod Wells Chronicle and Visitor's Directory*, 17 Aug. 1876; Gibson to Rendel, 5 May 1887, NLW MS 19450C/170.

210 W.H.Smith Archives, A.24, A.37, A.102, A.229, A.230, A.240, X.314, X.315; *The British Book Trade Directory, 1933*; Brown, *Victorian News*, p.29.

211 *Cardiff Hansard*, Dec. 1882; *Y Meddwl*, 27 Medi 1879.

212 G.R.Evans to Messrs. Davies and Evans, 3 Sept. 1906, MSZ/M/177/2, Gwyn. Arch. Dol.

213 Brynmor Jones, 'Argraffwyr Cymreig y Gororau', *JWBS*, July 1970, vol. x, no.3, p.123.

214 Arnot Reid, 'How a Provincial Paper is Managed', *Nineteenth Century*, vol. xx, Sept. 1886, p.392.

215 Rees, 'A History', p.373–80.

216 MS 3.348, CPL.

217 Rees, 'A History', p.376.

218 Owen, 'Cymdeithasau darllen', np.

219 In Gelliwig, Llŷn, in 1870, *Liverpool Mercury* was read by a gardener, and its contents relayed verbally to the rest of the community, J.O. Williams, *Stori 'Mywyd* (Lerpwl, 1932), p.213.

220 J. Thomas, *Cofiant y Parch. J. Davies, Caerdydd* (Merthyr Tydfil, 1883), p.124; R. Buick-Knox, *Wales and 'Y Goleuad'* (Caernarfon, 1969), p.64.

221 *Y Gweithiwr Cymreig*, 1 Awst 1860. A newspaper bearing the same title was launched independently in Aberdare in January 1885.

222 *Y Diwygiwr*, 1876, p.99.

223 Minutes, Aberstwyth Junior Radical Club, 9 Oct. 1888, NLW MS 5426C; 4 Nov. 1891, NLW MS 5425A.

224 William Hawkin Tilston to Rendel, 10 Dec. 1889, NLW MS 19455E/526.

225 Minutes, NWLF, 14 Oct. 1890, NLW MS 21,171D.

226 Invoices of Twentieth Century Press, held in the archives of the Marxian Club, Blaenclydach.

Chapter 3

1 A list of newspaper proprietors and editors who began as printers in Britain and the USA may be found in Mansfield, *Complete Journalist*, p.269; 'Notes on Printing of *Carmarthen Journal*', NLW MS 13475C;

Apprenticeship Indenture, 27 Sept. 1851, Mansel Coll. 849, SPL; *Cyfaill y Werin*, 13 Rhag. 1861.

2 *Tarian y Gweithiwr*, 15 Ion. 1875.

3 Strick, 'Newspaper Journalism', p. 249–50.

4 An Old Journalist, 'How to make a newspaper, without credit or cash', *Frazer's Magazine*, vol. xx, Dec. 1839, pp.746–52.

5 Mansel Coll. 723, SPL.

6 Rees, 'A History', pp. 162–208. Individual ownership could also be a temporary arrangement. The *Wrexham Free Press* was owned for a brief period by Hugh Davies, the town's ex-Mayor, and a man aptly described by a visiting printer as 'one of the most influential men connected with the management of the paper'. His ownership of the paper lasted only from the time the old company went into liquidation and the forming of a new company, PTA minute book of deputations, MRC 39A/TA/7/DEP/1, p.318.

7 NLW MS 3316A.

8 Rees, 'A History', p.488.

9 Account Book, *South Wales Reporter*, Apr. 1837, July 1838, NLW MS 3366D.

10 Mansel Coll. 761, SPL; local élites identified and aligned themselves with specific titles and their businesses, and would guard their interests jealously against the encroachment of others. Attempts by David Owen of Ash Hall, Cowbridge, for example, to buy the *Central Glamorgan Gazette* in Sept. 1890 was fiercely resisted and ultimately frustrated by the paper's Directors, Hemming to D. Owen, 4 Oct. 1880, GGLB, Glam RO.

11 L.Jones to John Ceiriog Hughes, 27 June 1864, NLW MS 10184D/75.

12 Mansel Coll. 739, 748, SPL.

13 Mansel Coll. 787, 786, SPL.

14 Merthyr Telegraph Printing Company, PRO BT31/11892/92529. See also B.C.Hunt, *The Development of the Business Corporation in England 1800–1867* (Cambridge, Mass., 1936), pp. 76–108.

15 J.E.Caerwyn Williams, 'Hanes Cychwyn y Traethodydd', *Llên Cymru*, cyf. xiv, Ion-Gorff. 1981–2, pp.111–142; *Y Cymro*, 17 Mai 1983.

16 Agreement between Revd Roger Edwards and Revd Daniel Rowlands, 9 Oct. 1865; *Y Traethodydd* Account Book, Bangor MS 223, UCNW.

17 *Ye Brython Cymreig*, launched in Lampeter in January 1892. *Y Brython* was started in Tremadog in 1858.

18 Cyril Parry, 'Socialism in Gwynedd 1900–1920', (Ph.D., University of Wales, 1967), p.72.

19 R.E.Prothero, 'The Attack on the Welsh Church', *Quarterly Review*, vol. 179, July 1894, p.175. For the growth of Nonconformity since 1830, see

Beriah Gwynfe Evans, *Diwygwyr Cymru*, (Caernarfon, 1900), p.312, and, since 1883, Thomas Rees, *History of Protestant Nonconformity, from its rise in 1633 to the present day* (1883), p.404.

20 NLW MS 4943B.

21 C. M. Arch., Bala Coll. 799, NLW.

22 From 'The Aims of Cymru Fydd', *Cymru Fydd*, July 1890, pp. 429–30.

23 Rees, *Protestant Nonconformity*, p.455, claims that £1.5 million had been spent by Welsh Nonconformists on building and renovating chapels in the previous twenty-five years. See also Ieuan Gwynedd Jones, *Communities. Essays in the Social History of Victorian Wales*, (Llandysul, 1987), Part 1, passim.

24 W.Evans, 'Y Methodistiaid Calfinaidd', in J.Morgan Jones (Ed.), *Trem ar y Ganrif, sef Adolwg ar y Bedwaredd Ganrif ar Bymtheg*, (Dolgellau, 1902), p.126; see also Buick Knox, *Y Goleuad*.

25 Bangor MS 15971, UCNW.

26 Thomas Charles Edwards to E.W.Evans, May 1892, NLW MS 10850C/54.

27 J.H.Jones to Hugh Lloyd, 31 Jan. 1902; James Venmore to Owen Eilian Owen, 31 Jan. 1902. Venmore, a Liverpool estate agent and accountant, later pulled out of the venture on the grounds that he had neither the 'time nor the inclination', James Venmore to Owen Eilian Owen, 7 Feb. 1902, NLW MS 3300D.

28 R.Tudur Jones, *Ffydd ac Argyfwng Cenedl*, cyf 1, (Abertawe, 1981), p. 110.

29 *Yr Efangylydd* was established in Llandovery in 1831, and *Y Diwygiwr* in Llanelli in August 1835.

30 O.L.Roberts, 'Yr Annibynwyr', in Morgan Jones, *Trem ar y Ganrif*, p.162–4.

31 *Y Tyst Cymreig*, 29 Mehef. 1867.

32 C.R.Jones to W.J.Parry, 25 Aug. 1891, NLW MS 8842D.

33 NLW MS 8842D.

34 J. Miles to W.J.Parry, 27 June 1893, NLW MS 8842D.

35 Accounts of payments to shareholders, the Celt Newspaper Company, NLW MS 4614A.

36 Memorandum of Association, Celt Newspaper Company, NLW MS 4618E.

37 W.J.Jeremy to D.S.Davies, 26 Sept. 1891 and 21 Mar. 1892, NLW MS 4616B.

38 *Seren Gomer*, Ion. 1851.

39 T.M.Bassett, *The Welsh Baptists* (Swansea, 1977), pp.342–5.

40 Percentages of all occupations declared by shareholders, (100% = 318), Wesleyan Arch. MS 395E, NLW.

41 J.J.Blunt to Earl of Powis, 11 Jan. 1843, Earl of Powis Corr., MS 33, NLW.

42 *Y Dywysogaeth*, 4 Mai 1877.

43 *North Wales Chronicle*, 8 June 1889; Adrian John Parry, 'The Church Defence Institution 1859–1896', (MA University of Wales, 1982), p.46.

44 Joint Stock Companies, *Parliamentary Returns*, 1899 (359) lxxxix, 69; NLW MS 7907E.

45 *Y Gloch*, 24 Gorff. 1898.

46 J. Myfenydd Morgan, 'Yr Eglwys Sefydliedig', in Morgan Jones, *Trem ar y Ganrif*, p.84.

47 Aspinall, *Politics*, pp.354–68.

48 P.Elliott, 'Professional ideology and organizational change: the journalist since 1800', in G. Boyce, J.Curran and P.Wingate, *Newspaper History from the seventeenth century to the present day*, (1978), p.177.

49 'A Newspaper Editor's Reminiscences', *Fraser's Magazine*, vol. xx, Nov. 1839, p.599.

50 Jefferies, *Hodge*, p.269.

51 Rees, 'A History', p.401.

52 Rees, 'A History', pp. 401–2.

53. Milne, 'Survival', p.214.

54 A.J.Lee, 'The Radical Press', *Edwardian Radicalism 1900–1914* (1974).

55 NWC 206, 207, Gwyn. Arch. Caer.

56 *Report of the Royal Commission on Land in Wales and Monmouthshire*, 1894, vol.ii, Qs. 22963, 22966, 22967. It was implied here that *Y gwalia* was subsidized for political reasons by its parent company, the North Wales Chronicle Co.

57 Kenyon was MP for Denbigh Boroughs in 1885–95 and 1901–6; D/KT/22, Clwyd Arch. Haw.

58 D/KT/22, Clwyd Arch. Haw.

59 Evan Morris to W. Lee Brooke, 12 July 1785, D/KT/22 Clwyd Arch. Haw.

60 Printed Circular, signed by George Kenyon and Owen J.Wynne, 24 Jan. 1878, D/KT/22, Clwyd Arch. Haw.; MRC MS39A/TA/1/8 p.325.

61 *The Times*, 9 and 12 May, 24 Oct. 1883; see also *Journalist*, 7 Jan. 1887.

62 Beriah Gwynfe Evans to T.E.Ellis, 3 Aug. 1892, T.E.Ellis Coll. 544, NLW.

63 T. W. Booker to Marquess of Bute, 18 Nov. 1839, Bute Coll. XX/73, CPL.

64 J.Bruce Pryce to Marquess of Bute, 23 Nov. 1839, Bute Coll. XX/80–81, CPL.

65 Henry Scale to Bute, 31 Dec. 1839, Bute Coll. XX/154, CPL.

66 Bute to E.P.Richards, 3 Aug. 1841, Bute Coll. IX/27/21/57, CPL; Ifano Jones referred to the *Cardiff Standard and County Chronicle* as 'the only Conservative Party newspaper in South Wales' in 1865, Jones, *Printers*, p.246.

67 Rees, 'A History', p.517.

68 Brown, *Victorian News*, p.70. See also John Davies, *Cardiff and the Marquesses of Bute* (Cardiff, 1981), pp. 25–6 and 135.

69 Bute Papers XX/73, 80, 154 (1830), CPL; Meeting of Directors, Daniel Owen and Co., 31 May 1894, Western Mail and Echo Ltd. Records 7, NLW; Sir William T. Lewis to Lascelles Carr, 8 June 1893, Western Mail and Echo Ltd. Records 29, NLW.

70 Western Mail and Echo Ltd., company file 46946, Companies Registration Office, London (CRO).

71 Minutes of meeting with Directors, Daniel Owen and Co., 7 Apr. 1892, 15 Jan. 1896, Western Mail and Echo Ltd, Records 7, N.L.W.

72 Obituary of David Duncan by Gwilym Williams, *Cambrian Daily Leader*, 16 Jan. 1888; *The Times*, 16 Jan.1888; *Udgorn Rhyddid*, 18 Ion. 1888.

73 Mitchell, *Press Directory*, 1915, p.28.

74 Joseph Chamberlain to Henry Tobit Evans, 9 Apr. 1887, NLW MS 18882B.

75 Henblas B. MS 711, UCNW.

76 M. Ostrogorski, *Democracy and the Organization of Political Parties*, vol. i, (1902), pp.236–8; Rees, 'South Wales . . . Newspapers', p.312.

77 A.C.Humphreys-Owen to Rendel, 28 Aug. 1885, NLW MS 19461C/262. Rendel was also approached in 1887 with an invitation to provide financial support to the *Star*: 'T.P.O'Connor is trying to start a Radical evening newspaper, and has asked me to ask you whether you wd. do anything to help it forward in the way of taking a share in the enterprise. I have done so to the tune of £1,000, and he tells me he has £27,000 subscribed for, but wishes to complete £40,000 before beginning. I know nothing abt. business matters, but it seems to me it wd. be a good thing politically and very lively financially', W.S.Blunt to Rendel, 13 Oct. 1887, NLW MS 1058; see also T.P.O'Connor, *Memoirs of an Old Parliamentarian* (1929), vol. ii, pp. 254–5 and 170.

78 A.C.Humphreys-Owen to Rendel, 25 Oct. 1888, NLW MS 19463C/466.

79 A.C.Humphreys-Owen to Rendel, 28 Oct. 1888, NLW MS 19463C/468; A.C.Humphreys-Owen to Rendel, 1 Nov. 1888, NLW MS 19463C/469.

80 Richard Williams to Rendel, 8 Apr.1889, NLW MS 19457C/ix 627.

81 Mason to Rendel, 8 Apr. 1889, NLW MS 19457C/ix 628; Mason to Rendel, 19 Apr. 1889, NLW MS 19457C/ix 629.

82 Mason to Rendel, 27 Apr. 1889, NLW MS 19457C/ix 631.

83 Rendel to Mason, 9 May 1889, NLW MS 19457C/ix 633.

84 Mason to Rendel, 10 May 1889, NLW MS 19457C/ix 634.

85 Mason to Rendel, 10 May 1890, NLW MS 1945D/432; J.Evans to A.C.Humphreys-Owen, 17 June 1893, Glansevern MS 6019, NLW. It was precisely in order to avoid such uncertainty regarding political ownership that the founders of the *Liverpool Daily Post* drew up some 'very unusual Articles' which made special provision for political control in the event of a takeover. As A.G. Jeans explained to the Royal Commission on the Press in 1962, 'Liverpool was a Conservative city, and the *Liverpool Daily Post* was started as a Liberal newspaper. The Company's founders were anxious the Conservatives should not be able to buy it up', *Royal Commission on the Press, 1962,* (HMSO, 1963) p.488.

86 Changes of title as follows: *Caernarvon Herald and North Wales Advertiser* Jan. 1831–Jan. 1836, *Caernarvon and Denbigh Herald and North and South Wales Independent* January 1836–June 1920. *Merioneth News* was incorporated in July 1920, and *North Wales Observer* in Apr. 1937, see *Yr Herald Cymraeg*, 23 Mai 1955; W.J.Parry, *Hanes fy Mywyd a'm Gwaith* (Caernarfon, n.d. ?1884), pp. 45,77; CRO 228N.

87 *The Times*, 21 Nov. 1932; *Caernarvon and Denbigh Herald*, 25 Nov. 1932.

88 Davies, *Atgofion*, p.114.

89 R. Maldwyn Thomas, 'Y Wasg Gyfnodol yn Nhref Caernarfon hyd 1875, gyda sylw arbennig i argraffwyr a chyhoeddwyr' (University of Wales MA 1979), p.178.

90 J.Roose Williams, *Quarryman's Champion. The Life and Activities of William John Parry of Coetmor* (Denbigh, 1978), pp. 132–5.

91 E.Morgan Humphreys, 'Profiadau Golygydd', *Caernarvonshire Historical Society Transactions*, 1950, vol.ii, pp. 82–3.

92 W.J.Parry, *Diary*, 14 and 30 Oct. 1889, NLW MS 8813D; R.M.Thomas, 'Y Wasg Gyfnodol', p.228, note 175.

93 Parry to Lloyd George, 26 Feb. 1891, NLW MS 8820C/305–6; Parry to Lloyd George, 14 Sept. 1891, NLW MS 8816C/94.

94 Parry to Lloyd George, 26 Feb. 1891, NLW MS 8820C/305–6.

95 Parry to Coplestone, 3 Mar. 1891, NLW MS 8820C/315; Parry to Coplestone, 14 May 1891, NLW MS 8820C/425; Parry to Coplestone, 21 May 1891, NLW MS 8820C/432; Parry to Coplestone, 18 Sept. 1891, NLW MS 8816C/107.

96 Parry to Coplestone, 2 Oct. 1891, NLW MS 8816C/140; the two companies were eventually merged in 1938 when *Y Genedl Gymreig* and its

associated newspapers were purchased by Marjorie Coplestone-Godfrey and the Caernarvon Herald andAssociated Newspapers Co. Ltd, CRO 346235/7.

97 Parry to Lloyd George, 28 Nov. 1891, NLW MS 8816C/231.

98 *Prospectus*, The Welsh National Press Company, Ltd., *Y Werin*, 24 June 1892; Parry to Lloyd George, 30 Dec. 1891, NLW MS 8816C/328; John Grigg, *The Young David Lloyd George* (1973), p.116; Parry to David Edwards, 16 Apr. 1892, NLW MS 8816C/634; Beriah Gwynfe Evans, *The Life Romance of Lloyd George* (1916), pp. 61–2; Parry to F.C.Lewis, 4 June 1892, and Parry to J.R.Pritchard, 4 June 1892, NLW MS 8816C/720.

99 T.E.Ellis to Rendel, 15 Oct. 1892, NLW MS 19449D/90.

100 NLW MS 19449D/90.

101 James Magarch, *The Abuse of Power. The War Between Fleet Street and the Media From Lloyd George to Callaghan* (1978), p.13; S.J. Koss, *The Rise and Fall of the Political Press in Britain*, vol. ii, p.5.

102 *Merthyr Times*, 10 Jan. 1895, 8 Jan. 1897. In 1888, and again in 1894, when the *Pall Mall Gazette* underwent a change in ownership and in politics, 'the staff left en bloc', Brown, *Victorian News*, p.87.

103 D.R.Hopkin, 'The Newspaper of the Independent Labour Party 1893–1906', (Ph.D., University of Wales, 1981), pp. 51, 84–6. See also R.Harrison, G.Woolven and R.Duncan, *The Warwick Guide to British Labour Periodicals 1790–1970* (Hassocks, Sussex, 1977). Other titles included the *South Wales Labour Times*, the *Western Valleys Labour Journal* and its predecessor, the *Monmouthshire Labour News*.

104 Parry, 'Socialism in Gwynedd', pp. 184–5; W.Eames, 'Brithgofion Newyddiadurwr', *Y Genhinen*, cyf. 13, 1962–3, p.75; articles by R.J. Derfel and E.W.Davies in *Y Genedl Gymreig*, cyf. 13. Chwef.–3 Ebrill, 1906.

105 Davies, *Atgofion*, p.129; *Liverpool Daily Post and Mercury*, 1 Feb. 1912; *Yr Herald Cymraeg*, 6 February 1912. Peter Angel represented the Caernarfon branch at PTA national meetings, for example in 1898, *Y Dinesydd Cymreig*, 8 May 1912 and Minutes, PTA Delegate Meeting, MRC 39A/TA/4/3/5/3. The 1911 printer's strike witnessed government intervention, through the Board of Trade, for the first time in idustrial bargaining, Musson, *Typographical Association*, p.167; Strick, 'Newspaper Journalism', p.151. See also J. H. Zeitlin, 'Craft Regulation and the Division of Labour: Engineers and Compositors in Britain 1890–1914' (Ph.D., University of Warwick, 1981).

106 *Liverpool Daily Post and Mercury*, 6 Feb. 1912.

107 *Liverpool Daily Post and Mercury*, 8 Feb. 1912. G.H. Roberts was Labour MP for Norwich from 1906, and was appointed Minister of Labour in 1917.

108 It was not unusual for printers to migrate during industrial disputes. In 1865 George Jenkin Jacobs worked as a printer at Peter Williams's *Merthyr Telegraph*, 'but a printer's strike occurring there, he, like all the other employees, left the town', Ifano Jones op. cit. p.282. £55 was paid by the Caernarfon branch of the PTA to defray the removal expenses of certain of its members and their families from Caernarfon to 'other branches', *Y Dinesydd Cymreig*, 26 Feb.1913.

109 MRC 39D/TA/4/8/22. Other recognized printing offices in north and mid-Wales in July 1924 included the following: North Wales Chronicle, Weekly News (Conway), Indispensable, Advertiser and North Wales Pioneer (Colwyn Bay), Advertiser and Circular (Llandudno), Wrexham Advertiser, Herald (Wrexham), Chronicle (Rhiwabon), Journal (Rhyl), Baner, North Wales Times and Free Press (Denbigh), Cambrian News (Aberystwyth), Montgomeryshire Express (Newtown). The list was again updated in 1935.

110 Parry, 'Socialism in Gwynedd', p.282.

111 *Y Dinesyddd Cymreig*, 8 May 1912, 3 July 1912.

112 Bangor MS 1219/189, UCNW.

113 Bangor MSS 1219/162, 1219/28. Percy Ogwen Jones explained to Kate Roberts that she would have to withdraw her investment in the paper by selling her shares in the company. For other details, consult the Dinesydd Publishing Co. Ltd. General Minute Book and the Dinesydd Directors' Minute Book, NLW MS 16723D.

114 Aspinall cites the example of the influence exerted by the Lowther family over the management of the *Westmorland Advertiser and Kendal Chronicle*, 'There is no evidence that the Lowthers themselves were shareholders in any of the local newspapers, but their agents and friends were, and they managed the Press as if it were their own property', Aspinall, *Politics*, pp.354–68.

115 'A Newspaper Editor's Reminiscences', *Fraser's Magazine*, vol. xx, Nov. 1839, p.599. See also Elliott, 'Professional ideology', p.177.

116 Jefferies, *Hodge*, p.269.

117 Rees, 'A History', p.401.

118 Rees, 'A History', p.402.

119 Writing of the north-east of England, Maurice Milne has observed that the 'absence of an editorial line was unlikely to command respect, allegiance or assistance in time of trouble . . . it was a case of rallying the faithful, as readers, advertisers, shareholders and directors', Milne, 'Survival', p.214.

120 Bute to E.P.Richards, 21 Mar. 1842, Bute Coll. IX/27/21/80, CPL.

121 H.C.Tierney to Sir Charles Phillips, 2 Feb. 1889, Picton Castle MS 561, NLW.

122 *Report of the Royal Commission on Land in Wales and Monmouthshire*, vol. ii, 1894, pars. 22964 to 22957.

123 Rendel to H. Owen, 2 Oct. 1879, Glensevern Coll., vol.i/35, NLW.

124 E.Morgan Humphreys, *Gwyr Enwog Gynt* (Llandysul,1950), p.44; Evan Jones, a printer turned Calvinistic Methodist minister, contributor to the *Cambrian News, Y Goleuad*, and associated with *Y Genedl*, established *Yr Amserau* in Caernarfon. Previously he had been associated with *Y Punch Cymraeg*.

125 T.R.Roberts to T.C.Lewis, 20 Apr. 1901, Bangor MS 15994, UCNW; see also T.C.Lewis to Thomas Jones, 16 Apr. 1901, Bangor MS 15995, UCNW.

126 Bangor MS 15971, UCNW.

127 Jones was formally described as a sub-editor, but in practice he was the executive editor of the paper, subject to the editorial guidance of the Dean of Bangor and his committee of clergymen.

128 MS by Lewis Jones (nd), see also his membership card for the Flintshire Constitutional Association (1872), and Diploma of an Associate of The Primrose League, NLW MS 6402D.

129 H.T.Edwards to W.Lewis Jones, 7 Nov. 1881; 19 Nov. 1881; 22 Nov. 1881, NLW MS 6402D.

130 Gibson to Rendel, 2 Dec. 1886, NLW MS 19450C/165.

131 Gibson to Rendel, 21 Jan. 1887, NLW MS 19450C/167.

132 NLW MS 19450C/167.

133 NLW MS 19450C/167. See also A. Jones, 'Reporting Nineteenth-Century Elections: The Gibson-Rendel Correspondence', *Journal of Newspaper and Periodical History*, vol. iii, no.i, winter 1986–87, pp. 17–22.

134 H.A.Latimer to Mansel, 22 Oct. 1904, Mansel Coll. 809, SPL.

135 John Rowlands to Rendel, 31 Oct. 1902, NLW MS 1945D/477; John Rowlands to Rendel, 3 Nov. 1902, NLW MS 1945D/478.

136 J.Timm to J.T.Jones, 13 Aug. and 6 Sept. 1853, NLW MS 3366D.

137 Thomas John Hughes (Adfyfyr) to Rendel, 1 Apr. 1889, NLW MS 19451D/276. For Rendel see Grahame V. Nelmes, 'Stuart Rendel and Welsh Liberal Political Organization in the late Nineteenth-century', *Welsh History Review*, vol. 9, 1978–9, pp 468–85.

138 Rendel Memo., 10 Mar. 1891, NLW MS 19451D/288; Adfyfyr to Rendel, 14 Dec. 1888, NLW MS 19451D/274.

139 Gibson to Rendel, 13 Mar. 1894, NLW MS 20571D/243.

140 John Rowlands to Rendel, 31 Oct. 1902, NLW MS 1945D/477.

141 William Cook to A.C.Humphreys-Owen, 2 May 1893, Glansevern Coll. 5660, NLW; Minutes, NWLF, 14 Dec. 1886, NLW MS 21,171D. The Executive Committee of the NWLF at this time also included Thomas Gee and W.J.Parry, both noted Liberal journalists.

142 Minutes, NWLF, 14 Dec. 1886, NLW MS 21,171D; also 27 Nov. 1886, 22 Jan. 1887, 30 Apr. 1887, 17 Sept. 1887, 12 Oct. 1887. 'In Cheshire

the printer who for years had received all the official contracts, dared to vote the Reform ticket on one occasion and immediately saw his functions transferred to a small but Conservative rival', *Parliamentary Papers*, 1835, no. 547, quoted in Charles Seymour, *Electoral Reform in England and Wales. The Development and Operation of the Parliamentary Franchise 1832–1885*, (1915, reprinted Oxford, 1970), p.186.

143 Minutes, NWLF, 24 Feb. 1891, NLW MS 21,171D.

144 Adfyfyr to Rendel, 7 Nov. 1888, NLW MS 19451D/272.

145 Ernest Bowen-Rowlands to Rendel, 28 Aug. 1891, NLW MS 19454D/476.

146 B.G.Evans to T.E.Ellis, 3 Aug. 1892, T.E.Ellis Coll. 544, NLW.

147 In support of his application, Hughes added the following: 'For years I was associated with Mr Abraham Mabon, and was the accredited writer on mining and other labour topics for the *South Wales Daily News*. I did all the industrial work, and this brought me into close contact with all the mining leaders', Adfyfyr to Rendel, 8 Aug. 1889, NLW MS 19451D/278; see also letter of 12 Oct. 1889, NLW MS 19451D/279; Adfyfyr to Rendel, 2 Sept. 1909, NLW MS 19451D/289.

148 B.G.Evans to T.E.Ellis, 12 Nov. 1893, T.E.Ellis Coll.545, NLW.

149 B.G.Evans to Lloyd George, 1 Jan. 1894, T.E.Ellis Coll. 546, 547, NLW.

150 Lloyd George to Parry, 11 May 1893, NLW MS 8824C.

151 B.G.Evans to Lloyd George, 25 May 1905, series A/box 1/folder 5/2, House of Lords Record Office, London.

Chapter 4

1 *The Periodical Press of Great Britain and Ireland, or an inquiry into the state of the Public Journals, chiefly as regards their moral and political influence* (1824), p.1 (henceforth *Periodical Press*).

2 Thomas Carlyle, 'Signs of the Times' (1829), in A.Shelston, *Thomas Carlyle: Selected Writings* (Harmondsworth,1971), p.80.

3 Prospectus, *Figaro in Wales*, Bangor MS 29598, UCNW.

4 Francois Guizot, *Memoirs of Sir Robert Peel* (1857), p.54.

5 *Periodical Press*, pp. 18, 57.

6 J. Bowring, *The Works of Jeremy Bentham*, vol. i (1843), p.568.

7 *Periodical Press*, p.12.

8 E.L. Bulwer, *England and the English* (1840), book iv, chapter i, 'The Influence of the Press', pp. 376–8, 398–400.

9 A Conservative Journalist, 'Why is the Provincial Press Radical?', *National Review*, 7, July 1886, pp. 678–82.

10 Arthur Murphy, 'The Tory Press', *Contemporary Review*, vol. 23, Apr. 1874, p.826.

11 *Printer*, 1 Feb. 1845, 1 Jan. 1845.

12 Reid, 'How a Provincial Paper is Managed', p.392.

13 *Printer*, 1 Mar. 1845.

14 Rendel to Grant-Duff, 7 Oct. 1884, NLW MS 20572D/382.

15 T.M.Jones, *Cofiant Y Parch. Roger Edwards* (Wrexham, 1908), pp. 258–9.

16 *Carmarthen Express*, 10 Apr. 1874.

17 R. Williams, 'The Church and Education in Wales', *Quarterly Review*, vol. 87, Sept. 1850, p.335; *Tarian y Gweithiwr*, 15 Ion. 1875; *Y Darian* 29 January 1925.

18 *South Wales Star*, 22 May 1891.

19 *Y Genedl Gymreig*, 1 Ion. 1895.

20 *Seren Cymru*, 13 Awst. 1851.

21 *Y Tŵr*, 22 Ebrill 1870.

22 *Ye Brython Cymreig*, 1 Ion. 1892.

23 Jones, *Roger Edwards*, p.20; *DWB* p.339.

24 Gibson to Rendel, 5 May 1887, NLW 19450C/170.

25 *Y Cymro*, 15 Medi 1892.

26 Aspinall, *Politics*, p.381; Brown, *Victorian News*, p. 134. Edmund Blunden, *Leigh Hunt's Examiner Examined* (1928) explores the objectives of the paper 'in producing Reform in Parliament'.

27 Oldcastle, *Journals*, pp.71–2.

28 Milne, 'Survival', p.216.

29 John Cornelius O'Callaghan, *The Green Book, or Gleanings from the Writing-Desk of a Literary Agitator*, (Dublin, 1845). See also Lauren Kessler, *The Dissident Press*, (1984), p.156; George S. Hage, *Newspapers on the Minnesota Frontier 1849–60* (Minnesota Historical Society, 1967), p.122; T.M.Kemnitz, 'Chartist Newspaper Editors', *Victorian Periodicals Newsletter*, no. 18, Dec. 1972, p.1.

30 'A Newspaper Editor's Reminiscences', *Fraser's*, p.591. See also Rees, 'A History', p.336.

31 'Notes on the Printing of the *Carmarthen Journal*'; John Evans died 25 May 1830, NLW 13475C.

32 Minutes, Aberystwyth Liberal Party, 5 May 1877, NLW 5424C; Aberystwyth Liberal Party Accounts 1877–78, NLW 5423B.

33 *Western Vindicator*, 8 June 1839; see also John O'Dwyer, *The Rise and Fall of Chartism in Monmouthshire* (1840).

34 Roberts, *Caledfryn*, passim.

35 NLW 3293E/13; for the establishment of County Councils, see Morgan, *Wales*, p.107.

36 J.Roose Williams, 'Quarryman's Champion', *Transactions of the Caernarvonshire Historical Society*, vol. 23, 1962; NLW MSS 8793D and 8813D.

37 Minutes, NWLF, 3 Sept. 1889, NLW MMS 21,171D.

38 Z/M/301/1, Gwyn. Arch. Dol.

39 *Y Werin*, 12 Ebrill 1890, 21 Mehef. 1890. See also David A. Pretty, *The Rural Revolt that Failed. Farm Workers' Trade Unionism in Wales 1889–1950*, (Cardiff, 1989), pp 20–44; *Merthyr Times,* 5 Dec. 1895; D.W. Howell, *Land and People in Nineteenth Century Wales* (Cardiff, 1977), p.109; D. Lleufer Thomas, *Royal Commission on Labour* (C.6894–xiv, 1893), ii, pp. 125–43; obituary in *Y Werin*, 11 Mawrth 1899.

40 T.E.Ellis to E.W.Evans, 26 Jan. 1889, NLW. 10851B/26; Minutes, Cymdeithas Cymru Fydd, Birmingham, (established 1 Sept. 1892), 9 Nov. 1897, NLW 21,216A.

41 Davies, *Reminscences*, p.148; *Y Gwir*, 1 Mawrth 1889; Lloyd George to Miss Gee, 29 Jan. 1895, NLW 8310D.

42 *Y Wyntyll*, 27 Mawrth 1884; *Cymru Fydd*, Mawrth 1888, p.163.

43 *Cymru Fydd*, Chwef. 1888, pp. 66–7; *Cymru Fydd*, Tach. 1890, p. 692. See also Tom Clarke, *My Northcliffe Diary* (1931), p.15, Clarke observed at close hand Northcliffe's 'ambition for power through his newspapers, though not necessarily for money'.

44 *Prospectus, Oswestry Herald*, Bangor MS 29590,UCNW.

45 Amlwch MS 4, UCNW.

46 *DWB,* p. 1066; for the ballad, see B.B.Thomas, 'Baledi Morgannwg' in *JWBS*, ii, pp. 50–55, 84–5, 151.

47 *DWB*, p.510.

48 *Usk Gleaner*, May 1878, quoted in Waters, *About Chepstow*, p. 11; Pat Hollis, *The Pauper Press. A Study in Working Class Radicalism of the 1830s* (Oxford, 1970), p.136; Joel H. Wiener, *A Descriptive Finding List of Unstamped Periodicals 1830–1836* (1970), passim.

49 Marquess of Bute to W. Thomas, 21 Dec. 1838, Bute Letter Book 13, p.88; Bute to Normanby, 5 Oct. 1840, Bute Letter Book 13, p.392; Bute to L. Lewis, 14 Dec. 1840, Bute Letter Book 13, p.458, Bute Coll., NLW; R. Reece to Bute, 6 Dec. 1839, Bute XX/110; H. Scale to Bute, 7 Dec. 1839, Bute XX/114; J.Coles, G.Hull, T.Hawkins to Home Secretary, 7 Dec. 1839, Bute MS XX/112, J.B.Pryce to Bute, 11 Dec. 1839, Bute XX/121, Glam RO.

50 Bute to L.Lewis, 15 Dec. 1840 and 11 Jan. 1841, Bute Letter Book 13, pp. 459 and 472; Bute to Normanby, 16 Jan. 1841, Bute Letter Book 13, p.474, Bute Coll., NLW.

51 E. Jenkins, *Chartism Unmasked* (Merthyr Tydfil, 1840), p.22.

52 David Williams, *The Rebecca Riots* (Cardiff, 1971), p.211.

53 *Udgorn Cymru*, 9 Ebrill, 14 Gorff., 8 Hyd., 22 Hyd. 1842.

54 Glyn Roberts 'Carmarthenshire: Political Affairs from 1536 to 1900', *Aspects of Welsh History* (Cardiff, 1969), p.107. Walter Griffith was

surprised that so few Welsh newspapers had taken up the cause of the Anti-Corn Law League, despite their declared support for the 'spirit of reform', *Clychgrawn Rhyddid*, 1 Mai 1841.

55 NLW MS 6402D.

56 J. Vincent, *The Formation of the British Liberal Party* (Harmondsworth, 1972), p.89.

57 Walter Yeldham, 'Diary and Memoranda', NLW MS 17935B.

58 *Blackwood's Edinburgh Magazine*, cxxvii, 1880, pp. 804–10; *The Times,* 24 Oct. 1883.

59 Printed Circular, 24 Jan. 1878, D/KT/22, Clwyd Arch. Haw.

60 Thomas Artemus Jones left Denbigh in 1889, and worked for newspapers in Hereford, East Anglia and Manchester before joining the Parliamentary staff of the *Daily Telegraph* in 1896. Shortly afterwards he joined the *Daily News*. In 1898 he entered the Middle Temple, and was called to the bar in 1901. He participated in Lord Penrhyn's libel action against W.J.Parry in 1903, and in the trial of Sir Roger Casement in 1916. He stood as a Liberal candidate in Macclesfield in 1922, East Swansea in 1923 and Keighley in 1924. In 1941 he served as Chairman of the Conscientious Objectors Tribunal in north Wales, and on 26 June 1943 published an open letter to Winston Churchill in *Y Cymro* putting forward the case for a Secretary of State for Wales.

61 *Report of the Royal Commission on Land in Wales*, vol. iv, 1895, par. 56337.

62 Lloyd George to T.E.Ellis, 11 Apr. 1891, Ellis Papers 683, NLW.

63 T.E.Ellis to the Editor, *Y Goleuad*, 21 Dec. 1887, NLW MS 10851C/20.

64 For example, T.J.Hughes to Rendel, 21 Dec. 1888, NLW MS 19451D/269.

65 Picton Castle Coll. 4829, NLW.

66 *The Times*, 8 Sept. 1866; H.L.Spring, *Lady Cambria* (1867), p.23; Morgan, *Wales*, p.96; H.A. Bruce considered the Welsh language to be 'a serious evil, a great obstruction to the moral and intellectual progress of my countrymen, H.A. Bruce, *The Present Position and Future Prospects of the Working classes in the manufacturing districts of South Wales* (Cardiff, 1851) p.12. See also John Coke Fowler, *The Characteristics and Civilization of South Wales* (Neath, 1873) pp.16–19, 27–31.

67 Picton Castle Coll. 4829, NLW.

68 From 1894 to 1897, Vincent edited *The National Observer*, and from 1897 to 1901, *Country Life*. His books include *Tenantry in Wales* (1887), *The Land Question in North Wales* (1896), and *The Life of the Duke of Clarence* (1893).

69 M.M.Bhownaggree, 'The Present Agitation in India and the Vernacular Press', *Fortnightly Review*, vol. lxii, new ser., 1897, p.310. Compare Bhownaggree's observation that 'the journalist and the congressite . . .

have so far worked hand in hand', p.313, with *The Times*' comment on the press in Wales ten years earlier, 'journalism [is] . . . hand in glove with the pulpit . . . the minister . . . walks straight from the chapel to the editorial room', *The Times*, 26 Dec. 1887. See also 'The Native Press in India', *Blackwood's*, Oct. 1897, pp. 584–6.

70 *North Wales Chronicle*, June 1889; A. Griffith-Boscawen, 'A Warning from Wales', *National Review*, vol. xxii, Sept.–Feb. 1893–4, pp. 97–103.

71 *Report of the Royal Commission on Land in Wales*, vol. iv, 1895, par. 64115.

72 *Report of the Royal Commission on Land in Wales*, vol. ii, 1894.

73 Ibid.

74 XM/622/1, XM/622/2, Gwyn. Arch. Caer.

75 Waters, *About Chepstow*, p.55; *WM*, 8 Oct. 1886.

76 Hemming to S.W.Henry, 20 Nov. 1877, GGLB, Glam RO.

77 *Workman's Advocate*, 21 Mar. 1874; *Cymru Fydd*, Rhag. 1890, p.754; Bassett, *Welsh Baptists*, p.322; O.M.Edwards to E.W.Evans, 16 Nov. 1889, NLW MS 10850C/29, and 6 Feb. 1891, NLW MS 10850C/24; *Cymru Fydd*, Ebrill 1891, p.234.

78 *Y Papur Newydd Cymraeg*, 16 Tach. 1836; Glanmor Williams, *Religion, Language and Nationality in Wales* (Cardiff, 1979), p.26.

79 'The State of Morals and Education in Wales', *Fraser's Magazine*, Mar. 1848, p.246.

80 'Travelling in Taffyland', *Blackwood's*, 63, Apr. 1848, p.462.

81 *Chambers's Edinburgh Journal*, Mar. 1849, p.158.

82 'State of Morals', p.254.

83 For example, the Wesleyan *Y Gwyliedydd*. 'Wesleyanism has figured prominently in the activities of the House of Commons in the past weeks', *Y Gwyliedydd* 25 April 1888.

84 David Davies, *Echoes from the Welsh Hills, or, Reminiscences of the Preachers and People of Wales* (1888), p.381.

85 John Williams, *A Defence of the Welsh People Against Misrepresentation of their English Critics* (Caernarfon, 1869), p.16.

86 *Seren Cymru*, 30 Hyd. 1851.

87 *Merthyr Times*, 14 Nov. 1895.

88 Beriah Gwynfe Evans, *Dafydd Dafis, sef Hunangofiant Ymgeisydd Seneddol* (Wrexham, 1898), pp. 53, 67.

89 Myfenydd, 'Cadwraeth y Iaith Gymreig', *Y Diwygiwr*, Mehef. 1874, p.181.

90 James Kenward, *An Account of the Life and Writing of the Revd John Williams, Ab Ithel* (Tenby, 1871), p.153.

91 *Yr Herald Cymraeg*, 23 Mai 1955.

92 *North Wales Observer and Express*, 7 Aug. 1888; *The Times*, 20 Aug. 1873.

93 *North Wales Observer and Express*, 13 Jan. 1888.

94 *WM*, 12 Oct. 1886, 13 Oct. 1886.

95 *WM*, 6 Nov. 1894.

96 Minutes, NWLF, NLW MS 21,171D. For example, the North Wales Liberals urged the Government to reconsider their decision not to allow Welsh to be used in agricultural examinations.

97 T.E.Ellis to Editor, *Y Goleuad*, 27 Sept. 1884, NLW MS 10851B/13; also NLW MS 10851B/9.

98 Abraham Roberts, 'Ein Pobl Ieuainc a Nodweddion yr Oes', *Y Traethodydd*, L, Mawrth 1894, p.124.

99 John Rhys and David Brynmor-Jones, *The Welsh People* (1906), p.608.

100 W.Eilir Evans, 'Newspapers and Magazines of Wales', in T. Stephens, *Wales To-day and To-morrow. 80 Writers, 80 Portraits* (Cardiff, 1907), p.347.

101 Jones, *O'r Mwg i'r Mynydd*, p.118.

102 D. Tecwyn Lloyd, *Barn*, vol. 121, Tach. 1972, pp. 122–3; see also vols 122, Nadolig 1972, and 123, Ion. 1973; D.Tecwyn Lloyd, 'The Welsh Language in Journalism', in Meic Stephens, *The Welsh Language Today* (Llandysul, revised edition, 1979), pp. 152–81; D. Tecwyn Lloyd, *Gysfenu i'r Wasg Gynt*, (BBC Cymru, 1980); Ian Hume, 'The Mass Media in Wales: Some Preliminary Explorations', in Ian Hume and W.T.R.Pryce, *The Welsh and their Country. Selected readings in the social sciences*, (Llandysul, 1986), pp. 325–7.

103 Thackray Bunce, 'Church and Press', p.389.

104 Iorwerth Jones, *David Rees, Y Cynhyrfwr* (Swansea, 1971), pp. 69–75; Glanmor Williams, *David Rees, Llanelli. Detholiad o'i Waith* (Cardiff, 1950), pp. 58–62; *Y Gloch a'r Amserau Eglwysig*, 6 Mai 1898.

105 Davies, *Atgofion*, p.82.

106 Jones, *Ffydd ac Argyfwng*, p. 161.

107 *Y Byd Cymreig*, 25 Rhag. 1862. Newspaper criticism was also articulated in rhyme: thus 'Pwll Scott' in *Y Gweithiwr Cymreig*, 19 Ion. 1888, advising fellow workers to abandon John Mills's *Tarian y Gweithiwr*,

'Gwybydded pawb drwy'r eang fyd
Fod *Tarian* Mills yn dyllau i gyd;
Rhaid newid hon a bloeddio'n hy,
Y Gweithiwr fydd ein tarian ni.'

108 Minutes, Corwen Debating Society, 8 Jan. 1894, Z/M/705/2, Gwyn. Arch. Dol. The Society was renamed the Corwen Literary Society in Sept. 1894.

109 *Glamorgan Free Press*, 9 May 1891.

110 E. Morgan Humphreys, *Cymru a'r Wasg* (Wrexham, 1924), p.3; W.Lewis Jones, 'Y Wasg Gymreig a Chymru Fydd', *Cymru*

Fydd, Gorff. 1888, p.385; R.E Prothero, 'The Attack on the Welsh Church' *Quarterly Review*, vol. 179, July 1894, p.173.

111 Paul John Jenkins, *Moesoldeb Gwleidyddol* (Carmarthen, 1896), pp. 40–42; *Forester*, 17 Sept. 1874.

112 Jones, *Ffydd ac Argyfwng*, pp. 136, 143, 172; J. Evans Owen, 'The Welsh Newspaper', in Stephens, *Wales*, p.343; W.T. Stead, *The Revival in the West: A Narrative of Facts* (London, 1905).

113 Oldcastle, *Journals*, p.39.

114 H.D.Traill, 'Newspapers and English: a Dialogue', *Macmillan's Magazine*, vol. 50, Oct. 1884, p.445. In Wales these concerns had been expressed as early as 1836, when *Y Papyr Newydd Cymraeg* complained of the 'stuffy, old-fashioned style of *Seren Gomer*, and advocated the establishment of a new, non-partisan literary journal, *Y Papyr Newydd Cymraeg*, Medi. 1836.

115 T.E.Ellis to the Editor, *Y Goleuad*, 23 Aug. 1892, NLW MS 10851B/34.

116 Some of the most important teachers of poetry in nineteenth-century Wales were editors of newspaper poetry columns, Ben Davies, 'Colofn Barddoniaeth y Newyddiaduron, 1814–1870', *JWBS*, vol. iv, no. 3., Aug. 1933, p.90. Huw Menai (A Welsh Miner), *Through the Upcast Shaft* (1920), and *The Simple Vision* (1945). Payment for poems and songs varied from paper to paper. Ap Glaslyn (John Owen) received £1.11*s*. 6*d*. for the copyright of the words and music of his song 'I Godi'r Hen Wlad Yn Ei Hol' from the Welsh National Press in Apr. 1894, but by 1904 the same writer received £3 from the same company for the words and music of another song. In addition to selling music and song manuscripts, newspaper publishing houses also published novels in book form, and commissioned educational text books. John Edward Lloyd was commissioned in Apr. 1900 to write a bi-lingual History of Wales for schools for £45, NLW MS 8843E/1,/2,/3,/6, NLW MS 10183D/1. See also Nigel Cross, *The Common Writer, Life in Nineteenth-Century Grub Street* (Cambridge, 1985), pp. 126–8.

117 *DWB*, p.1083.

118 *National Vindicator*, 12 Feb. 1842; Jones, *Roger Edwards*, p.259; *Y Drysorfa*, Chwef. 1866–Ebrill 1867; *Y Dydd*, 5 Mehef. 1868; *Y Gweithiwr Cymreig*, 29 Ion. 1885; John Owen, *Cofiant Daniel Owen* (Wrexham, 1899), p.26; *Y Cymro*, 22 Mai 1890; *Cymru Fydd*, Gorff. 1890, p.431; *Y Werin*, 26 Mawrth 1892, 24 Rhag. 1892, 24 Mehef. 1893; T. Hudson Williams, *Atgofion am Gaernarfon* (Aberystwyth, 1950), pp. 32, 56–7.

119 *Merthyr Times*, 24 Jan. 1895, 18 July 1895, 19 Dec. 1895.

120 *Young Wales*, 22 Oct. 1896.

121 A. Jones, 'Tillotson's Fiction Bureau: the Manchester Manuscripts', *Victorian Periodicals Review*, vol. xvii, nos. 1 and 2, Spring and Summer 1984, pp. 44–5.

122 Hemming to Tillotson, 11 Mar. 1878, 13 Mar. 1878, 9 Sept. 1879, Hemming to W. Andrews, 23 Sept. 1879, Hemming to Cassell, Potter and Galpin, 9 Sept. 1879, 1 Feb. 1881, GGLB, Glam RO.

123 *Y Genedl Gymreig*, 31 Rhag. 1890; R.J.Rowlands to the Welsh National Press Co., 14 Sept. 1901, NLW MS 8843E/8, on transfer of copyright to the company of his novel *Dyrysu Dau Fywyd*; *DWB*, pp. 371, 810. Howard Spring worked for the *South Wales Daily News* for nine years, and following successive periods spent on the *Yorkshire Observer*, C.P.Scott's *Manchester Guardian* and Beaverbrook's *Evening Standard*, he retired from journalism to take up full-time writing. *Fame is the Spur!* was published in 1940, Marian Howard Spring, *Howard* (1967), H. Spring, *The Autobiography of Howard Spring* (new edition, 1972); see also Glenn H. Jordan, 'Images of Tiger Bay: Did Howard Spring tell the truth?', *Llafur*, vol.5, no.1, 1988.

124 See for example, in one sample week in the *Western Mail* 1 to 8 Nov. 1894, reviews of a Grand Concert in Cardiff, the re-opening of the Empire Music Hall in London, short notices on performances in the Empires in Cardiff, Newport, Swansea, and the Panopticon in Cardiff, and a review of orchestral music in Wales by Joseph Parry.

125 *DWB*, pp. 734, 142.

126 R. Williams, 'Methodism in Wales', *Quarterly Review*, vol. 85, Sept. 1849, p.336; Thomas Edwards, *Geirlyfr Saesoneg a Chymraeg. An English and Welsh Dictionary* (Holywell, 1850), William Williams, *Grammadeg Gymreig* (Caerdydd, 1851). Lucien Febvre observed that the emergence of the printing press in early modern Europe consolidated 'the rise of the vernacular languages', Lucien Febvre and Henri-Jean Martin, *The Coming of the Book. The Impact of Printing 1450–1800*, trans. David Gerard, (1976), p.332.

127 *Seren Cymru*, 13 Nov. 1851; Saunders Lewis, *Detholiad o Waith Ieuan Glan Geirionydd* (Cardiff, 1931), p.6; *Gwron Cymreig*, 1 Ion. 1852; Jones, *O'r Mwg i'r Mynydd*, p.277.

128 *Merthyr Times*, 20 June 1895; *DWB* pp. 490, 500.

129 Rhys and Brynmor-Jones, *Welsh People*, p.510; *DWB*, p.500.

130 *National Vindicator*, 18 Sept. 1841; *Cymru Fydd*, Chwef. 1888, p.71; D.E.Jenkins, *Bedd Gelert. Its Facts, Fairies and Folk-lore* (Porthmadog, 1899).

131 *Amddiffynydd y Gweithiwr*, 3 Ebrill 1875, reprinted a winning essay from the Llanberis Eisteddfod of 1873 on 'Poverty in Wales'. *Y Chwarelwr*, 27 Rhag. 1876, set an essay competition on the chief characteristics of the city and people of Ephesus; *Udgorn Rhyddid*, 25 Ion. 1888, published the results of a readers' poll on the most popular ministers and preachers in Llŷn and Eifionydd.

132 Dudley Baines, *Migration in a Mature Economy. Emigration and Internal Migration in England and Wales 1861–1900* (Cambridge, 1985) p.171; Rowland Berthoff, 'The Welsh' in Stephan Therstrom (ed.), *Harvard Encyclopaedia of American Ethnic Groups* (Bambridge, Mass., 1980), p.1012. For the Welsh press in the USA see p.1016.

133 *Y Cymro*, 12 Mehef. 1890.

134 *Report of the Royal Commission on Land in Wales*, vol. ii, 1894, par. 22836. On anonymous journalism, see Bulwer, *England*, p.384; John Duncan to T.E.Ellis, 27 July 1885, T.E.Ellis Papers 36, NLW.

135 *Y Rhedegydd*, 8 Chwef. 1879; *Y Traethodydd*, xxxix, 1884, p.188; M.Jeune, 'Amusements of the Poor', *National Review*, vol. 21, Mar.–Aug. 1893, p.306.

136 Bulwer, *England*, pp. 379–81.

137 *Y Chwarelwr*, 1 Nov. 1876; *Amddiffynydd y Gweithiwr*, 25 July 1874; *Glamorgan Free Press*, 9 May 1891.

138 Benedict Anderson, *Imagined Communities. Reflections on the Origin and Spread of Nationalism* (1983), p.39.

139 W.J.Fox, 'Addressed Chiefly to the Working Classes . . . On the Duties of the Press Towards the People', *People's Journal*, 3 Jan. 1846, p.4.

140 James Curran, 'Press History as Political Myth', in J.Curran and J. Seaton, *Power Without Responsibility. The Press and Broadcasting in Britain*, (Glasgow, 1981), p.17.

141 *Cymru Fydd*, Mawrth 1888, p.126.

142 J. Evans Owen, *Wales Today and Tomorrow* (1907), pp. 341, 344, 348.

143 Jones, *O'r Mwg i'r Mynydd*, p. 11, 'rhyngom ein dau ... fe gedwir ein gwlad' ('Between us . . . our country will be safe').

144 Richard Hoggart refers to these sudden shifts in format and style as the 'distressing dance' of the modern journalist, Richard Hoggart, *The Uses of Literacy* (Harmondsworth, 1959), p.173.

145 Peter Burke maintains that 'language is an active force in society, used by individuals and groups to control others or to defend themselves against being controlled, to change society or to prevent others from changing it . . . the social history of language cannot be divorced from questions of power', Peter Burke and Roy Porter (Eds.), *The Social History of Language* (Cambridge, 1987), p.13. For the disjunction between communicators and audiences, see Allan Bell, *The Language of the News Media* (Oxford, 1991), p.85.

Chapter 5

1 *Western Mail*, 4 Aug. 1914, 5 Aug. 1914; for press censorship see Phillip Knightley, *The First Casualty. The war correspondent as hero,*

propagandist, and myth maker from the Crimea to Vietnam (1975), pp.3–18, 79–112; D.R.Hopkin, 'Domestic censorship in World War I', *Journal of Contemporary History*, vol. 5, no. 4, 1970, pp. 328–52; James Michael, *The Politics of Secrecy. Confidential Government and the Public Right to Know* (Harmondsworth, 1982), pp.38–40.

2 Aled Eirug, 'Agweddau ar y Gwrthwyneb i'r Rhyfel Byd Cyntaf yng Nghymru', *Llafur*, vol. 4, no.4., 1987, pp. 58–68; A. Mor-O'Brien, '"Conchie": Emrys Hughes and the First World War', *Welsh History Review*, vol. 13, 1986–7, pp, 328–9. See also S.E. Koss, *Fleet Street Radical : A. G. Gardiner and the Daily News* (1973), pp. 148.

3 Koss, *Rise and Fall*, ii, p.293.

4 *WM*, 17 Sept. 1914.

5 *Caernarvon and Denbigh Herald,* 25 Nov. 1932.

6 Davies, *Atgofion*, p.132.

7 *Merthyr Express*, 15 Aug. 1914, quoted in Colin Lovelace in Boyce et al, *Newspaper History*, p.311.

8 C.F. Carr and F.E.Stevens, *Modern Journalism. A Complete Guide to the Newspaper Craft* (1931), p.1.

9 *Yr Herald Cymraeg*, 23 Mai 1955.

10 *Report of the Royal Commission on the Press (*RCP), 1947–9 (1949), chapter vii.

11 Koss, *Rise and Fall*, ii, p.354–7.

12 Koss, *Rise and Fall*, ii, pp. 370–1.

13 David Cannadine, *The Decline and Fall of the British Aristocracy* (Yale, 1990), p. 215.

14 Herbert Tracey (ed.), *The British Press. A Survey, a newspaper directory, and a who's who in journalism* (1929), p.17.

15 Tracey, *British Press*, p. 20.

16 D. Jeffrey Williams, *Capitalist Combinations in the Coal Industry* (1924), p.118.

17 Viscount Camrose, *British Newspapers and Their Controllers* (1947), p. 67.

18 Joint Managing Director to E. Jacobson, 31 Aug. 1928, Western Mail and Echo Ltd., Records 33, NLW.

19 Tracey, *British Press*, pp. 32–4, 60; Francis Williams, *Dangerous Estate. The Anatomy of Newspapers* (1957), p.177. See also 'The Contemporary British Press', *The Economist*, Nov. 3, 10, 17, 21, 28, 1928. Also on the Berry family, see M. Mackworth, *D. A. Thomas, Viscount, by his Daughter and Others* (1921), pp. 137–8 (for purchase of the *Cambrian News* in 1915 see p.215); Christine Shaw, 'William Ewart Berry, James Gomer Berry' and Graeme M. Holmes, 'Henry Seymour Berry' in David J. Jeremy (ed.) *Dictionary of Business History* (1984), vol. i, pp. 301–9; *Willings's Press Guide*, 1930.

20 Cudlipp recalls that 'the difference in the Berry conception of proprietorship was due to Camrose's regard for journalistic ethics, a consideration which hadn't kept the Harmsworth's awake at night.' Camrose and his son Michael Berry, Lord Hartwell, were both interventionist editors-in-chief of the *Daily Telegraph*, 'a grey newspaper for the grey middle classes', and both were trained journalists. Cudlipp argues that Camrose was the creative force, and dismissed Kemsley as a 'book-keeper'. Kemsley's editorial role as a proprietor in his own right when the empire was amicably divided is bereft of interest', Hugh Cudlipp, 'The Deathbed Repentance', *British Journalism Review*, vol. i, no.2, winter 1990, p.6.

21 Tracey, *British Press*, p.40.

22 Jane Soames, *The English Press: newspapers and news* (1936), pp. 53–5.

23 *Who Was Who? 1961–1970* (1972), p.264; *Who's Who? 1976* (1976), p.560.

24 Koss, *Rise and Fall*, ii, p.497.

25 Koss, *Rise and Fall*, ii, p.559; Bangor MS 16009, UCNW.

26 Sir Alfred Robbins, *The Press* (1928), p.76.

27 Soames, *English Press*, p.52.

28 Koss, *Rise and Fall*, pp. 488–9.

29 Hywel Francis and David B. Smith, *The Fed, a history of the South Wales Miners in the twentieth century*, (1980), p.268. For a wry insight into local journalism in the south Wales coalfield in the 1930s, see Gwyn Thomas's account of life inside the office of the fictional *Clarioneer*, 'nobody more to the left than a Lib-Lab and nobody more to the right than a corpse', Gwyn Thomas, *Sorrow For Thy Sons* (1986), p.199. My thanks to Professor David B. Smith for drawing my attention to this reference.

30 Francis and Smith, *The Fed*, p.208.

31 Francis and Smith, *The Fed,* p.269.

32 Francis and Smith, *The Fed,* p.163.

33 Mark Hollingsworth, *The Press and Political Dissent. A Question of Censorship* (1986), p.242.

34 Francis and Smith, *The Fed*, pp. 132, 113, 269.

35 D. Hywel Davies, *The Welsh Nationalist Party 1925–1945. A Call to Nationhood* (Cardiff, 1983), pp. 23, 38, 64, 71.

36 Hywel Francis, *Miners against Fascism. Wales and the Spanish Civil War* (1984), pp. 86–94; Colin Holmes, *Anti-Semitism in British Society 1876–1939* (1979), pp. 99–101.

37 *Y Crwt* won a degree of outside recognition by being reviewed in the *Sunday Observer,* W.D. Williams, 'Cydathro', in Meredydd Evans (gol.), *Gwr Wrth Grefft* (Aberystwyth, 1974), p.27; E. M. Humphreys,

'Report to the Directors', 30 June 1924, Bangor MS 16009, UCNW.

38 Tracey, *British Press*, p.38.

39 R.D. Blumenfeld, *What is a Journalist?* (1930), p.3. For a lively debate on the value of journalism courses, see John Roberts Williams and Vaughan Hughes in Guto Roberts, *Dwy Genhedlaeth* (Caernarfon, 1983), pp. 28–51.

40 *The Woman Journalist*, Apr.–May 1929. See also Gertrude M. Allen, 'The Woman's Page Specialist', *The Writer*, Aug. 1925, and A Woman Journalist, 'Women in Journalism', *The Writer*, June 1926.

41 Dylan Thomas, 'Return Journey', p.109; Ralph Maud, *Dylan Thomas in Print. A Bibliographical History*, (1970), p.49.

42 Leonard Fletcher, *They Never Failed. The Story of the Provincial Press in Wartime* (1946), pp. 38–41.

43 Fletcher, *They Never Failed*, pp. 11–13.

44 The Newsprint Supply Co. Ltd was formed in 1940. A non-profit-making co-operative organization chaired by Beaverbrook, but which also included other major proprietors, it arranged the importation of newsprint from Canada. Its Rationing Commmittee, initially chaired by Stanley Bell of the *Daily Mail*, sought to supply newsprint to all newspapers in the United Kingdom, Camrose *British Newspapers*, p.153.

45 The Labour party, *Your Own Journal. A Guide for Labour Parties*, 1948, p.1.

46 *RCP*, 1949, p.89.

47 *RCP*, 1949 p.9; R.T.Jenkins, 'Edward Morgan Humphreys', *Y Traethodydd*, Hydref, 1955, p.160.

48 *Newsprint 1939–1949. The Crisis of the British Press* in *RCP*, 1949, p.18.

49 Emrys Jones, 'Tregaron: A Sociological Study of a Welsh Rural Community, (Ph.D., University of Wales, 1947), pp. 172–6. D. Tecwyn Lloyd conducted a similar survey in east Carmarthenshire in January 1973, by which time both the *Daily Mirror* (137 copies) and the *Sun* (122) were outselling *WM* (107). For further details, see D.Tecwyn Lloyd, 'The Welsh Language in Journalism', in Meic Stephens, *The Welsh Language Today* (Llandysul, 1979), pp. 175–6. For circulation figures of Welsh newspapers in the 1980s, see Ian Hume, 'The Mass Media in Wales', in Hume and Pryce, *The Welsh*, p.344.

50 The Newspaper Society, *Regional Readership Survey among housewives*, Feb. 1959, pp.338–9.

51 Royal Commission on the Press, *Attitudes to the Press. A Report by Social and Community Planning Research*, Research Series 3, (HMSO, 1977), *RCP* 1977, *Attitudes*, p.18.

52 *RCP* 1949 p.28.

53 Op. cit. p.19.

54 Op. cit. p.xxx.

55 Op. cit. p.148.

56 Royal Commission on the Press, *The Concentration of Ownership in the Provincial Press*, by Nicholas Hartley, Peter Gudgeon, Rosemary Crafts, Research Series 5 (HMSO, 1977) [*RCP Ownership 1977*], pp. 52–8. The 'big five' in 1977 were Thomson Regional, Westminster Press, the Associated Newspapers Group, United Newspapers and the Iliffe family chain.

57 *RCP* 1947, p.176; *RCP* 1962, p.20; *RCP* 1960, p.400.

58 *RCP* 1977, *Att*, p.88.

59 *RCP* 1962, p.247.

60 *RCP 1977, Ownership*, pp. 121, 183.*RCP* 1962, p.238.

61 *RCP* 1962, p.175; *RCP 1977, Ownership*, pp. 6, 114.

62 Decreasing from 154,137 in 1956 to 145,791 in 1957, *RCP* 1962, pp. 237–52.

63 *RCP* 1962, p.228.

64 *Football Argus*, owned by the South Wales Argus Ltd, was a Saturday paper that enjoyed a circulation of 24,000 in 1961, *RCP* 1962, pp. 168, 399. By 1974 the circulations of these papers stood as follows: *Western Mail*, 95,000; *South Wales Echo*, 126,000; *South Wales Argus*, 56,000; *South Wales Evening Post*, 73,000, *RCP* 1977, *Ownership*, pp. 97, 101.

65 *RCP* 1962, pp. 491, 248.

66 *Empire News*, 3 Oct. 1954; *RCP* 1962, p.248.

67 Lord Thomson of Fleet, *After I was Sixty. A Chapter of Autobiography* (1975), pp. 84–5, 68.

68 See for example the editorial of the Christmas issue 1982, 'Mae'n ymddangos nad cuddio'r gwir rhag pobol ydi'r gamp ond troi a phlygu eu meddyliau nhw fel nad ydyn nhw ddim eisiau'i weld o' (It appears that the trick is not to hide the truth, but to twist and bend people's minds so that they do not wish to see it), *Sulyn*, 17 Hyd. 1982, Rhifyn Nadolig 1982.

69 D.H. Simpson *Commercialisation of the Regional Press. The Development of Monopoly, Profit and Control* (Aldershot, 1981), pp. 69, 106.

70 *RCP* 1977, p.160.

71 Carl E. Lindstrom, *The Fading American Newspaper* (New York, 1960), pp. 7–9.

72 Rachel Low and Roger Manvell, *The History of the British Film 1896–1906* (1948), p.21.

73 Rachel Low, *The History of the British Film 1906–1914* (1948), pp. 22, 51; see also the *Kinematograph Year Book Directory*, (1915).

74 Rachel Low, *The History of the British Film 1914–1918* (1948), p.134.

75 Jeffrey Richards, *The Age of the Dream Palace. Cinema and Society in Britain 1930–1939* (1984), pp. 70–74.

76 *Liverpool Daily Post*, 14 Feb. 1912.

77 *Liverpool Daily Post*, 29 Dec. 1917.

78 Rachel Low, *The History of the British Film 1918–1929* (1971), pp. 33, 42.

79 Low, *British Film 1918–1929*, pp. 151, 153, 156.

80 Low, *British Film 1918–1929*, p.286. By 1948 this style had lost its edge, and G. Vlement Cave, Editor of *Pathe News*, argued that 'The formal method of title and then story is as old and out of date as some of the news carried. It needs streamlining, and tricks used to give the reel punch. News is always urgent, and often vital. It should be handled in that way', in 'Newsreel must find a new Policy', *Penguin Film Review*, 7, Sept. 1948, p.54.

81 Low, *British Film 1918–1929*, p.44.

82 J.Ellis Williams, 'Cyfansoddi Lluniau Llafar', *Y Ford Gron*, Mehef. 1935, pp. 175, 192; Carol Reed's treatment of such A.J.Cronin novels as *The Stars Look Down*, censored until the mid-1940s, and Penrose Tennyson's *The Proud Valley*, also demonstrate the extent to which the Welsh working class, and in particular the south Wales miners, had become a powerful subject matter for film-makers outside Wales. See also P.Stead, 'Wales in the Movies', in Tony Curtis, *Wales: The Imagined Nation. Studies in Cultural and National Identity* (Bridgend, 1986), pp. 161–71, and Bert Hogenkamp, 'Today We Live: The making of a documentary in a Welsh mining valley', *Llafur*, vol. 5 no. 1, 1980.

83 Asa Briggs, *History of Broadcasting, vol 2, The Golden Age of Wireless*, p.154. For a comprehensive account of radio and television broadcasting in Wales, see James Medhurst, 'Hanes Darlledu a Llyfrgelloedd i'r Byd Darlledu yng Nghymru', (M.Lib, University of Wales, 1991).

84 Rowland Lucas, *The Voice of a Nation?*, (Llandysul, 1981), p.60.

85 *The Times*, 18 Oct. 1988; Angus MacDermid to the author, 27 Mar. 1987.

86 Tommy Eyton Evans, *Cyw o Frid. Atgofion Newyddiadurwr* (Dinbych, 1985), pp. 7, 14.

87 Bedwyr Lewis Jones, 'Blynyddoedd Mawr John Eilian 1930–34', *Y Faner*, 29 Mawrth 1985.

88 Paul Ferris, *Sir Huge, The Life of Huw Wheldon* (1990), pp. 4–13. Wheldon was controller of programmes from 1965 to 1968, and managing director from 1968 to 1975.

89 'Programmes as Broadcast from the West Region', *BBC Schedules*, 11 Jan. 1935, 26 Feb. 1935, BBC Wales Records Centre, Cardiff (*BBC Schedules*, WRC).

90 *BBC Schedules*, WRC 1935–39, passim.

91 *BBC Schedules*, WRC 1935–39, passim.

92 Asa Briggs, *The History of Broadcasting in the United Kingdom. Sound and Vision*, vol. iv, (Oxford, 1979), p.91.

93 Briggs, *History of Broadcasting*, iv, p.91.

94 Briggs, *History of Broadcasting*, iv, p.101. See also Jeremy Tunstall, *The Media in Britain* (1983), p.230.

95 Directors of the Caernarvon Herald and Associated Newspapers Ltd., 20 Oct. 1961, CRO 346235/36. See also 4 Dec. 1970, CRO 346235/46.

96 Tunstall, *Media in Britain*, p.33.

97 Bernard Sendall, *Independent Television in Britain. Origin and Foundation, 1946–62*, vol. i, (1982), p.210–21.

98 Bernard Sendall, *Independent Television in Britain. Expansion and Change, 1958–68*, vol. ii, (1983), pp. 70–82.

99 Sendall, *Independent Television*, ii, p.357.

100 Sendall, op. cit. ii, pp. 354–366.

101 David A. Patten, *Newspapers and the New Media* (White Plains, 1986), pp. 3, 3–13.

102 Sendall, *Independent Television*, ii, p.124.

103 D. Bevan, 'The mobilization of cultural minorities: the case of Sianel Pedwar Cymru', *Media, Culture and Society*, 1984, vol vi, pp. 103–117. For Welsh radio and television consumption patterns in the late 1970s, see Stephen Wyn Williams, 'Culture and Ethnicity in Wales: a spatial perspective' (Ph.D., University of Wales, 1980), p 352.

104 Charles Curran, *A Seamless Robe. Broadcasting – Philosophy and Practice* (1979), p.155.

105 Tunstall, *Media in Britain*, p.231.

106 Patrick Hannan, *Wales on the Wireless. A Broadcasting Anthology* (Llandysul, 1988), p.viii.

107 Patrick Hannan, *Wales in Vision. The People and Politics of Television* (Llandysul, 1990) p. ix.

A glossary of Welsh-language titles

Amddiffynydd y Gweithiwr	(The Workman's Advocate)
Yr Amserau	(The Times)
Baner ac Amserau Cymru	(The Banner and Times of Wales)
Y Brython	(The Briton)
Y Byd Cymreig	(The Welsh World)
Y Celt	(The Celt)
Cronicl yr Oes	(Chronicle of the Age)
Cyfaill y Werin	(The Friend of the People)
Cylchgrawn Rhyddid	(The Journal of Freedom)
Y Cymro	(The Welshman)
Y Chwarelwr	(The Quarryman)
Y Drysorfa	(The Treasury)
Y Dydd	(The Day)
Y Diwygiwr	(The Reformer)
Y Drych	(The Mirror)
Y Dywysogaeth	(The Principality)
Y Frythones	(The British Woman)
Y Genedl Gymreig	(The Welsh Nation)
Y Genhinen	(The Leek)
Y Gloch a'r Amserau Eglwysig	(The Bell and the Church Times)
Y Goleuad	*(The Illuminator)*
Y Gweithiwr Cymreig	(The Welsh Worker)
Y Gwir	(The Truth)
Y Gwladgarwr	(The Patriot)
Y Gwron Cymreig	(The Welsh Hero)
Y Gwyliedydd	(The Observer)
Y Gymraes	(The Welsh Woman)
Yr Haul	(The Sun)
Yr Herald Cymraeg	(The Herald of Wales)
Llais y Wlad	(Voice of the Nation)
Y Llan	(The Church)
Y Meddwl	(The Mind)
Y Papyr Newydd Cymraeg	(The Welsh Newspaper)
Y Rhedegydd	(The Bobbin)
Seren Cymru	(The Star of Wales)
Seren Gomer	(The Star of Gomer)

Tarian y Gweithiwr	(The Worker's Shield)
Y Tŵr	(The Tower)
Y Tyst a'r Dydd	(The Witness and the Day)
Y Tyst Cymreig	(The Welsh Witness)
Udgorn Rhyddid	(The Clarion of Freedom)
Y Wawr	(The Dawn)
Y Werin	(The People)
Yr Ymofynydd	(The Inquirer)

Bibliography

(All books published in London, unless otherwise stated)

Manuscripts

BBC Wales Records Centre, Cardiff
BBC Schedules, West Region, 1935–1939

Cardiff Public Library
Bute Coll.

Clwyd Archives, Hawarden
W.Williams and Sons
Kenyon Papers

Companies Registration Office, Cardiff
Caernarvon Herald and Associated Newspapers Co. Ltd.

Companies Registration Office, London
Western Mail and Echo Ltd.

Glamorgan Record Office, Cardiff
Glamorgan Gazette Letter Book
Letters and Accounts, The Cambrian office

Gwynedd Archive Service, Caernarfon
Gorddinog
North Wales Chronicle Co. Ltd.
Vaynol Estate Papers
Moriah
Poole

Gwynedd Archive Service, Dolgellau
Y Dydd Papers

The Marxian Club, Blaenclydach
Invoices, Twentieth Century Press

National Library of Wales, Aberystwyth
Bala
Baker-Gabb
Broom-Hall
Calvinistic Methodists Archive, General Coll.
Chwibren

Cwrt Mawr
Cyfarthfa
D.R. Daniel
D.S. Davies
Earl of Powis
Thomas Edwards
T.E.Ellis
Frondirion
A.O. Evans
George Eyre Evans
Glansevern
House of Lords Record Office, Schedule to the David Lloyd George Papers
Ivor James
Josiah Thomas Jones
Lleufer Thomas
NLW Misc. MSS
Nefydd
Neuadd Wen
North Wales Liberal Federation
Picton Castle
A.I.Pryse
D.R.Daniel Coll.
W.J.Parry
Rendel
Western Mail and Echo Ltd. Records
Wesleyan Arch.
Harris Williams

Newberry Library, Chicago
Prince Louis-Lucien Bonaparte Coll.

Public Record Office, Kew
Board of Trade:
Merthyr Newspaper Co.
Merthyr Telegraph Printing Co. Ltd

Friendly Societies:
Rules of the Labour Press Industrial and Provident Society Ltd.

Home Office:
Election Riots in Wales, 1868–1869

Swansea Public Library
Mansel Coll.

University College of North Wales, Bangor
Amlwch
Bala–Bangor

Bangor
Belmont
Coetmor
Henblas B.
UCNW Misc. MSS
Dinesydd papers

University of Warwick Modern Records Centre
Minutes, Typographical Association

W.H.Smith Archives, Abingdon, Oxfordshire
Bookstall receipts, South Wales Area
Bookstall receipts, North and Mid Wales Area

Theses

V. S. Berridge, 'Popular Journalism and working class attitudes 1854–1883: a study of *Reynolds's Newspaper*, *Lloyd's Weekly Newspaper* and *The Weekly Times*'(Ph.D., University of London, 1976).

Catherine Evans, 'The Rise of the Periodical Press in Wales up to 1860' (MA, University of Wales, 1926).

D. R. Hopkin, 'The Newspaper of the Independent Labour Party 1893–1906' (Ph.D., University of Wales, 1981).

D. M. Jones, 'The Liberal Press and the Rise of Labour. A study with particular reference to Leeds and Bradford, 1850–1895' (PhD., University of Leeds, 1973).

Emrys Jones, 'Tregaron: A Sociological Study of a Welsh Rural Community (Ph.D., University of Wales, 1947).

G. T. Jones, 'Bywyd a Gwaith Roger Edwards o'r Wyddgrug' (MA, University of Wales, 1933).

Philip Henry Jones, 'A nineteenth-century Welsh printer; some aspects of the career of Thomas Gee, 1815–1898' (Fellowship of the Library Association, 1977).

James Medhurst, 'Hanes Darlledu a Llyfrgelloedd i'r Byd Darlledu yng Nghymru' (M. Lib, University of Wales, 1991).

J. M. Milne, 'The Politics of *Blackwood's*, 1817–1846: a study of the political, economic and social articles in *Blackwood's Magazine* and of selected contributors' (Ph.D., University of Newcastle upon Tyne, 1985).

Thomas Geoffrey Morgan, 'The Welsh Press and Prince Louis Napoleon Bonaparte, 1815–1871' (MA, University of Wales, 1979).

Adrian John Parry, 'The Church Defence Institution 1859–1896' (MA, University of Wales, 1982).

Cyril Parry, 'Socialism in Gwynedd 1900–1920' (Ph.D., University of Wales, 1967).

R. D. Rees, 'A History of South Wales Newspapers to 1855' (Ph.D., University of Reading, 1954).

H. C. Strick, 'British Newspaper Journalism, 1900–1956: a study in industrial relations' (Ph.D., University of London, 1957).

R. Maldwyn Thomas, 'Y Wasg Gyfnodol yn Nhref Caernarfon hyd 1875, gyda sylw arbennig i argraffwyr a chyhoeddwyr' (MA University of Wales, 1979).

Siân Rhiannon Williams, 'Rhai agweddau cymdeithasol ar hanes yr iaith Gymraeg yn ardal ddiwydiannol Sir Fynwy yn y bedwaredd ganrif ar bymtheg' (Ph.D., University of Wales, 1985).

Stephen Wyn Williams, 'Culture and Ethnicity in Wales: a spatial perspective' (Ph.D., University of Wales, 1980).

J. H. Zeitlin, 'Craft Regulation and the Division of Labour: Engineers and Compositors in Britain 1890–1914' (Ph.D., University of Warwick, 1981).

Articles

'The Advertising Agent', *The Newspaper Press*, Mar. 1871.

Jeremy Adze, 'The Methods of the New Journalism', *Welsh Review*, Feb. 1892.

'The Aims of Cymru Fydd', *Cymru Fydd*, July 1890.

Gertrude M. Allen, 'The Woman's Page Specialist', *The Writer*, Aug. 1925.

P. Archer, 'The Post in Wales', *Old Wales*, vol. ii, no. i.

C. Baggs, ' "Well done Cymmer workmen!" The Cymmer Collieries Workmen's Library 1893–1920', *Llafur*, vol. v, no. iii, 1990.

Rowland Berthoff, 'The Welsh' in Stephan Therstrom (ed.), *Harvard Encyclopaedia of American Ethnic Groups* (Bambridge, Mass., 1980).

Beta, 'The Vernacular Press of Wales', *Young Wales*, Feb. 1892.

D. Bevan, 'The mobilization of cultural minorities: the case of Sianel Pedwar Cymru', *Media, Culture and Society*, 1984, vol. vi.

M. M. Bhownaggree, 'The Present Agitation in India and the Vernacular Press', *Fortnightly Review*, vol. lxii, new ser., 1897.

Lenore O'Boyle, 'The Image of the Journalist in France, Germany, and England, 1815–1848', *Comparative Studies in Society and History*, x, 1968.

A. Mór-O'Brien, '"Conchie": Emrys Hughes and the First World War', *Welsh History Review*, vol. xiii.

J. Thackeray Bunce, 'Church and People', *National Review*, vol. xxii, Sept.-Feb. 1893–94.

G. Clement Cave, 'Newsreel must find a new Policy', *Penguin Film Review*, 7, Sept. 1948.

Stephen Coltham, 'English Working-Class Newspapers in 1867', *Victorian Studies*, vol. xiii, no. ii, Dec. 1969.

A Conservative Journalist, 'Why is the Provincial Press Radical?', *National Review*, vol. vii, July 1886.

'The Contemporary British Press', *The Economist*, Nov. 3, 10, 17, 21, 28, 1928.

Creswick R. Corbitt in *People's Journal, Annals of Progress*, vol. 3, 17 Apr. 1847.

Emily Crawford, 'Journalism as a profession for women', *Contemporary Review*, vol. lxiv, Sept. 1893.

Hugh Cudlipp, 'The Deathbed Repentance', *British Journalism Review*, vol. i, no. ii, winter 1990.

Richard Cust, 'News and Politics in Early Seventeenth-Century England', *Past and Present*, no. 112, August 1986.

Alun Oldfield-Davies, 'Y BBC a Chymru', *Y Genhinen*, cyf. cii, rhif. i, Gaeaf 1961–2.

Ben Davies, 'Colofn Barddoniaeth y Newyddiaduron, 1814–1870', *J.W.B.S.*, vol. iv, no. iii., Aug. 1933.

David Davies, 'The Journalism of Wales during the Victorian Era', *Young Wales*, Aug. 1897.

John Davies (Gwyneddon), 'Llenyddiaeth Newyddiadurol Cymru', *Y Traethodydd*, xxxix, 1884.

William Davies and Evan Lloyd Jones, (joint winners), 'The Periodical Literature of Wales during the present century', *Transactions of the Royal National Eisteddfod of Wales, Cardiff 1883* (Cardiff, 1884).

R. J. Derfel, 'Papur Newydd Dyddiol Cymraeg', *Traethodau ac Areithiau* (1864), reprinted in D.Gwenallt Jones (ed.), *Detholiad o Ryddiaith Gymraeg R.J.Derfel* (Dinbych, 1945).

William Eames, 'Brithgofion Newyddiadurwr', *Y Genhinen*, cyf. xiii, 1962–3, xiv, 1963–4.

Lewis Edwards, 'Cyhoeddiadau Cyfnodol y Cymry', *Y Traethodydd*, iv, 1848.

—— 'Dr Edwards ac Eben Fardd', *Y Traethodydd*, l, Mawrth 1894.

A. Elliott, 'Newspapers, Statesmen, and the Public', *Edinburgh Review*, vol. clxxxv, Jan. 1897.

P.Elliott, 'Professional ideology and organisational change: the journalist since 1800', in G. Boyce, J.Curran and P. Wingate, *Newspaper History from the seventeenth century to the present day*, (1978).

Griffith Ellis, 'Llenyddiaeth Gymreig y Triugain Mlynedd Diweddaf', *Y Genhinen*, xvi, 1898.

Aled Eirug, 'Agweddau ar y Gwrthwyneb i'r Rhyfel Byd Cyntaf yng Nghymru', *Llafur*, vol. iv, no. iv, 1987.

D. Tudur Evans, 'Welsh Periodical Literature', *Welsh Review*, Dec. 1891.

W. J. Fox, 'Addressed Chiefly to the Working Classes...On the Duties of the Press Towards the People', *People's Journal*, 3 Jan. 1846.

Isaac Foulkes, 'Llenyddiaeth Gyfnodol Gymreig', *Transactions of the Liverpool Welsh National Society*, 3rd session, 1887–88 (Liverpool, 1888).

'The Fourth Estate', *The Rambler*, vol.iii, pt. xv, Mar. 1849.

'The Frontiers of Tradition', *British Journalism Review*, vol. i, no. iv, Summer 1990.

A. Griffith-Boscawen, 'A Warning from Wales', *National Review*, vol. xxii, Sept. – Feb. 1893–4.

Gwyliedydd, 'Y Newyddiadur Cymreig, a Materion Crefyddol', *Y Genhinen*, xi, 1893.

T. W. Hancock, 'The First Shrewsbury Newspaper', *Bye-gones*, May 1881.

Francis Hitchman, 'The Penny Press', *Macmillan's Magazine*, vol. xliii, April 1881.

Bert Hogenkamp, 'Today We Live: The making of a documentary in a Welsh mining valley', *Llafur*, vol. v no. i, 1980.

D. R. Hopkin, 'Domestic censorship in World War I', *Journal of Contemporary History*, vol. v, no. iv, 1970.

J. E. Hughes, 'Dylanwad y Wasg Newyddiadurol ar Fywyd Cymdeithasol y Genedl', *Y Traethodydd*, lxv, Medi 1910.

E. Morgan Humphreys, 'Profiadau Golygydd', *Caernarvonshire Historical Society Transactions*, 1950, vol. ii.

'Ieuan Gwynedd ac Eben Fardd', *Y Traethodydd*, l, Gorff. 1894.

R. T. Jenkins, 'Edward Morgan Humphreys', *Y Traethodydd*, Hydref, 1955.

M. Jeune, 'Amusements of the Poor', *National Review*, vol. xxi, Mar. – Aug. 1893.

Aled Jones, 'Reporting Nineteenth-Century Elections: The Gibson – Rendel Correspondence', *Journal of Newspaper and Periodical History*, vol. iii, no. i, winter 1986–87.

—— 'Tillotson's Fiction Bureau: the Manchester Manuscripts', *Victorian Periodicals Review*, vol. xvii, nos. i and ii, Spring and Summer 1984.

Bedwyr Lewis Jones, 'Blynyddoedd Mawr John Eilian 1930–34', *Y Faner*, 29 Mawrth 1985.

Brynmor Jones, 'Argraffwyr Cymreig y Gororau', *JWBS*, July 1970, vol. x, no. iii.

Edward Jones, 'Argraffwyr Cymru', *Y Traethodydd*, lvi, Gorff. 1901.

Ieuan Gwynedd Jones, 'The Dynamics of Politics in Mid-Nineteenth Century Wales', *Explorations and Explanations. Essays in the Social History of Victorian Wales* (Llandysul, 1981).

J. J. Jones, 'The Welsh Church periodical press', *National Library of Wales Journal*, vol. iv, 1945.

J. O. Jones, 'The National Awakening in Wales IV: in its relations to the Welsh press', *Young Wales*, Dec. 1895.

W. Lewis Jones, 'Y Wasg Gymreig a Chymru Fydd', *Cymru Fydd*, Gorff. 1888.

Glenn Jordan, 'Images of Tiger Bay: did Howard Spring tell the truth ?', *Llafur*, vol.5, no.1, 1988.

T. M. Kemnitz, 'Chartist Newspaper Editors', *Victorian Periodicals Newsletter,* no. 18, Dec. 1972.

Lord Kemsley, 'Journalism as a Career', *The Welsh Anvil/Yr Einion*, vol.i, Apr. 1949.

A. J. Lee, 'The British press and its historians', *Journalism Studies Review*, no. iii, June 1978.

—— 'The Radical Press', in A.J.A. Morris (ed.), *Edwardian Radicalism 1900–1914: some aspects of British radicalism* (1974).

Roper Lethbridge, 'The Vernacular Press of India', *Contemporary Review*, vol. xxxvii, Mar. 1880.

Idwal Lewis, 'Welsh Newspapers and Journals in the United States', *National Library of Wales Journal*, vol. ii, 1941–2.

T. H. Lewis, 'Y Wasg Gymraeg a Bywyd Cymru 1850–1901', *Transactions of the Honourable Society of Cymmrodorion*, Session 1964, part i (1964).

D. Tecwyn Lloyd, 'Newyddiaduraeth yng Nghymru', *Barn*, cyf. 121–3.

—— 'The Welsh Language in Journalism', in Meic Stephens, *The Welsh Language Today* (Llandysul, revised edition, 1979).

J. H. Lloyd (Peryddon), 'Hen Argraffdai a Hen Argraffwyr y Bala', *Journal of the Merioneth Historical and Record Society*, vol. ii, 1957–60.

S. Maccoby, 'Newspaper Politics: A Footnote to Nineteenth-Century History', *Politica*, August 1934.

Michael MacDonagh, 'The Bye-Ways of Journalism', *Cornhill Magazine*, new series, vol. vi, Jan. to June 1899.

F. Mayne, 'The Literature of the Working Classes', *Englishwoman's Magazine*, vol. v, 1850.

Maurice Milne, 'Survival of the Fittest?', in J. Shattock and Michael Wolff, *The Victorian Periodical Press: Samplings and Soundings* (Leicester/Toronto, 1982).

G. Osborne Morgan, 'Welsh Nationality', *Contemporary Review*, vol. liii, Jan. 1888.

Arthur Murphy, 'The Tory Press', *Contemporary Review*, vol. xxiii, Apr. 1874.

Myfenydd, 'Cadwraeth y Iaith Gymreig', *Y Diwygiwr*, Mehef., 1874.

'The Native Press in India', *Blackwood's*, Oct. 1897.

Grahame V. Nelmes, 'Stuart Rendel and Welsh Liberal Political Organization in the late Nineteenth-century', *The Welsh History Review*, vol. ix, 1978–9.

'A Newspaper Editor's Reminiscences', *Fraser's Magazine*, vol. xx, Nov. 1839.

W. Odell, Jr., 'Free Libraries and their Workings', *Macmillan's Magazine*, vol. 43, Apr. 1881.

An Old Journalist, 'How to make a newspaper, without credit or cash', *Frazer's Magazine*, vol. xx, Dec. 1839.

Bob Owen, 'Welsh American Newspapers and Periodicals', *National Library of Wales Journal*, vol. iv, 1950.

Pierce Owen, 'Can Mlynedd Newyddiaduraeth Gymreig', *Y Traethodydd*, cyf. newydd iv, 1916.

'The Peasant Literature of Wales', *The Athenaeum*, 8 Nov. 1856 and 27 December 1856.

William E. Pegg, 'The Conductors of the *Western Mail*', *Wales*, May-Dec. 1911.

J. S. R. Phillips, 'The Growth of Journalism', in A.W.Ward and A.R. Waller (Eds.), *Cambridge History of English Literature*, vol. xiv (Cambridge, 1916).

Paul A. Pickering, 'Class Without Words: symbolic communication in the Chartist movement', *Past and Present*, 112, August 1986.

Emyr Price, 'Lloyd George a'r Wasg', *Barn*, Ebrill 1976.

R. E. Prothero, 'The Attack on the Welsh Church', *Quarterly Review*, vol. xlxxix, July 1894.

R. D. Rees, 'South Wales and Monmouthshire Newspapers under the Stamp Acts', *Welsh History Review*, vol i, no. iii, 1962.

Arnot Reid, 'How a Provincial Paper is Managed', *Nineteenth Century*, vol. xx, Sept. 1886.

'Representative Government – what is it good for ?', *The Westminster Review*, new ser., vol. xii, Oct. 1857.

Abraham Roberts, 'Ein Pobl Ieuainc a Nodweddion yr Oes', *Y Traethodydd*, cyf. l, Mawrth 1894.

Glyn Roberts 'Carmarthenshire: Political Affairs from 1536 to 1900', *Aspects of Welsh History* (Cardiff, 1969).

G. W. Roderick, 'Education, Culture and Industry in Wales in the Nineteenth-Century', *Welsh History Review*, vol. xiii, 1986–7.

E. G. Salmon, 'What the Working Classes Read', *Nineteenth Century*, vol. xx, July 1886.

S. C. 'A few remarks on the "Fourth Estate" ', *Welsh Review*, July 1892.

'The State of Morals and Education in Wales', *Fraser's Magazine*, Mar. 1848.

P. Stead, 'Wales in the Movies', in Tony Curtis, *Wales: The Imagined Nation. Studies in Cultural and National Identity* (Bridgend, 1986).

Sir J. F. Stephens, 'Journalism', *Cornhill Magazine*, vol. vi, July 1862.

Simon Thomas, 'Gwaith Geoff Charles', *Barn*, Ion. 1988.

H. D. Traill, 'Newspapers and English: a Dialogue', *Macmillan's Magazine*, vol. l, Oct. 1884.

'Travelling in Taffyland', *Blackwood's*, vol. lxiii, Apr. 1848.

J. E. Vincent, 'The Vernacular Press of Wales', *National Review*, vol. xii, 1888–9.

Huw Walters, 'Cyfarpar Llyfryddol Gwasg Gyfnodol Gymreig y Bedwaredd Ganrif ar Bymtheg', *Cylchgrawn Llyfrgell Genedlaethol Cymru*, cyf. xxv, 1987–8.

'Welsh Language and Literature', *The Penny Cyclopaedia of the Society for the Diffusion of Christian Knowledge*, vol. xxvii, 1843.

Dafydd Wyn Wiliam, 'Y Wasg Argraffu ym Modedern, Mon', *Journal of the Welsh Bibliographical Society,* June 1971, vol.x, no.4.

J. Ellis Williams, 'Cyfansoddi Lluniau Llafar', *Y Ford Gron*, Mehef. 1935.

J. E. Caerwyn Williams, 'Hanes Cychwyn Y Traethodydd', *Llên Cymru*, cyf. xiv, Ion.–Gorff. 1981–2.

J. Roose Williams, 'Quarryman's Champion', *Transactions of the Caernarvonshire Historical Society*, vol. xxiii, 1962.

R. Williams, 'The Church and Education in Wales', *Quarterly Review*, vol. lxxxvii, Sept. 1850.

—— 'Methodism in Wales', *Quarterly Review*, vol. lxxxv, Sept. 1849.

—— 'Montgomeryshire Newspapers', *Montgomeryshire Collection*, vols v and x

Siân Rhiannon Williams, '*Y Frythones*: Portread Cyfnodolion Merched y Bedwaredd Ganrif ar Bymtheg o Gymraes yr Oes', *Llafur*, vol.iv, no. i, 1984.

W. E. Williams, 'Trem ar y Papurau Newyddion', *Cymru Fydd*, Awst 1890.

A Woman Journalist, 'Women in Journalism', *The Writer*, June 1926.

Books and pamphlets

Benedict Anderson, *Imagined Communities. Reflections on the Origin and Spread of Nationalism* (1983).

Hartley Aspden, *Fifty Years a Journalist* (Clitheroe, 1930).

A. Aspinall, *Politics and the Press, c.1780–1850* (1949).

Cyril Bainbridge, *One Hundred Years of Journalism* (1984).

T. M. Bassett, *Braslun o Hanes Hughes a'i Fab* (Oswestry, 1946).

—— *The Welsh Baptists* (Swansea, 1977).

Allan Bell, *The Language of the News Media* (Oxford, 1991).

Enoch Arnold Bennett, *Journalism for Women. A Practical Guide* (1898).

R. D. Blumenfeld, *What is a Journalist?* (1930).

John Boon, *Victorians, Edwardians and Georgians. The Impressions of a Journalist Extending Over Forty Years* (1928).

H. R. Pratt Boorman, *Newspaper Society. 125 Years of Progress* (Maidstone, 1961).

Borough of Aberystwyth, *Annual Report of the Public Free Library and Reading Room Committee, 1883–4* (1884).

Andrew Boyd, *Broadcast Journalism. Techniques of Radio and TV News* (Oxford, 1988).

Laurel Brake, Aled Jones and Lionel Madden (eds.), *Investigating Victorian Journalism* (1990).

T. B. Browne, *The Geography of the Provincial Press* (1891).

Lucy Brown, *Victorian News and Newspapers* (Oxford, 1985).

H. A. Bruce, *The Present Position and Future Prospects of the Working Classes in the Manufacturing Districts of South Wales* (Cardiff, 1851).

Asa Briggs, *The History of Broadcasting in the United Kingdom, vol. ii, The Golden Age of Wireless* (1965).

Asa Briggs, *The History of Broadcasting in the United Kingdom. vol. iii, Sound and Vision* (1979).

Clement J. Bundock, *The National Union of Journalists. A Jubilee History 1907–1957* (Oxford, 1957).

E. L. Bulwer, *England and the English* (1840).

Peter Burke and Roy Porter (eds.), *The Social History of Language* (Cambridge, 1987).

H. Findlater Bussey, *Sixty Years of Journalism* (1906).

James A. Carey, *Communications as Culture. Essays on Media and Society* (Boston, 1988).

T. Catling, *My Life's Pilgrimage* (1911).

James Henry Clark, *Reminiscences*, (1908).

Tom Clarke, *My Northcliffe Diary* (1931).

M. Clement, *The SPCK and Wales 1699–1740* (1954).

Collet D. Collet, *History of the Taxes on Knowledge. Their origin and Repeal* (1933).

Mary Elizabeth Craig, *The Scottish Periodical Press 1750–1789* (1931).

Myfanwy I. Crawshay, *Journalism for Women* (1932).

Nigel Cross, *The Common Writer, Life in Nineteenth-Century Grub Street* (Cambridge, 1985).

J. Curran and J. Seaton, *Power Without Responsibility. The Press and Broadcasting in Britain* (Glasgow, 1981).

Cymric Mytton-Davies, *Journalist Alone* (Newtown, 1968).

David Davies, *Reminiscences of my Country and People* (Cardiff, 1925).

—— *Echoes from the Welsh Hills, or, Reminiscences of the Preachers and People of Wales* (1888).

E. W. Davies, *The Newspaper Society, 1836–1936* (1936).

D. Hywel Davies, *The Welsh Nationalist Party 1925–1945. A Call to Nationhood* (Cardiff, 1983).

J. A. Davies, *Education in a Welsh Rural County 1870–1973* (Cardiff, 1973).

John Davies, *Cardiff and the Marquesses of Bute* (Cardiff, 1981).

Picton Davies, *Atgofion Dyn Papur Newydd* (Lerpwl, 1962).

Elizabeth L. Eisenstein, *The Printing Press as an Agent of Change*, vols. i and ii, (Cambridge, 1979).

Beriah Gwynfe Evans, *Cymro, Cymru a Chymraeg, yn eu cysylltiad ag addysg* (Liverpool, 1889).

Chris J. Evans (ed.), *The Book of Cardiff* (Oxford, 1937)

Meredydd Evans (Gol.), *Gwr Wrth Grefft* (Aberystwyth, 1974).

Tommy Eyton Evans, *Cyw o Frid. Atgofion Newyddiadurwr* (Dinbych, 1985).

Leslie Wynne Evans, *Education in Industrial Wales 1700–1900. A study of the Works Schools System in Wales during the Industrial Revolution* (Cardiff, 1971).

Lucien Febvre and Henri-Jean Martin, *The Coming of the Book. The Impact of Printing 1450–1800*, trans. David Gerard, (1976).

Paul Ferris, *Sir Huge, The Life of Huw Wheldon* (1990).

Leonard Fletcher, *They Never Failed. The Story of the Provincial Press in Wartime* (1946).

John Coke Fowler, *The Characteristics and Civilization of South Wales* (Neath, 1873).

Hywel Francis and David Smith, *The Fed, a history of the South Wales Miners in the twentieth century* (1980).

T. Frost, *Reminiscences of a Country Journalist* (1886).

J. Ginswick (ed.), *Labour and the Poor in England and Wales, 1849–1851, vol. iii, The Mining and Manufacturing Districts of South Wales and North Wales* (reprinted 1983).

R. Griffith, *Cofiant y Gohebydd* (Dinbych, 1905).

Richard Griffith (Carneddog), *Gwaith Glaslyn. Detholiad o'i Farddoniaeth a'i Ryddiaeth* (Caernarfon, 1914).

Mark Hollingsworth, *The Press and Political Dissent. A Question of Censorship* (1986).

Richard Hoggart, *The Uses of Literacy* (Harmondsworth, 1959).

D. W. Howell, *Land and People in Nineteenth Century Wales* (Cardiff, 1977).

Ian Hume and W. T. R. Pryce, *The Welsh and their Country. Selected readings in the social sciences*, (Llandysul, 1986).

Geraint H. Jenkins, *Thomas Jones yr Almanaciwr 1648–1713* (Cardiff, 1980).

Peter Henessy, *What the Papers Never Said* (1985).

James Hibbert (ed.), *Notes on Free Public Libraries and Museums* (Preston, 1881).

Pat Hollis, *The Pauper Press. A Study in Working Class Radicalism of the 1830s* (Oxford, 1970).

E. Morgan Humphreys, *Cymru a'r Wasg* (Wrexham, 1924).

—— *Y Wasg Gymraeg* (Caernarfon, 1944).

W. Hunt, *Then and Now. Fifty Years of Newspaper Work* (Hull, 1887).

Mason Jackson, *The Pictorial Press. Its Origins and Progress* (1885).

E. Jenkins, *Chartism Unmasked* (Merthyr Tydfil, 1840).

Paul John Jenkins, *Moesoldeb Gwleidyddol* (Carmarthen, 1896).

David J. V. Jones, *Before Rebecca: popular protest in Wales 1793–1835* (1973).

Ieuan Gwynedd Jones, *Communities: The Observers and the Observed*, Annual Gwyn Jones Lecture (Cardiff, 1985).

—— *Communities. Essays in the Social History of Victorian Wales*, (Llandysul, 1987).

—— *Explorations and Explanations. Essays in the Social History of Victorian Wales* (Llandysul, 1981).

Iorwerth Jones, *David Rees, Y Cynhyrfwr* (Swansea, 1971).

J. E. Jones, *Ieuan Gwyllt, ei fywyd, ei lafur, ei athrylith, ei nodweddion, a'i ddylanwad ar Gymru* (Treffynnon, 1881).

J. H. Jones, *O'r Mwg i'r Mynydd* (Lerpwl, 1913).

J. Morgan Jones (ed.), *Trem ar y Ganrif, sef Adolwg ar y Bedwaredd Ganrif ar Bymtheg* (Dolgellau, 1902).

R. Tudur Jones, *Ffydd ac Argyfwng Cenedl*, cyf i, (Abertawe, 1981).

T. M. Jones, *Cofiant Y Parch. Roger Edwards* (Wrexham, 1908).

—— *Llenyddiaeth Fy Ngwlad* (Treffynnon, 1893).

T. Gwynn Jones, *Cofiant Thomas Gee*, cyf i a ii, (Dinbych, 1913).

Joseph Keating, *My Struggle for Life* (1916).

James Kenward, *An Account of the Life and Writing of the Rev. John Williams, Ab Ithel* (Tenby, 1871).

Phillip Knightley, *The First Casualty. The war correspondent as hero, propagandist, and myth maker from the Crimea to Vietnam* (1975).

R. Buick-Knox, *Wales and 'Y Goleuad'* (Caernarfon, 1969).

Stephen A. Koss, *The Rise and Fall of the Political Press in Britain*, vols. i (1981) and ii (1984).

S. E. Koss, *Fleet Street Radical: A. G. Gardiner and the Daily News* (1973).

D. Tecwyn Lloyd, *Gysfenu i'r Wasg Gynt*, (BBC Cymru, 1980).

Llyfrgell Genedlaethol Cymru, *Y Wasg Gyfnodol Gymreig / The Welsh Periodical Press 1735–1900* (Aberystwyth, 1987).

Rachel Low and Roger Manvell, *The History of the British Film*, vols. i-iii (1948), vol. iv (1971).

Rowland Lucas, *The Voice of a Nation?* (Llandysul, 1981).

M. Mackworth, *D. A. Thomas, Viscount, by his Daughter and Others* (1921).

F. J. Mansfield, *Sub-editing, A book mainly for young journalists* (1932).

—— *Gentlemen, the Press!* (1943).

—— *The Complete Journalist* (1936).

William Haslam Mills, *The Manchester Guardian. A Century of History* (1921).

Kenneth O. Morgan, *Wales in British Politics 1868–1922* (Cardiff, 1970).

—— *Rebirth of a Nation: Wales 1880–1980 (Oxford, 1981).*

Vyrnwy Morgan, *Kilsby Jones* (Wrexham, 1897).

Claude Morris, *I Bought a Newspaper* (1963).

Robert Munter, *The History of the Irish Newspaper* 1685–1760 (Cambridge, 1967).

A. E. Musson, *The Typographical Association. Origins and History up to 1949* (Oxford, 1954).

Ralph Negrine, *Politics and the Mass Media in Britain* (1989).

The Newspaper Society, *A Centenary Retrospect 1836–1936* (1936).

—— *Regional Readership Survey among housewives* (1959).

John Oldcastle (Wilfrid Meynell), *Journals and Journalism: with a guide for literary beginners* (1880).

J. Evans Owen, *Wales Today and Tomorrow* (1907).

W. J. Parry, *Hanes fy Mywyd a'm Gwaith* (Caernarfon, n.d. ?1884).

Thomas Parry, *Hanes Llenyddiaeth Gymraeg hyd 1900* (Caerdydd, 1945).

The Periodical Press of Great Britain and Ireland, or an inquiry into the state of the Public Journals, chiefly as regards their moral and political influence (1824).

David A. Pretty, *The Rural Revolt that Failed. Farm Workers' Trade Unionism in Wales 1889–1950* (Cardiff, 1989).

D. Ben Rees, *Wales: The Cultural Heritage* (Ormskirk, 1981).

Eiluned Rees, *The Welsh Book Trade Before 1820* (Aberystwyth, 1988).

John Rhys and David Brynmor-Jones, *The Welsh People* (1906).

Jeffrey Richards, *The Age of the Dream Palace. Cinema and Society in Britain 1930–1939* (1984).

Thomas Richards, 'Dinbych a'r Wasg Gymraeg', *Transactions of the Honourable Society of Cymmrodorion*, Session 1939 (1940).

Lord Riddell, *The Story of the Western Mail* (Cardiff, 1929).

Sir Alfred Robbins, *The Press* (1928).

Thomas Roberts (Scorpion), *Cofiant Caledfryn* (Bala, 1877).

Saunders, Otley and Co, *The Newspaper Press of the Present Day* (1860).

Bernard Sendall, *Independent Television in Britain. Origin and Foundation*, vols. i and ii (1982, 1983).

Charles Seymour, *Electoral Reform in England and Wales. The Development and Operation of the Parliamentary Franchise 1832– 1885* (1915, reprinted Oxford, 1970).

J. Shattock and Michael Wolff, *The Victorian Periodical Press: Samplings and Soundings* (Leicester/Toronto, 1982).

J. E. Southall, *Bi-lingual Teaching in Welsh Elementary Schools* (1888).

—— *Wales and Her Language* (Newport, 1892).

D. H. Simpson *Commercialisation of the Regional Press. The Development of Monopoly, Profit and Control* (Aldershot, 1981).

Jane Soames, *The English Press: newspapers and news* (1936).

H. L. Spring, *Lady Cambria* (1867).

Howard Spring, *The Autobiography of Howard Spring* (new edition, 1972).

T. Stephens, *Wales To-day and To-morrow. 80 Writers, 80 Portraits* (Cardiff, 1907).

W.T. Stead, *The Revival in the West: A Narrative of Facts* (London, 1905).

C. Tawelfryn Thomas, *Cofiant Ieuan Gwynedd* (Dolgellau, 1909).

Lord Thomson of Fleet, *After I was Sixty. A Chapter of Autobiography* (1975).

Herbert Tracey (ed.), *The British Press. A Survey, a newspaper directory, and a who's who in journalism* (1929).

Jeremy Tunstall, *The Westminster Lobby Correspondents* (1970).

—— *The Media in Britain* (1983).

Bill Twamley, *Cardiff and Me Sixty Years Ago* (Newport, 1984).

J. Don Vann and R. T. VanArsdel (eds.), *Victorian Periodicals. A Guide to Research*, vol. i (New York, 1978).

J. E. Vincent, *The Land Question in North Wales* (1896).

—— *Letters from Wales* 1889).

Ivor Waters, *Chepstow Printers and Newspapers* (Chepstow, 1981).

Aaron Watson, *A Newspaper Man's Memories* (1925).

H. Whorlow, *The Provincial Press Society 1836–1886. A Jubilee Retrospect* (1886).

Joel H. Wiener, (ed.), *Innovators and Preachers. The role of the Editor in Victorian England* (Westport, Connecticut, 1985).

—— *A Descriptive Finding List of Unstamped Periodicals 1830–1836* (1970).

David Williams, *The Rebecca Riots* (Cardiff, 1971).

Francis Williams, *Dangerous Estate. The Anatomy of Newspapers* (1957).

G. J. Williams, *Y Wasg Gymraeg Ddoe a Heddiw* (Bala, 1970).

Glanmor Williams, *David Rees, Llanelli. Detholiad o'i Waith* (Cardiff, 1950).

—— *Religion, Language and Nationality in Wales* (Cardiff, 1979).

Gwyn A. Williams, *When was Wales?* (Harmondsworth, 1985).

John Williams, *A Defence of the Welsh People Against Misrepresentation of their English Critics* (Caernarfon, 1869).

D. Jeffrey Williams, *Capitalist Combinations in the Coal Industry* (1924).

J. O. Williams, *Stori Mywyd* (Lerpwl, 1932).

John Roberts Williams, *O Wythnos i Wythnos* (Caernarfon, 1987).

J. Roose Williams, *Quarryman's Champion. The Life and Activities of William John Parry of Coetmor* (Denbigh, 1978).

Raymond Williams, *Culture* (1981).

—— *The Long Revolution* (1961).

T. Hudson Williams, *Atgofion am Gaernarfon* (Aberystwyth, 1950).

F. J. F. Wilson and D.Grey, *Modern Printing Machinery* (1888).

C. F. Wingate, *Views and Interviews on Journalism* (New York, 1875).

Index

Aberdare Times 31, 89
Abergavenny Telephone 29
Aberystwyth Observer 34, 75
A Collection of All the Material News 12
Adolygydd, Yr 18
Adsain 70
Advertiser of Wales 41
Alliance News 24
Allied Newspapers 211–13
Amddiffynydd yr Eglwys 123
Amserau, Yr 2, 42, 43, 160, 179, 193, 196
Amserau Wythnosol, Yr 63
Anglican Church 17, 18, 51, 93, 122–3, 189–90
Arcade 227
Athraw, Yr 25, 101

Baner Cymru 43
Baner ac Amserau Cymru 2, 24, 33, 41, 51, 68, 106, 111, 169. See also *Y Faner*
Bedwas Rebel 214
Bedyddiwr, Y 15, 101, 122
Beirniad, Y 79
Berry, Gomer (Viscount Kemsley) 210–13
Berry, Henry (Lord Buckland of Bwlch) 210, 314
Berry, William Ewart (Lord Camrose) 210–14
Bird, John 13
Blaenavon and Brynmawr Express 17
Bransby, James Hews 16
Brecon County Times 14
Breden, John 12
Breiz Atao 215
Bristol Journal 1, 128
Bristol Chronicle 110
British Workman 111
British Broadcasting Corporation (BBC) 232–5
Broster, Charles 13, 110, 126
Brython, Y 18, 34, 41, 71,117, 185, 188, 197, 200
Brython Press 77
Brython Cymreig, Ye 30, 71, 75, 117, 157, 188
Burges, Francis 11
Byd Cymreig, Y 8, 188

Caernarfon printers' strike (1893), 87
Caernarvon Advertiser 7, 126, 191
Caernarvon and Denbigh Herald 22, 24, 52, 68, 96, 139–40
Caernarvon Herald 16, 38, 110, 130, 133
Cambria Daily Leader (*Cambrian Daily Leader* for first four issues, May 1861) 2, 116, 211, 212
Cambrian 2, 13, 14, 69, 73, 75, 90, 95, 96, 102, 106, 114, 115, 116, 148, 163
Cambrian Bay Visitor 109
Cambrian Journal 15
Cambrian Messenger 13
Cambrian News 16, 34, 46, 75, 76, 145–9
Cambrian Newspaper Co. 75, 116
Cambrian Quarterly Magazine 14
Cambro-Briton 14
Cardiff and South Wales Times 225
Cardiff Argus 97
Cardiff Hansard 109
Cardiff Times 16
Cardiff and Merthyr Guardian 79, 96, 143
Carmarthen Express 100, 156
Carmarthen Journal 2, 13, 14, 17, 19, 44, 73, 75, 78, 95, 114, 115, 158, 163, 188
Carr, Lascelles 16, 59, 87–8
Carter, Isaac 12

cartoonists 55
Celt, Y 68, 101, 121–2, 160
Cennad Catholig Cymru 124
Cenhadwr Americanaidd, Y (Rensen, New York, USA) 101
censorship 204, 218
Central News Agency 26, 29–30
Cerddor Cymreig, Y 43, 100
Charles, Thomas 1, 93
Chepstow Weekly Advertiser 14
Chester Chronicle 22, 45
Christian World 112
Church of England Catholic Chronicle and Monastic Times 123
cinema, influence of 230
Clark family, Chepstow 14
Cloriannydd, Y 32, 34, 51
Collet, Collet Dobson 4, 82, 95
Colliery Guardian 105
Colliery Workers' Magazine 214
Colwyn Bay and District Advertising and Bill Posting Co. Ltd. 68
Coplestone, Frederick 22, 68, 70, 133–7, 205
Cronicl Cymru 63, 126
Cronicl yr Oes 2
Crawford Committee (1974) 238
Crwt, Y 216
Cudlipp family 212–13
Cwmtillery Searchlight 214
Cyfaill y Werin 114
Cyfaill yr Aelwyd 44
Cyfarthfa Castle 90
Cylchgrawn, Y 14
Cylchgrawn Cynmraeg, Y 1, 13
Cylchgrawn Rhyddid 23, 62, 101, 163
Cymru 97
Cymru Fydd 41, 88, 148, 160, 161, 179
Cymru'r Plant 102, 216

Daniel, D. R. 21, 30
Daily Courant 11
Daily News 6, 16, 20, 24, 27, 41, 46, 70, 111, 190, 205, 208
Davies, David 1
Davies, David John (Dyer) 55
Davies, John (Gwyneddon) 19
Davies, Picton 42, 44, 49, 50, 51, 232
Davies, T.A. 50, 58–9
Davies, William 31, 36, 42, 44, 57, 65, 114
Ddraig Goch, Y 216
Derfel, R. J. 98, 158
Deyrnas, Y 106
Dinesydd Cymreig, Y 24, 46, 105, 138–41, 215
Dirwestydd, Y 101
Diwygiwr, Y 79, 111, 120, 182, 187
Dobbins, Edward 15–16
Douglas, John Kenmuir 87, 126
Douglas, Kenmuir Whitworth 47, 65, 126
Drafod, Y (Patagonia) 44
drunkenness 57
Drych, Y (Utica, USA) 24, 101, 193
Drych Cristnogol, Y 11
Drysorfa, Y 2, 96, 102
Duncan, David 16, 38, 53, 57, 59, 80, 85, 87,88, 114, 129–30
Dydd, Y 37, 42,
Dyddiadur Wesleyaidd, Y 72
Dysgedydd, Y 2, 90, 110, 120
Dywysogaeth, Y 66, 123, 167

Eames, William 45
educational provision and literacy 93–4
Edwards, David 16, 45
Edwards, Lewis 42
Edwards, Roger 156, 193, 196
Edwards, O. M. 97, 102, 179, 184, 204, 216, 227
Efangylydd, Yr 14, 120, 187
Eglwysydd, Yr 106
Eilian, John 232–3
eisteddfod 34, 51, 77, 192, 195, 196
Ellis, T. E. 32, 38, 54, 149–150, 156, 160, 169, 185, 191
Empire News 226
Eurgrawn Wesleyaidd, Yr 2
Evans, Beriah Gwynfe 46, 49, 64, 160, 182, 184, 193; on circulation figures 96–7, 150–51; 'Dafydd Dafis' 55
Evans, Daniel 13
Evans, Evan 12
Evans, George Eyre 104
Evans, Henry Tobit 17, 44, 130, 188

Evans, John 14, 15, 114
Evans, Samuel (Gomerydd) 15
Evans, Samuel 45
Evans, Thomas (Tomos Glyn Cothi) 1
Evening Express 55
Eyre and Spottiswoode 15

Faner, Y 216, 227. See also *Baner ac Amserau Cymru*
Fargher, Robert 63
Federation of Southern Newspaper Owners 86
Fellten, Y 80
Ffenestr, Y 100
fiction, serialization of 192–5
Figaro in Wales 154, 157
Ford Gron, Y 216, 233
Frythones, Y 44

Gad-lef, Y 124
Gee, Thomas 2, 15, 24, 39, 43, 71, 73, 74, 79, 114, 160, 168–76
Geirgrawn, Y 1, 13
Genedl Gymreig, Y 21, 22, 33, 45, 67, 68, 72, 75, 86, 96, 98, 128, 133–7, 144, 150, 157, 168–76, 195, 213
Genhinen, Y 216
Geninen, Y 20
George, David Lloyd 21, 22, 31, 51, 64, 96, 101, 126, 133–7, 151, 168–76, 179, 182, 205–6, 208–9, 233–4
Gibson, John 16, 23, 46, 76, 108, 109, 114, 145–9, 157, 158
Glamorgan Free Press 34, 92, 189, 199
Glamorgan Gazette 25, 26, 28, 35, 43, 68, 78, 106, 178, 194
Gloch, Y 71, 187
Glorian, Y 92
Gloucester Journal 14, 97, 110
Goleuad, Y 19, 43, 90, 111, 119–20, 144, 169, 185, 189, 191, 196
Goleuad Cymru 2
Golwg 227
Good Templars' Advocate 105
Griffith, John (Y Gohebydd) 24, 90
Griffiths, Richard (Carneddog) 33
Gutemberg, Johann Gensfleisch zum 11
Gwalia 22, 25, 29,32, 67,68, 74, 98, 167
Gweithiwr, Y 15, 79
Gweithiwr Cymreig, Y 17, 24, 107
Gwirionedd, Y 167
Gwladgarwr, Y 18, 43, 100, 114, 122
Gwron Cymreig, Y 38, 79, 148, 196
Gwyliedydd, Y 14, 21, 24, 36–7, 99, 107, 188
Gwynne, H. A. 27,
Gymraes, Y 18, 44, 93

Haggar, Walter 229
Hamer, F. E. 45, 159
Harlech Television (HTV) 236
Harris, Joseph (Gomer) 2
Harry, Miles 12
Haul, Yr 14, 17, 54, 120, 122, 184, 187
Haverfordwest and Milford Haven Telegraph 39
Haylings, William Roderick 64
Heath, Charles 13
Heddiw 216
Hemming, J. 25, 28–30, 35–6, 43, 68, 106, 178
Herald Cymraeg, Yr 17, 22, 33, 34, 52, 90, 96, 98, 104, 133–7, 160, 183, 192, 204
Herald of Wales 116
Hereford Journal 1
Howell, Jenkin 17, 89
Hughes, Hugh 62, 63
Hughes, John James (Alfardd) 17
Hughes, Thomas John (Adfyfyr) 19, 41, 51, 148–50
Hughes and Son, Oswestry 79

Illustrated Usk Observer 14
Independent Television (ITV) 235–7
Independent Television Authority (ITA) 237
Institute of Journalists (National Association of Journalists) 60

Jacobs, George Jenkin 79–80
jobbing 73, 77

Jenkins, Thomas 14
Jones, Alice Gray (Ceridwen Peris) 44
Jones, David Watkin (Dafydd Morgannwg) 192
Jones, Evan (Ieuan Gwynedd) 18, 93, 101, 107, 188, 196
Jones, Hugh (Erfyl) 18, 21, 25, 99
Jones, John Gwyndaf 45
Jones, J. O. (Ap Ffarmwr) 45, 70, 89, 137, 158, 160
Jones, J. H. 71
Jones, Josiah Thomas 15, 61, 76, 79, 116, 148, 188
Jones, Kilsby 93
Jones, Owen (Meudwy Mon) 90
Jones, Robert Isaac (Alltud Eifion) 18, 117
Jones, Thomas 2
Jones, Thomas ('The Almanacker') 11
Jones, Thomas (Glan Alun) 17
Jones, W. E. (Cawrdaf) 69
journalism, definitions 7
Journalist and Newspaper Proprietor 33

Lewis, Lewis William (Llew Llwyfo) 51
Lewis, Rees 80
Liberal Press Agency 26
linage 50
Linotype Users' Association 86, 87
Liverpool Daily Post 16, 24, 25, 110, 226, 230, 235
Liverpool Mercury 110, 111
Lobby journalism 52–4
London Mercury 12
Llais Llafur 138
Llais y Wlad 126
Llan, Y 25, 72–3, 101, 123, 144, 184
Llan a'r Dywysogaeth, Y 85
Llandrindod Wells Chronicle and Visitors' Directory 109
Llandudno Chronicle 126
Lloyd, John 63
Lloyd's Weekly Newspaper 110

Manchester Guardian 20, 41, 45, 110, 112
Mansel, William 75
Mason, Frank 49
Mason, Fred B. 19, 30, 131–3
Meddwl, Y 74, 109
Merthyr and Cardiff Chronicle 15, 61, 69, 75, 76
Merthyr and Cardiff Reporter 100, 102, 115
Merthyr Express 34, 38, 70, 87, 159, 206, 222
Merthyr Guardian 13, 128
Merthyr Pioneer 24, 138
Merthyr Star 71
Merthyr Telegraph 31, 79
Merthyr Times 45, 70, 89, 137, 160, 193–4
Merthyr Tydfil Times 210
Methodist Times 24
Mid-Glamorgan Herald 116
Midland Federation of Newspaper Owners 86
Miners' Monthly 214
Miscellaneous Repository, neu y Drysorfa Gymmysgedig 1
Monmouthshire Beacon 128
Monmouthshire Merlin 13, 15, 96, 159, 176
Monmouthshire and South Wales Newspaper Co. Ltd. 41
Monmouthshire Guardian 80
Monthly Advertiser 82
Monthly Herald 96
Montgomeryshire Express 30, 75, 76, 131–3, 144, 231
Montgomeryshire Herald 159
Morgan, Eluned 44
Morgan, Haydn 46
Morgan, John Thomas (Cymro Tawel) 51, 70, 77, 97, 104, 238
Morgan, Richard Humphrey, (adapted Pitman's shorthand into Welsh) 45
Morris, Claude 8
Morris, Lewis 1
music journalism 192

National Press Agency 26, 28
National Typographical Association 81. *See also* Provincial Typographical Association
National Union of Journalists (NUJ)

33, 57, 60
National Union of Railwaymen (NUR) 105
Neath Gazette 116
New Journalism 41, 55, 186, 190, 240
News of the World 110, 111, 207, 212–13, 226, 235
Newspaper legislation: Licensing Act (1662) 11; Stamp Act (1712) 61; Six Acts (1819) 61; Newspapers Act (1836) 22, 61, 69; Printers and Publishers Act (1839) 22; Libel Act (1843) 22; Postage on Newspapers (Channel Islands) Act (1848) 63; Repeal of the Stamp Act (1855) 2, 4, 7, 114, 204; Newspaper Libel and Registration Act (1881) 22; Admission of the Press Act (1908) 49
Newspaper Federation (Lancashire Newspaper Society, Northern Federation of Newspaper Owners) 86
Newspaper Society 45, 86
Newspaper Stamp Returns 95–6
Nonconformity 118–22, 157, 168–77, 186–90; Baptists 2, 35, 78, 104; Calvinistic Methodists 2, 17, 93, 96, 111; Independents 2, 15; Unitarians 2; Wesleyans 2, 59
Northcliffe Newspapers 211–212
North Wales Advertiser and Vale of Clwyd Gazette 126
North Wales Chronicle 22, 26, 32, 45, 47, 58, 65, 67, 72, 74, 87, 108, 110, 126, 143, 166, 232, 233
North Wales Chronicle Co. Ltd (North Wales Newspapers Ltd.) 223
North Wales Constitutional Press Co. Ltd. 126–8
North Wales Gazette 2, 13, 99, 126, 178, 191
North Wales Liberal Federation 104, 149
North Wales Observer 67, 96
North Wales Property Defence Association (PDA) 170–77
Northern Union of Printers 80. See also Provincial Typographical Association
Norwich Post 11

Oswestry Advertiser 19, 131–3
Owen, Bob (Croesor) 39
Owen, David (Brutus) 120, 122, 180, 187
Owen, Richard Jones (Glaslyn) 38

Pall Mall Gazette 24, 185
papurau bro 227
Papur y Cymry 17
Papyr Newydd Cymraeg 20, 23, 62, 63, 69, 95, 99, 179
Parry, Robert (Robyn Ddu Eryri) 17
Parry, W. J. 21, 22, 64, 133–7, 144, 176
Pembrokeshire Herald 12, 74, 163
Penny Magazine 14
Philipps, Sir Charles 39
Pilkington Committee (1961) 237
poetry columns 191–2
Pontypridd Chronicle and Workmen's News 92
Pontypridd Observer 222
population growth 91
Potter, John Theophilus 12
Potter, Joseph 12
Principality 83, 187
Printer 56, 155
Printer's Register 97
Printers' Society of North Wales and the Border Counties 83
printing machines 73
Pritchard Catherine (Buddug) 52
Probert, Evan 17
Provincial Typographical Association (PTA) 80–85, 139–40. *See also* Typographical Association
Prys, Sir Siôn 11
Pryse, Robert John (Gweirydd ap Rhys) 17
Punch Cymraeg, Y 55, 116

railways 107–8
readership surveys, 220–21
reading rooms 103–5
Rebecca 227

Rebecca Riots 4, 164–5, 188
Rees, David (Y Cynhyrfwr) 120, 180, 187
Rees, Ebenezer 138
Rees, Josiah 1
Rees family, Llandovery 14
Rees, Sarah Jane (Cranogwen) 44
Rees, William (Gwilym Hiraethog), 24, 43, 63, 121, 160, 161, 196
Reith, John 234
Rendel, Lord 19, 30,130–33, 145–50, 156
reporting of elections 145–48
Reynolds, Jonathan Owain (Nathan Dyfed) 38
Reynolds's Newspaper 110, 111
Rhondda Clarion 215
Rhondda Socialist Newspaper 138
Rhys, Morgan John 1, 13
Roberts, Ellis (Elis Wyn o Wyrfai) 17, 123
Roberts, John (Ieuan Gwyllt) 42
Roberts, John (Lanbryn-mair) 24
Roberts, William (Nefydd) 15, 38, 72, 77, 78
Roman Catholicism 11, 123
Rowland, Robert David (Anthropos) 34
Ross, John 12
Royal Commissions on the Press (1949) 219, 222–3; (1962, 1977) 223–7

Sabbatarianism 101, 226
Salesbury, William 11
schools of journalism 217
Seren Cymru 15, 91, 106, 122, 157, 182, 192, 196
Seren Gomer 2, 15, 69, 72, 96, 101, 104, 107, 114, 122, 158, 205
Shropshire and North Wales Owners' Association 86
Sianel Pedwar Cymru (S4C) 3, 238
Silurian 7, 73, 82
Smith and Son, W. H. 109
Society for the Diffusion of Useful Knowledge (SDUK) 14
Society for the Propagation of Christian Knowledge (SPCK) 12
South Wales and Monmouthshire Association of Newspaper Proprietors 86
South Wales Argus 87, 176, 225, 226
South Wales Argus Ltd 222–3
South Wales Critic 51
South Wales Daily News 16, 26, 32, 34, 36, 38, 41, 44, 46, 50, 51, 57, 58, 59, 60, 74, 80, 85, 87, 88, 97, 129–30, 178, 182, 190, 192, 195, 211, 215
South Wales Daily Post 46, 211, 212, 217
South Wales Echo 52, 92, 130, 178, 212, 213, 218, 222, 225
South Wales Evening Telegram 92
South Wales Gazette 65, 92
South Wales Graphic 15
South Wales Liberal Federation 104
South Wales Morning News 15
South Wales Miner 214
South Wales Newspaper Co. 15
South Wales Radical 104
South Wales Radical and Nonconformist 52
South Wales Reporter 18, 23, 31, 62, 76, 115
South Wales Star 156, 178
South Wales Weekly News 52
South Wales Weekly Telegram 15
South Wales Worker 138
sport reporting 52
Star of Gwent 73, 74, 79, 96
Sussex Daily News 15
Sulyn 226
Swansea Herald 90, 96
Swansea Journal 75
Swansea and District Workers' Journal 138
Swansea and Glamorgan Herald 25
Swansea Press Ltd. 223

Tarian Rhyddid 100
Tarian y Gweithiwr 23, 39, 89, 96, 108, 114, 138, 156, 192, 196
Television Wales and the West (TWW) 235–6
Temlydd Cymreig, Y 105
Tenby Observer 49
Thomas, David (Dafydd Ddu Eryri) 191
Thomas, D. A., (Viscount Rhondda) 210

Thomas, Dylan 217, 234
Thomas, John (Eifionydd) 20
Thomas, Nicholas 12
Thomas, Rhys 12
Thomson, Roy 212, 224–7
Times, The 41, 66, 73, 110, 111, 164, 171–6, 179, 182, 204, 207, 213
tithe agitation 168–76
Tlysau yr Hen Oesoedd 1
Traethodydd, Y 35, 102, 110, 117, 198
Transport and General Workers' Union (TGWU) 105
Tredegar Guardian 80
Tredegar Iron Times 92
Tredegar Telegraph 80
Trysorfa Gwybodaeth, neu Eurgrawn Cymraeg 1, 13
Trysorfa y Plant 102
Trysorfa Ysprydol 2
typesetting machines 74
Typographical Association 27, 80, 85–90. *See also* the Provincial Typographical Association
Tyst a'r Dydd, Y 19, 68, 71, 96, 101
Tyst Cymreig, Y 63, 121

Udgorn Cymru 52, 138
Udgorn Rhyddid 21, 101
Usk Gleaner and Monmouthshire Record 14

Vanguard 215
Vincent, John Edmund 173–6

Wales, regions 6
Wales 55, 216
Wales on Sunday 227
Wasg Americanaidd, Y (Pittsburg, USA) 101, 193
Wawr, Y 17, 215
Weekly Mail 97
Welsh Arts Council 227
Welsh Catholic Herald 123
Welsh Catholic Times 123
Welsh Coast Pioneer 34
Welsh Gazette 148
Welsh language: almanacs 11; bilingualism 6; census returns 92–3; difficulties of editors 18; neologisms 195–6; use in journalism 168–87
Welshman 13, 73, 84–5, 95, 130, 188
Welsh National Press Co. (Welsh National Newspaper Co.) 22, 46, 64, 72, 75, 77, 100, 119, 121, 150, 193
Welsh Nationalist 216
Welsh Review 216
Wenynen, Y 17
Werin, Y 45, 67, 96, 160, 161, 189
Western Counties Graphic 16
Western Mail 16, 25, 26, 27, 31, 32, 34, 36, 42, 44, 45, 45, 46, 49, 50, 52, 55, 57, 65, 70, 76, 80, 85, 87, 88, 98, 101, 128–9, 143, 166, 176, 178, 182, 184, 185, 190, 191, 192, 195, 197, 198, 204, 206, 207, 211, 212, 213, 215, 218, 220, 222, 225, 233, 235
Western Valleys News 92
Western Vindicator 95, 110, 163
Wheldon, Huw 233
Williams, Joseph 96
Williams, Peter 79
Williams, Raymond ix, 101
Williams, Richard Hughes (Dic Tryfan) 34
Williams, William (Caledfryn) 19, 159, 196
Wilmot, William 13
women journalists 44–5, 52
Woodall's Newspapers Ltd 223, 231, 236
Workman's Advocate 34, 51, 70, 77, 84, 104–5, 138, 178, 192
Wrexham Evening Leader 226
Wrexham Guardian 75, 126–8, 167

Ymofynydd, Yr 2
Young Wales 179
Yspiwr, Yr 95